Adventure Guide to

Hawai`i

John Penisten

HUNTER

HUNTER PUBLISHING, INC.
130 Campus Drive, Edison NJ 08818
(732) 225 1900, (800) 255 0343, fax (732) 417 0482

1220 Nicholson Rd., Newmarket, Ontario,
Canada L3Y 7V1, (800) 399 6858

The Boundary, Wheatley Road, Garsington
Oxford, OX44 9EJ England
01865-361122; fax 01865-361133

ISBN 1-55650-841-7

©1999 John Penisten

Maps by Kim André, © 1999 Hunter Publishing, Inc.
All photos by John Penisten, Pacific Pictures,
unless otherwise indicated.

Cartoons by Joe Kohl

Cover: *Winter Surf, Oahu* (Ron Dahlquist, SuperStock)

For complete information about the hundreds of other travel guides
offered by Hunter Publishing, visit our Web site at:
www.hunterpublishing.com

4 3 2 1

Contents

Maps

Acknowledgements

This book couldn't have been completed without the help of many good folks throughout the Hawaiian Islands. I'd like to thank them all for the many ways in which they individually assisted me with this project, their insights into experiencing all the adventures of the islands and their expertise in providing information to aid my research as I traveled around these beautiful islands of Aloha.

A special Mahalo to:

Sonja Swenson, Lori Michimoto, Reece Olayvar, Sandi Yara, Nancy Daniels, Lynette Lo Tom, Aaron Placourakis, Erica MacGuyer, Annette Kaohelaulii, Sancie De Mattos, Connie Wright, Caroline Witherspoon, Linn Nishikawa, Brett Huske, Lawrence Aki, Barbara Sheehan, Bernie Caalim-Polanzi, Joyce Matsumoto, Dave Sayre, Shari Chang, Claire Akau, Buzzy Sproat, Glen Grant, Ruth Tamura, B.J. Whitman.

And a special thanks and "shaka" to Grace and Gilbert Fujiyoshi for their insights into dining out in Hawai`i and to Milton Fujiuchi whose wide knowledge of island culture and the outdoors and generous help and assistance allowed me to experience the real outdoors of Lana`i and Kaua`i.

About the Author

John Penisten is an independent photojournalist and writer and lives in Hilo, Hawai`i, with his wife, Susan, and two daughters, Janelle and Joelle. He manages his own photo agency, Pacific Pictures, which specializes in images of Hawai`i and the Pacific Rim region. He is the author of two other books on Hawai`i travel, culture and history. He has traveled throughout the Pacific Islands, Australia, New Zealand and parts of Asia. His self-illustrated articles appear regularly in national and international publications. He has lived in Hawai`i for 25 years and wouldn't think of living anywhere else.

Introduction

The Islands of Hawai`i

They are known the world over as the "Islands of Aloha," for their custom of welcoming visitors to their sunny, tropical shores. Most island residents (population: 1,186,000) take pride in the "Aloha Spirit" – an attitude of openness and friendliness, especially to visitors. Hawai`i's multi-cultural community has been able to evolve, develop and grow over the generations because of the embracing "Aloha Spirit." It has allowed them to overcome differences with dignity and respect and enabled its cosmopolitan community to live together harmoniously. That spirit will remain with you long after you return home.

Hawai`i is an archipelago of incredible natural beauty and sharp contrasts. Mountains, volcanoes mostly, some jagged peaks, some gracefully sloping, reach through puffy layers of clouds into the Pacific blue sky. Where land meets sea, there is an explosion of bright blues and greens from water, reef and sky, mixed with the white, golden, black and even green sands of the beaches, and with the black lava rock and sheer cliffs that plunge into the sea.

There are lush tropical valleys, high cascading waterfalls tumbling into jungle pools, upland rain forests dense with tropical vegetation and a high tree canopy. There are arid lava deserts nearly devoid of plantlife, volcanic craters still steaming, lava flows exploding in steam and pumice as they roll into the sea, remote tranquil beaches where only the sound of breaking surf on the shore disturbs the quiet. Underwater marine reserves and coral reefs teem with tropical marinelife, while coastal or mountain hiking trails lead to views that are unsurpassed. These are the things that make for adventure in Hawai`i.

First time and returning visitors will find a Hawai`i that has a wide ranging selection of soft to hard adventure activities. From Hilo to Hanalei, there are any number of exciting, educational and adrenalin-pumping activities. You can ride a bike down a volcano, scuba or snorkel a reef or underwater cave, follow a trail through the rain forest, ride a mule down a 3,000-foot switchback trail, picnic at an isolated beach, troll for a Pacific blue marlin and with luck get a "hook up," take a sunset cocktail cruise off fabled Waikiki Beach, visit an ancient Hawaiian he-

The Hawaiian Islands

iau and touch history, ride a kayak down an old sugar plantation irrigation flume, explore the summit of Hawai`i's tallest mountain, and the list goes on.

Hawai'i is no longer just a beach resort. It all depends how active or inactive you want to be. If you're looking for adventure and excitement, you'll find it on all of the Hawaiian Islands. If you're into more sedentary adventure activities, like laying about on a beautiful beach sipping a maitai, well, you won't have to go far in Hawai'i to do that either.

There are eight islands that make up the main Hawaiian chain: Kaua`i, O`ahu, Moloka`i, Lana`i, Maui, Hawai`i, Kaho`olawe and Ni`ihau. This main group of islands is traditionally known as the Windward Islands. There is also a cluster of small islands and atolls known as the Northwestern Hawaiian Islands or the Leeward Islands, which lie far to the northwest of the main group. This group has no permanent human inhabitants but is a refuge for seabirds and animals like Hawaiian monk seals, sea turtles and other marinelife species.

Kaua`i is the "Garden Island" and has some of the grandest and most magnificent scenery in the islands. Its rugged mountainous interior and forests have lush vegetation, beautiful waterfalls, and quiet rain forest streams. There are also attractions like the spectacular Waimea Canyon, the hidden valley of Kalalau, Hanalei Bay, Wailua River, the Na Pali Coast, Poipu Beach and much more.

Diamond Head, O`ahu
(Waikiki / O`ahu Visitors Association).

O`ahu is the "Gathering Place," the most populated island and the location of the state's capital, Honolulu. Honolulu is the principal shipping port, site of the major international airport, the business, financial and government center, and the educational heart of the state. O`ahu is also the US military command center for the Pacific region. The Waikiki Beach area is the prime visitor center with its many hotels, restaurants, activities and more. Attractions abound on O`ahu, with places like Diamond Head, Pearl Harbor, Nu`uanu Pali Lookout, Punchbowl National Cemetery, the Ko`olau Mountains, the North Shore, surfing beaches, and much more.

Moloka`i is the "Friendly Isle," which is perhaps the most endearing trait of this small Hawaiian country community. Moloka`i has cattle ranching, small family farms, coffee orchards and a very rural laid-back atmosphere. It's a place to unwind and escape life's hectic pace. On the North Shore are some of the world's highest seacliffs, towering to 3,000 feet. Below the cliffs, on the Makanalua Peninsula, is the famed Hansen's disease settlement at Kalaupapa where leprosy victims were banished in the 1800s.

Lana`i is a privately owned island, formerly a pineapple plantation until the industry closed in the 1980s. Since then, Castle & Cooke, Inc. has built two world-class hotels on the island and has transformed it into a luxury resort destination for those who want to see something of a small, remote island while indulging in first-class accommodations, dining, championship golf, and more. And for those who are so inclined, Lana`i can provide an adventurous experience exploring remote beaches, a cross-island mountain backcountry road and more.

Maui is the "Valley Isle," with sugar and pineapple plantations and up-country mountain cattle ranches. The 10,023-foot Mt. Haleakala is the world's largest dormant volcano and dominates Maui's landscape. Its last eruption was about 1790. Lahaina in West Maui was Hawai`i's capital until 1845. It was a rowdy whaling port in the mid-1800s and still retains something of its whaling town atmosphere, which visitors find appealing. Maui's world-class resorts at Ka`anapali, Kapalua, Kihei, Wailea and Makena attract visitors from around the globe. And Haleakala National Park, the Hana Coast, Iao Valley and other sites on Maui provide visitors with much to experience.

Hawai`i is the "Big Island" because it is, in fact, bigger than all the other Hawaiian Islands combined. But it is also known as the "Orchid Isle" and the "Volcano Isle" for obvious reasons. The island's dominant features are the twin towering peaks of Mauna Kea (13,796 feet) and Mauna Loa (13,677 feet). But those aren't the island's only volcano mountains. The others are Kohala (5,480 feet), Hualalai (8,271 feet) and Kilauea (4,093 feet). The island has a large tropical flower industry which produces millions of orchids, anthuriums and other tropical blooms annually. The island also produces coffee, macadamia nuts, papaya, ginger, cattle and much more. Hawai`i Volcanoes National Park is a much visited attraction, along with Akaka Falls, Parker Ranch, Waipio Valley, Kealakekua Bay, Pu`uhonua O Honaunau National Historical Park in Kona and others.

**Kaho`olawe** is uninhabited and until a few years ago was used by the US Navy for target practice. Ships would regularly bombard the island in practice while airplanes would bomb and strafe it. The US Navy finally relinquished control of the island and returned it to the State of Hawai`i. But it will not be used for anything until bomb squads remove all active and potentially dangerous ordnance and the island is declared safe.

Ni`ihau is sometimes called The Forbidden Island, simply because few are ever allowed onto it. The island is privately owned by the reclusive Robinson family, who run a cattle ranch there and strictly guard access to the island. However, in the last couple of years there have been indications that the island may be opening more to the outside, even with a very small tourism program and reports of military installations being considered as a way to bring income to the island. There are about 200 Hawaiians who call Ni`ihau home. They follow a mostly traditional Hawaiian lifestyle on this small, remote island.

The Northwestern Hawaiian Islands or **Leeward Islands** lie far to the northwest of the main islands. They extend in a chain over 1,000 miles from Nihoa in the southeast to Kure Atoll in the northwest, almost to the International Dateline in the middle of the Pacific. The group includes the islands of Necker, French Frigate Shoals, Gardner Pinnacles, Maro Reef, Laysan, Lisianski, Pearl and Hermes Atoll, and Midway Atoll. The islands are primarily a national wildlife refuge, home to many thousands of seabirds, plus the endangered Hawaiian green sea turtle, rare Hawaiian monk seal and other land birds and marinelife species, some found nowhere else on earth. The Midway Atoll National Wildlife Refuge was only recently opened in 1997 for the public to experience the birdlife and refuge eco-system. The National Park Service contracted with a private company to run eco/tours to Midway using the former military airbase and facilities as a tourism center. See the Kaua`i section of this book for details.

The Hawaiian Language

One of the more positive things the early missionaries did for the Hawaiians was to standardize their Polynesian, up to then only a spoken language, into a written language. Hawaiian shares much with the languages of other Pacific islands.

The missionaries organized the Hawaiian language into an alphabet of 12 letters, five vowels (a, e, i, o, u) and seven consonants (h, k, l, m, n, p and w). Every letter of a word is sounded. Syllables end in vowels and many syllables contain only vowels. All Hawaiian words end in a vowel. There are no double consonants in Hawaiian. A vowel always separates consonants.

The accent generally falls on the next-to-last syllable, although some words are unaccented. Called an "okina," it is used in some words to indicate the "glottal stop," a sign that a "k" sound found in other Polynesian dialects has disappeared in Hawaiian usage. Where this mark appears, the accent falls on the preceding vowel, as in the following: Ka`u (Kah`oo), Kapa`au (Kahpah`ow), Ho`okena (Ho`okenah).

The consonants are pronounced as they are in English, with "w" being the only exception. When "w" introduces the last syllable of a word, it sometimes is sounded as a "v." Examples are the famous Polynesian ceremonial drink, awa, actually pronounced "ava," and the area on O`ahu called Ewa is pronounced "Ehva." Likewise, the name of the islands, Hawai`i, is actually pronounced "Havai`i"

Pronouncing Hawaiian

The five vowels are pronounced as follows:

a as in father, above

o as in note, own

e as in obey, weigh

u as in rule, true (oo)

i as in marine (ee)

In addition, there are some vowel combinations which resemble diphthongs and are pronounced as follows:

ai and *ae* (eye) as in mile, line

ao and *au* (ow) as in cow, how

ei (ay) as in day, say

oe (oy) as in boy, toy

Learning to pronounce and use some Hawaiian words on your visit will certainly prove to be an adventure and add a whole new dimension to your travel experience. Listening for and using some of the local language can also prove useful in interpreting road maps, street signs, and place names.

In addition to Hawaiian, the unofficial language of the islands is "pidgin English." This language evolved over generations as ethnic groups migrated to Hawai`i and ended up living and working together on the sugar and pineapple plantations. Most of these immigrant laborers knew little or no English, nor did they know the languages of the other immigrant groups. A hodge-podge, mixed language of English, Chinese, Hawaiian, Japanese, Filipino, etc., evolved. You'll probably hear bits and pieces of this pidgin English as you travel through the islands. Even though they know standard English, many islanders use pidgin when speaking to each other. It's traditional.

Geography & Geology

The Islands of Hawai`i are among the most isolated inhabited lands in the world, far from any other major land mass with their mid-ocean location. They are located in the North Pacific Ocean at approximately 155-160° west longitude and 18-22° north latitude, just below the Tropic of

Cancer. The islands are about 2,400 miles southwest of North America and over 5,000 miles east of any major land mass in Asia.

The Hawaiian Islands are volcanic high islands, each a mountain summit rising from the depths of the Pacific. The mountains and islands were built over the millennia by successive eruptions and overlaying lava flows. The islands lie in a general northwest-to-southeast curving arc, stretching 1,523 miles from Kure Atoll in the northwest to the easternmost point on the Island of Hawai`i. Scientists estimate that eruptive activity began building the islands some 30 million years ago in the low-lying coral atolls of Kure, Midway, Laysan and others which lie far to the northwest of the main Hawaiian Islands.

■ Plate Tectonics

Today, volcanic activity is centered on the Island of Hawai`i and its Mauna Loa and Kilauea volcanoes. Recently, volcanologists and marine geologists have been studying the developing island of Lo`ihi, which lies just a few miles south of the Island of Hawai`i. Using deep-diving submarines, scientists have observed underwater lava flows and eruptive activity from that volcano to study how the islands are formed. Lo`ihi is still several thousand feet below the surface of the ocean, so it will be a few thousand years before it pokes above the water as Hawai`i's newest island.

"Safe" Volcanoes

Hawai`i's volcanoes do not usually have violent explosive eruptions. These volcanoes are, in fact, relatively safe because of the low amount of gas they emit. The magma forms streams of flowing lava that spreads over several acres once it breaks out on the surface. There may be some spectacular fountaining and bubbling of lava at the eruption point, a crack or crater, but for the most part Hawai`i eruptions are relatively mild affairs. This is why volcanologists can study Hawai`i volcanic eruptions close up, taking samples of lava, temperatures and gathering other data. This is also why visitors are allowed to get relatively close to eruption sites.

The volcanology of Hawai`i can be explained by the geologic theory of plate tectonics. The theory sees the Earth's surface as being composed of an interconnecting series of plates overlaying one another. These plates float over a liquid core of molten rock or magma. As these plates slide and bump against each other, the magma is forced up through the openings, resulting in volcanic eruptions and lava flows. The theory also holds that the Hawaiian Islands are located on a large Pacific plate centered over a "hot spot," a vast reservoir of magma that is continually being released. As the Pacific plate moves and slides, magma is released and lava flows through cracks or openings, adding to old islands or forming new ones.

Visitors to Hawai`i Volcanoes National Park on the Big Island of Hawai`i may get a chance to see volcanic activity, but no one can predict what a volcano may or may not do. But for the last several years, since 1983, volcanic activity in the national park's southeast flank has been ongoing. There have been a number of surface eruptions and surface lava flows that have made their way downslope to the sea. These flows, over the years, have destroyed a number of homes in residential subdivisions, covered power lines and highways. The lava has actually added several hundred acres to the island. Visitors have been able to see the lava flow into the sea at various points on the national park's southern boundary.

Hawai`i Volcanoes National Park provides opportunities to learn more about volcanoes, their natural history and geology at the park's visitors center museum and exhibits. You can also hike some of the park's trails across still-steaming craters and vast fields of lava. There are two types of lava produced by Hawai`i volcanoes. Pahoehoe is a heavy free-flowing fluid in its molten state; when cooled, it has a smooth surface that is hard and black. What is called `a`a lava is a jumbled mass of clinker rocks with rough surfaces and sharp edges.

The Goddess Pele

Visitors to the national park can also learn about the Hawaiian goddess of fire, Pele, who is said to reside in and controls the forces of the volcano. Pele is one of the more tempestuous and fanciful figures of Hawaiian legend. She is goddess of fire, ruler of the wild and unpredictable world of the volcanoes.

Self-assured and assertive, Pele is said to appear as either a beautiful young girl or as a wrinkled old hag walking her white dog along the backroads of the Big Island. In a place where legends are as important as history and where people still believe in the supernatural, stories are hard to ignore. Pele is said to have arrived in Hawai`i in a sailing canoe, probably from somewhere in the Society Islands group far to the south of Hawai`i. According to legend, Pele lived on the other Hawaiian Islands before taking up residence on the Big Island. She also once lived on Mauna Kea but was driven out by her rival, Poliahu, the goddess of snow. After that, Pele settled into the firepits of Kilauea Volcano. From there she guards her domain and lashes out from time to time.

Legend has it that removing pieces of lava rock from the volcano will bring the wrath of Pele. It is said she will place a curse of bad luck on anyone taking her lava. Warning signs attest to this. Rangers at Hawai`i Volcanoes National Park frequently get packages of lava rocks in the mail. These are sent by visitors who did not heed the warnings, removed some rocks for souvenirs, and soon had a series of accidents and just plain bad luck. Returning the rocks, they ask the rangers to put them back at the volcano. There are many other legends associated with Pele, part of the adventure of exploring and discovering these magical islands.

Hawaiian Folklore

The islands of Hawai`i are rich in folklore. Hawai`i shares a common heritage with the other Polynesian islands. Part of that heritage is an oral folklore and history handed down through the generations. Hawai`i had no written language until the arrival of the missionaries in the 1800's. Only then was the heritage and culture recorded.

Island folklore revolves around a tradition of storytelling. These tales are both myths and legends. The myths are generally stories of the deeds of godlike beings while legends generally deal with the feats of heroes and other human beings with god-like powers. In many cases, the terms blend to become interchangeable.

Religious belief in pre-missionary Hawai`i centered on the supernatural. The Hawaiians were children of nature and believed that much of life and fate was controlled by nature's forces and supernatural beings. It was their belief that these supernatural beings, gods and goddesses, could be invoked with prayer and homage and placated with sacrifice, human or otherwise.

The Four Gods

Traditional Hawaiian folklore recognizes four gods who controlled or influenced much of life in early Hawai`i. **Kane** was the father of life and living creatures and associated with sunlight, fresh water and forests. **Ku** was the fearsome god of war who demanded human sacrifice in exchange for conciliation. **Lono** was the god of growing things – rain, harvest, sports and peace – and was honored with an annual makahiki festival to celebrate the autumn harvest. **Kanaloa** was the spirit of evil and ruler of the land of departed souls.

There were also many other important mythical figures, some who had superhuman attributes. **Pele** is the goddess of fire and dwells in the volcanoes of the Island of Hawai`i. She is recognized as controlling the destructive powers of the volcanoes. **Maui**, widely known in Polynesian folklore, is a demi-god known for heroic feats. **Laka** is the goddess of hula and **Kuula** the god of fishermen. And throughout Hawaiian culture, there are numerous deities recognized as having power over various aspects of life.

It was traditional for each family to have an ancestral guardian spirit, ghost or supernatural being called an **aumakua**. This aumakua was prayed to and its power invoked when help was needed in any situation. Such beings were honored with a family shrine or altar at which offerings were occasionally provided. Fishermen prayed for safety and good luck at the village shrine and left part of their catch as homage to the gods after a successful trip. The ruling village or island district ali`i (chief) had a heiau (temple) built and sacrifices made to the god or gods as a way of invoking their help in ensuring a good harvest, good weather, many children or victory in war.

Throughout early Hawaiian culture, people and their lives were influenced by strong beliefs in gods and goddesses, heroes and heroines, ghosts and ghost-gods or aumakuas. Lacking the written language and conveniences of Western civilization, Hawai`i refined its heritage with oral histories handed down through the generations.

📖 For those who want to learn more about Hawai`i's folklore, consult *Myths and Legends of Hawai`i*, William D. Westervelt, Mutual Publishing, Honolulu, 1987; and *The Legends and Myths of Hawai`i*, King David Kalakaua, Charles Tuttle Company, Rutland, Vermont, 1972.

Waimea Bay (Robert Coelho).

History

■ The First Hawaiians

No one knows for sure exactly when, but the islands of Hawai`i were first settled by Polynesian migrants several hundred years before Columbus discovered America and before European navigators explored and circled the globe during the age of discovery. The first settlers of Hawai`i probably came from the Marquesas Islands, near today's French Polynesia, far to the south of Hawai`i. They are said to have arrived in Hawai`i around 500 AD. Some of Hawai`i's oldest archaeological sites date back to about that time. Later settlers probably came from the Society Islands, also part of today's French Polynesia.

The early Polynesians were master navigators and sailors and their world was dominated by the Pacific Ocean. They are believed to have originated in Southeast Asia and Indonesia. They migrated across the Pacific by island-hopping in their simple double-hulled sailing canoes, settling the islands along the way. They crossed vast stretches of open unknown ocean in simple craft using only their knowledge of ocean currents, winds and stars to navigate. That fact is undisputed. What anthropologists and historians do dispute are the routes, times and other details as to when this all happened.

Warrior print by Jacques Arago, 1819.

It is thought, at least by some, that the first Polynesians landed along the southern shores of the Big Island of Hawai`i. Some feel the Big Island would have been the first visible landmark when coming from the south because of the high peaks of Mauna Kea and Mauna Loa. The southern shore of the Big Island would have made for a natural landing site after a long sail across the ocean. Ka Lae, or South Point, is traditionally believed to be where those first migrants stepped ashore. From there, over succeeding generations, they spread among all the islands of Hawai`i.

The first settlers, and those that came in later migratory waves, arrived in a Hawai`i that was, up until then, uninhabited, an undisturbed tropical ecosystem. The islands had evolved through undersea volcanic action over tens of thousands of years. As the islands grew and evolved above water, they developed a unique indigenous ecosystem. Thousands of species had arrived by wind and ocean current to become established and adapt to the island environment. Everything from the tiniest insects and plants to the tallest rain forest trees had evolved in complete isolation.

Into this environment came the first settlers, who lived here, equally undisturbed and unaware of the outside world for generations. These original Hawaiians lived a communal lifestyle, following a rigid pagan religion in which they believed their lives were controlled by supernatural gods of the earth, sea and sky. Their daily lives were also regimented by a social and political system, known as the kapu system, of ruling ali`i (royalty), kahuna (priests and sorcerers) and a warrior-class that controlled the commoners through fear and intimidation. Their world revolved around daily events of fishing, hunting, farming and gathering, tight-knit village and clan life, and adherence to strict ceremonial protocol. Violations of the system brought severe penalties and dire consequences, often death, at the hands of the ruling ali`i and kahuna.

Each island had its hereditary ali`i or ruling chiefs, who ruled their respective chiefdoms. But these rival ali`i and their clans continuously fought among themselves for control and power. Civil war was widespread among ruling ali`i and their warrior clans. Kamehameha the Great, from Kohala on the Big Island of Hawai`i, was known as a fierce warrior and became a prominent ruling chief. Around 1790, Kamehameha consolidated his power on the island of Hawai`i by defeating rival chiefs in battle. He then went on to raise a large army and conquered the islands of Maui, Moloka`i and O`ahu over the next few years. While he failed to conquer Kaua`i in battle (his army was turned back by a storm at sea), in 1810 Kaua`i recognized Kamehameha as king of all the islands. Thus was founded the Hawaiian monarchy, which ruled over a united kingdom of the islands until it was deposed in 1893.

Hawaiian warrior by Sarah Stone, c. 1800.

■ Discovery by the Western World

King Kamehameha ruled his realm of islands from Kona on the island of Hawai`i until his death in 1819. But, even before this, change was in the air. Unbeknownst to the Hawaiians, forces were gathering that would end their isolation and alter their culture forever.

Captain Cook

The islands of Hawai`i basked in total isolation from the rest of the world until early in 1778, when famed British explorer Captain James Cook sighted O`ahu and landed on Kaua`i. Cook named the group the Sandwich Islands after his patron, the Earl of Sandwich. For many years thereafter, the islands were known by that name. The Hawaiians on Kaua`i had greeted Cook as an incarnation of their god Lono, since he had appeared at the time of the Makahiki, an important social-religious celebration.

Cook eventually sailed north to continue his search for the fabled Northwest Passage through North America – a passage that would shorten the voyage from Europe to Asia. He spent the next several months exploring the northwest coast of America up to the Arctic, but returned to Hawai`i later that year. He planned on cruising through the islands, charting them and resting his crew from the rigors of the northwest and the Arctic. In January, 1779, Cook anchored in Kealakekua Bay on the island of Hawai`i. Once again, Cook was received as Lono and rendered

Captain James Cook.

great honors and respect by the Hawaiians. In February, after resupplying his ships, he sailed north, but a freak storm forced him back to Kealakekua Bay to repair his ships. This was to prove a fateful event.

The Hawaiians were surprised to see the god Lono return so soon and became uneasy, thinking it a bad sign. While Cook's men went about their repair work to the ships, altercations occurred between them and the Hawaiians. One of the ship's small boats soon turned up missing, supposedly taken by the Hawaiians. One thing led to another and Captain Cook himself took a landing party ashore at Kealakekua Bay to see about resolving the matter. Cook planned to take a chief hostage until the boat was returned, a tactic that had worked previously in such incidents.

However, when Cook landed with armed guards, the Hawaiians became more restless and agitated. Things got out of hand rapidly. The Hawaiians were alarmed at the hostile intent of Lono (Cook) and his armed guards. It was soon learned that a chief elsewhere had been killed by a shot from another boat. The Hawaiians became visibly angered and made threatening advances toward Cook's party. Cook and his guards, huddled on the shore facing a large menacing throng, retreated to their boats. A Hawaiian threw his dagger at Cook, who then turned and fired one barrel of his pistol. He missed, but succeeded in angering the crowd even more. Cook then fired his second barrel, killing a native. At this point, Cook's guards opened fire and a general melée broke out. Cook, still ashore, turned to run toward the boat, but was struck down by a club and stabbed in the back with a dagger. He fell into the water and died. The armed guards who made it to the boat hurried back to the ships and set sail away from Kealakekua Bay, never to return.

So ended the life of Captain James Cook, superb navigator and explorer. And while he never lived to realize it, his "discovery" of the islands of Hawai`i would prove to be a monumental event of Pacific exploration. In something of an ironic gesture, a monument stands today on the shore of Kealakekua Bay on the Kona Coast of Hawai`i, marking the exact spot where Captain James Cook met his fate.

■ The Coming of Change

After Cook introduced Hawai`i to the world, it wasn't long before influences, both good and bad, made their impact on the islands. More ships from more countries began to pass through the islands during the years when King Kamehameha rose to prominence. Kamehameha did not entirely conquer and unite the islands under one kingdom on his own. He had outside help in the form of two English sailors, John Young and Isaac Davis, who acted as advisors on the operation of foreign weapons and on modern warfare, thus giving him an advantage over his rivals.

Kamehameha defeated one chief after another, taking control of the island of Hawai`i, and then Maui, Moloka`i and O`ahu – all by 1795. In the battle for O`ahu, Kamehameha's forces annihilated the defenders, forcing them up the Nu`uanu Valley and over a sheer cliff.

Kamehameha the Great.

During these years, there was growing influence from contact with the world beyond Hawai`i's shores. Ship captains and sailors, traders and merchants, rascals and scalawags descended upon the islands and left their mark. The Hawaiians themselves were changing, cultural mores were slowly breaking down, the old system of ruling ali`i with control over commoners was cracking and the old religious beliefs in supernatural gods began to break up. It was a time of social upheaval among the Hawaiians, who found themselves and their ways under assault by an outside world they barely understood.

■ The Kings & the Missionaries

With this maelstrom raging, King Kamehameha died in 1819. He was succeeded by his eldest son, Liholiho, who took the title of Kamehameha II. The new king was assisted by Kamehameha's favorite wife, the powerful Ka`ahumanu, who served as co-ruler with the new king. It was Li- ho-

Kamehameha II.

liho who initiated the overthrow of the kapu system, the old system of strict religious, social and political rules governing the lives of all Hawaiians. It was into this maelstrom, in 1820, just a year after the death of Kamehameha the Great, that the first American missionaries arrived from New England. Liholiho gave the arriving missionaries permission to stay in Hawai`i for one year on a trial basis. This proved to be a fateful decision.

Not only did the missionaries bring Christianity to a Hawaiian people becoming disillusioned with their own ancient gods, but they represented the first of several migrations that led to the modern cosmopolitan makeup of Hawai`i today. In the years since Cook's arrival, Hawai`i had become a haven for trading vessels. A trade in sandalwood had opened with China, which proved profitable for the King and the chiefs, but a burden on the common people, who had to gather the wood far up into the forests. The introduction of Western diseases and alcohol, along with the breakdown of the ancient morality, had created a chaotic situation. The missionaries gained an easy foothold because they aligned themselves with the chiefs against some of these evils.

Just five years into his reign, in 1824, Kamehameha II and his Queen, Kamamalu, traveled to London, England. They had little time to enjoy their visit nor did they get to meet the British king, George IV. Both Hawaiians contracted measles and died within a few days of each other.

A second son of Kamehameha the Great, Kauikeaouli, was soon proclaimed King and took the title of Kamehameha III. During his 30-year reign, the kingdom of Hawai`i grew in stature and was recognized by the world's great powers, France, Britain and the United States. These countries saw Honolulu grow from a small village to an important and strategic trading and naval port and they had an interest in its control. During Kamehameha III's reign, in 1840, Hawai`i's political system was transformed from an absolute to a constitutional monarchy.

In 1843, a British naval fleet forced the cession of Hawai`i to Great Britain as a result of a dispute over leased lands to foreigners. For about six months, the Hawaiian Islands were in British hands, until the arrival of

British Rear Admiral Richard Thomas. He reconciled the dispute and restored Kamehameha III to his throne.

Until 1845, the capital of Hawai`i had been in Lahaina, Maui. Kamehameha III and the Legislature moved to Honolulu that year, recognizing the growing value of Honolulu as a commercial port. In 1850, the King declared Honolulu the official capital of the kingdom.

■ Immigrant Influx

Whaling

In the early to mid-19th century, Hawai`i was a center of the whaling industry and its main port was Lahaina, Maui. Hundreds of whaling ships plied the Pacific in search of whales, whose oil and other products were much sought after. This activity prompted the rise of shipping-related businesses that brought economic benefits to Hawai`i. Many of the new businesses were actually undertaken by the missionaries and their descendants. The missionaries were shrewd enough to manipulate things to their advantage. It has often been said that the missionaries came to Hawai`i to do good, and that they did very well indeed. Some of Hawai`i's largest business corporations of today had their beginnings with missionary founders.

But the whaling industry also brought unintended costs. The influx of thousands of rowdy seamen into the small towns of Honolulu, Lahaina and even Hilo, brought drunkenness, debauchery and riotous behavior as had never been seen before. The seamen also brought diseases to which the Hawaiians had no immunity and for which there was no effective medical treatment: influenza, measles, typhoid, smallpox and venereal diseases. Fortunately, with the discovery of oil in Pennsylvania in 1859, the whaling industry's days were numbered and by 1870 the whaling era had ended. But the damage had already been done.

Sugar

During the early to mid-1800s, the sugarcane industry was established and began to prosper. But one problem that hindered its development was a shortage of labor. Sugar planters, unable to secure enough labor locally, began lobbying to bring in foreign contract laborers. In 1852, a group of Chinese contract laborers were the first of many immigrants that came to labor in the sugar plantations. This tide of immigrant labor continued until 1946 and was perhaps the single biggest factor in the development of Hawai`i's modern multi-cultural population. The Japanese first came in 1868, with Filipinos, Koreans, Portuguese and Puerto Ricans following over the years.

Sugar soon became important to Hawai`i's economy. The sugar planters, mostly American businessmen – many the direct descendants of the first American missionaries – felt constrained by the policies of the monarchy. The planters wielded much political clout and favored annexation of Hawai`i by the United States in order to provide a guaranteed protected market for their product. This put them at odds with the Hawaiian monarchists who intended to keep Hawai`i for the Hawaiians. Thus was set the course for an inevitable collision.

■ The Last Kamehamehas & Kalakaua

After the death of Kamehameha III, Alexander Liholiho became Kamehameha IV. He was a grandson of Kamehameha the Great and ruled from 1855-1863. He and his wife, Queen Emma, were greatly concerned with looking after the general welfare and well-being of the Hawaiian people. One of their greatest accomplishments was the founding of Queen's Hospital to provide medical care for Hawaiians. The hospital is still thriving in today's Honolulu.

Kamehameha IV was succeeded by his brother, Lot, who became Kamehameha V. Lot reigned from 1863-1872, and was to be the last of the Kamehamehas to rule the Hawaiian Kingdom established by his grandfather. During this time there were political struggles over the constitution between those wanting to limit democracy and strengthen the monarchy's power as against those wanting to increase democratic measures and limit the monarch's powers.

With the death of Kamehameha V, the line of direct descendants of Kamehameha the Great ended. The Legislature, after a popular vote, confirmed William Charles Lunalilo as King. However, Lunalilo's reign was to be the shortest of any Hawaiian monarch – only one year. The Legislature set about electing a new king and chose David Kalakaua as successor. But supporters of former Queen Emma, widow of Kamehameha IV, rose up in anger with the announcement and sparked general disorder and riots. Order was finally restored by British and American troops, who came ashore from ships in the harbor. King Kalakaua was inaugurated as the seventh monarch of the Hawaiian Kingdom on February 13, 1874.

King Kalakaua ruled from 1874 to 1891. Kalakaua continued negotiations that had begun earlier with the United States and in 1875 completed a treaty of reciprocity between the two nations. The treaty assured Hawai`i of a market for its sugar in the US; upon its renewal in 1887, the US secured the exclusive use of Pearl Harbor in Honolulu as a coaling station for its navy.

Kalakaua, known as the Merry Monarch for his love of the hula (which the missionaries had long sought to ban) and who enjoyed luaus and social gatherings, had a stormy political reign. The American businessmen who controlled much of Hawai`i's commerce, and the sugar industry, saw Kalakaua as an obstructionist to their plans. With his affinity for the hula and attempts to revive Hawaiian culture and traditions, they saw him as someone who was stirring up native Hawaiians against non-Hawaiians. Among Kalakaua's major accomplishments was the construction of Iolani Palace in 1882.

The Bayonet Constitution

In 1887, through crafty political intrigue, Kalakaua was forced to accept a new constitution. It was called the Bayonet Constitution because it was imposed by force, and took many of the king's powers away. He could no longer appoint the House of Nobles, no longer had absolute veto power and the king's cabinet became responsible to the Legislature, not to the king. The new constitution also gave voting rights to all male residents of the Kingdom, thus giving foreigners the right to vote. At the same time, it set up a property qualification in order to vote. This stipulation effectively reduced the power of Hawaiians in the political life of the Kingdom and increased the control of resident foreign businessmen. The loss of his royal powers greatly affected Kalakaua. He died during a visit to San Francisco in 1891 and was succeeded by his sister, Liliuokalani, who became queen.

■ Monarchy Deposed

Queen Liliuokalani was to be Hawai`i's last monarch. She reigned from 1891 to 1893. She made great efforts to eliminate the restrictions which had been imposed on the monarchy and had reduced the participation of Hawaiians in their own government. In 1892, she attempted to proclaim another constitution to restore the monarchy's powers. This action led her opponents, mostly American businessmen, to stage a bloodless "revolution." On January 17, 1893, with the assistance of US marines from the USS *Boston* anchored in Honolulu Harbor and, with the support of the resident US minister, Queen Liliuokalani was deposed and a provisional government was formed. The Hawaiian Monarchy had effectively ended.

The new provisional government, under the leadership of Sanford Ballard Dole, requested annexation by the United States, but was turned down by President Grover Cleveland. The leaders of the revolution then declared Hawai`i a Republic and Dole was proclaimed President in 1894.

■ Annexation

Hawai`i's strategic military importance in the Pacific area continued to grow as the 19th century drew to a close. The United States was keenly aware of the importance of maintaining close ties with Hawai`i or even controlling the islands outright. President William McKinley was more favorable toward annexation than his predecessor. Thus, by a joint resolution of Congress on August 12, 1898, the islands of Hawai`i were formally annexed by the United States. The new possession was then reorganized as the Territory of Hawai`i and Dole was appointed its first Governor on June 14, 1900. The first Territorial Legislature convened in 1901.

■ The 20th Century

With annexation, Hawai`i's growth and development seemed assured. The sugar industry and the new pineapple industry, developed by James Dole, a young cousin of Governor S.B. Dole, took off and prospered. Foreign laborers continued to flow into Hawai`i from Asia and elsewhere as old laborers served out their contracts and elected to say on doing other work.

World War I only marginally affected Hawai`i. The '20s saw the first attempts at promoting Hawai`i as a tourist destination with the advent of ocean liners. The first non-stop flight from the mainland to Hawai`i was in 1927, marking the arrival of the trans-Pacific air age and giving Hawai`i a closer link to the outside world. Commercial inter-island air service began in 1929. Pan American World Airways linked Hawai`i directly with the mainland in 1936 when it began regular commercial passenger service with its huge flying boats. During the '30s, communication services expanded rapidly and linked the islands closer to the mainland and the world.

The Great Depression years of the '30s were not as serious in Hawai`i's agriculture-based economy as in more industrialized areas. With growing international tensions around the world and especially with Japan in the Far East, the US began to build its military power in Hawai`i.

■ Pearl Harbor & World War II

The first 40 years of the Territory of Hawai`i's existence were relatively peaceful and obscure. But Hawai`i burst upon the American consciousness with a rude awakening on the morning of December 7, 1941, when air and naval forces of the Empire of Japan attacked US forces at Pearl Harbor and other installations on O`ahu. The attack cost nearly 4,000 casualties and caused great damage to the US naval fleet berthed there. In one quick change of scene, Hawai`i went from a land of quiet tranquil sugar and pineapple plantations to a bristling armed camp and the command center for US operations in the Pacific war. The islands would never quite be the same again.

■ Hawai`i & the Modern Era

Hawai`i celebrated the end of World War II with the rest of the world on August 14, 1945. It was the end of a stirring drama in which the islands had played a pivotal role. Like the rest of post-war America, Hawai`i was on the threshold of great social, cultural and economic change and development. The rise of labor unions, rapid development and expansion of communications, air transportation, construction, and the beginning of modern mass tourism greatly impacted on Hawai`i.

A political changing of the guard also took place after the war. From its inception, the Territory of Hawai`i was dominated by old guard Republicans. However, in 1954, Democrats took control of both houses of the Territorial Legislature, then the Governorship in 1962, and they have yet to lose control of either. However, the last few elections have seen Republicans make inroads and regain a few seats in the legislature. Who knows what the future might bring?

■ Hawai`i - The 50th State

From the '30s to the '50s, Hawai`i had pushed hard for statehood in the US Congress. A succession of Hawai`i delegates to Congress had actively lobbied for the idea. The efforts resulted in success when both the US House and Senate passed the necessary legislation. Hawai`i officially entered the Union as the 50th state on August 12, 1959. Statehood was recognition of Hawai`i's achievements and future potential as part of the United States.

The last several years have seen a renaissance of Hawaiian culture, language, arts, hula and more in the "Aloha State." This revitalization of Hawaiiana has resulted in a new pride of the Hawaiian people. This cultural reawakening has also prompted calls from some to reassess Hawai`i's political alignment and sovereignty, even to questioning whether Hawai`i should remain a part of the United States.

Debate has raged in the media over the 1893 abolishment of Hawai`i's monarchy and government, the establishment of the provisional government and the annexation by the US. The public debate continue today.

In 1993, the centennial observance of the overthrow of the Hawaiian monarchy, the US Congress, in an ironic gesture, officially offered an apology for the overthrow of the sovereign government of Hawai`i and recognized the act as illegal. Various native Hawaiian groups and organizations had long pursued such action, hoping to gain recognition for a Hawaiian sovereignty movement and to reestablish a Hawaiian nation and reclaim native land rights. The political groups, pro and con, are assessing what the next steps are to be and what direction to take the debate on sovereignty for Hawai`i.

How to Use This Book

Each of the six major islands, Kaua`i, O`ahu, Maui, Moloka`i, Lana`i and Hawai`i, has its own chapter. The Kaua`i chapter includes information on Ni`ihau Island and Midway Atoll and its national wildlife refuge visitor program.

Each chapter begins with sections on *Geography, Climate* and *History*, which serve as an introduction to the island. This is followed by *Information Sources* and *References* sections providing additional contacts and sources of information for each island. This includes visitors' bureau offices, resort destination offices, chambers of commerce, travel industry associations, and travel-related books. There is also a *Getting There* section detailing airline service to the island as well as inter-island air service. Full airline contact information, telephone numbers, and Internet Web site and e-mail addresses are also provided where available. There are sections on transportation details like buses, rental cars, motorcycles and bicycles. *Touring* covers the main highways and routes around each island as well as touching on the major attractions of each area and land tour operators.

Adventures details the many adventure activities and options for each island. Full contact information is included for making reservations or obtaining information, and where available and appropriate, addresses, telephone numbers, and Internet Web site and/or e-mail addresses. Adventures and activities listed include everything from hiking, golf, tennis, shopping, and museums through biking, beaches and water sports activities, scenic air tours, horseback trail ride adventures and unique island eco/cultural activities.

Each chapter ends with a detailed listing of *Camping, Lodging*, and *Dining* options.

Adventure Island-Style

■ On Foot

The islands have an amazing diversity of hiking trails and adventures and this book lists a number of the most popular walks and hikes for each island as well as a few of the lesser known backcountry trails and treks. While it's impossible to list them all, there is a good cross-section of hiking adventures included with something for everyone, from novice, to experienced hiker, to the challenging backpacker who relishes remote overnight campouts in the wilderness.

In Hawai`i or any other area you don't know well, use common sense before striking out on a trail. Get a trail map and study it, consult with the local island visitors' bureau office, resort destination office, your hotel concierge, or park service rangers for information on the area or specific trail you plan to hike. While some walks and trails may appear easy and short, there may be special conditions such as freak rainstorms that could make them downright dangerous. Find out about any special weather factors that could affect your planned hike, what sort of gear you might need, how much water and food to carry. And if you're thinking of going it alone, think twice.

Some island trails are fraught with danger because of the terrain, climate and other conditions. Trails across open lava fields often have cracks and deep chasms into which hikers can fall and get severely injured. Some trails are susceptible to foggy, cloudy conditions during storms, causing hikers to lose their way. Some mountain ridge trails are narrow, steep and winding, with sharp vertical dropoffs. If a hiker steps off the trail, a fall would surely cause injury and the thick rain forest vegetation can hide and muffle any sounds made by an injured hiker, even though rescuers may be only a few feet away.

Hiking Tips

■ Use common sense and be prepared. Realize that help and rescue can be hours away, especially on a remote difficult trail.

■ Learn about the conditions to be expected on the trail you're hiking before you depart.

■ Begin hiking early, allowing plenty of time to reach your destination and return, or to set up camp for the night.

■ It's always best to hike with a companion. Be sure to let someone know where you're going, what trail you're taking and how long you expect to be gone.

■ Know your limits and capabilities. Don't challenge yourself and your physical condition beyond them.

■ Know that some of Hawai`i's backcountry trails are used by local fishermen and hunters, sometimes traveling with horses and/or mules. Be cautious and do nothing to frighten or spook the animals, especially on dangerous cliffside or ridge trails. Get off the trail if you do encounter horses or mules and give them the right of way.

■ Take plenty of water with you. The heat, humidity and physical exertion of hiking Hawai`i can be punishing. Don't drink water from streams and ponds because Hawai`i's watersheds have high levels of foreign bacteria. Stream and pond water must be boiled first or have purification tablets added to make it safe to drink.

■ Take lots of snacks and food along, in case you're gone longer than expected.

■ Use good judgement and enjoy Hawai`i's many fantastic hiking trails and adventures.

In addition to details on hiking, each chapter's *On Foot* section also covers activities like golf and tennis plus more sedate pursuits like shopping, museums and touring historic sites. For some, these are adventures in themselves.

■ On Wheels

 You will find many adventures on wheels in the islands, including bus or van tours, individual rental cars, off-road 4WD sport utility vehicles, motorcycles, motorscooters and mopeds, bicycles and even a few horse-drawn wagon rides.

Each island chapter lists the tour operators and details the itineraries offered. There are also listings of rental agencies for cars, motorcycles-mopeds, bicycles and others. Some of the car rental agencies have off-road 4WD vehicles available for backcountry trails and roads. A few have exotic luxury and sports cars available for those whose definition of an adventure is cruising the islands in a Corvette or a Ferrari.

Biking, on the streets and off-road, has become increasingly popular in the islands. More and more visitors are opting for bicycle adventures, through organized group excursions offered by tour operators or as individual outings. Some serious bikers even bring their own bikes with them, shipping them as part of their baggage on the airlines. Bike lanes on Hawai`i's streets and highways are becoming more common. But some island roads still pose problems for bikers in that they can be narrow, winding and steep. So bikers need to be aware of vehicle traffic and use special caution to stay out of vehicle lanes as much as possible.

Each island chapter has a section on bicycle rentals and shops plus a descriptive listing of trails suitable for bikers. It's impossible to list all the biking trails but this book's listings by island are a good cross-section. Some of the more rugged backcountry trails are a special challenge and will appeal to mountain bikers. Most trails open to hikers are open to bikers, but there are exceptions. And restrictions vary from time to time, being enforced and then rescinded by local governing authorities. So, as much as possible, check ahead to see what restrictions, if any, apply to trails you plan on biking.

Trails for hiking and biking vary widely throughout the islands from easy to difficult, flat to hilly, hard-packed dirt to slippery mud in rainy conditions. Trails listed in this book are open to the public but some may cross private land and may be marked with a "Kapu" sign, meaning no trespassing. Check ahead to see if you need a permit or permission to follow a specific trail.

The tour operators listed for each island run a variety of itineraries, taking advantage of each island's attractions and geophysical attributes. The tours offered are usually comprehensive and include the bike and all necessary equipment, helmet, raingear, water, snacks and/or lunch, etc. The bike shops and others listed can also provide additional information on biking the islands, so don't hesitate to call on them.

The rules that govern hiking trails can generally be applied to biking trails as well. Common sense prevails.

Biking Tips

■ Keep to the trails and don't venture off on your own into unknown territory, especially in deep forests, valleys, gulches and lava fields. Respect private property and requirements for permits and/or obtaining permission. Realize that some national and state park trails may be off-limits to bikers.

■ Avoid marring or damaging trail surfaces. Avoid loosening rocks, soil, roots, stairs. Leave nothing behind; take only pictures.

■ Be aware of trail conditions, ride responsibly and avoid actions that cause danger or harm to hikers and others riding with you.

■ Yield to hikers; don't come upon them by surprise. Share the trail and the joy of being outdoors with others.

■ Know that some of Hawai`i's backcountry trails are used by local fishermen and hunters, sometimes traveling with horses and/or mules. Be cautious and do nothing to frighten the animals, especially on dangerous cliffside or ridge trails. Give animals the right of way.

- Be prepared. Know your bike and equipment and keep all in good working condition so there is no hazard to you or others.

■ On Water

One of Hawai`i's biggest recreational resources is, of course, the ocean. Both visitors and residents flock to the beaches and coastlines, protected bays and coves. The *On Water* section of each chapter details all the many types of activities available. Included are listings of beaches by region on each island, cruises, sailing and rafting excursions, kayaking, parasailing and jet ski adventures, scuba diving and snorkeling cruises, whale watching cruises, surfing and windsurfing, and deep sea fishing charters.

On Water Tips

- An old Hawaiian saying states: "Never turn your back to the sea." Many have been knocked over by unexpectedly large and powerful waves. Some survive but many drown. Always be on guard when at the coast or beach.

- Not all Hawai`i beaches have lifeguards. And nowhere are they on duty all the time. Try to choose one that does have a lifeguard on duty.

- Ask lifeguards or local folks about surf conditions. Ask about currents, riptides and undertows. Study the waves, their frequency and size. Look for signs of currents and riptides. Pay attention to warning signs of heavy surf or other hazardous conditions. Read and heed signs about large waves, undertows, slippery rocks, jellyfish or other unsafe conditions.

- Use the buddy system and never swim or snorkel alone.

- If you're unsure of your ability in the ocean, use a flotation device that you wear rather than an air mattress or other device from which you may become separated.

- Use extreme caution with small children as well. Put a flotation device on them. Don't let them wander into rough water or near breaking surf.

- Tidal pools and shallow reef areas are great places to explore and observe marinelife, but always wear protective footwear and keep an eye on any high surf action. Avoid the sharp rocks and corals of the reef as cuts can be dangerous and very painful. Also keep in mind that some marine animals have natural defenses like sharp spines, stingers, or poisons. Don't stick your fingers or hands into crevices in the reef where creatures may lurk.

- Respect the sea and its power. Don't take unnecessary risks like getting close to a blowhole or posing for pictures near a big surf breaking in the background.

Hawai'i's sun emits powerful ultra-violet rays that can cause serious damage to unprotected skin. This is true whether you're swimming at the beach, lounging around the hotel pool, or hiking through the lavafields. Many folks learn the hard way that Hawai'i's sun can bake and burn in a very short time. Always use a good sunscreen or sunblock, hat and light coverup clothing where possible. An after-sun product is also helpful.

■ In the Air

Beautiful to behold from the ground, the Islands of Aloha are something else again from the air. Magnificent is almost too tame a description. Suffice it to say that the green-clad mountains, deep lush valleys and sheer plunging cliffs make for some truly awesome viewing experiences. Each island chapter lists a number of scenic air tour and helicopter flightseeing adventures.

■ Eco/Cultural Excursions

There are a considerable number of eco/cultural activities throughout the islands. Each island chapter lists activities, with details, location and full contact information. Included are river cruises, botanical gardens, fruit farms, coffee farms, wineries, historic old towns, aquariums and marinelife parks, zoos, historic churches and heiau (temples), cultural centers, nature centers, historic parks and fish market auctions. Many of these provide a special perspective on Hawai`i's unique history, multi-cultural heritage or environment.

Lodging, Camping & Dining

There are far too many accommodations and restaurants of all types around the islands to list them all in this book. Each island chapter has a cross-section of accommodations and restaurant listings organized by region. The listings are chosen for cleanliness, quality, value, ambience, surroundings, location, good service, great food, menu variety, available amenities or a combination of these. Keep in mind that hotels and restaurants can and do change rates/prices, services, menus, and times of operation frequently.

Accommodations and restaurants listed cover the range from budget, to moderate, to first-class. The listings are categorized by a price scale listed at the beginning of each section. The hotel rate scale is based on the standard nightly rate for a double-occupancy room as follows:

Accommodations Price Scale
$ . . . . up to $100 per night
$$ . . . . $100-199 per night
$$$ . . . . $200-299 per night
$$$$ . . . . $300 and up per night

The restaurant price scale below is for the average dinner meal per person with no alcohol or dessert included:

Dining Price Scale
$ . . . . under $10 per person
$$ . . . . $10-25 per person
$$$ . . . . $25 and up per person

Hawaiian Foods

The following glossary should be helpful in your culinary adventures.

Adobo - Filipino seasoned meat, poultry or seafood.

Ahi - Hawaiian name for yellowfin tuna.

Aku - Hawaiian name for skipjack tuna.

Bean thread noodles - also called long rice, this is fine vegetable-based Asian pasta used in a variety of dishes.

Black beans - Chinese fermented salted soybeans used as a flavoring.

Char siu - Chinese-style sweet flavored roast pork.

Coconut milk - rich, creamy liquid squeezed from grated coconut, available fresh, frozen or canned.

Dim sum - Chinese-style steamed or fried dumplings with various fillings.

Furikake - Japanese condiment of dried seaweed flakes and sesame seeds.

Ginger - spicy, pungent root used for flavoring.

Haupia - Hawaiian coconut pudding.

Hawaiian red chile pepper - small, very hot chile pepper grown and used in Hawai`i to add spice flavoring.

Hawaiian salt - white or pinkish coarse sea salt traditionally harvested on Kaua`i Island.

Huli huli - Hawaiian term for cooking over an open fire or barbecuing.

Kalbi - Korean-style barbecued short ribs.

Kalua pig - traditional Hawaiian roast pig flavored with Hawaiian salt and cooked in an underground oven (imu), a luau staple.

Kamaboko - Japanese steamed fish cake, used as ingredient in other dishes such as saimin noodles.

Katsu - breaded and fried chicken, pork or beef, usually with Oriental-style soy flavored barbecue sauce.

Kiawe - Hawaiian name for the algaroba or mesquite tree whose hard wood and chips make charcoal used for grilling and smoking meats.

Lilikoi - egg-shaped, yellow fruit with a zesty citrus flavor, full of seedy, juicy pulp, used for flavoring dishes; passionfruit.

Limu - Hawaiian word for seaweed.

Luau - young taro leaves used in preparing certain luau dishes such as laulau; also refers to the large festive meal where luau foods and other traditional Hawaiian dishes are served.

Laulau - bundles of meat such as pork, beef or fish wrapped in luau leaves; bundles are then wrapped in ti leaves and cooked in traditional Hawaiian underground oven (imu) or steamed.

Lomi salmon - Hawaiian salad made from salted salmon and diced onions and tomatoes.

Macadamia nut - native of Australia but grown widely in Hawai`i; round, creamy, light-brown nut noted for rich, oily flavor and used in a variety of dishes.

Mahimahi - Hawaiian name for the dolphinfish.

Malasada - Portuguese fried doughnut.

Manapua - Chinese steamed bun with sweet pork filling.

Mandoo - Korean-style dumplings filled with vegetables or meat.

Manju - Japanese sweet bun filled with bean-paste.

Miso - fermented soybean paste.

Misoyaki - Japanese dish of meat or fish marinated in miso, then broiled.

Mochi - sticky glutinous rice cake.

Nabemono - Japanese-style dish with ingredients such as vegetables, seafood, meat.

Nori - paper-thin green/black sheets of dried seaweed; used to wrap sushi (rice) rolls.

Ogo - a type of edible Hawaiian seaweed.

Onaga - Hawaiian name for red snapper fish.

Ono - Hawaiian name for long fish of the mackerel family, also called wahoo.

Opakapaka - Hawaiian name for pink or ruby snapper fish.

Opihi - limpet shellfish which grows on rocks along shorelines; considered a delicacy for Hawaiian luaus and eaten raw.

Pinacbet - Filipino mixed vegetable dish.

Pipikaula - Hawaiian beef jerky.

Poi - a starchy, purplish-gray paste akin to mashed potatoes and made from cooked taro root, a staple of the Hawaiian luau.

Poke - Hawaiian word for "slice," referring to traditional Hawaiian-style sliced raw seafood such as ahi tuna, squid or octopus with fresh seaweed, Hawaiian salt and red chile peppers; usually eaten as an appetizer.

Portuguese sausage - Hawaiian-made pork sausage spiced with chili pepper, garlic, salt and other flavorings; comes in mild to very hot versions; used in a variety of dishes.

Pulehu - charcoal broiled meats usually seasoned with Hawaiian sea salt.

Pupu - any finger food served as an appetizer.

Saimin noodles - also called ramen, a common variety of thin Asian wheat noodles, often served with pieces of fish cake, cabbage, egg; served in soup or as an entrée.

Sashimi - Japanese word for thinly sliced and very fresh raw fish, usually ahi tuna, served with soy sauce and horseradish paste.

Soy sauce - known in Hawai`i as shoyu, an essential dark brown liquid flavoring made from fermented soy beans, salt, flour and water and used widely in Asian cookery.

Sushi - Japanese vinegared rice; various styles of rice cakes and rolls with different vegetable, meat and seafood fillings.

Taro - a traditional Hawaiian food; large, purplish tuber used for making poi, a starchy edible paste dish and a staple of the traditional Hawaiian diet and luau.

Tempura - Japanese style of deep frying.

Teriyaki - a Japanese sauce or marinade made from soy sauce, sugar and fresh grated ginger; beef, chicken, pork or fish that has been marinated in the sauce and then baked or broiled.

Tofu - fresh soybean curd, used in various Asia/Pacific dishes.

Won ton or Wun tun - Chinese meat-filled dumplings.

Yakitori - Japanese-style grilled or broiled chicken.

Hawaiian Regional Cuisine

Hawai`i has a wonderfully diverse tradition in cuisine and foods. Dining out all over the Hawaiian Islands is truly an adventure, whether you are a genuine gourmet or someone who simply enjoys good food. Hawai`i's ethnically diverse population has, over the years, helped to blend and meld many differents cuisines into a truly delightful marriage. This has given rise over the last few years to what culinary experts recognize as "Hawaiian Regional Cuisine," a trend which utilizes fresh local produce, meats, seafood and incorporates the culinary influences of Hawai`i's diverse population. You'll find restaurants, cafés, coffee shops and local-style eateries featuring dishes with flavors from Hawai`i, China, Japan, Korea, southeast Asia, Europe and America. You're in for a real culinary adventure.

Traveling to Hawai`i & Inter-Island

Hawai`i is about five hours flying time from the US west coast. Each island chapter details the airlines and services to/from that island and the US mainland. The main gateway to the Hawaiian Islands is, of course, Honolulu. It has the greatest number of direct flights to/from the US mainland. However, Kaua`i, Maui and Hawai`i have direct US mainland flights as well, although not as many. Most inter-island flights are about 30 minutes. Hilo to Honolulu is the longest route and takes 40-45 minutes.

For the romantics who yearn for a slower more leisurely mode of transport, there is a section on cruise ships that sail to Hawai`i and inter-island.

Hawai`i's Visitor Seasons

With a continuous mild climate, Hawai`i is a year-round destination. The islands have two separate peak visitor seasons during the year when demand for flights, hotels, restaurants, rental cars and tours is heaviest. The first is during the winter months, roughly from mid-November through the end of March. The other busy season is during the summer months, from June through the end of August. The rest of the year is generally slower and quieter. The months of April and May or September and October are great times to visit Hawai`i because the crowds are gone and the weather is pleasant.

Climate & Weather

As the old cliche about the weather goes, if you stick around long enough it'll change. That's pretty much true of the islands as well. Hawai`i is blessed with generally mild temperatures and moderate humidity the year around. The temperature variation from day to night and season to season is relatively small. Weather conditions and temperatures vary by elevation and area of the island.

Hawai`i basically has two seasons. Summer is May to October, when the sun is close to directly overhead. The weather during this period is warmer and drier than the rest of the year and the northeast tradewinds (which cool and temper the islands) blow more regularly.

The winter months are November to March. During this time, the sun is farther to the south and the weather, both day and night, is noticeably cooler. The northeast tradewind pattern is often interrupted and "kona" (south) winds, cloudy periods and rainstorms rumble through the islands.

■ Rainfall

Rainfall varies greatly between the islands and within each individual island. The eastern, windward sides of the islands generally receive the greatest amount of rainfall because the prevailing northeast tradewinds (at least in the summer) bring the rainclouds over the eastern coasts. The clouds are then carried up and over the interior mountains and the rain is released. That's why the windward sides of the islands are so lush and green with rain forests and dense vegetation. The western or leeward sides of all the islands tend to be much drier, with considerably less vegetation and more desert-like conditions.

Rainfall varies by elevation and location but along the windward coastal areas it can be 50-130 inches or more annually. Hana on Maui's east coast averages about 70 inches annually, while Hilo on Hawai`i's east coast averages 130 inches per year. Higher elevation areas generally receive much higher annual rainfalls. By contrast, Lahaina on Maui's leeward coast averages just 14 inches annually while the Kohala Coast on the Big Island of Hawai`i averages less than 10 inches per year and is recognized as the driest region in the islands. Rainfall is equally distributed throughout the year, with no real wet and dry season.

■ Temperatures

Average daytime temperatures in summer range from the upper 70s to low 80s in most areas of the islands. In winter, daytime temperatures range from the upper 60s to lower 70s. However, temperatures can vary more significantly at higher elevations throughout the islands, particularly in high mountain areas.

Clothing & Gear

For most occasions, dress in the islands is casual. For men, an Aloha shirt (made from that colorful, flowery art print fabric) and slacks are appropriate for almost any occasion. For women, the same can be said of a mu`umu`u (a full-length dress made from that same Aloha fabric). Comfort and fit should be important guidelines in selecting what clothing to bring. Generally, lightweight cotton and blend materials, and permanent press wash-and-wear clothes are the most versatile. The emphasis should be on keeping cool and comfortable in the tropics. Jeans or shorts and tee shirts are the daily wear here.

The only time men might need a more formal coat and tie and ladies an evening dress would be for that special night out at one of the more plush resorts or fine-dining restaurants. But many of the better restaurants that used to require jackets for men have rescinded the rule and have gone more casual.

Beachwear, swimsuits and the like are appropriate for the beach and pool areas, but most resorts require coverups for the lobby, public areas, shops and restaurants, so plan accordingly.

You will need warm clothes if you plan to visit higher-elevation national parks, ranches or rain forests. And on the mountain summits of Haleakala on Maui or Mauna Kea and Mauna Loa on the Big Island freezing temperatures and snow are not unusual. Warm water-repellent jackets would also be useful for rainy days and cool temperatures.

Comfortable walking or hiking shoes are definitely a must for hiking. Any other special clothing and/or gear necessary for activities you plan to participate in should be brought with you. Most tour operators or outfitters will provide any special clothing or gear necessary for their activity.

Driving & Road Conditions

There is a comprehensive highway, road and street system linking all regions of each major island. The highways essentially encircle the islands. Roads and highways are maintained by either the island county or the State of Hawai`i. Honolulu on O`ahu is the only area with a multi-lane freeway system, but it is limited mostly to the densely populated central island region. The major highways and roads on all the islands are paved.

Driving on island highways and roads is no different than driving elsewhere. Just remember to drive defensively and with caution. Some roads, especially in rugged coastal areas, gulches and valleys, tend to be narrow, winding and steep in places, often with little or no shoulder margin.

Also, in some places with steep cliffsides along coastal areas or in gulches, heavy rainfall can cause landslides and road closures. Some low-lying places near stream beds and natural drainages are subject to flooding in heavy rain. So be aware of the route you are taking and the weather conditions. Heed any hazard warnings or posted signs. If you are unsure, make inquiries about local road and weather conditions. In each major island chapter, the Information Sources section lists the telephone contact for the National Weather Service office on that island. A call will provide the current weather conditions and immediate area forecast.

DID YOU KNOW?

**Hawai`i Warrior Road Signs:** While driving around the islands, be on the lookout for the distinctive red and yellow cloaked Hawaiian Warrior road signs. These have been erected by the Hawai`i Visitors Bureau to note special historic sites, places of interest to visitors and scenic attractions.

Tropical Photography

Be familiar with your camera equipment before taking a trip. If you're using a new camera or lens, run a roll or two of film through to make sure it works properly and that you know how to use it. You wouldn't try to break in a new pair of hiking boots on a trip to Hawai`i would you? Don't do it with new photography equipment either.

If it's equipment you've used and are familiar with, check it over to make sure all is in working order. Install a fresh set of batteries and take along an extra set. Nothing's worse than to be in the field ready for that shot-of-a-lifetime and then have the camera fail due to a dead set of $3 batteries.

One hazard for photographers in the islands is rain. Depending on the season and locale, rain can be frequent and heavy. However, with caution and adequate rain gear, you can still shoot pictures. One good thing about rainy days is that subtle overcast lighting can create special effects on your subjects and give your pictures a different mood.

At the other extreme of Hawaiian weather is the glaring hot sun. The usual midday lighting is harsh and brilliant. In this light, heavy shadows almost always enter photographs. Be aware of them and learn to compensate for dark shadowy areas in your pictures. Use your camera's light meter to take a reading for both light and shadow areas of your scene and then average it out. Take additional shots one aperture stop above and below the meter reading to ensure that one of your photos will be perfect. You can also use your camera's built-in flash or a portable flash to fill in and brighten dark shadow areas.

Keep in mind that early morning and late afternoon or early evening hours are the best times for picture-taking because the natural outdoor lighting is usually mellow and golden. These are the best times to take dramatic outdoor pictures.

The sun produces heat very fast in the tropics. Leaving your camera and film to "bake" in a closed car can ruin the emulsions of your film and adversely affect the operation of your camera and lens mechanisms.

Sand from the beach is another problem. Fine gritty sand can get into the camera's mechanism, on the mirror or in the lens. Protect your camera when you're on the beach. Avoid putting it down on the sand.

Finally, the fine misty salt spray from ocean surf is very corrosive to camera bodies and lenses. After shooting ocean-beach scenes, or if you've been out on the water, thoroughly clean your camera with a soft cloth, lens cleaner and tissues.

You can easily buy film in the islands but keep a good supply on hand. Film is cheap in comparison to the other costs of travel like airplane tickets, hotels, car rentals and food. After the trip when you're back home, your photos will help you relive your experience. So enjoy your adventures in these splendid islands and shoot lots of film.

Information Sources

For most practical purposes, the statewide Hawai`i Visitors and Convention Bureau is the main resource for travel information on all islands. The HVCB offices are listed here, as well as in each chapter. They will provide free information. For quick access, check out their Web site listed below.

Telephone Access in the Islands: Hawai`i's area code is 808.

Hawai`i Visitors & Convention Bureau Offices

Honolulu, O`ahu (Corporate Office)

Waikiki Business Plaza, 2270 Kalakaua Avenue, 8th floor, Honolulu, HI 96815, ☎ 800/GO-Hawai`i, 808/923-1811; Fax 808/922-899; Web site (for all islands) http://www.goHawaii.com.

Big Island of Hawai`i

250 Kwawe Street, Hilo, HI 96720, ☎ 808/961-5797; Fax 808/961-2126.

75-5719 W. Alii Drive, Kailua-Kona, HI 96740, ☎ 808/329-7787; Fax 808/326-7563.

Kaua`i

3016 Umi St., Suite 207, Lihue, HI 96766, ☎ 808/245-3971; Fax 808/246-9235.

Maui

1727 Wili Pa Loop, Wailuku, HI 96793, ☎ 808/244-3530; Fax 808/244-1337.

References

The following may prove helpful in planning your trip and your adventures.

Ball, Stuart. *The Backpackers Guide to Hawai`i,* University of Hawai`i Press, Honolulu, HI. 1996.

Berger, Andrew J. *Hawaiian Birdlife,* University of Hawai`i Press, Honolulu, HI. 1994.

Fielding, Ann and Robinson, Ed. *An Underwater Guide to Hawai`i,* University of Hawai`i Press, Honolulu, HI. 1991.

Introduction

Grant, Glen. *Obake Files: Ghostly Stories from the Supernatural of Hawai`i,* Mutual Publishing, Honolulu, HI. 1996.

Grant, Glen. *Waikiki Yesteryear,* Mutual Publishing, Honolulu, HI. 1996.

Harper, Stephan K. *Hawai`i Golf Guide,* Teebox Publishing, 1994.

Hawai`i Audubon Society. *Hawai`i's Birds,* Hawai`i Audubon Society, Honolulu, HI. 1993.

Henderson, Janice Wald. *The New Cuisine of Hawai`i,* Random House, Inc. New York, NY. 1993.

Hobson, E. and Chave, E.H. *Hawaiian Reef Animals,* University of Hawai`i Press, Honolulu, HI. 1979.

Judd, Gerrit P. *Hawai`i: An Informal History,* Macmillan Publishing Co., New York, NY. 1979.

McMahon Richard. *Camping Hawai`i - A Complete Guide,* University of Hawai`i Press, Honolulu, HI. 1994.

Menton, Linda and Tamura, Eileen. *A History of Hawai`i,* University of Hawai`i, Honolulu, HI. 1993.

Merlin, Mark. *Hawaiian Forest Plants,* University of Hawai`i Press, Honolulu, HI. 1996.

Olsen, Brad. *Extreme Adventures Hawai`i,* Hunter Publishing, Edison, NJ. 1998.

Pratt, Douglas. *Enjoying Birds in Hawai`i,* Mutual Publishing Co., Honolulu, HI. 1993.

Smith, Rodney. *Hawai`i: A Walker's Guide,* Hunter Publishing, Edison, NJ. 1997.

Soehren, Rick. *The Birdwatcher's Guide to Hawai`i,* University of Hawai`i Press, Honolulu, HI. 1996.

Vogelsberger, Paul. *Golf Hawai`i: The Complete Guide,* Printech Hawai`i, 1995.

Wallin, Doug. *Diving & Snorkeling Guide to the Hawaiian Islands,* Gulf Publishing Company, 1991.

Kaua`i

The Garden Island

Geography

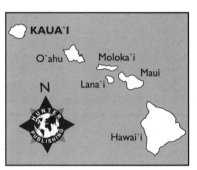

Kaua`i, the Garden Isle, has a land mass of 553.3 square miles and is the fourth largest of the seven major populated Hawaiian Islands. It is also the oldest of the inhabited islands and has a population of about 56,000. The County of Kaua`i is comprised of the Island of Kaua`i and the county seat is Lihue. The island was formed by the eruption of one massive volcano. Mt. Waialeale, at 5,148 feet, is the largest remaining portion. The island's remarkable landscape includes the scenic Waimea Canyon, a deep gorge on the west side and the spectacular Na Pali Coast on the north shore, with cliffs rising 2,700 feet and white sand beaches scattered in clefts of the dazzling coastline. The age of the island, as measured by comparison of its structural lava flows, ranges from 3.8 to 5.6 million years. Kaua`i has some 90 miles of alternating rugged rocky coastal areas, seacliffs and beautiful sandy beaches.

Climate

Average temperatures range from 70° near the coast in February and March to 77° in August and September. Cooler temperatures in the mountain areas offer a pleasant contrast. The world's wettest spot is at Mt. Waialeale, with an average annual rainfall of 450-475 inches. The rainfall record there is 665.5 inches in a single year. Elsewhere on Kaua`i, the east and north shores get 30-45 inches annually, while the south and west shores get only 5-20 inches.

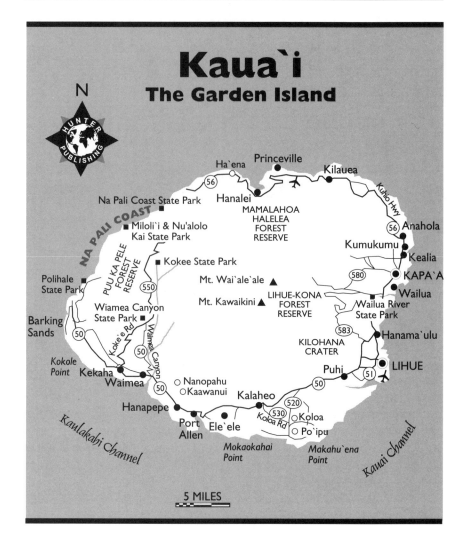

Kaua`i
The Garden Island

N

Ha`ena Princeville Kilauea

56

Na Pali Coast State Park Hanalei
MAMALAHOA
HALELEA
FOREST
RESERVE 56 Anahola
Miloli`i & Nu'alolo
Kai State Park
Kumukumu
Kealia
Kokee State Park 580 KAPA`A
Polihale
State Park 550 Mt. Wai`ale`ale ▲ Wailua
LIHUE-KONA
FOREST
RESERVE Wailua River
State Park
Mt. Kawaikini ▲
Wiamea Canyon
State Park ■
Barking
Sands 50 583 Hanama`ulu
KILOHANA
CRATER
Kokole
Point Kekaha Puhi 51 LIHUE
Waimea 50
Nanopahu
Kaawanui 50
Kalaheo
Hanapepe 530 520
Koloa Rd Koloa
Port
Allen Ele`ele  Po`ipu
Mokaokahai
Point Makahu`ena
Point

NA PALI COAST
PUU KA PELE FOREST RESERVE
Koke`e Rd
Waimea Canyon
Kuhio Hwy
Kaulakahi Channel
Kauai Channel

5 MILES

History

The first settlers, Polynesians, probably arrived on Kaua`i around 800 AD. The islanders enjoyed a healthy environment overall, even though they lived under the rigid kapu system of rules. The island prospered under a succession of ruling ali`i (kings and chiefs). The Hawaiians knew nothing about the world beyond their shores until Captain James Cook came ashore at Waimea in January, 1778. Kaua`i remained independent until 1810, when King Kaumuali`i conceded the island to Kamehameha the Great in order to avoid the devastation and bloodshed of war. Thus, Kaua`i was the only island that Kamehameha did not conquer in battle and it was the last to recognize and join a united kingdom of Hawai`i.

Sugarcane and pineapples were its primary industries for generations, until the demise of pineapple cultivation in the 1960s and '70s. Sugar is still important in some areas of Kaua`i, while other crops like coffee, papaya and guava are expanding rapidly. Tourism became an important part of the island economy after statehood. Visitors found the "Garden Island" had beautiful tropical scenery and a friendly ambiance which made it a relaxing vacation spot. Over the past few years, Kaua`i has been in the movies and on TV, having provided scenic backdrops for a number of full-length features.

Information Sources

**Kaua`i Visitors Bureau,** 3016 Umi Street, Suite 207, Lihue, Hi 96766; Kaua`i Hotline Visitor Information, ☎ 800/262-1400, 808/245-3971; www.visit.Hawai`i.org/.

Poipu Beach Resort Association, PO Box 730, Koloa, HI 96756, ☎ 808/742-7444; e-mail info@poipu-beach.org; http://poipu-beach.org.

Princeville Resort, PO Box 3069, Princeville, HI 96722, ☎ 800/826-4400; http://www.Hawai`i-travel.com/Princeville.htm.

Kalapaki Bay Resort Association, Kaua`i Marriott, Kalapaki, Lihue, HI 96766, ☎ 808/826-9343.

Economic Development Office, County of Kaua`i, 4280A Rice St., Lihue, HI 96766, ☎ 808/241-6390; http://Kaua`i-Hawaii.com.

Kaua`i County Information Office, 4444 Rice St., Suite 245, Lihue, HI 96766, ☎ 808/241-6303.

Parks & Recreation Department, Camping Permits, County of Kaua`i, 444 Rice St., #150, Lihue, HI 96766, ☎ 808/241-6660.

Division of State Parks, Department of Land & Natural Resources, Camping Permits, 3060 Eiwa Street, Room 306, Lihue, HI 96766, ☎ 808/241-3444.

Kaua`i Chamber of Commerce, 4272B Rice St., Lihue, HI 96766, ☎ 808/245-7363.

Kaua`i Vacation Planner, http://www.hsHawaii.com/kvp/.

National Weather Service, daily forecasts for Kaua`i, ☎ 808/245-6001.

References

Alford, John. *Mountain Biking the Hawaiian Islands: Mauka to Makai,* Ohana Publishing, Honolulu, HI. 1997.

Chisholm, Craig. *Kaua`i Hiking Trails,* The Fernglen Press, Lake Oswego, Oregon, 1994.

Carter, Frances. *Hawai`i on Foot,* Bess Press, Inc., Honolulu, HI, 1990.

Early, Dona, and Stilson, Christie. *Kaua`i: A Paradise Family Guide,* Prima Publishing, Rocklin, CA, 1997.

Koch, Tom. *Six Islands on Two Wheels: A Cycling Guide to Hawai`i,* Bess Press, Honolulu, HI, 1990.

Morey, Kathy. *Kaua`i Trails: Walks, Strolls and Treks on the Garden Isle,* Wilderness Press, Berkeley, CA, 1997.

Olsen, Brad. *Extreme Adventures Hawai`i,* Hunter Publishing, Edison, NJ. 1998.

Smith, Robert. *Hiking Kaua`i,* Hawaiian Outdoor Adventures Publications, Maui, Hawai`i, 1997.

Smith, Rodney. *Hawai`i: A Walker's Guide,* Hunter Publishing, Edison, NJ. 1997.

Stone, Robert. *Day Hikes on Kaua`i,* Day Hike Books, Inc., Red Lodge, Montana, 1997.

Zurick, David. *Hawai`i, Naturally,* Wilderness Press, Berkeley, CA. 1990.

Getting There

■ Inter-Island Airlines

Inter-island airlines provide numerous daily regularly scheduled flights between Honolulu, Kaua`i's Lihue Airport, Princeville Airport and other destinations within the islands.

- **Aloha Airlines,** US ☎ 800/367-5250, Canada ☎ 800/235-0936, on Kaua`i ☎ 808/245-3691; e-mail aloha@alohaair.com; www.alohaair.com/.

- **Hawaiian Airlines,** US and Canada ☎ 800/367-5320, on Kaua`i ☎ 808/245-1813; www.Hawaiianair.com/.

- **Island Air,** US ☎ 800/323-3345, Canada ☎ 800/235-0936, within Hawai`i ☎ 800/652-6541; e-mail aloha@alohaair.com; www.alohaair.com/. This subsidiary of Aloha Airlines provides shuttle service between Honolulu and Princeville Airport in north Kaua`i.

■ US Mainland & Kaua`i

Presently, United Airlines is the only major air carrier providing flights to Kaua`i's Lihue Airport, with direct service from the US west coast via Honolulu.

- **United Airlines,** in the US at ☎ 800/241-6522; www.ual.com

- **Pleasant Hawaiian Holidays,** ☎ 800/242-9244, in Hawai`i at ☎ 808/923-7611; www.pleasantholidays.com. This tour operator specializes in complete air/hotel packages to Kaua`i with flights via Honolulu.

Kaua`i

■ Cruise Ships

The last few years have seen an increase in international cruise ships making port calls in the Hawaiian Islands. So, once again, it is possible to sail to the islands on a luxurious ocean liner. Several cruise lines now regularly route their ships into Honolulu on a seasonal basis, as well as to the neighbor islands of Kaua`i, Maui and the Big Island of Hawai`i at Kona and Hilo. Schedules vary as do itineraries. For details, it is recommended that you check with a travel agent or cruise tour reservation specialist.

Among the ships that have made Hawai`i port calls on regular sailings recently from North America and other points are: **Princess Cruise Lines'** *Island Princess, Sea Princess* and *Golden Princess* (☎ 800-PRINCESS/774-6237)*;* **Royal Viking Lines'** *Sagafjord* and *Royal Viking Sun* (☎ 800-426-0821); **Holland America Lines'** *Statendam, Rotterdam* and *Maasdam* (☎ 800-426-0327); **Cunard Lines'** *Queen Elizabeth II* (☎ 800-221-4770); **Royal Caribbean Lines'** *Legend of the Seas* (☎ 800-327-6700); and **Carnival Cruise Lines'** *MS Tropicale* (☎ 800-327-9501).

In addition, within the Hawaiian Islands, American Hawai`i Cruises offers exclusive inter-island cruises between Honolulu and the neighbor islands aboard the *SS Independence*. There are three-day and week-long packages. The ship spends a day in each port at Kaua`i, Maui and the Big Island's Kona and Hilo. There are shore excursions and tours available from dockside at each port. For details and information, contact your travel agent or: **American Hawai`i Cruises**, 550 Kearny St., San Francisco, CA 94108, ☎ 800/765-7000.

Getting Around

You can drive almost the entire way around Kaua`i except where the road is blocked by the rugged and beautiful Na Pali Coast area on the northwest side of the island. The road extends from Polihale Beach

State Park on the west side to Ke`e Beach at Ha`ena State Park on the north end. From one end to the other is a distance of roughly 75-80 miles.

Lihue, the main town and airport, is on the southeast side of the island. The Kuhio Highway #56 follows the east coast to the north through the old plantation towns of Wailua and Kap`aa to Anahola, Kilauea, Princeville Resort and Hanalei on the North Shore, a distance of about 31 miles. The road winds along the coast for another nine miles past Hanalei, where it terminates at Ha`ena State Park. This portion of the road is quite narrow, winding and hilly.

Southwest out of Lihue, the Kaumualii Highway #50 follows overland through sugar plantation country to the turnoff to Koloa and the Poipu Beach resort area. The road continues west to Kalaheo, Hanapepe, Waimea and the west coast, where it terminates at Polihale Beach State Park, a distance of about 40 miles. At Waimea, there are turnoffs onto Koke`e Road and Waimea Canyon Road, which connect and follow up the spectacular Waimea Canyon to Koke`e and Kalalau Valley Lookout, where the road terminates. This is a distance of 20 miles one way.

Essentially, there is one main highway around the island. And there are few branch roads off the main highway, so you shouldn't get lost, or at least if you do, it shouldn't be for long. Keep in mind that even though Kaua`i is small and there are few roads, there is a lot of traffic. Also, heavy trucks and tour buses use the same highway around the island, so be aware of traffic ahead and behind at all times.

Just remember when driving around Kaua`i, always lock your car when you park and never leave valuables inside unattended.

> Car rental agencies will provide a detailed map of Kaua`i. Available in Kaua`i bookstores and many other shops is the latest edition of the excellent full color topographic *Map of Kaua`i,* by James Bier and published by the University of Hawai`i Press.

■ Bus/Taxi Service

There are some local tour bus and taxi operators that provide airport/hotel transportation and general island tours. Call them in advance for reservations and information.

- **Akiko's Taxi,** 5258 Laipo Road, Kapa`a, ☎ 808/822-7588.

- **North Shore Cab & Tours,** PO Box 757, Hanalei, ☎ 808/826-6189.

- **Poipu Taxi,** PO Box 173, Kaumakani, ☎ 808/639-2044, 639-2042.

- **South Shore Taxi & Tour,** Poipu Beach, ☎ 808/742-1525.

- **City Cab,** Lihue, ☎ 808/245-3227.

- **Al's VIP Limo Taxi,** Poipu Road in Poipu, ☎ 808/742-1390.

- **Scotty Taxi,** three-3400 Kuhio Highway, Lihue, ☎ 808/245-7888.

- **Roberts Hawai`i Tours,** ☎ 800/831-5541, on Kaua`i ☎ 808/245-9101.

- **Trans Hawaiian Kaua`i,** 3601 Ahukini Road, Kaua`i, ☎ 808/245-5108.

■ Limousine Service

If you want to go first-class with airport/hotel transportation or even a customized island tour or special excursion, you might consider hiring a private luxury stretch limousine. If you're so inclined, contact any of the following:

- **Kaua`i North Shore Limousine,** PO Box 757, Hanalei, HI 96714, ☎ 808/826-6189.

- **Rocky's Limousine Service,** 3-2087 Kaumualii Highway, Lihue, HI 96766, ☎ 808/246-0662.

- **Custom Limousine,** PO Box 3267, Lihue, HI 96766, ☎ 808/246-6318.

- **Kaua`i Limousine,** Lihue, Kaua`i, ☎ 808/245-4855.

■ Car & Truck Rentals

Since Kaua`i is relatively small and has essentially one highway following the coast around the island, a rental car is probably your best value in ground transportation. Having your own car gives you flexibility in arranging your own adventures and planning your own schedule.

There are several national car rental agencies on Kaua`i and most are located at Lihue Airport. Some of the agencies have rental desks in hotels and shopping centers.

- **AA Aloha Cars-R-Us,** ☎ 800/655-7989, on Kaua`i ☎ 808/879-7989.

- **AA Paradise Network,** ☎ 800/942-2242, on Kaua`i ☎ 808/579-8277.

- **Alamo Rent a Car,** ☎ 800/327-9633, on Kaua`i ☎ 808/246-0645.

- **Avis Rent a Car,** ☎ 800/321-3712, on Kaua`i ☎ 808/245-3512.

- **Budget Rent a Car,** ☎ 800/527-0700, on Kaua`i ☎ 808/245-1901.

- **Dollar Rent a Car,** ☎ 800/800-4000, on Kaua`i ☎ 808/245-3651.

- **Hertz Rent a Car,** ☎ 800/654-3011, on Kaua`i ☎ 808/245-3356.

- **Ho`okipa Haven Vacation Service,** for all Hawaiian Islands, ☎ 800/398-6284.

- **National Car Rental,** ☎ 800/227-7368, on Kaua`i ☎ 808/245-5636.

- **Westside U-Drive,** 4562 Ehako, Poipu Beach area, ☎ 808/332-8644.

■ Motorcycle & Scooter Rentals

There is only one operator renting motorcycles and scooters on Kaua`i. Call them for the current daily and weekly rates.

- **Ray's Motorcycle Rentals,** 4558 Kukui, Kapa`a, HI 96746, ☎ 808/822-HOGG. Open seven days a week with daily or weekly rentals of Harley-Davidson motorcycles.

■ Bicycle Rentals

Kaua`i has only a couple of operators renting bicycles and related equipment. Call them for current daily and weekly rental rates.

- **Kaua`i Cycle and Tour,** 1379 Kuhio Highway, Kapa`a, HI 96746, ☎ 808/821-2115.

- **Outfitters Kaua`i,** 2827A Poipu Road, Poipu, Koloa, HI 96756, ☎ 808/742-9667.

Touring Kaua`i

Regardless of where you stay in Kaua`i, you'll have easy access to the rest of the island. Since it is relatively small, driving distances are short between areas and attractions.

■ Lihue, the County Seat

Lihue is the government and commercial center for all of Kaua`i. County of Kaua`i and State of Hawai`i government office complexes are located in town. One of Lihue's noteworthy features is the large **Kaua`i Marriott Hotel** at Kalapaki Beach. Adjacent to the hotel complex are the Kiele Golf Club and Lagoon Golf Club (☎ 808/241-6000), both championship courses. The hotel beach area fronts on Nawiliwili Bay and Harbor. The Hule`ia River flows into Nawiliwili Bay and upstream is the **national wildlife refuge** and the **Menehune Fishpond**, which can be seen from a lookout off Hulemalu Road leading up from the harbor. Lihue has several older shops and restaurants in the downtown area as well as newer shopping complexes around town. With its central location on the southeast side of the island, Lihue is within easy reach of all areas of Kaua`i.

Kalalau Valley Lookout, Waimea Valley.

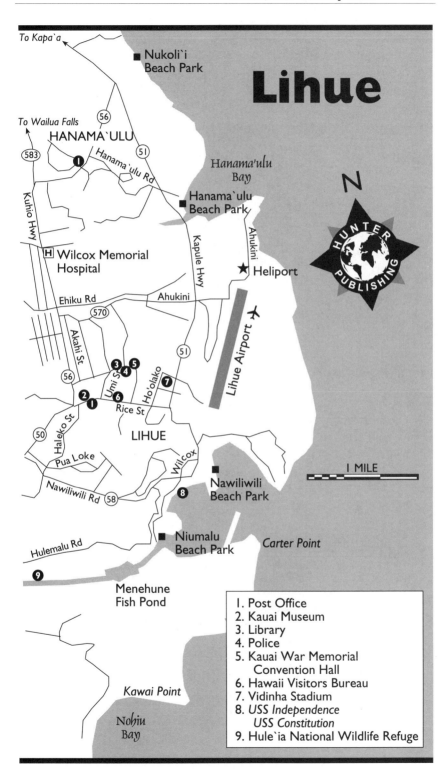

Lihue

Kaua'i

1. Post Office
2. Kauai Museum
3. Library
4. Police
5. Kauai War Memorial
   Convention Hall
6. Hawaii Visitors Bureau
7. Vidinha Stadium
8. *USS Independence*
   USS Constitution
9. Hule'ia National Wildlife Refuge

Kalalau Valley & Mountains, Waimea.

■ The Coconut Coast

From Lihue, if you're heading north on Kuhio Highway 56, the Wailua River area has a number of river activities including cruises to the famous **Fern Grotto**. There are also kayak and hiking excursions along the river plus the **Keahua Arboretum** on Kuamo`o Road behind Wailua. **Wailua Falls** and **Opaeka`a Falls** in this area are both worth seeing. There are several nice beaches in the Wailua and Kapa`a areas, known as the Coconut Coast.

The Sleeping Giant

Near Kapa`a is a mountain profile view of the sleeping giant, a local legend. According to local legend, a giant named Puni lay down to rest near the banks of the Wailua River. Villagers from the area, frightened by the giant, tried to wake Puni and scare him away by throwing rocks at him. The rocks landed in his mouth and choked him to death. He still lies there today.

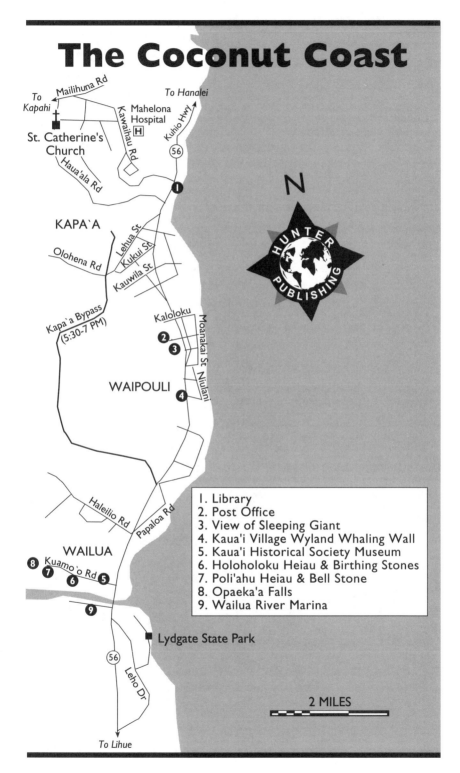

The Coconut Coast

To Kapahi
Mailihuna Rd
To Hanalei
Mahelona Hospital [H]
Kawaihau Rd
Kuhio Hwy
St. Catherine's Church
Haua'ala Rd
[56]
❶

KAPA'A
Olohena Rd
Lehua St
Kukui St
Kauwila St

Kapa'a Bypass (5:30-7 PM)
Kaloloku
❷
❸
Moanakai St
Niulani

WAIPOULI
❹

Haleilio Rd
Papaloa Rd

WAILUA
❽ Kuamo'o Rd
❼
❻ ❺
❾

1. Library
2. Post Office
3. View of Sleeping Giant
4. Kaua'i Village Wyland Whaling Wall
5. Kaua'i Historical Society Museum
6. Holoholoku Heiau & Birthing Stones
7. Poli'ahu Heiau & Bell Stone
8. Opaeka'a Falls
9. Wailua River Marina

■ Lydgate State Park

[56]
Leho Dr

2 MILES

To Lihue

Kaua'i

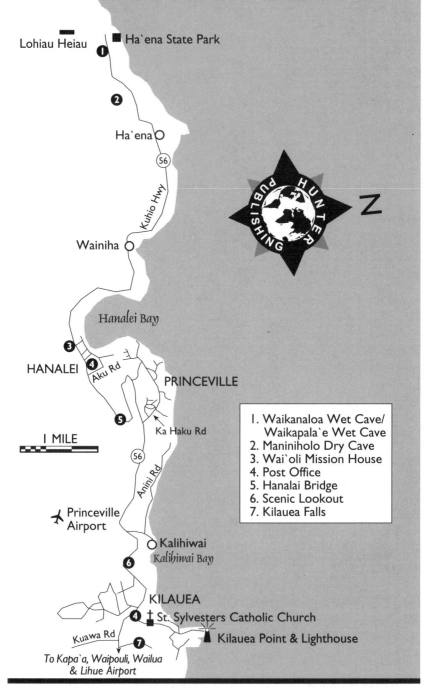

The North Shore

Lohiau Heiau

■ Ha`ena State Park

❶

❷

Ha`ena ○

56

Kuhio Hwy

Wainiha ○

Hanalei Bay

❸

HANALEI ❹ Aku Rd

PRINCEVILLE

❺

I MILE

Ka Haku Rd

56

Anini Rd

✈ Princeville
Airport

○ Kalihiwai
Kalihiwai Bay

❻

KILAUEA

❹ ✝ St. Sylvesters Catholic Church

Kuawa Rd

❼

▲ Kilauea Point & Lighthouse

*To Kapa`a, Waipouli, Wailua
& Lihue Airport*

1. Waikanaloa Wet Cave/
   Waikapala`e Wet Cave
2. Maniniholo Dry Cave
3. Wai`oli Mission House
4. Post Office
5. Hanalai Bridge
6. Scenic Lookout
7. Kilauea Falls

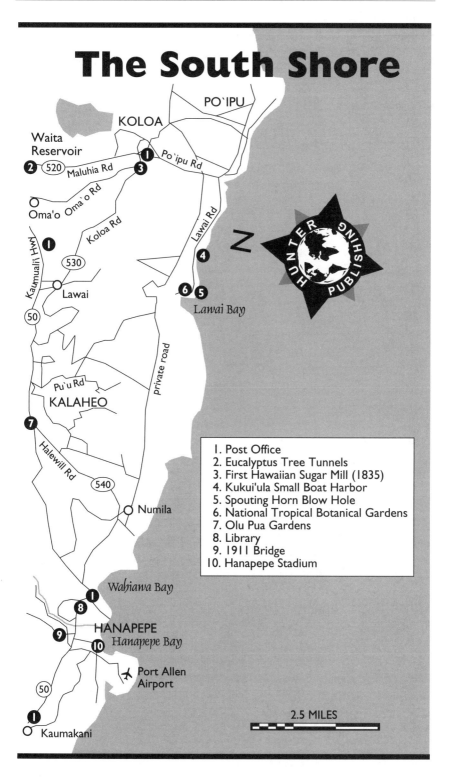

The South Shore

PO`IPU

KOLOA

Waita Reservoir

② ⑳520 Maluhia Rd

Po `ipu Rd ①

③

Oma'o Oma`o Rd

Koloa Rd

Lawai Rd

N

Kaumualii Hwy

① ⑤530

Lawai

④

⑥⑤

Lawai Bay

⑤50

Private road

Pu`u Rd

KALAHEO

⑦

Halewill Rd

⑤540

Numila

1. Post Office
2. Eucalyptus Tree Tunnels
3. First Hawaiian Sugar Mill (1835)
4. Kukui'ula Small Boat Harbor
5. Spouting Horn Blow Hole
6. National Tropical Botanical Gardens
7. Olu Pua Gardens
8. Library
9. 1911 Bridge
10. Hanapepe Stadium

Wahiawa Bay

①

⑧

HANAPEPE
⑨   Hanapepe Bay
⑩

Port Allen
Airport

⑤50

①
Kaumakani

2.5 MILES

Kaua`i

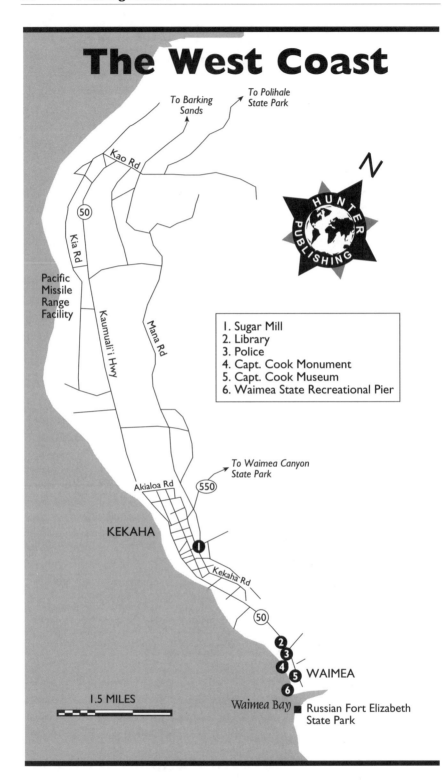

The West Coast

To Barking Sands

To Polihale State Park

Kao Rd

50

Kia Rd

Pacific Missile Range Facility

Kaumuali`i Hwy

Mana Rd

1. Sugar Mill
2. Library
3. Police
4. Capt. Cook Monument
5. Capt. Cook Museum
6. Waimea State Recreational Pier

To Waimea Canyon State Park

Akialoa Rd

550

KEKAHA

Kekaha Rd

50

2
3
4
5 WAIMEA
6

1.5 MILES

Waimea Bay

Russian Fort Elizabeth State Park

■ The North Shore

Further up the coast at Kilauea, be sure to stop at **Kilauea Point National Wildlife Refuge**. There are lots of seabirds nesting on this high seacliff area near the old lighthouse. The drive onward to Princeville and Hanalei passes through cattle ranches and rolling hill country as you get near the North Shore area. **Hanalei** has beautiful tropical mountain and coastal scenery with lovely white and golden sand beaches all along the coast. Princeville and Hanalei have several resorts and vacation condos throughout the area. Over the years, this area has been used for several movies and TV shows as background scenery. Distances between the sights and attractions are short. The views at **Hanalei Bay** are beautiful, with rugged tropical mountain peaks serving as a backdrop to a lovely crescent beach and bay. The Hanalei River flows through the Hanalei Valley and the view from the Princeville lookout is spectacular. Hanalei town is a funky beach town with colorful shops and restaurants worth exploring. Your drive ends at **Haena State Park** and before you is the rugged Na Pali Coast. You can hike the **Kalalau Trail** along the coast either as a day-trip or overnight.

■ Koloa & Poipu Beach

Leading south and west out of Lihue is the Kaumualii Highway 50. South of the highway and across the Hule`ia River valley is a profile of Queen Victoria in the Hoary Head mountain range, visible as you're leaving town. The south coast is noted for the famous **Poipu Beach** area, with its classy hotels, condos and golf courses and historic old Koloa town, where the sugar industry on Kaua`i got its start. There is much history in this area plus such attractions as the spouting horn blowhole. The famous **National Tropical Botanical Garden** is at Lawai and the **Olu Pua Botanical Garden** is also nearby at Kalaheo.

■ Waimea & the West Coast

Further along the coast is the old plantation town of Hanapepe, now something of an artists' colony with several interesting art shops and galleries. Waimea is the gateway to the scenic **Waimea Canyon** and all the hiking, biking, nature walks and camping that it offers – plus the spectacular **Kalalau Valley lookout**. The mouth of **Waimea Bay** is recognized as the first landing place of **Captain James Cook** in the Hawaiian Islands in 1778. There is a monument to Captain Cook in town and many of Waimea's buildings are on the National Register of Historic

Kaua`i

Waimea Canyon & Koke`e State Park

KOKE`E
STATE
PARK

WAIMEA
CANYON
STATE
PARK

550

Veterans
Memorial
Hospital H

KEKAHA

Russian Fort 50
Elizabeth ■

Waimea Bay

1. Waimea Canyon Lookout
2. Pu`u Hinahina Lookout
3. Koke`e Lodge
4. Kalalau Lookout
5. Pu`u o Kila Lookout
6. Waipo`o Falls

Places. It's an interesting town to explore. Also on a bluff overlooking Waimea Bay are the ruins of a **Russian Fort** dating back to 1817 when, for a brief time, Kaua`i was a Russian protectorate. On the west coast near the end of the road is the **Pacific Missile Range Facility at Barking Sands** (so called for the curious sound made by the sand when rubbed between the hands – caused by cavities in the sand pebbles). **Polihale Beach State Park** is a beautiful wild area at the end of the road on the west coast. This is a broad expanse of golden sand and rugged surf. Like the route to the North Shore, the south and west sights and attractions are relatively close to one another.

■ Land Tours

The following tour operators offer half-day and full-day coach and van tours around Kaua`i visiting the island's main sights and attractions, Waimea Canyon, Wailua River, Coconut Coast, West Coast, Poipu Beach, the North Shore and more. Contact the operators for current details. Standard half-day island tours range from $33 to $43 per person; full-day tours are $60 to $73 per person.

- **Polynesian Adventure Tours,** 3113 B Oihana Street, Lihue, HI 96766, ☎ 808/246-0122.

- **Roberts Hawai`i Tours**, Lihue, Kaua'i, HI 96766, ☎ 800/831-5541, on Kaua`i ☎ 808/245-9101.

- **Trans Hawaiian Kaua`i,** 3601 Ahukini Road, Kaua`i, HI 96766, ☎ 808/245-5108.

- **Kaua`i Mountain Tours,** PO Box 3069, Lihue, HI 96766, ☎ 808/245-7224.

- **Activities Unlimited Kaua`i Inc.,** 6281C Hauaala Road, Kapa`a, HI 96746, ☎ 808/821-1313.

- **Hawai`i Movie Tours,** 356 Kuhio Highway, Kapa`a, HI 96746, ☎ 808/822-1192.

Adventures

Kaua`i's Best Adventures

Following are a dozen of Kaua`i's best, listed in no particular order.

- Take a bike tour down the **Waimea Canyon Road**.

- Kayak the **Wailua River** to the **Fern Grotto** and hike to a jungle waterfall.

- Hike the famed **Kalalau Trail** on the Na Pali Coast.

- Take a **scenic boat or raft ride** along the **Na Pali Coast**.

- Hike any of the trails in the **Waimea Canyon**.

- Visit the **Kilauea Lighthouse and National Wildlife Refuge**.

- Go **horseback riding** in east Kaua`i.

- Take a spectacular **helicopter ride** along the **Na Pali Coast**.

- Explore Kaua`i's **National Tropical Botanical Garden** at Lawai and Haena.

- Hike the historic **Poipu Beach Trail**.

- Enjoy an authentic Hawaiian **luau and hula show**.

- Stroll any of the famed **North Shore beaches**.

■ On Foot

 Kaua`i has a number of hiking trails, ranging from coastal beach trails, to pali (cliff) trails and rain forest walks. The trails pass through different eco-climate zones around the island, presenting spectacular scenic views of beach and coast, forest and mountain, streams and waterfalls.

The North Shore

DON'T MISS **Kalalau Trail** begins at the end of Kuhio Highway 56 at Haena State Park, Ke`e Beach. This is Kaua`i's premier hiking trail, leading into some of its most spectacular wilderness along the famed Na Pali Coast. The 11-mile trail passes through five lush valleys, winding along towering seacliffs, isolated beaches and old Hawaiian ruins. The first section, Ke`e Beach to Hanakapiai Beach, is a two-mile walk in, 2½ hours. Side trails lead off into valleys and secluded waterfalls. Midway is a campground for those packing camping gear. No facilities, so hikers must carry water and supplies. The trail ends at Kalalau Beach and return is along the same route. This is a difficult trail, with some stretches over rocky terrain and stream crossings. Muddy and slippery when raining. Camping permits required: **Department of Land & Natural Resources**, State Parks Division, 3060 Eiwa St., Room 306, Lihue, HI 96766, ☎ 808 241-3444.

The Coconut Coast

Kuilau Ridge Trail is just opposite the Keahua Arboretum on Highway 580, Kuamoo Road, 5½ miles above Wailua. This is a 2.4-mile, two-hour round-trip moderate uphill hike to a picnic shelter. The rest stop overlooks the surrounding tropical rain forest and mountains. Take some time to wander through the arboretum to enjoy the mountain views and exotic trees and plants. This is a good mountain biking trail also.

Nounou Mountain Trail-East Side, turn left off Kuhio Highway 56 at second stoplight past Wailua River Bridge onto Haleilio Road. From the intersection, drive two miles and look for trailhead on right at telephone pole #38. The trail winds its way up, climbing through dense rain forest. The moderate 3½-mile, two-hour round-trip walk ends at a picnic shelter on the chest of the "Sleeping Giant" mountain. Nice panoramic views of ocean, the Wailua River and Mt. Waialeale on clear days. **Nounou Mountain Trail-West Side** begins along Kamalu Road, Highway 581, in the Wailua Homesteads at telephone pole #11. The three-mile round-trip, 1½-hour trail climbs up the mountain and joins the East Side Trail, passing through replanted forest. The trail is quite steep in areas.

**Kapa`a Coastal Walk** begins at the north end of Kapa`a town off Kuhio Highway 56 opposite Haua`ala Road near the Kapa`a Jodo Mission Church. Near the roadside parking area, there is an old roadway which meanders along the coastline. The old roadway rises along the ocean ridge with trails leading off to the beach below. There is a ridge overlook at about one mile with nice coastal and beach views. This is an easy two-mile round-trip, one-hour hike. Ocean breezes and sun can be strong at mid-day here.

Waimea Canyon Area

Iliau Nature Loop. This easy quarter-mile 20-min. loop trail is on Waimea Canyon's western edge and begins at Kukui Trail. There are native upland plants identified and scenic canyon vistas.

Awaawapuhi Trail. This is a more serious and strenuous 6½-mile round-trip, probably requiring three-four hours or more. It begins on Highway 550, Waimea Canyon Road, at the 17-mile marker. Native dryland plants are identified. The trail ends at a grassy picnic spot at 2,500 feet elevation. Beautiful vistas of valleys and Na Pali Coast.

**Halemanu-Koke`e Trail.** This easy 2½-mile round-trip begins off Halemanu Road, Koke`e State Park in Waimea Canyon. This is a self-guided nature trail through native forest with lots of birdlife.

Pihea Trail. This is a strenuous, difficult 7½-mile trail which begins at the end of Highway 550, Waimea Canyon Road, at Puu O Kila, Koke`e State Park Lookout. There are scenic canyon views, native forest and birds, and wet swamp terrain to traverse.

___

Hiking Resources

Sierra Club-Hawai`i Chapter/Kaua`i Group, PO Box 3412, Lihue, HI 96766, ☎ 808/822-9238 or 246-8748. This group has regular outings, walks, hikes and excursions around Kaua`i and visitors may be able to join their activities. Call or write for information.

Kaua`i

Golf Courses

There are public and private resort golf courses on Kaua`i with beautiful ocean and mountain landscape views. Greens fees at the resort courses range from $70 to $150, with public course fees much less.

- **Princeville Makai Golf Course,** Princeville Resort, has three courses – Woods Nine, Lakes Nine, and Ocean Nine; ☎ 808/826-3580.

- **Prince Golf and Country Club,** Princeville Resort, is a par-72 championship layout, ☎ 808/826-5000.

- **Wailua Golf Course,** Wailua, is a municipal par-72 layout, ☎ 808/241-6666.

- **Kaua`i Lagoons Golf Club,** Kalapaki Beach, Lihue, adjacent to Marriott Hotel, has two courses, Kiele Course and Lagoons Course, ☎ 808/241-6000. These championship courses have hosted PGA tournaments in the last few years.

- **Kiahuna Golf Club,** Poipu Beach Resort, is a par-70 layout, ☎ 808/742-9595.

- **Poipu Bay Resort Golf Course,** Poipu Beach Resort, is a par-72 course, ☎ 808/742-8711.

- **Kukuiolono Golf Course,** Kalaheo, is a nine-hole par-36 public course, ☎ 808/332-9151.

Tennis Courts

Kaua`i has both public tennis courts operated by the County of Kaua`i and private resort courts that are open to the public. Some county courts are lighted for night play and resort courts require advance reservations and charge use fees. Many hotels and condos have their own tennis facilities for guests, which range from $8 to $20 per hour.

- **Hanalei Bay Resort,** 5380 Honoiki Road, Princeville Resort, ☎ 808/826-6522.

- **Kaua`i Lagoons Racquet Club,** at the Kaua`i Marriott Hotel, Lihue, ☎ 808/241-6000.

- **Kiahuna Tennis Club,** Poipu Beach Resort, ☎ 808/742-9533.

- **Princeville Tennis Complex,** Princeville Resort, ☎ 808/826-3620.

- **Hyatt Regency Kaua`i Tennis Club,** 1571 Poipu Road, Poipu Beach Resort, ☎ 808/742-1234.

County of Kaua`i tennis courts are located in parks in the following areas: Waimea, Kekaha, Koloa, Kalaheo, Lihue, Wailua and Kapa`a.

Shopping

Kukui Grove Shopping Center, Kaumuali`i Highway 50 on the west edge of Lihue, ☎ 808/245-7784, is Kaua`i's largest traditional shopping complex, with Liberty House department store, Sears, K-Mart, Borders Bookstore, Longs Drugs plus fashion, jewelry, shoe, and specialty gift shops.

**Kaua`i Village Plantation Shops,** Kuhio Highway 56, Kapa`a, ☎ 808/822-4904. This complex of over 40 shops and restaurants features arts and crafts galleries, jewelry, apparel and gift stores, plus Longs Drugs, Safeway and popular restaurants like A Pacific Café.

Coconut Marketplace, Kuhio Highway 56, near Kapa`a, ☎ 808/822-3641. This is a pleasant complex of small shops and boutiques featuring resort fashions, jewelry, arts and crafts galleries, specialty gifts and a number of restaurant and food outlets.

Waipouli Town Center, 771 Kuhio Highway 56, Waipouli, has several shops and food concessions.

Ching Young Village, in the heart of historic Hanalei, North Shore, Kuhio Highway 56, ☎ 808/826-7222. There are several interesting shops and food outlets from art to apparel, groceries to gifts and pizza to local-style plate lunches.

Kinipopo Shopping Village, Kuhio Highway 56, Wailua. There are jewelry, surf, tattoo, resort wear and other shops, plus restaurants in this small complex across from Sizzler's.

Kilohana, one mile west of Lihue on Kaumuali`i Highway 50, ☎ 808/245-5608. This historic plantation estate is a tudor-style manor house and has a number of fine boutique shops including arts and crafts, jewelry, fashion and specialty gifts, plus Gaylord's Restaurant.

Anchor Cove Shopping Center, 3416 Rice Street, near Nawiliwili Harbor and Kalapaki Beach, Lihue, ☎ 808/246-0634. There are a number of specialty shops ranging from arts and crafts to resort wear, plus restaurants and food outlets.

Kaua`i

Hawaiian Arts and Crafts

Hawaiian Trading Post, Lawai, ☎ 808/332-7404.

Kaua`i Museum Gift Shop, 4428 Rice Street, Lihue, ☎ 808/246-2470.

Lehuanani Designs, 5361 Kuapapa, Kapa`a, ☎ 808/821-0696.

**Products of Hawai`i,** 4-484 Kuhio Highway, C-13, Kapa`a, ☎ 808/821-0384.

House of Handcraft, 4-484 Kuhio Highway, C-10, Kapa`a, ☎ 808/822-2566.

Sandra's Crafts, 4473 Kukui Street, Kapa`a, ☎ 808/822-1555.

Island Gifts, 4-484 Kuhio Highway, Kapa`a, ☎ 808/821-0193.

The Country Store, Kilohana, Highway 50, ☎ 808/246-2778.

**Gifts of Kaua`i,** 4-484 Kuhio Highway, Kapa`a, ☎ 808/822-0851.

Aloha Oe Island Gifts, 9875 Waimea Road, Waimea, ☎ 808/338-9946.

Avana's at Hanalei, 5-5190 Kuhio Highway, B4, Hanalei, ☎ 808/826-6867.

Lana's Hawaiian Shop, 4-1477 Kuhio Highway, #B, Kapa`a, ☎ 808/821-2017.

Uncle Eddie's Aloha Angels, 3830 Hanapepe Road, Hanapepe, ☎ 808/335-0713.

J & J Ohana, 4520 Kukui, #103, Kapa`a, ☎ 808/822-7525.

Museums

Explore and discover the early history of Kaua`i with a visit to **Kaua`i Museum,** 4428 Rice Street, Lihue, HI 96766, ☎ 808/245-6931. Learn about the geological history of Kaua`i and the Hawaiian Islands. Get the story of the early Hawaiian people, their culture, arts and lifestyle. See how the islands have changed since Captain Cook first landed in Waimea in 1778. The Kaua`i Museum will help you gain an incredible appreciation for the wonderful diverse heritage of the people and islands of Hawai`i. The Museum Shop has an excellent collection of Hawaiiana books and local crafts.

**Koke`e Natural History Museum,** Koke`e State Park, Waimea Canyon, ☎ 808/335-9975. There are informative exhibits and displays relating to Waimea Canyon and Koke`e's natural history, flora and fauna and the area's unique ecosystem.

Waimea Sugar Mill Camp Museum, PO Box 1178, Waimea, HI 96796, ☎ 808/338-0006, on Kaua`i's west side, offers walking tours through a real sugar mill camp, a residential housing complex for plantation workers' families built between 1900 and 1930. Visitors learn about the plantation lifestyle of an earlier era and how these hardworking immigrants created an industry that in turn led to the multicultural society of Hawai`i today.

■ On Wheels

Biking Kaua`i

 The following can provide you with all the details, maps, information, bikes and equipment enjoy Kaua`i's great biking trails. They also offer organized biking excursions. Half-day tours including the popular Waimea Canyon downhill bike ride begin at $65 per person. Check with the outfitters for details.

Outfitters Kaua`i, 2827A Poipu Road, Koloa, HI 96756, ☎ 808/742-9667. This outfitter offers a spectacular 12-mile winding Bicycle Downhill Canyon to Coast adventure through the Waimea Canyon to Kekaha Beach Park; bike and equipment rentals too.

Kaua`i Coasters, PO Box 3038, Lihue, HI 96766, ☎ 808/639-2412; e-mail coast@aloha.net; www.aloha.net/~coast This bike outfitter offers 12-mile half-day cruises down Waimea Canyon.

Bicycle Downhill, ☎ 808/742-7421. This bike outfitter has 12-mile cruises down Waimea Canyon to the coast at Kekaha.

**Kaua`i Cycle and Tours,** 1379 Kuhio Highway, Kapa`a, HI 96746, ☎ 808/821-2115. This outfitter offers a variety of guided mountain bike tours on scenic trails around Kaua`i; also guided night rides.

Bicycle John, 3215 Kuhio Highway, Lihue, HI 96766, ☎ 808/245-7579; http://Kaua`i.net/~kwc9/bicyclejohn/bjmain. This is a full-service bike sales and repair shop, with equipment and parts.

Lihue Area

Hulemalu Road and Menehune Fish Pond Ride. This ride begins at Lihue's Nawiliwili Harbor Beach Park. Across the harbor is the Mar-

In the Fern Grotto, Wailua River.

riott Hotel and Kalapaki Beach. Follow the road west past the ship docks and Matson Navigation Company. Past a small bridge, hang right onto Hulemalu Road at Niumalu Park. This winding road lies below the Hoary Head Mountains and parallels the Huleia Stream National Wildlife Refuge. There is an overlook at the famous Menehune Pond on the stream. The road continues through warm, dry and dusty sugarcane fields to the area of Puhi where it meets the Kaumuali`i Highway 50. Turn right to head back to Lihue, and return to Nawiliwili Harbor via Nawiliwili Road #58, a 10-mile round-trip, moderate difficulty, two-three hours.

The Coconut Coast

Wailua Falls Ride. Just north of Lihue turn off Kuhio Highway #56 at Hanamaulu onto Highway #583; watch for sign. Ride four miles to the end of the road through old sugarcane fields and stream gulches. This is a winding, hilly and narrow country road. At road's end is Wailua Falls, a beautiful twin falls (depending on rainfall) set amidst lush tropical vegetation. There is a rough trail leading to the waterfall base, but it is dangerous, especially when wet and muddy, and not recommended. Return to Kuhio Highway the same way. This moderate round-trip is eight miles, two hours.

**Opaeka`a Falls and Keahua Arboretum.** North of Lihue turn off Kuhio Highway #56 at first right past Wailua River Bridge onto Kuamoo Road #580; watch for sign. It's two miles of gradual uphill to the Opaeka`a Falls overlook. Along this stretch are some historic old Hawaiian heiau (temples). There are nice overlook views of the Wailua River Valley. You'll also see lots of boat traffic on the river, from kayaks to ski boats to cruise boats shuttling tourists up to the famous fern grotto. It's another five miles on a winding and hilly road to Keahua Arboretum. There are foot trails through the botanical gardens, picnic facilities and even some swimming holes on Keahua Stream, which runs through the arboretum. Return to Kuhio Highway the same way. This moderate round-trip is 14 miles, four to five hours.

Moalepe Trail starts in the Wailua Homesteads at the end of the paving on Olohena Road. It begins as a right-of-way crossing a pasture within the Wailua Game Management Area. The trail enters the forest reserve for about a mile. It joins the Kuilau Trail (see hiking section above) at about 2.15 miles.

Kuamoo-Nounou Trail starts at .5 mile past Opaeka`a Falls on Kuamoo Road, Highway 580. It connects with the Nounou Mountain West Side Trail and follows the west side of Nounou Forest Reserve through replanted forest groves.

The North Shore

DON'T MISS **Kilauea Point National Wildlife Refuge** explores the seabird refuge and historic lighthouse at Kilauea Point. Turn off Kuhio Highway 56 at Kilauea, follow signs to Kilauea Road. It's about 1½ miles to the refuge entrance through residential areas and pastureland. Leave bikes at the visitors center and explore the high seacliff bluff, a short walk away. The lighthouse is on the National Register of Historic Places. The bird refuge is home to the red-footed booby, wedge-tailed shearwater, Laysan albatross and other Hawaiian seabirds. They'll be soaring and riding the rising air currents over the cliffs and pounding surf. Some of the birds burrow into the ground to build nests. Just offshore is Mokuaeae Islet, also a seabird refuge. Length of ride from Kilauea town round-trip, three miles and one-two hours.

Hanalei Valley Lookout and Valley Ride begins at the Hanalei Valley Lookout on Kuhio Highway 56 at Princeville Resort. Adjacent to the shopping center, an overlook has nice valley vistas of taro fields, mountains and the Hanalei River. Winding down the highway a mile or so, an old steel-frame bridge crosses the river. Turn left after crossing the bridge and follow the Hanalei River Road through taro patches to the national wildlife refuge wetlands to look for endangered Hawaiian water birds. The two-mile paved road ends at a hunter check station. Foot trails lead to the river wetlands. Return to the highway, turn left to Hanalei town

Kilauea Lighthouse.

Kaua`i

Na Pali Coast Hiking Trail.

and ride to the end of the road at Haena. Pass through the quiet town of Hanalei and check out Hanalei Pier on the bay for nice scenic views. Continue west past many fine beaches and the Haena wet and dry caves. The Na Pali Coast trail begins at road's end and there are nice views of the coast from here. Biking the Na Pali Coast trail is not advised. Caution is advised on the narrow winding highway; some hills and sharp curves. Be prepared for hot sun and/or rain showers throughout. Princeville to Haena round-trip on this route is about 16 miles, moderate difficulty, five-six hours.

Princeville Resort Ride is a casual exploration ride through the meandering roads of this large residential resort complex of hotels, vacation condominiums, tennis courts and golf courses. While most of the area sits above the ocean on seacliffs, access is available to small beaches below Sealodge Condo, Pali Ke Kua Condo, the Princeville Resort and Hanalei Bay Resort. Vantage points allow views of Hanalei Bay to watch surfers and windsurfers challenge the surf. The resort roads meander in and around residences and golf course fairways. Nice views and easy ride on paved roads, with gentle tradewinds that cool the area; varying length and duration of ride, three-seven miles, two-four hours. Begin and end at Princeville Shopping Center.

Hanalei Valley taro fields.

The South Shore

The Mahaulepu Ride is a three-six-hour 17-mile round-trip ride along the beautiful Poipu Beach resort area on Kaua`i's sunny south shore. The ride begins at Poipu and Lawai Road intersection and follows the coastal access roads east through the resort area and back onto Poipu Road near the Hyatt Regency. The paved road turns to dirt passing coastal sand dunes and the golf course. The dirt road leads to Kawailoa Bay and Pao`o Point and Haula Cove, with a nice beach. It's a moderate ride with lots of interesting historical sites along the way. Check with Outfitters Kaua`i above for details on this and other rides.

The Spouting Horn Ride is an easy ride of one to two hours covering five- miles round-trip. This ride is also in the Poipu Beach area and begins on the Lawai Road just below the intersection with Poipu Road. Follow the paved Lawai Road along the coast. The route passes the birthplace, now a park, of Prince Jonah Kuhio Kalanianaole, who served as Hawai`i's first delegate to the US Congress. The road meanders along the coast and past a number of vacation homes and condominiums. The route terminates at the famed Spouting Horn Park.

Waimea Canyon & Koke`e Park

DON'T MISS The most exciting bike rides on Kaua`i are the **Waimea Canyon to Coast Downhill Cruise** and the **Koke`e Mountain Bike Ecotour.** These rides take place at Waimea Canyon, on Kaua`i's west side. The canyon downhill ride is two-three hours and 12 miles of casual cruising down the winding road in the "Grand Canyon of the Pacific." Stops are made along the way to take in the natural history and culture of the area. The downhill ride starts at Koke`e up in the Waimea Canyon and terminates at Kekaha on the coast. The mountain bike ride takes place at Koke`e and explores the cool high forest backroads of the state park area. Riders can learn about the natural history and culture and see rare Hawaiian flora and fauna. The bike shop outfitters provide transportation pickups for the ride up to Koke`e in the Waimea Canyon.

■ On Water

Beaches

Kaua`i has a wonderful variety of beaches, big and small, some next to the highways with lots of parking, some that are secluded, with little or no parking. You may have to park and walk a ways to reach some beaches. Ocean conditions vary by season, location and weather. Read and heed beach warning signs. Some beaches on Kaua`i have lifeguards, but not all. Check on water and surf conditions with lifeguards if available.

North Shore

Haena Beach Park is near the end of Kuhio Highway 56 at Haena across from Maniniholo Dry Cave; swimming, snorkeling, picnics.

DID YOU KNOW?

Hanalei Beach is on Kuhio Highway 56 at Hanalei town on the bay. This is a wide sandy expanse highlighted by the Hanalei Pier, seen in the movie *South Pacific*. Park has restrooms and picnic facilities. This beach was listed in the annual "Top 10 Best Beaches" national survey conducted by the University of Maryland; it is one of six Hawai`i beaches so honored.

Tunnels, at Haena next door to Haena Beach Park, is also good for swimming, scuba underwater caves, surfing.

Anini Beach Park, just below Princeville Resort on Anini Road, has windsurfing, snorkeling and fishing (best in summer and calm weather), along with picnic facilities.

East Shore

Anahola Beach Park, at Anahola Bay, has good year-round snorkeling, swimming, boogie boarding and surfing.

Lydgate State Park, at Wailua near mouth of Wailua River, offers good swimming for kids, beginning snorkelers, picnics, pavilion, old Hawaiian heaiu (temple) ruins.

Kalapaki Beach fronts the Kaua`i Marriott Hotel at Nawiliwili Harbor, Lihue, with good boogie boarding, surfing, windsurfing and swimming on calm days.

South Shore

Poipu Beach Park, good for kids and beginning boogie boarders, surfers and windsurfers.

Salt Pond Park, good swimming and snorkeling when calm, surfing and windsurfing.

Prince Kuhio Park, Lawai Road, good swimming, snorkeling and relaxing in calm weather.

Mahaulepu Beach adjoins Keoniloa Beach fronting the Hyatt Regency Hotel; snorkeling best in calm surf; surfing and windsurfing.

West Shore

Kekaha Beach Park stretches for 15 miles; known for strong currents, so use caution when swimming, snorkeling, surfing.

Polihale Beach State Park, past end of Kaumuali`i Highway 50, is a large expanse of golden sand; surf and currents dangerous, good for picnics, viewing south end of Na Pali Coast.

Cruises & Sailing

Several cruise outfitters offer ocean excursions via catamaran, powerboat or sailboat along the famed Na Pali Coast and other areas of Kaua`i. Per person rates for a standard two-hour to half-day cruise range from $55 to $75; longer cruises are $99 and up.

Hanalei Beach.

Hanalei Sea Tours, PO Box 1437, Hanalei, HI 96714, ☎ 800/733-7997, 808/826-7254. This cruise operator has raft and catamaran cruises from two hours to a half-day or longer.

Na Pali Adventures, Hanalei, ☎ 800/659-6804. This operator has catamaran cruises on the Na Pali Coast; winner of Green Star Award for environmentally sensitive tours; its vessels use recycled vegetable oil for engine fuel.

Liko Kaua`i Cruises, PO Box 18, Waimea, HI 96796, ☎ 800/238-6831, 808/338-0333; e-mail liko@aloha.net; www.extreme-Hawaii.com/activities/liko/. Locally owned cruises feature Na Pali Coast highlights and narration on history and culture of the area.

Capt. Andy's Kaua`i, PO Box 1291, Koloa, HI 96756, ☎ 808/822-7833. This luxury 55-foot sailing catamaran does seasonal whale watching cruises, picnic/snorkeling excursions and Na Pali Coast scenic cruises.

Na Pali Explorer, 9600 Kaumuali`i Highway, Waimea, HI 96796, ☎ 808/335-9909. This cruise operator uses open powerboats for half-day or longer seasonal whale watching, snorkel excursions and cruises along the Na Pali Coast.

Bluewater Sailing, PO Box 1318, Hanalei, HI 96714, ☎ 808/828-1142. The 42-foot *Lady Leanne II* ketch-rigged yacht does half-day scenic sails, two-hour sunset sails and private charters in Kaua`i's pristine waters.

Kayaking & Rafting

Kayak paddling and inflatable raft excursions are a popular adventure on Kaua`i's inland and coastal waterways. The following outfitters provide guided excursions on the ocean, rivers, walkways and remote coastlines. Standard half-day kayak adventures range from $40 to $65; raft adventures range from $55 to $80.

**Outfitters Kaua`i,** 2827A Poipu Road, Koloa, HI 96756, ☎ 808/742-9667. This outfitter on Kaua`i's sunny southern coast provides half-day sea kayak and all-day deep jungle kayaking adventures, plus hikes to waterfalls, bike trips on mountain trails or ocean shorelines; rentals.

Kayak Kaua`i, PO Box 508, Hanalei, HI 96714, ☎ 800/437-3507, 808/826-9844, 822-9179; e-mail outbound@aloha.net. Wailua River paddling excursions to fern grotto or jungle waterfalls hikes; also Hanalei River national wildlife refuge excursions and Na Pali Coast kayak voyages, plus other hiking and biking excursions and rentals.

Pedal 'n Paddle, ☎ 808/826-9069 in Hanalei on the North Shore. Rental kayaks for the Na Pali Coast or exploring the Hanalei River or other area streams. Full range of camping and sporting equipment for rent.

Paradise Outdoor Adventures, ☎ 808/822-1112; www.kayakers.com. Tours and rental kayaks for Wailua River paddling excursions, motor boats, and seacycles.

Kayak Adventures, ☎ 808/826-9340. Kayaks available for river paddling or sea kayaks for coastal cruising adventures to hike tropical jungle trails.

**Kaua`i Z-TourZ,** ☎ 808/742-6331, PO Box 1082, Kalaheo, HI 96741; e-mail z-tourz@aloha.net; http://planet-Hawaii.com/z-tourz/index.htm. Inflatable raft tours up the Huleia River past the national wildlife refuge and the Menehune Fishpond. Explore magnificent scenery of Mahaulepu and Kipu Kai along Kaua`i's southeast shores.

Captain Zodiac, PO Box 456, Hanalei, HI 96714, ☎ 800/422-7824, 808/826-9371. Half-day and longer raft cruises on the Na Pali Coast, plus seasonal sunrise and sunset cruises for photographers.

Scuba Diving & Snorkeling

Several scuba diving outfitters offer diving tours to Kaua`i's ocean sanctuaries and coral reefs for closeup looks at the incredible tropical marine life. An introductory one-tank scuba dive begins at $85; two-tank dives are around $100-125. Snorkeling adventure standard cruises are 2½ hours to a half-day and range from $55 to $75 per person, scuba equipment included, plus snacks and lunch (on half-day cruises).

Sunrise Diving Adventures, PO Box 1255, Kapa`a, HI 96746, ☎ 808/822-REEF. Specializes in first-time divers. Complete PADI instruction and equipment provided. Transportation, snacks provided. Snorkelers welcome too.

Wet-n-Wonderful Ocean Sports, PO Box 840, Kapa`a, HI 96746, ☎ 808/822-0211. First-time PADI diving instruction and equipment rentals. Dive excursions around Kaua`i, including spectacular night dives.

Fathom Five Divers, PO Box 907, 3450 Poipu Road, Koloa, HI 96756, ☎ 800/972-3078. Custom dive boats, PADI certification and refresher classes and dives plus a variety of half-day dives and snorkeling at Kaua`i's best reef locations.

**Dive Kaua`i,** 976 Kuhio Highway, Kapa`a, HI 96746, ☎ 808/822-0452. A full range of PADI instructional dives, equipment rentals, and dive/snorkel excursions.

Nitrox Tropical Divers, PO Box 1255, Kapa`a, HI 96746, ☎ 800/NX5-DIVE, ☎ 808/822-REEF. PADI guided dive tours and all gear plus equipment rentals and underwater scooter vehicles that allow faster and further travel.

Surfing, Windsurfing & Water Skiing

Kaua`i's beaches are inviting to surfers of all levels. There are lots of surfing hotspots around the island, but conditions are weather-dependent. Check with lifeguards, hotel activities desks, surf shops for the latest conditions in each area as well as instructional programs. One outfitter, Kaua`i Water Ski listed below, also does water-skiing excursions on the Wailua River. Surfing and wind-surfing instruction packages begin at $65 per person for sessions of two-three hours. Water skiing packages for up to six people are $55 for a half-hour, $100 for one hour, boat included.

- **Nukamoi Beach & Surf Shop,** 2080 Ho`one Road, Koloa, ☎ 808/742-8019.

- **Progressive Expressions,** Old Koloa Town, ☎ 808/742-6041.

- **Windsurf Kaua`i,** ☎ 808/828-6838.

- **Anini Beach Windsurfing,** ☎ 808/826-WIND.

- **Sea Star Kaua`i,** Kalaheo, ☎ 808/332-8189.

- **Kaua`i Water Ski,** Kinipopo Shopping Village, Kuhio Highway 56, Wailua, ☎ 808/822-3574.

Fishing - Deep Sea & Freshwater

There are several fishing charter boat operators and fishing outfitters on Kaua`i for anglers looking to hook a big one on either the ocean or in freshwater ponds. Deep sea fishing charters begin at about $85 per person for a half-day, $125 and up for a full-day charter. Fresh water bass fishing charters range from a half-day at $105-175 for one-two fisher-men to a full-day at $200-275, everything included.

Kaua`i Cono's, PO Box 391, Anahola, HI 96703, ☎ 808/822-9355. This locally owned charter boat has half- and full-day fishing charters for up to six people. All gear and tackle provided.

True Blue, Lihue, ☎ 808/246-6333. This charter operator use the 30-foot Force Sportfisher *Pamelita* and has half- and full-day charters, in-cluding all gear and tackle.

Anini Fishing Charters, Anini Beach, Princeville, ☎ 808/828-1285, uses the 33-foot Sportfisher *Sea Breeze V* and offers half- and full-day charters; live bait, lure trolling and bottom fishing available.

JJ's Big Bass Tours, ☎ 808/332-9219. Bass fishing champion John Jardin takes guests on Kaua`i's scenic freshwater reservoirs to angle for smallmouth, bigmouth and peacock bass. All equipment provided.

Cast & Catch Bass Guides, ☎ 808/332-9707. Bass master Tom Christy has bass boats on Kaua`i's freshwater reservoirs and angles for smallmouth, bigmouth and peacock bass. Half- and full-day charters, all equipment provided.

■ In the Air

Scenic Flightseeing & Helicopter Tours

Flightseeing Kaua`i can be a fantastic visual experience – for many perhaps the most memorable adventure of a Kaua`i visit. An air tour of the famed Na Pali Coast presents a stun-ning vista of rippling mountains, jagged ridges, deep gorges and valleys, waterfalls, remote secluded beaches and wilderness coast-line. Additional air tours cover Kaua`i's noted beaches and lush green interior mountains and valleys or the colorful hues of the Waimea Can-yon on Kaua`i's west side – the "Grand Canyon of the Pacific." The operators are based either at Lihue, Princeville or Port Allen Airports. Try any of the following helicopter or air tour lines. Air tour rates vary from point of origin. Typical one-hour scenic coastal-interior tours range from $60 to $99. Deluxe Circle Island tours range from $109 to $169 and include the Na Pali Coast and Waimea Canyon.

- **Hawai`i Helicopters,** ☎ 800/367-7095, ☎ 808/826-6591; www.Hawaiiheli.com.

- **Island Helicopters,** ☎ 800/829-5999, ☎ 808/245-8588; e-mail island@aloha.net; http://planet-Hawaii.com/island.

- **Jack Harter Helicopters, ☎** 808/245-3774.

- **Will Squyres Helicopter Tours, ☎** 808/245-8881 or 245-7541.

- **Safari Helicopters, ☎** 800/326-3356, **☎** 808/246-0136; e-mail safari@aloha.net; http://planet-Hawaii.com/~safari/.

- **'Ohana Helicopter Tours, ☎** 800/222-6989, 808/245-3996.

- **Bali Hai Helicopter Tours, ☎** 800/325-TOUR, 808/335-3166; e-mail blh@aloha.net; http://aloha-Hawaii.com/balihai.

- **Kumulani Air, ☎** 808/246-9123, specializes in a unique three-island air tour of Kaua`i, Ni`ihau (The Forbidden Island) and Lehua aboard a deluxe Piper Chieftain twin-engine airplane.

■ On Horseback

Trail Rides

There are several horseback outfitters on Kaua`i, offering guided trail rides into some of the Garden Island's most spectacular scenic country. Enjoy a casual, relaxing horseback ride while discovering the natural physical beauty of Kaua`i. Ride along quiet beaches, upland ranch pastures, mountain ridges, along tropical streams, pools and waterfalls amidst Kaua`i's lush tropical forests and grasslands. Standard two-hour trail rides range from $56 to $79 per person. Longer three- and four-hour rides and all-day adventures range from $95 and up.

Silver Falls Ranch, Inc., PO Box 1541, Hanalei, HI 96714, ☎ 808/828-6718, offers two separate trail rides of two and three hours each; private excursions available. Ranch is just minutes from Kilauea town at foot of Mount Namahana with vistas of Kaua`i's most spectacular peaks.

Princeville Ranch Stables, PO Box 888, Hanalei, HI 96714, ☎ 808/826-6777; e-mail pstable@aloha.net; www.Kaua`i.net/~kwc4. This outfitter has a number of two- to three-hour trail rides to waterfalls, beaches and bluffs overlooking the ocean, mountains and valley. They also have a cowboy cattle drive.

Esprit de Corps Riding Academy, PO Box 269, Kapa`a, HI 96746, ☎ 808/822-4688. Two- to four-hour and full-day rides through lush backcountry; great for photographers.

CJM Country Stables, 1731 Kelaukia St., Koloa, HI 96756, ☎ 808/742-6096. Two- to three-hour trail rides past some of Poipu's most spectacular beach scenery.

■ Eco/Cultural Activities

 Among Kaua`i's most adventurous excursions are the backcountry 4WD mountain tours into the Waimea Canyon, Koke`e State Park and the Na Pali-Kona Forest Reserve. The winding backroads pass through tropical forests abundant with native orchids, lilies, ferns and native trees. The forest comes alive with rare Hawaiian birdlife, tropical fruits, remote canyons, quiet streams and secluded waterfalls. Guests get closeup views of Kaua`i's magnificent tropical forest environment.

**Kaua`i Mountain Tours,** PO Box 3069, Lihue, HI 96766, ☎ 808/245-7224, offers full-day backcountry tours through the Waimea Canyon, Koke`e State Park and the Na Pali-Kona Forest Reserve; picnic lunch included. Guests bring a camera, walking shoes and jacket. Rates begin at $50-60 per person.

The Wailua River and Fern Grotto Cruise is a sedate but worthwhile adventure. **Smith's Motor Boat Service,** Wailua Marina, ☎ 808/821-6892, is the original tour operator for this cruise, having started the cruises many years ago. The Wailua River cruises to the exotic fern grotto, a large cavern with a fern-covered ceiling in a lush tropical forest setting, is a romantic and popular activity, especially with the older set. They also arrange weddings in the fern grotto, complete with Hawaiian musicians singing the fabled "Hawaiian Wedding Song." They sing for each boatload of visitors too and provide entertainment while you cruise up and down the river. It's a bit touristy,

Wailua River cruise.

but good fun anyway. Cruises operate several times daily. Rates are $15 per person.

Waialeale Boat Tours, Wailua Marina, ☎ 808/822-4908, also operates Wailua River cruises to the fern grotto. The river cruise is pleasant and relaxing, watching the tropical forest and mountain peaks of Kaua`i's rugged interior slide by. Rates are $15 per person.

 DON'T MISS Those who enjoy getting close to nature and the botanical world will find much to appreciate at Kaua`i's botanical gardens. It's no wonder they call it "The Garden Island." **The National Tropical Botanical Garden** has two sites on Kaua`i. On the south shore at Lawai, the **Allerton Garden,** ☎ 808/742-2623, is open several times weekly for guided tours only. The garden has a premier collection of tropical palms, erythrinas, breadfruit and native Hawaiian plants, plus many rare and endangered species of the tropical world. On the north shore at Haena, the **Limahuli Garden,** ☎ 808/826-1053, maintains an old Hawaiian system of terraces for growing taro and keeps a collection of traditional useful Hawaiian plants. There are both guided and self-guided tours available several times weekly. Reservations required in advance for both garden guided tours.

Olu Pua Gardens and Plantation, PO Box 518, Kalaheo, HI 96741, ☎ 808/332-8182, is another fascinating and beautiful tropical botanical garden. Olu Pua is located just a mile west of Kalaheo on Kaumuali`i Highway 50 in south Kaua`i. The gardens and grounds are the old Alexander family estate, which was built in the 1930s.

DID YOU KNOW?

With their ties to Hawai`i's missionary era, the Alexander family came to prominence early, establishing Kaua`i's largest pineapple plantation and later helping to found Alexander & Baldwin, a prosperous international corporation.

There is a handsome old main residence, a visitors center and the sprawling grounds, with acres of heliconias, orchids, bromiliads, anthuriums, palms and tropical plants of all types.

Waiakalua Palm Nursery, PO Box 501, Kilauea, HI 96754, ☎ 808/828-1334; e-mail wpn@aloha.net. This is at the 21-mile marker off Kuhio Highway 56 on Waiakalua Street, Kilauea Farms area. These picturesque grounds include a tropical garden with a large variety of mature palms and tropical plants. Plants can be purchased and shipped to the mainland.

Guava Kai Plantation, off Kuhio Highway 56 on Kuawa Road, Kilauea, ☎ 808/828-1925. This 480-acre commercial guava orchard is the undisputed "Guava Capital of the World." Free tours of visitors center, processing plant, nature walk and gift shop. Learn about guava production and the wide range of luscious tropical products, ranging from sherbet to jams and jellies to baked goods and more.

DID YOU KNOW?

Kaua`i has a diverse and colorful socio-cultural history and heritage with its multi-ethnic immigrant population. The ethnic groups who came to Kaua`i over the years to work in the pineapple and sugar plantations all left their marks on Kaua`i's community. The old plantation lifestyle, while significantly changed from generations ago, can still be seen around Kaua`i.

Old Town Hanapepe, southwest shore, is a turn off the Kaumuali`i Highway 5 but a big step back into an earlier time. Stroll at your leisure and discover the rustic charm of "Kaua`i's biggest little town." Hanapepe was once a thriving center of commerce and entertainment in the late 1800s and early 1900s. It boasted two movie theaters, three skating rinks and over 60 stores and businesses to serve the busy plantation community of the day. Today, Hanapepe is a quiet place full of historic buildings that house quaint arts and crafts shops, clothing and gift shops, coffee bars, restaurants and more. Kaua`i's sunny southern shore is enjoying a rebirth as an artisans' colony.

Old Koloa Town, located off Kaumuali`i Highway 50 on Highway 520 on the way to Poipu Beach, is another of Kaua`i's old plantation towns that has been revived in recent years. Stroll through the colorful main street town and enjoy the complex of shops, restaurants and stores housed in the original old plantation town buildings. Visit the Koloa History Center and learn more about the early plantation town lifestyle.

Midway Atoll National Wildlife Refuge

For information and details about this adventure tour, contact: **Midway Atoll,** PO Box 3028, Lihue, Kaua`i, HI 96766, 888/574-9000, ☎ 808/245-4718.

Laysan albatross, Midway Atoll.

The Midway Atoll National Wildlife Refuge lies over a thousand miles northwest of the main Hawaiian Islands. These eroded volcanic islands are now just coral atolls reaching above the ocean a few feet. Ringed by coral reefs and turquoise lagoons, they are a haven for hundreds of thousands of sea birds, endangered Hawaiian monk seals and threatened Hawaiian green sea turtles. The waters surrounding these atolls are full of big game fish and colorful reeflife and provide a unique scuba diving and snorkeling environment.

Midway is famous for its pivotal role in World War II, but the tiny mid-Pacific atoll is now carving out a new future in wildlife conservation and environmental tourism. Established in 1988 as a National Wildlife Refuge, Midway Atoll opened to visitors in mid-1996, making history as the first remote Pacific island refuge to do so. Midway now welcomes birdwatchers, wildlife enthusiasts, snorkelers, scuba divers, World War II history buffs, researchers, sport fishermen, photographers, nature lovers and anyone who seeks a unique travel experience on one of the most remote atolls on earth.

The US Department of Defense closed the former Midway Naval Air Facility in 1992. Jurisdiction and control of Midway was transferred to the Department of the Interior for management as a national wildlife refuge by the US Fish and Wildlife Service. The Service then entered into a cooperative agreement with the Midway Phoenix Corporation to operate the infrastructure at Midway and to provide a visitor program to help defray costs. As a result of this unique government/private sector cooperation, Midway's spectacular resources are now available to 100 guests per week.

Guests joining a tour to Midway meet up at Lihue, Kaua`i airport, from where the adventure begins. Travel to Midway is via Phoenix Air on a spacious Gulfstream turboprop airplane. The flight time is four-five hours from Lihue, Kaua`i to Midway.

On-island transportation is on foot, by bicycle, or by an occasional golf cart. But Midway is so small, you'll enjoy just wandering around on your own. Midway guests are housed in a remodeled military Bachelor Officer's Quarters dating from the 1950s. The island's earlier history is still visible in the turn-of-the-century buildings of the old Commercial Pacific Cable Company.

DID YOU KNOW?

Midway is best known for the World War II "Battle of Midway" on June 4, 1942, when the US Navy ambushed the Japanese Fleet north of the island, inflicting heavy losses and destroying four Japanese aircraft carriers. Historians have called the Battle of Midway the turning point in the war, eventually leading to US victory. Midway lies at the far northwest end of the Hawaiian archipelago. The base of Midway's volcano, which built the island, lies submerged under 500 feet of old coral reef. Above the surface is the coral reef that rings the atoll and three sandy islands. The largest is Sand Island, about 1,200 acres (one by two miles) and the only populated island in the atoll. The smaller islands, Eastern and Spit, are inhabited only by wildlife.

Activities

The island offers a variety of activities, including a bowling alley, movie theater, library, tennis, racquetball, weight room, and gymnasium. There is also a small convenience store, an All-Hands Club pub, and meals are enjoyed in the old Navy Galley, a caféteria-style dining hall with plenty of great food. The beachside Pavilion offers continental breakfasts and buffet dinners, with lovely lagoon views. There is also the gourmet Ironwood Restaurant, which offers delightful French cuisine.

Midway has other adventure activities as well, including big game fishing, shore fishing, scuba diving and snorkeling, wildlife observing, and photography. Guests can also just do nothing and enjoy the tranquility of Midway's remote mid-Pacific location. The refuge's future plans include creation of a historical museum, interpretive exhibits, self-guided nature trails, outdoor classroom programs and satellite links that will share this special place with the world.

Kaua'i

Albatross chick, Midway Atoll.

Wildlife

Midway offers one of the most incredible wildlife experiences in the world. The seabirds that nest here have been protected for decades and show little fear of humans. Approximately 45 highly endangered Hawaiian monk seals make their home on Midway. A large number of threatened Hawaiian green sea turtles use the lagoon as a feeding area and are easily seen around the waters and harbor area. Midway also has about 200 spinner dolphins in surrounding waters. The lagoon supports more than 200 species of fish, including an abundance of bright colorful reef fish.

Bird lovers will have no trouble finding birds to observe. They're literally all over the place. Midway is the nesting and resting place for 15 species of seabirds including the largest colony of Laysan albatross, the world famous "gooney bird." Some 400,000 pair of Laysan albatross share Midway with their near cousin, the black-footed albatross. Other birds include red-tailed tropicbirds, white terns, black and brown noddies, gray-backed terns, sooty terns, red-footed boobies, masked boobies, great frigate birds, Bonin petrels, and wedge-tailed shearwaters.

Independent travelers are welcome on Midway and there are several free guided tours available for the enjoyment and education of all visitors. However, most visitors take advantage of the guided programs and activities offered by Ocean Society Expeditions, Midway Sport Fishing, and Midway Diving Corporation.

Rates for Midway Packages

Airfare, Hawai`i-Midway-Hawai`i: $750

Single/double room, shared bath: $120 nightly

Single/double room, private bath: $155-225

VIP Suite: $300

Standard meals: $25 per person, daily

Deluxe meals: $38

Check when you make reservations as to other fees for golf cart, bicycle and cellular phone rental.

These operators can be contacted directly for information and details.

Ocean Society Expeditions, Fort Mason Center, Building E, San Francisco, CA 94123, ☎ 800/326-7491, 415/441-1106.

Midway Sport Fishing, 3 East Broad Street, Newnan, GA 30264; ☎ 888/BIG-ULUA, 770/254-8326.

Midway Diving, PO Box 3028, Lihue, HI 96766; ☎ 888/574-9000.

US Fish and Wildlife Service, Box 50167, Honolulu, HI 96850, ☎ 808/541-1201 or 541-2749; for general information on Midway Atoll National Wildlife Refuge.

Lodging

Kaua`i offers a variety of lodging to fit every taste and budget, from first class hotels and vacation condominiums to budget motels and bed and breakfast inns. The rates below are for a standard double-occupancy room.

Accommodations Price Scale	
$	less than $100 per night
$$	$100-199 per night
$$$	$200-299 per night
$$$$	$300 and up per night

Bed & Breakfasts

Bed & Breakfast Hawai`i-Kaua`i, PO Box 449, Kapa`a, HI 96746, ☎ 800/733-1632; e-mail bandb@aloha.net; www.planet-Hawaii.com/bandb. They have B&B listings for the entire island of Kaua`i.

**Bed & Breakfast Kaua`i,** 6436 Kalama Road, Kapa`a, HI 96746, ☎ 800/822-1176, 808/822-1177. They provide B&B listings for all of Kaua`i.

Lihue Area

Motel Lani, 4240 Rice Street, Lihue, ☎ 808/245-2965, is a centrally located budget accommodation. The motel is two miles from the airport and one mile from Kalapaki Bay and beach. There are restaurants, shopping and other attractions within walking distance. These are clean, comfortable, simple rooms for the budget-minded traveler. $

Tip Top Motel, 3173 Akahi Street, Lihue, ☎ 808/245-2333, is one of Kaua`i's original budget lodgings. It has several rooms in two-story modern buildings. It's located right in town and just five minutes from the airport. Clean, comfortable, affordable rooms all have air conditioning and cable TV. The well-known Tip Top Café is on premises. $

Garden Island Inn, 3445 Wilcox Road, Lihue, ☎ 800/648-0154, 808/245-7227; e-mail garden@aloha.net; www.planet-Hawaii.com/g-i-inn; located just across from Kalapaki Bay. This is a small 21-room hotel with newly renovated oceanview rooms. Rooms are bright, comfortable and very well furnished. Convenient to beach, shopping, restaurants, activities, town and more. $

**Kaua`i Marriott Resort and Beach Club,** Kalapaki Beach, Lihue, ☎ 800/220-2925, 808/245-5050; www.marriott.com. This is one of Kaua`i's largest deluxe resorts and the only one located just minutes from the airport and town. It is a full-service beach resort with all the related amenities and activities, plus golf courses, and is right on the beach. $$$

The Coconut Coast

**Outrigger Kaua`i Beach,** 4331 Kaua`i Beach Drive, Lihue, ☎ 800/688-7444, ☎ 808/245-1955; e-mail reservations@outrigger.com; www.outrigger.com. This full-service resort is on the Coconut Coast beach just north of Lihue. It features newly renovated guest rooms, restaurant and large pool; close to major attractions, shopping and dining. $$

**Aston Kaua`i Beach Villas,** 4330 Kaua`i Beach Drive, Lihue, ☎ 800/922-7866, 808/245-7711; www.aston-hotels.com. This deluxe oceanfront condo complex has nice tropical grounds and lagoons and fully-furnished 1-2BR units. It has tennis courts, pool and spa and is near major attractions, shopping and dining. $$

**Aston Kaua`i Beachboy Hotel,** 4-484 Kuhio Highway, Kapa`a, ☎ 800/922-7866, 808/822-3441; www.aston-hotels.com. This affordable beachfront hotel is on the Coconut Coast. Rooms are air-conditioned, with fridges and private Lana`is. There are tennis courts, pool, restaurant on the grounds. It's convenient to shopping and area attractions. $$

Kakalina's Bed & Breakfast, 6781 Kawaihau Road, Kapa`a, HI 96746, ☎ 808/822-2328; email klinas@aloha.net; www.kexotix.com/kakalina.html. Located near Kapa`a town on a working tropical flower farm in the foothills of Mount Waialeale just five minutes from the beach. One studio and a two-room unit available. Convenient to town shopping, dining and activities. $

Lampy's Bed & Breakfast, 6078 Kolopua Street, Kapa`a, HI 96746, ☎/fax 808/822-0478. This country B&B is nestled behind Sleeping Giant Mountain just five minutes from Wailua Bay. Comfortable, cozy, well-furnished rooms have private baths and entrances. Nearby to shopping, restaurants and attractions. $

Keapana Center Bed & Breakfast, 5620 Keapana Road, Kapa`a, HI 96746, ☎ 800/822-7968, ☎/fax 808/822-7968. This large hilltop home on six acres has great views of surrounding mountains and country just five minutes from Kapa`a town and the beach. Convenient to town shopping, dining and attractions. $

Hale Makana, PO Box 3671, Lihue, HI 96766, ☎ 808/245-6500. This vacation cottage is located on a one-acre tropical fruit farm just eight minutes from Wailua Bay. Pick fruit, stroll the neighborhood and soak up the ambiance of country Kaua`i. Near to restaurants, shopping and activities. $

Lanikai Resort, 390 Papaloa Road, Kapa`a, HI 96746, ☎ 800/755-2824 or Castle Resorts, ☎ 800/367-5004, 808/822-7700; www.castle-group.com. This is a luxury beachfront condo with large spacious 1/2BR units. Garden units are very near to the beach. Units have full kitchens and Lana`is overlooking the water; walking distance to restaurants and shops. $$$

The North Shore

Bed & Bay Hanalei, PO Box 508, Hanalei, HI 96714, ☎ 800/437-3507, 808/826-9844; e-mail outbound@aloha.net. This rustic old-fashioned plantation-style cottage is just a block from Hanalei Bay and within walking distance of Hanalei town. It's fully furnished with kitchen, laundry, etc. Convenient to all North Shore activities, town, shopping, restaurants. $

Hanalei Bay Resort, 5380 Honoiki Road, Princeville, HI 96722; Castle Resorts, ☎ 800/367-5004, 808/826-6585; www.castle-group.com. This vacation condo complex located in the Princeville resort area has studio and 1-2BR units available. Units are fully furnished; pool, golf course, tennis courts, restaurants, shops are nearby. $$

Pali Ke Kua at Princeville, 5300 Ka Haku Road, PO Box 899, Princeville, HI 96714; Marc Resort Hawai`i, ☎ 800/535-0085; 808/922-9700; e-mail marc@aloha.net; www.planet-Hawaii.com/marcresorts/. This deluxe condo complex has 1-2BR units, fully furnished, in Princeville resort. Near to shopping, restaurants, tennis, golf course, pool and attractions. $$

The Historic Bed & Breakfast, PO Box 1662, Hanalei, HI 96714, ☎ 808/826-4622. This unique B&B is in a 1901 Buddhist mission church, which is on the National and State Historic Register. Renovated guest rooms are modestly decorated. Right in Hanalei town, convenient to everything on the North Shore. $

Hanalei Inn, 5-5468 Kuhio Highway, PO Box 1373, Hanalei, HI 96714, ☎ 808/826-9333. This simply furnished beach house lodge has studio units with kitchenettes and ceiling fans. A strictly budget accommodation, it is just a block from Hanalei Bay. $

Hanalei Colony Resort, PO Box 206, Hanalei, HI 96714, ☎ 800/628-3004; e-mail hcr@aloha.net. This vacation condo complex is located beachfront at Haena near the end of the Hanalei Highway at the Na Pali area. The rooms are modestly appointed and have nice views of ocean or garden. No phones, TV, stereos or other intrusions on the country peace and quiet. Poolside continental breakfast is complimentary. $$

Cliffs at Princeville, 3811 Edward Road, Hanalei, HI 96714, ☎ 800/367-7052, 808/826-6219. This vacation condo complex is in the Princeville resort and has 1-4BR units. The units are well-equipped and have full kitchens. The complex has pool, tennis courts, jacuzzi-sauna, BBQ area and guest pavilion. Near to resort services, golf, restaurants. $$

The South Shore & West

Outrigger Kiahuna Plantation, 2253 Poipu Road, Koloa, HI 96756, ☎ 800/688-7444, ☎ 808/742-6411; e-mail reservations@outrigger.com; www.outrigger.com. This is a first-class condo complex with several buildings on or near the beach. The 1-2BR units are spacious, airy and fully furnished; 2BR units can sleep up to six; great place for families right on the beach. $$

Kiahuna Plantation Resort/Beach Bungalows at Kiahuna, 2253B Poipu Road, Koloa, HI 96756; Castle Resorts, ☎ 800/367-5004, 808/742-2200; www.castle-group.com. This is a lovely condo complex on

35 acres of wide lawns and tropical gardens. Fronted by a sandy swimming beach; great for adventure-seeking groups, golfers and tennis buffs. 1-2BR units have all amenities. Near to Poipu area resorts, restaurants and shops. $$

Hyatt Regency Kaua`i, 1571 Poipu Road, Koloa, HI 96756, ☎ 800/233-1234, 808/742-1234, is a full-service resort; facilities include pool, tennis courts, golf course, health club/spa, restaurants and more. $$$

Baytown Loft, 3559 Hanapepe Road, Hanapepe, ☎ 800/510-8684 or 808/335-5562. This family-operated small inn has four newly renovated 1BR apartments with kitchenettes; ideal for couples and small groups. Located in historic old Hanapepe town. $

Poipu Bed & Breakfast Inn, 2720 Ho`onani Road, Poipu Beach, HI 96756, ☎ 800/22-POIPU or 808/742-1146, e-mail poipu@aloha.net. This is an old 1933-era plantation-style home renovated with theme/decor guest rooms, all comfortably furnished. Other nearby guest cottages and condo units also available. $$

Gloria's Spouting Horn Bed & Breakfast, 4464 Lawai Beach Road, Poipu, HI 96756, ☎ 808/742-6995. This handsome cedar B&B is right on the oceanfront very close to Poipu's famed spouting horn blowhole. It's also convenient to many other area attractions. $$

Koloa Landing Cottages, 2704-B Ho`onani Road, Poipu, HI 96756, ☎ 808/742-1470. The studio and 1BR cottages sleep two or three and the 2BR cottages sleep four people. The main house has more space and can sleep up to six. All units have full kitchens. The cottages are in a tropical garden setting across from Koloa Landing, a popular place for diving, snorkeling and canoeing. $

Hale Kua, 4896-E Kua Road, PO Box 649, Lawai, ☎ 800/440-4353 or 808/332-8570; e-mail halekua@aloha.net. A 1BR cottage or condo unit available. Nice views of the ocean and Lawai Valley in a tropical setting, with lots of quiet and privacy. Minutes from town, shopping, attractions, restaurants. $

**Koke`e Lodge,** 3600 Koke`e Road, Waimea, HI 96796, ☎ 808/335-6061. This rustic state park lodge has a dozen completely furnished housekeeping cabins. Everything except food is included. Cabin sizes vary, sleeping up to six or seven people. $

Makahuena at Poipu, 1661 Pe`e Road, Poipu, HI 96756; Castle Resorts, ☎ 800/367-5004, 808/742-2482; www.castle-group.com. This oceanfront all-suite condo has very nice 1-3BR units. Resort amenities include pool, sun deck, spa, tennis court and BBQ facilities. Beaches

Kaua`i

surround this oceanfront location on the sunny Poipu shore. Sunrises and sunsets are a bonus. $$

Poipu Shores, 1775 Pe`e Road, Poipu, HI 96756; Castle Resorts, ☎ 800/367-5004, 808/742-7700; www.castle-group.com. This is an oceanfront condo in the sunny Poipu Resort area. 1-3BR units are spacious, with oceanfront views, full kitchens, island decor, laundry, private Lana`i, pool, BBQ facilities and other amenities. Near resort activities, attractions, dining, shopping. $$

Camping

■ State Parks

Camping permits are required for all state parks. There's no charge, but permits must be applied for through: **Hawai`i State Department of Land and Natural Resources,** Division of State Parks, 3060 Eiwa Street, Room 306, Lihue, HI 96766-1875, ☎ 808/241-3444. State park campgrounds all have restrooms, showers, drinking water, fireplaces and picnic tables, except the Na Pali Coast/Kalalau Trail campgrounds, which have no facilities.

Campgrounds include **Koke`e Park** at Waimea Canyon, which has four separate campground areas, and **Polihale State Park**. There are also state cabins at Koke`e Park, which accommodate up to six people for $35-45 per night. Cabins are fully furnished with hot showers, kitchen facilities, linens and fireplaces. Koke`e Lodge handles reservations at PO Box 819, Waimea, HI 96790, ☎ 808/335-6061.

■ County Parks

The County of Kaua`i also has campgrounds at its county-maintained parks. Camping permits are also required and cost $3 per person per night. Contact: **Department of Public Works, Division of Parks & Recreation,** County of Kaua`i, 4444 Rice St., Mo`ikeha Bldg. #150, Lihue, HI 96766, ☎ 808/241-6660.

Camping is permitted at these county parks: **Haena Beach Park, Anini Beach Park, Hanamaulu Beach Park, Salt Pond Park, Lucy Wright Park**. Parks have restrooms, picnic tables, showers and drinking water available. Other county parks do not allow overnight camping. Campers must use tents.

Dining

Dining out on Kaua`i is a culinary adventure. The island has lots of choices, ranging from first-class fine dining restaurants at the better resorts to the local-style budget plate lunch shops in the towns and villages around the island. And like the rest of Hawai`i, the attraction here is the diversity and blend of Asian/Pacific cuisines, which reflect Hawai`i's multi-cultural community. The restaurant price ranges, as in the other sections of this book are based on the average dinner meal, exclusive of tax, alcoholic beverages and desserts.

Dining Price Scale

$	under $10 per person
$$	$10-25 per person
$$$	$25 and up per person

The Luau & Its History

The Hawaiian luau dates from the early days of Hawaii's communal lifestyle. It was common practice for a large extended village family and clan to join together in a harvest of the land and sea's abundance and to celebrate by sharing a large festive meal. Luaus were also held on special holidays and to mark special ceremonies and events. It's not much different in today's Hawaii. Luaus are held to mark holidays, ceremonies, and celebrations such as weddings, anniversaries, birthdays, graduations and so on.

Over the years, Hawaii's ethnic groups have left their own culinary influences on the luau. But an authentic Hawaiian luau usually consists of the following foods:

- **Poi**, a thick gray paste-like substance much like mashed potatoes and made from cooked taro root, a luau staple;
- **Baked sweet potatoes**;
- **Kalua pig**, a whole roast pig cooked in a traditional underground imu oven;

- **Poke**, any raw fish that has been marinated and spiced with local flavors such as chili pepper or soy sauce;

- **Lau lau**, chunks of kalua pig, chicken or fish flavored with coconut milk and wrapped in taro leaves, which is then wrapped in ti leaves and steamed in the imu oven;

- **Lomilomi salmon**, diced salted salmon with tomatoes and green onions, sort of a Hawaiian salsa;

- **Opihi**, small salt water limpets (shellfish) which are considered a luau delicacy and eaten raw;

- **A`ama crab**, also a delicacy and eaten steamed;

- **Luau chicken**, which is chicken cooked with luau (taro) leaves;

- **Kulolo**, a steamed pudding made from grated cooked taro root and coconut milk;

- **Haupia**, a sweet custard made from coconut milk.

Luaus are noted for huge amounts of food and usually include Hawaiian music, song and hula dance performances.

Luau roast pig in the imu oven.

■ Luaus

Reflections of Paradise, Kilohana Carriage House, Kaumuali`i Highway 50, one mile west of Lihue, ☎ 808/245-9595. This luau show includes a full Polynesian Review of dance and music of Hawai`i, Tahiti, Samoa and New Zealand, plus an all-you-can-eat buffet of Hawaiian foods like kalua pig, mahimahi, teriyaki beef, pineapple chicken, sweet potatoes, rice and more. Call for times. $$$

Kaua`i Coconut Beach Resort, ☎ 808/822-3455, presents a nightly "All Hawaiian Luau Show," including all-you-can-eat buffet of roast kalua pig, Polynesian chicken, mahimahi, teri beef, lomi salmon, veggies and fruit salad, haupia coconut pudding and more. Enjoy a torch lighting ceremony, lei greeting and a full program of song and dance capturing the legend and lore of the "Garden Island." $$$

■ Restaurants

Lihue Area

Lihue, being the county seat and main population center of Kaua`i has a number of interesting cafés and restaurants.

Hanamaulu Restaurant & Tea House, Highway 56 just north of Lihue Airport, ☎ 808/245-2511, is one of Kaua`i's oldest and best Oriental restaurants. The menu features both Japanese and Chinese dishes. Oriental decor adds a pleasant atmosphere to this country-style inn dining room. $

Oki Diner, 3125 Kuhio Highway in Lihue, ☎ 808/245-5899, is a real local-style plate lunch café with table seating. The extensive menu features burgers and sandwiches, saimin and won ton noodles, and local plate lunch favorites like beef stew, chicken tofu, BBQ ribs and more. Nothing fancy here, just good filling food. Many of the dishes are named for some of Kaua`i's former mayors and politicians. It's popular with the locals, a sign that the food is good. $

Tip Top Café, 3173 Akahi Street in Lihue, ☎ 808/245-2333, is part of the Tip Top Motel operation. This is probably Kaua`i's most famous coffee shop. The menu offers typical coffee shop fare and homemade desserts from the in-house bakery as well. $

Hamura Saimin, 2956 Kress, just off Rice Street in Lihue, ☎ 808/245-3271, is a typical "hole-in-the-wall" place with a back alley location. They are renowned for their fresh-made saimin noodle soup, won ton soup, fried noodles and beef or chicken sticks. The place may be a bit worn looking but the local-style food is great. $

Café Portofino, 3501 Rice Street, Lihue, ☎ 808/245-2121, is an authentic Northern Italian restaurant. The menu offers a wide range of pastas, fresh seafood and Italian specialties like veal osso bucco and shrimp scampi, plus homemade desserts, gelati and sorbets. $$

JJ's Broiler, 4416 Rice Street, Lihue, ☎ 808/246-4422, has a menu of regional Pacific cuisine and American fare, including steaks and seafood, plus sandwiches and a salad bar. Their Slavonic steak is a popular selection. There are nice views along Kalapaki Beach to enjoy with lunch or dinner. $$

Ma's, 4277 Halenani Street, Lihue, is another of those "hole-in-the-wall" places with good local-style food. In fact, it's just around the corner from Hamura Saimin noted earlier. They offer great breakfast and lunch specials. Nothing fancy in this diner lunch-counter operation, but the food is worth a stop and it won't put a huge dent in your wallet either. $

Gaylord's Restaurant, at Kilohana Plantation, Highway 50 west, Lihue, ☎ 808/245-5608, is one of Kaua`i's more elegant restaurants. It features an extensive American-continental menu for lunch and dinner in a relaxed, casual old plantation home atmosphere. The ambiance is nice and the food is excellent. $$$

The Coconut Coast

A Pacific Café, Kuhio Highway, Kaua`i Village Shopping Center, Kapa`a, ☎ 808/822-0013. This is the famed restaurant of noted chef, Jean-Marie Josselin, a leader of the Hawaiian Regional Cuisine trend, noted for creative use of local products. A new menu each night ensures variety. Reservations necessary. $$$

JR's Plantation Restaurant, 3-4221 Kuhio Highway, Hanama`ulu, ☎ 808/245-1606, also brings a creative touch and imaginative approach to local cuisine. Menu highlights are a Hawaiian Dinner Platter of traditional kalua roast pig, steamed chicken laulau, lomi salmon with poi and rice. Fresh island fish, seafood, garlic rack of lamb, prime rib, filet mignon and homemade desserts complete the menu. $$

The Bull Shed, 796 Kuhio Highway, Kapa`a, ☎ 808/822-3791. This popular restaurant has been serving up terrific steaks and seafood since 1979. The food is great, as is the relaxing oceanfront setting. Prime rib, tenderloin filet, top sirloin plus shrimp, lobster and fresh fish highlight the menu. $$

Local's Fast Food, 733 Kuhio Highway, Kapa`a, ☎ 808/822-3100. This eatery specializes in local-style breakfast items, plate lunches, sandwiches, burgers, saimin and specialty bowl meals. $

Mema Thai & Chinese Cuisine, Wailua Shopping Plaza, Kapa`a, ☎ 808/823-0899. The menu features authentic Thai spicy and hot cuisine. Most entrées available with chicken, beef, pork, shrimp, scallops, calamari or a combination. Curries, noodles, fried rice, salads and soups round out the extensive menu. $$

Ono Family Restaurant, 1292 Kuhio Highway, Kapa`a, ☎ 808/822-1710. This is a local-style café serving up generous portions of good simple food. Entrées include spaghetti and meat balls, salisbury steak, fried chicken, sandwiches, burgers and more. The homemade pies are always fresh and tasty. Warm Aloha-style service too. $$

Eggbert's, 4-484 Kuhio Highway, Coconut Marketplace, Kapa`a, ☎ 808/822-3787. This is a popular family specialty restaurant open daily for breakfast, lunch and dinner. The menu includes breakfast traditionals, plus sandwiches, salads and a variety of daily dinner entrée specials. $

Restaurant Kintaro, 370 Kuhio Highway, Kapa`a, ☎ 808/822-3341. This traditional Japanese cuisine restaurant has contemporary Japanese decor and a menu of authentic cuisine. Choose from teriyaki, tempura, yakitori, nabemono seafood, noodles and fresh-made sushi. Teppanyaki tables provide tableside cookery. $$

Rocco's, 4405 Kukui Street, Kapa`a, ☎ 808/822-4422. This Italian restaurant is open daily for lunch and dinner and has an extensive menu of Italian specialties such as eggplant marsala, shrimp caesar, lasagna, ravioli, scampi, pizza, plus fresh island fish. $$

Violet's Place, Kuhio Highway, Kaua`i Village Shopping Center, ☎ 808/822-2456. Open daily for breakfast, lunch and dinner, they serve traditional breakfast items and, for lunch or dinner, sandwiches, burgers, Filipino entrées like pork adobo, chicken paria, pinacbet, plus Chinese, Thai and Hawaiian specialties. $

The North Shore

Hanalei Dolphin, Hanalei, ☎ 808/826-6113. The emphasis here is on fresh fish and seafood. Menu features fresh island catch and seafood selections plus chicken and steaks. There are some interesting appetizers, chowder, casseroles and other items. $$

Casa di Amici, 2484 Keneke Street & Lighthouse Road, Kong Lung Center, Kilauea, ☎ 808/828-1555. This Italian restaurant has casual al fresco country dining. Varied appetizers, salads and soups are on menu with mains like grilled duck breast, lamb, beef filet, chicken and seafood served in creative preparations. $$

The Hanalei Gourmet, 5161 Kuhio Highway, Hanalei, ☎ 808/826-2524. This restaurant is located in the historic old Hanalei school building. Menu features Pacific Rim cuisine using fresh local products, herbs, spices; burgers, sandwiches, salads, seafood and more. $

Kilauea Bakery & Pau Hana Pizza, Kong Lung Center off Kilauea Lighthouse Road, Kilauea, ☎ 808/828-2020. Along with their excellent fresh bakery products and breads, they have a menu of traditional and specialty pizzas, soup of the day and salads. $$

Zelo's Beach House, Kuhio Highway & Aku Road, Hanalei, ☎ 808/826-9700. This is a funky beach house-style dining room, open-air, with beach and island decor accents all around. The menu offers a variety of fresh island fish, seafood, pastas, steaks and nightly dinner specials plus gourmet burgers, salads, desserts. Generally good food and good service. $$

Hanalei Wake-Up Café, Aku Road, Hanalei, ☎ 808/826-5551. This small family-operated café serves breakfast, lunch and dinner daily. Lunch-dinner mains feature Mexican specials. Very casual laid-back atmosphere. $

Duane's Ono Burgers, Kuhio Highway, Anahola, ☎ 808/822-9181. This is a popular local eatery right on the highway. The main event is the teriyaki burger piled high with all sorts of fixings. They also feature several varieties of burgers and other sandwiches as well. $

Hanalei Mixed Plate, Kuhio Highway, Ching Young Shopping Center, Hanalei, ☎ 808/826-7888. This is your typical hole-in-the-wall sort of place. It's a tiny lunch-counter operation with daily mixed plate specials, fresh island fish, sandwiches, salads, burgers. $

The South Shore & West

Joe's Café, in the Kiahuna Tennis Club, Poipu Beach, ☎ 808/742-6363, is a small place open for breakfast and lunch. The menu has traditional breakfast items plus salads, Portuguese bean soup, fresh sandwiches and hot daily specials. $

Roy's Poipu Bar & Grill, 2360 Kiahuna Plantation Drive, Poipu, ☎ 808/742-5000, is the Kaua`i location of this popular fine dining chain. The food is fresh, creative, superbly crafted and presented, hallmarks of a Roy's meal. Roy's features Hawai`i grown and produced foodstuffs and Asian/Pacific flavorings done with a French flair. Everything is good here. $$$

Tidepools, at the Hyatt Regency Kaua`i, 1571 Poipu Road, Poipu Beach, ☎ 808/742-1234, is the resort's signature dining room. The ambiance is "old Hawai`i," with open air thatched huts set among tumbling waterfalls and fish lagoons. The menu features fresh island seafood, grilled steaks and other specials. $$$

Koloa Fish Market, 5482 Koloa Road, Koloa, ☎ 808/742-6199, is a small local-style eatery serving up excellent plate lunch fare. The menu changes daily with specials like teriyaki chicken, meat loaf, fresh island fish and there is always a Hawaiian mixed plate of laulau, kalua pig and lomi salmon. Take outs only. $

Green Garden, Highway 50 in Hanapepe town, ☎ 808/335-5422, is one of those old family-run Kaua`i cafés, dating back to 1948. They serve breakfast, lunch and dinner and feature a menu of American fare and local-style cuisine. Popular with both residents and tour groups. They're famous for "mile high" cream pies for dessert. It's not fancy but functional and the food is great. $$

Kalaheo Steak House, 4444 Papalina Road, ☎ 808/332-9780, is in the small upcountry town of Kalaheo, west of Lihue. The menu features choice mainland beefsteaks and prime rib plus fresh island fish, seafood, pork and poultry specials. Try the homemade Portuguese bean soup. $$

The House of Seafood, 1941 Poipu Road, Poipu, ☎ 808/742-6433, has a large selection of seafood, fresh local and imported. The daily fresh catch is prepared in various ways. The menu also has several creative appetizers, salads and soups. $$$

O`ahu

The Gathering Place

Geography

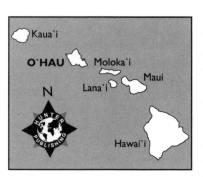

O`ahu, the Gathering Place, has a land mass of 608 square miles and is the third largest of the Hawaiian Islands. It has a population of about 875,000. The island rises from sea level to the highest point at 4,020 feet on Mt. Kaala in the Waianae Range. O`ahu has a 112-mile coastline of beautiful sandy beaches, sheer rocky cliffs and rugged lava fields. The City and County of Honolulu is comprised of the Island of O`ahu and the county seat is in Honolulu. It is also the capital city of the State of Hawai`i. Based on comparison of its structural lava flows, the island is 2.2 to 3.4 million years old.

Climate

Average temperatures on O`ahu range from 71-80°, with variable rainfall in different sectors of the island. The winters, from November to March, generally bring more frequent rains and cooler temperatures.

History

It is believed that the first Polynesians arrived on O`ahu before 1000 AD. The Hawaiians followed their communal lifestyle over the generations and were subservient to the ruling ali`i (kings and chiefs). O`ahu remained an independent kingdom until Kamehameha the Great from the Island of Hawai`i invaded and conquered the defenders in a decisive

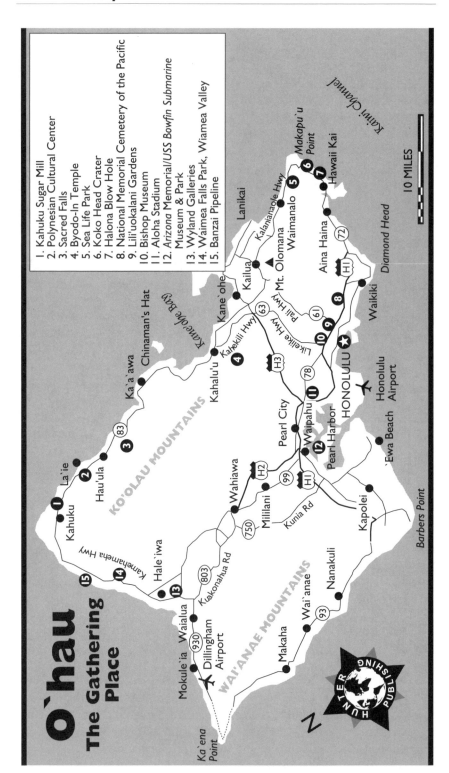

O'hau
The Gathering Place

1. Kahuku Sugar Mill
2. Polynesian Cultural Center
3. Sacred Falls
4. Byodo-In Temple
5. Sea Life Park
6. Koko Head Crater
7. Halona Blow Hole
8. National Memorial Cemetery of the Pacific
9. Lili'uokalani Gardens
10. Bishop Museum
11. Aloha Stadium
12. Arizona Memorial/USS Bowfin Submarine Museum & Park
13. Wyland Galleries
14. Waimea Falls Park, Wiamea Valley
15. Banzai Pipeline

10 MILES

battle at the Nu`uanu Valley in 1795. With this, Kamehameha brought O`ahu into his united kingdom of Hawai`i.

With its fine harbors, O`ahu gradually became the state's political, economic, military, educational and cultural center. Honolulu Harbor, discovered before 1800, became a key Pacific port for whalers, sandalwood and fur traders. Pearl Harbor became known to the world's powers for its strategic importance as a port in the middle of the vast Pacific. By 1850, the Hawaiian monarchy had moved permanently to Honolulu from its former capital in Lahaina, Maui. It has been the capital ever since. O`ahu has long led the way in business, government, banking, shipping, transportation, and tourism.

Hawaiian in gourd mask, sketched in 1779 by John Webber, who accompanied Captain Cook.

Information Sources

**Hawai`i Visitors and Convention Bureau,** 2270 Kalakaua Avenue, 8th floor, Waikiki Business Plaza, Honolulu, HI 96815, ☎ 800/GO-Hawai`i, 808/923-1811; www.visit.Hawaii.org; for meetings information, www.goHawaii.com

Visitors Information Service Desk, Hawai`i Visitors and Convention Bureau, Royal Hawaiian Shopping Center, 2201 Kalakaua Ave., Suite A401-A, Honolulu, HI 96815, ☎ 808/923-1811.

Waikiki/O`ahu Visitors Association, 1001 Bishop Street, Suite 477, Pauahi Tower, Honolulu, HI 96813, ☎ 808/524-0722.

**Hawai`i Attractions Association,** 615 Pi`ikoi Street, Suite 1812, Honolulu, HI 96714, ☎ 808/596-7733; www.Hawaiiattractions.com

Information Office, City and County of Honolulu, 530 S. King St., Honolulu, HI 96813, ☎ 808/523-4385.

Parks and Recreation Department, City and County of Honolulu, 650 S. King St., Honolulu, HI 96813, ☎ 808/547-7275; for permits, ☎ 808/523-4525.

Department of Lands and Natural Resources, State of Hawai`i, Division of State Parks-Camping, 1151 Punchbowl, Honolulu, HI 96813, ☎ 808/587-0300; for hiking information, ☎ 808/587-0166.

The Chamber of Commerce of Hawai`i, 1132 Bishop St., Suite 200, Honolulu, HI 96813, ☎ 808/545-4300.

National Weather Service, daily weather forecasts for Honolulu, ☎ 808/973-4380; for Island of O`ahu, ☎ 808/973-4381; marine forecast, ☎ 808/973-4382; surf forecast, ☎ 808/973-4383.

References

Alford, John. *The Mountain Biker's Guide to O`ahu,* Ohana Publishing, Honolulu, HI, 1995.

Carter, Frances. *Hawai`i on Foot,* Bess Press, Inc., Honolulu, HI, 1990.

Clark, John. *The Beaches of O`ahu,* University of Hawai`i Press, Honolulu, HI. 1994.

Koch, Tom. *Six Islands on Two Wheels: A Cycling Guide to Hawai`i,* Bess Press, Honolulu, HI, 1990.

Morey, Kathy. *O`ahu Trails: Walks, Strolls and Treks on the Capital Isle,* Wilderness Press, Berkeley, CA, 1994.

Olsen, Brad. *Extreme Adventures Hawai`i,* Hunter Publishing, Edison, NJ. 1998.

Smith, Robert. *Hawai`i's Best Hiking Trails,* Hawaiian Outdoor Adventures Publications, Maui, Hawai`i. 1994.

Stone, Robert. *Day Hikes on O`ahu,* Day Hike Books, Red Lodge, Montana, 1994.

Smith, Rodney. *Hawai`i: A Walker's Guide,* Hunter Publishing, Edison, NJ. 1997.

Zurick, David. *Hawai`i, Naturally,* Wilderness Press, Berkeley, CA. 1990.

Getting There

■ Inter-Island Air Service

These airlines provide numerous daily scheduled flights between Honolulu, O`ahu, and other destinations within the Hawaiian Islands. All
flights operate from Honolulu International Airport.

- **Aloha Airlines,** US, ☎ 800/367-5250, Canada, ☎ 800/235-
  0936, on O`ahu, ☎ 808/244-9071; e-mail aloha@alo-
  haair.com; www.alohaair.com/

- **Island Air,** US, ☎ 800/323-3345, Canada, ☎ 800/235-0936,
  on O`ahu, ☎ 808/484-2222, within Hawai`i, ☎ 800/652-6541;
  e-mail aloha@alohaair.com; www.alohaair.com/. This subsidiary of Aloha Airlines operates shuttle flights from Honolulu to smaller airports throughout the Neighbor Islands of
  Kaua`i, Maui, Moloka`i and Lana`i.

- **Hawaiian Airlines,** US and Canada, ☎ 800/367-5320, on
  O`ahu, ☎ 808/838-1555; www.Hawaiianair.com/

■ US Mainland & Honolulu

These airlines operate regularly scheduled flights between Honolulu International Airport and the US mainland and Canada. Some airlines
also operate flights to Maui, Kaua`i and the Big Island of Hawai`i via
Honolulu with stopover flights or connecting to inter-island carrier
flights.

- **Hawaiian Airlines,** US and Canada, ☎ 800/367-5320, on
  O`ahu, ☎ 808/838-1555; www.Hawaiianair.com/.

- **American Airlines,** US and Canada, ☎ 800/433-7300, on
  O`ahu, ☎ 808/833-7600; www.americanair.com/.

- **Air Canada,** US, ☎ 800/776-3000; www.aircanada.ca/.

- **Continental Airlines,** US, ☎ 800/523-3273; www.flyconti-
  nental.com/.

O`ahu

- **Canadian Airlines,** US, ☎ 800/426-7000, on O`ahu, ☎ 808/681-5000; www.cdnair.ca/.

- **Delta Airlines,** US, ☎ 800/221-1212; www.delta-air.com/.

- **America West Airlines,** US, ☎ 800/235-9292; www.americawest.com/.

- **Northwest Airlines,** US, ☎ 800/225-2525, Canada, ☎ 800/447-4747, on O`ahu, ☎ 808/955-2255; www.nwa.com/.

- **Trans World Airlines,** US, ☎ 800/221-2000; www.twa.com/.

- **United Airlines,** US, ☎ 800/241-6522; www.ual.com.

- **Pleasant Hawaiian Holidays,** US, ☎ 800/242-9244, on O`ahu, ☎ 808/923-7611 or 926-1833; www.pleasantholidays.com; this operator offers room/car/fly package tours and flights on scheduled services.

■ Cruise Ships

Once upon a time, luxury cruise ships were the only way to get to the Hawaiian Islands. Back in the days before World War II, Hawai`i's tourism industry developed as a result of the cruise ship industry. Then, cruise liner travel was for the affluent. The rise of the jet age and modern mass tourism made a trip to Hawai`i affordable for many and the old luxury cruise liners were mothballed.

However, the last few years have seen an increase in international cruise ships making port calls in the Hawaiian Islands. So, once again, it is possible to sail to the islands on a luxurious ocean liner. Several cruise lines now regularly route their ships on a seasonal basis into Honolulu as well as the neighbor islands of Kaua`i, Maui and the Big Island of Hawai`i at Kona and Hilo. Schedules vary, as do itineraries. For details, it is recommended that you check with a travel agent or cruise tour reservation specialist.

Among the ships that have made Hawai`i port calls on regular sailings recently from North America and other points are: **Princess Cruise Lines'** *Island Princess, Sea Princess* and *Golden Princess* (☎ 800-PRINCESS/774-6237); **Royal Viking Lines'** *Sagafjord* and *Royal Viking Sun* (☎ 800-426-0821); **Holland America Lines'** *Statendam, Rotterdam* and *Maasdam* (☎ 800-426-0327); **Cunard Lines'** *Queen Elizabeth II* (☎ 800-221-4770); **Royal Caribbean Lines'** *Legend of the*

Seas (☎ 800-327-6700); and **Carnival Cruise Lines'** *MS Tropicale* (☎ 800-327-9501).

In addition, within the Hawaiian Islands, **American Hawai`i Cruises** offers exclusive inter-island cruises between Honolulu and the neighbor islands aboard the *SS Independence.* There are three-day and week-long packages. The ship spends a day in each port at Kaua`i, Maui and the Big Island's Kona and Hilo. There are shore excursions and tours available from dockside at each port. For details and information, contact your travel agent or: American Hawai`i Cruises, 550 Kearny St., San Francisco, CA 94108, ☎ 800/765-7000.

Getting Around

Upon arrival at Honolulu International Airport, look for the visitor information, car rental and transportation counters in the baggage claim areas. You should be able to make arrangements for your ground transportation if you've not already done so. There are also phone banks for hotels in case you need to make a reservation or contact the hotel. Taxi stands are located in front of the baggage claim area. You can meet your coach shuttle, taxi or car rental shuttle in front of the baggage claim area.

If you are connecting to an inter-island flight for another island destination on Aloha or Hawaiian Airlines, or a commuter line, you need to proceed to the inter-island terminal, which will be to your left as you exit the baggage claim area of the main terminal. Depending upon your exit location, it will be a five-10 minute walk to the inter-island terminal, a block or more away. There are also free WikiWiki Shuttle Buses if you would rather ride. Catch one in front of the baggage claim area.

If you didn't have your baggage checked through to your final island destination, you need to pick it up. You might want to get one of the baggage carts. It'll save you some trouble. Walkways also lead directly to the inter-island terminal from inside the main overseas terminal concourse. Just follow the signs inside the main terminal and/or ask for directions from any airport personnel.

■ Airport Transportation

There are several airport/hotel shuttle and taxi services available. For reservations and information, contact any of the following.

- **Airport-Island Shuttle,** Mililani, Honolulu, ☎ 808/623-8855.

- **Americab,** Honolulu, ☎ 808/591-8830.

- **The Cab,** Honolulu, ☎ 808/422-2222.

- **1st Choice Shuttle,** Honolulu, ☎ 808/988-9293.

- **Robert's Taxi,** Leeward, ☎ 808/486-4609; Windward, ☎ 808/261-8555.

- **Hawai`i Kai AAA Hui/Koko Head Taxi,** Honolulu, ☎ 808/396-6633.

- **Hawai`i Kai Taxi & Airport Express,** Honolulu, ☎ 808/396-8294.

- **Leeward AAA Hui/Airport Express,** Waipahu, ☎ 808/676-6996.

- **Leeward Airport Shuttle,** Honolulu, ☎ 808/422-2222.

- **Windward Airport Shuttle,** Kane`ohe, ☎ 808/235-9464.

■ Bus & Trolley Service

There are a couple of bus options from Honolulu Airport to Waikiki Beach area hotels or to other locations on O`ahu.

- For information or advance reservations for airport/hotel bus transport, try **H&M Shuttle Service,** 2550 Kuhio Avenue, Honolulu, ☎ 808/924-8882.

- The City and County of Honolulu also operates its own public bus transit system, called **TheBus.** This bus system covers the entire island of O`ahu and all major attractions. One can also catch a bus from the airport to Waikiki area hotels. The public bus system is an excellent and inexpensive way of seeing the sights of Waikiki, Honolulu and greater O`ahu. For complete information and schedules, contact their 24-hour information line, ☎ 808/296-1818, then press 8287; for baggage information, ☎ 808/848-4500; for general information and bike rack information, ☎ 808/848-5555. They even have a Web site: www.thebus.org

- **Waikiki Trolley,** 1141 Waimanu Street, Honolulu, HI 96814, ☎ 800/824-8804, 808/596-2199. This operator runs a fleet of open-air trolleys on a route connecting the Waikiki Beach area with downtown Honolulu and all major sites and attractions. There is all-day service, with frequent stops at each attraction. There are two different routings, a Honolulu Sightseeing Tour and a Shopping Trolley Tour. Single-day or multi-day passes are available. One-day pass is $18, multi-day pass is $30. Special shopping trolleys run out to the Waikele Shopping Outlets at Pearl City. Call for details.

■ Limousine Service

For those who want to mix adventure with luxury (and have the deep pockets necessary!), arranging a private luxury limousine for airport/hotel transport and/or tours around Oʻahu would certainly be a memorable experience. These operators can custom-package almost any sort of excursion or outing, including airport planeside pickups, golf tours, circle-island tours, beach tours, picnics, weddings and much more. Take a VIP ride in a Rolls Royce or Jaguar limo or a Lincoln Towncar super-stretch limo. Check with any of the following operators.

- **Aloha Limousines,** PO Box 88043, Honolulu, HI 96830, ☎ 800/345-9344, 808/955-0055.

- **Rocky's Limousine Service,** 975 Kapiolani Blvd., Honolulu, HI 96814, ☎ 808/596-8488 or 596-8484.

- **A-1 limousines by Neven,** 320 Ohua Avenue, Honolulu, ☎ 808/922-1531.

- **Lowy Limousine Service,** PO Box 6201, Honolulu, HI 96818, ☎ 808/455-2444.

- **Imperial Limousine Inc.,** PO Box 29420, Honolulu, HI 96820, ☎ 808/836-0011.

- **Cloud 9 Limousine,** Honolulu, ☎ 808/235-7999 or 524-7999.

- **Sharp Limousine Tours Inc.,** 1777 Ala Moana, Honolulu, ☎ 808/951-6144.

- **Platinum Limousine,** 1124A-20th. Avenue, Honolulu, ☎ 808/735-9980.

- **Islands Limousine Service Inc.,** 1281 S. King St., Honolulu, ☎ 808/596-9811.

- **Rex Limousine,** 2240 Kuhio Avenue, Waikiki, ☎ 808/924-7110.

- **Duke's Limousine,** 876 Curtis St., Honolulu, ☎ 808/597-1552.

- **Hawai`i I Limousines,** PO Box 88694, Honolulu, HI 96830. ☎ 808/678-2337.

■ Car & Truck Rentals

For rental cars and trucks on O`ahu, check with any of the following for compact, economy, mid-size, full-size, convertible, 4WD vehicles and trucks. Several of the national chains have multiple locations and outlets in Waikiki hotels and shopping centers; call for details.

A WORD TO
THE WISE

Most Waikiki hotels have parking garages but they charge extra for a parking space. Street parking in Waikiki is next to impossible so it would be wise to confirm with your hotel in advance to make sure they have parking available. Wherever you go on O`ahu, remember to lock your car and never leave valuables inside unattended.

- **AA Aloha Cars-R-Us,** for Honolulu Airport pick-up, ☎ 800/655-7989.

- **AA Paradise Network,** for Honolulu Airport pick-up, ☎ 800/942-2242.

- **Adventure Rentals,** 1946 Ala Moana Blvd., Honolulu, ☎ 808/944-3131.

- **Alamo Rent a Car,** ☎ 800/GO-ALAMO, Honolulu Airport, ☎ 808/833-4585, and other Honolulu locations; www.goalamo.com.

- **Avis Rent a Car,** ☎ 800/321-3712, Honolulu Airport, ☎ 808/834-5536, and other Honolulu locations.

- **Budget Rent a Car,** ☎ 800/527-0700, all Hawaiian Island locations, ☎ 808/537-3600.

- **Classic Car Rentals,** 2139 Kuhio Avenue, Waikiki, ☎ 808/923-1983; rent a classic like a Cobra, Viper, Ferrari, Porsche or Corvette.

- **Courtesy Car and Truck Rental,** Honolulu Airport, ☎ 808/831-2277; Waikiki location, ☎ 808/971-2660.

- **Dollar Rent a Car,** ☎ 800/800-4000, Honolulu Airport, ☎ 808/831-2330; other Honolulu/Hawai`i locations, ☎ 808/944-1544.

- **Enterprise Rent a Car,** ☎ 800/325-8007, Honolulu Airport, ☎ 808/836-7722; Waikiki and other locations, ☎ 808/922-0090.

- **Ferrari Rentals,** 1879 Kalakaua Avenue, Waikiki, ☎ 808/942-8725.

- **Funway Exotic Car Rentals,** 325 Seaside Avenue, Waikiki, ☎ 808/971-2660; rent an exotic car like a Viper, Ferrari, BMW, Porsche, Corvette, Jaguar or Mercedes.

- **Hertz Rent a Car,** ☎ 800/654-3011, Honolulu Airport, ☎ 808/831-3500.

- **Ho`okipa Haven Vacation Service,** ☎ 800/398-6284, serving all the Hawaiian Islands with discount car rentals.

- **National Car Rental,** ☎ 800/227-7368, Honolulu Airport, ☎ 808/831-3800.

- **Paradise Isle Rentals,** 151 Uluniu, Waikiki, ☎ 808/922-2224; rent a Jeep, Mustang, convertibles and more.

- **Thrifty Car Rental,** ☎ 800/367-2277, Honolulu Airport, ☎ 808/833-0046.

- **Tradewinds U-Drive,** 2875A Koapaka, Honolulu, ☎ 808/834-1465.

- **VIP Car Rental,** Honolulu Airport, ☎ 808/488-6187; Waikiki location, ☎ 808/922-4605, 924-6500.

O`ahu

Waikiki Beach.

▪ Motorcycle & Moped Rentals

Check with any of the following for daily or weekly rentals of motorcycles, mopeds and motorscooters.

- **Adventure Moped Rentals,** 1705 Kalakaua Avene, Waikiki, ☎ 808/941-2222.

- **Adventure Rentals,** 1946 Ala Moana, Honolulu, ☎ 808/944-3131; a full line of motorcycles, mopeds and scooters.

- **Funway Exotic Car Rentals,** 325 Seaside Avenue, Waikiki, ☎ 808/971-2660; in addition to exotic dream cars, they also rent Honda and Harley-Davidson motorcycles by the day or week.

- **Big Mountain Rentals,** 2426 Kuhio Avenue, Waikiki, ☎ 808/926-1644; they have a wide range of motorcycles and mopeds for rent.

- **Island Motorcycle,** 512-B Atkinson Drive, Honolulu, ☎ 808/957-0517; Harley-Davidson motorcycles by the day or week.

- **The Moped Connection,** 750-A Kapahulu Avenue, Kapahulu, ☎ 808/732-3366; half- and full-day moped rentals available.

- **Coconut Cruisers,** 2301 Kalakaua Avenue, Waikiki, ☎ 808/924-1644; a full range of mopeds and scooters available for rent.

- **Paradise Isle Rentals,** 151 Uluniu Avenue, Waikiki, ☎ 808/922-2224; a full line of Harley-Davidson motorcycles and moped rentals.

Waimea Bay.

■ Bicycle Rentals

Check with any of the following bike shops for a full line of bicycles and related equipment rentals.

- **Big Mountain Rentals,** 2426 Kuhio Avenue, Waikiki, ☎ 808/926-1644.

- **Blue Sky Rentals & Sports Center,** 1920 Ala Moana, Waikiki, ☎ 808/947-0101.

- **Island Triathlon & Bike,** 569 Kapahulu Avenue, Kapahulu, ☎ 808/732-7227; a full line of bike and equipment rentals for everyone from beginners to pro biker competitors.

- **Paradise Isle Rentals,** 151 Uluniu Avenue, Waikiki, ☎ 808/922-2224.

- **Barnfield's Raging Isle Surf & Cycle,** 66-250 Kamehameha Highway, Haleiwa, ☎ 808/637-7707; this well stocked shop has bike and bike equipment rentals from beginner to pro level.

Touring O`ahu

■ Metro Honolulu

A WORD TO
THE WISE

If you're used to driving in a large hectic urban environment or on busy freeways, you'll feel right at home in O`ahu. If you're used to driving in a tamer environment, you may be in for a surprise. Honolulu traffic is notorious for congestion. In fact, you'll find most of its major thoroughfares, freeways and main streets, even the side streets, clogged with traffic at most any time of the day or night – especially during the business rush hours. So, plan accordingly.

Get a good map of the city and island and study it well. Most car rental agencies provide a map with each car rental. The Hawaiian-named streets may cause you some problems but try to learn the major through streets that connect Waikiki (where you will most likely be staying) with the rest of Honolulu, downtown, outlying districts and the highways that go around the island.

Two maps that are especially good are: **Map of O`ahu,** by James Bier, University of Hawai`i Press. This is a full color topographic map with detail on all of O`ahu, major attractions and street names. Another choice is **Bryan's Sectional Maps of O`ahu,** (get the latest edition) by J. R. Clere, an excellent guide to streets and roads all around O`ahu. These are available at bookstores and shops all over Honolulu.

■ Waikiki Beach

From the airport to Waikiki is about 10 miles via Nimitz Highway, which runs right outside the airport. The ride to Waikiki usually takes 20-30 minutes, depending on traffic. Nimitz Highway becomes Ala Moana Boulevard as it passes through downtown Honolulu and along Honolulu Harbor. From there it heads straight into Waikiki. From the airport, you can also take the H-1 Freeway into Waikiki. Exit the H-1 at

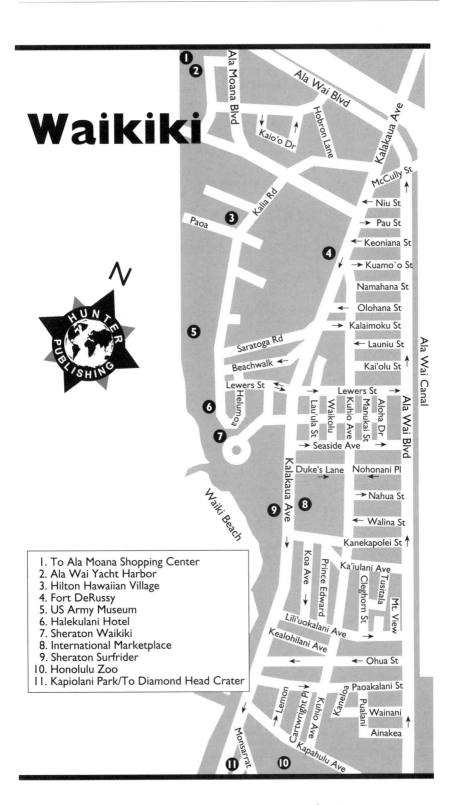

Waikiki

O'ahu

1. To Ala Moana Shopping Center
2. Ala Wai Yacht Harbor
3. Hilton Hawaiian Village
4. Fort DeRussy
5. US Army Museum
6. Halekulani Hotel
7. Sheraton Waikiki
8. International Marketplace
9. Sheraton Surfrider
10. Honolulu Zoo
11. Kapiolani Park/To Diamond Head Crater

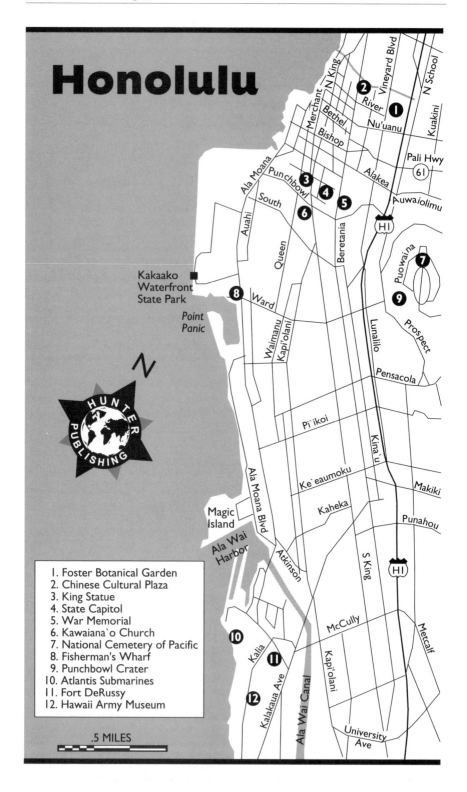

Honolulu

Kakaako Waterfront State Park

Point Panic

1. Foster Botanical Garden
2. Chinese Cultural Plaza
3. King Statue
4. State Capitol
5. War Memorial
6. Kawaiana`o Church
7. National Cemetery of Pacific
8. Fisherman's Wharf
9. Punchbowl Crater
10. Atlantis Submarines
11. Fort DeRussy
12. Hawaii Army Museum

.5 MILES

Punahou Street, turn right and make another right on Beretania, then a quick left onto Kalakaua Avenue. This leads right to the heart of Waikiki.

Waikiki is on the south shore of O`ahu. North-south main streets and freeways connect the Waikiki resort area with downtown Honolulu, Honolulu International Airport, Pearl Harbor and the central O`ahu plain. Highways and freeways also connect Waikiki and downtown Honolulu with the famous North Shore beach areas, the eastern Windward Coast and the western Leeward Coast. There are also highways leading to the eastern Windward Coast, Waimanalo, Kailua and Kane`ohe, plus routes to the western Leeward Coast and Waipahu, Kapolei, and Waianae.

Waikiki is an excellent central location with easy access to many major attractions, either by walking, trolley, bus or your own rental car.

■ Downtown Honolulu

Located just two miles north of the Waikiki Beach resort area is historic downtown Honolulu. Within a short distance of the center of downtown are a number of Honolulu's major attractions. A street map will enable you to locate these easily and most of them are within walking distance of one another. These attractions include the **State Capitol** and adjacent **Iolani Palace, Washington Place, King Kamehameha Statue** and **Ali`iolani Hale**, the **Mission Houses Museum, Kawaiahao Church, Honolulu Hale, National Memorial Cemetery of the Pacific at Punchbowl, Chinatown** and its unique shops and open-air markets, the **Aloha Tower Marketplace, Hawai`i Maritime Museum** and **Falls of Clyde** sailing ship and **Kewalo Basin** boat harbor.

■ Central O`ahu

This central O`ahu corridor is flanked on the east by the **Ko`olau Mountain Range**, which runs the full length of the windward coast from Hawai`i Kai and Makapu`u on the southeast to Kahuku on the northeast point. To the west of the central corridor is the **Waianae Mountain Range**, stretching from the Waipahu-Makakilo area through Nanakuli, Waianae, and Makaha to Ka`ena Point on the remote northwest tip of the island.

O`ahu has a limited freeway system that is heavily used and always busy. The **H-1 Freeway** connects the Kahala area behind Diamond Head with Waikiki, downtown Honolulu, the airport, Pearl Harbor and

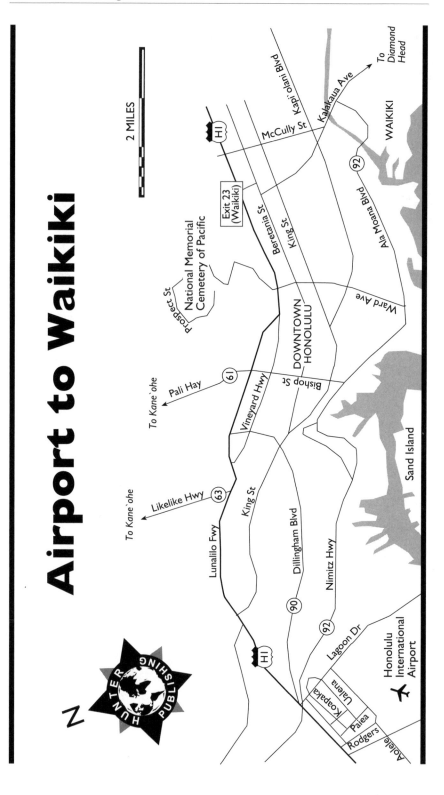

Airport to Waikiki

extends west out to Waipahu and the Kapolei near Barber's Point Naval Air Station. The **H-2 Freeway** links the central corridor of Pearl City and Wahiawa area. And the new **H-3 Freeway**, just opened in late 1997 after years of delay, links Kane`ohe and Kailua on the windward coast with the Halawa and Pearl Harbor areas on the leeward coast via a spectacular route up and over (through tunnels) the Ko`olau Mountains. This new route provides some spectacular views of forest, valleys and mountains. Two other trans-Ko`olau routes link the windward coast with the leeward coast. These are the **Pali Highway 61** and the **Likelike Highway 63**. Both routes connect downtown Honolulu with the Kane`ohe and Kailua areas.

■ The South & the Windward Coast

Finding one's way around O`ahu from Waikiki is not too difficult as long as you stick to the main routes. There is only one road, the **Kalanianaole Highway 72**, that follows the coast from Waikiki southeast around the island and continues up the length of the east windward coast. The road changes to the **Kamehameha Highway 83** up the Windward Coast at Kane`ohe and follows around to the North Shore and Haleiwa. The road, still the Kamehameha Highway but changed to #99, then turns back south to Waikiki through the central corridor of O`ahu, linking up with the H-2 freeway at Wahiawa.

The drive along the southeast coast is scenic, with lots of beaches and mountain scenery. The route passes through the residential areas of Kaimuki, Kahala, Waialae, Aina Haina, Niu and Hawai`i Kai, past Maunalua Bay, Koko Head Crater, Hanauma Bay, Sandy Beach, to Makapu`u Point and Sea Life Park. From Makapu`u, the coastal route follows up the Windward Coast through Waimanalo, with numerous beach parks, to the Kailua and Kane`ohe areas, providing views of the Ko`olau Mountain Range and Rabbit Island.

The Windward Coast route follows along the beaches of northeast O`ahu and through the farming communities of Waiahole and Waikane, past Mokoli`i (Chinaman's Hat) Island, Ka`a`awa, Kahana Bay, Hau`ula, La`ie (home of the Polynesian Cultural Center and Brigham Young University-Hawai`i), and the former sugar plantation area of Kahuku, before turning west to the North Shore. Along the North Shore the route passes the world famous surfing beaches of Sunset Beach, Ehukai, the Banzai Pipeline and Waimea Bay, Waimea Valley and Adventure Park, then on to the surf center of Haleiwa and former sugarcane center of Waialua. From Waialua, the **Farrington Highway 930** extends west

O`ahu

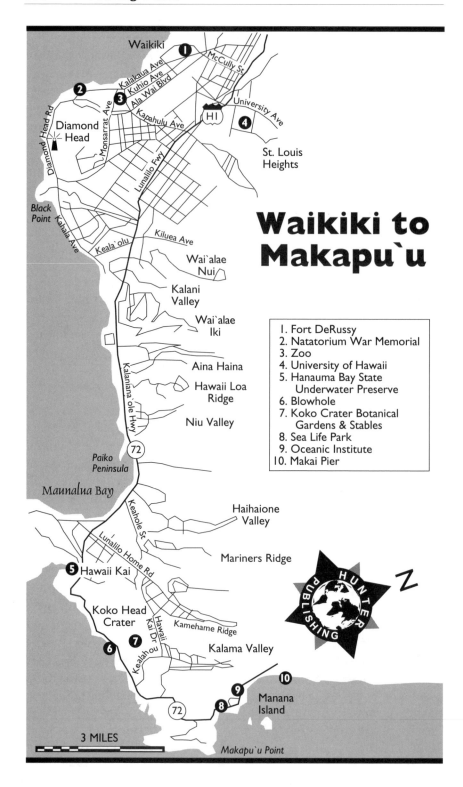

Waikiki to Makapu`u

1. Fort DeRussy
2. Natatorium War Memorial
3. Zoo
4. University of Hawaii
5. Hanauma Bay State Underwater Preserve
6. Blowhole
7. Koko Crater Botanical Gardens & Stables
8. Sea Life Park
9. Oceanic Institute
10. Makai Pier

Waikiki

McCully St

Kalakaua Ave
Kuhio Ave
Ala Wai Blvd

University Ave

Kapahulu Ave

HI

Diamond Head Rd

Monsarrat Ave

Diamond Head

St. Louis Heights

Lunalilo Fwy

Black Point

Kahala Ave

Keala`olu

Kiluea Ave

Wai`alae Nui

Kalani Valley

Wai`alae Iki

Aina Haina

Kalaniana`ole Hwy

Hawaii Loa Ridge

Niu Valley

72

Paiko Peninsula

Maunalua Bay

Keahole St

Lunalilo Home Rd

Haihaione Valley

Mariners Ridge

Hawaii Kai

Koko Head Crater

Hawaii Kai Dr

Kamehame Ridge

Kealahou

Kalama Valley

HUNTER PUBLISHING

N

Manana Island

72

Makapu`u Point

3 MILES

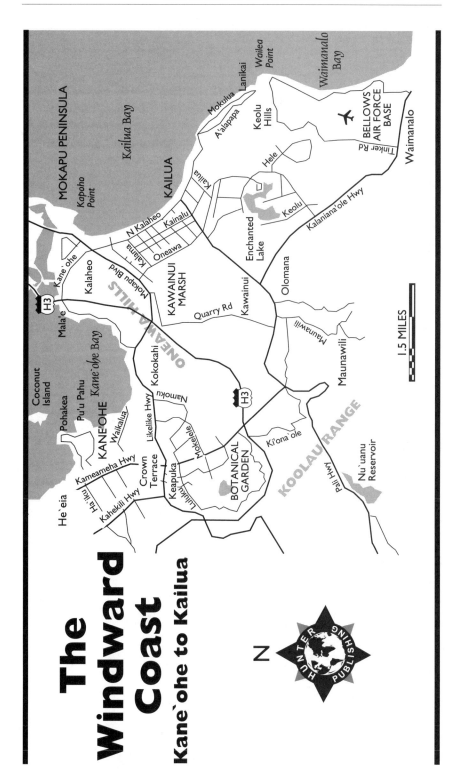

The Windward Coast
Kane'ohe to Kailua

O'ahu

N

1.5 MILES

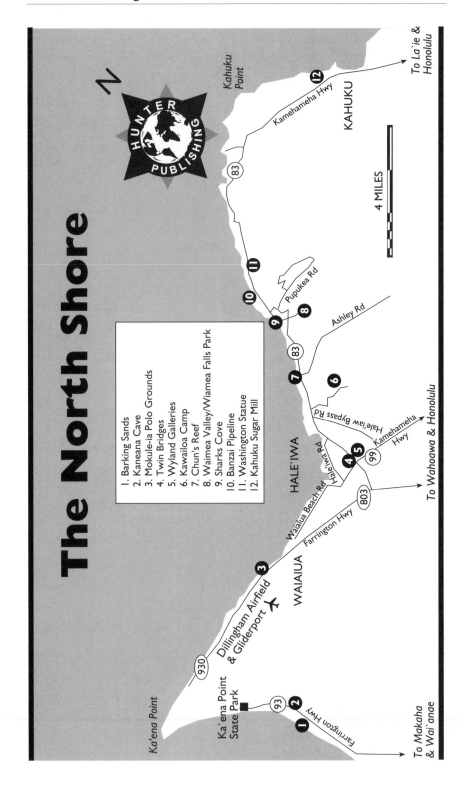

The North Shore

1. Barking Sands
2. Kaneana Cave
3. Mokule-ia Polo Grounds
4. Twin Bridges
5. Wyland Galleries
6. Kawailoa Camp
7. Chun's Reef
8. Waimea Valley/Wiamea Falls Park
9. Sharks Cove
10. Banzai Pipeline
11. Washington Statue
12. Kahuku Sugar Mill

through the Mokuleia area, past Dillingham Airfield, where the road terminates. From here, it is a five-mile hike to **Ka`ena Point Natural Area Preserve**, the remote westernmost point of O`ahu.

From the North Shore, the route heads south to the central plain of O`ahu and through the pineapple plantations of the Wahiawa and Mililani areas, with mountain views of the Ko`olau Range to the east.

■ The Leeward Coast

From the central area of O`ahu, you can take the western coastal drive along the leeward Waianae Coast. This road deadends just short of the far northwest Ka`ena Point (approached from the south side) and you must return the same way. Take the H-1 Freeway or Farrington Highway 93 west from Pearl City. This route passes through the Ewa Plain area around the north side of Pearl Harbor and through Waipahu to Makakilo. There are turnoffs to the Ewa Beach, Barbers Point Naval Air Station, Kapolei and Ko Olina Resort areas along the southwest coast of O`ahu. This route skirts around the southern end of the Waianae Mountain Range, which runs the length of the Leeward (Waianae) Coast. This is a drier, warmer area compared to the Windward Coast, devoid of the lush tropical vegetation and rain forest of the eastern coast. There are a number of beautiful sandy beach parks along the Waianae Coast. The route continues north, following the coast through the communities of Nanakuli, Lualualei, Ma`ili, Waianae and Makaha to the end of the road near Ka`ena Point.

From Waikiki to **Hanauma Bay** is 11 miles/30 minutes via Kalanianaole Highway 72; to **Sea Life Park** via Kalanianaole Highway 72 is 15 miles/40 minutes; to **Historical Downtown Honolulu** is four miles/15 minutes; to **Punchbowl National Cemetery** is five miles/20 minutes; to **USS Arizona Memorial** is 11 miles/30 minutes; to the **Nu`uanu Valley and Pali Lookout** via Pali Highway 61 is 11 miles/30 minutes; to **Polynesian Cultural Center**, Laie, via Pali Highway 61 and Kamehameha Highway 83, is 35 miles/one hour and 15 minutes; to **Waimea Valley and Adventure Park** via H-2 Freeway and Highway 99 to North Shore is 36 miles/one hour.

■ Land Tours/Operators

There are several tour operators offering half-day and full-day narrated, guided coach and van tours around O`ahu. Contact any of the following operators for details. Half- and full-day tours vary according to specific

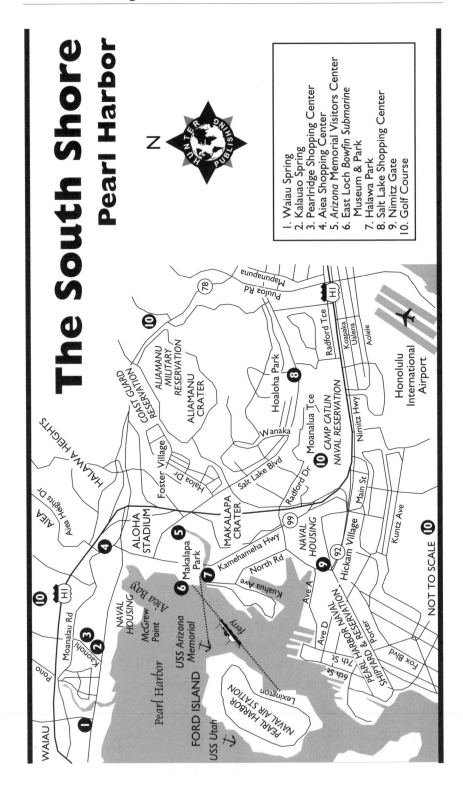

The South Shore
Pearl Harbor

N

1. Waiau Spring
2. Kalauao Spring
3. Pearlridge Shopping Center
4. Aiea Shopping Center
5. Arizona Memorial Visitors Center
6. East Loch Bowfin Submarine
   Museum & Park
7. Halawa Park
8. Salt Lake Shopping Center
9. Nimitz Gate
10. Golf Course

itinerary. Half-day tours to sites like Arizona Memorial, downtown Honolulu, Diamond Head, Tantalus and Nuuanu Valley, Pali Lookout and Punchbowl Cemetery range from $15 to $23 per person. Full-day tours to outlying sites like the Windward Coast, Polynesian Cultural Center, the North Shore and Circle Island tours range from $55-75 per person.

Annette's Adventures, 45-403 Koa Kahiko Street, Kaneohe, HI 96744, ☎ 808/235-5431. This operator specializes in custom-designed island tours and excursions to out-of-the-way places emphasizing ecotourism activities; day trips, hiking and camping trips, overnight discovery trips, and neighbor island trips. Complete air and ground transportation packages with bed and breakfast accommodations or other small, locally owned inns and lodges.

**O`ahu Expeditions,** 44-409 Kaneohe Bay Drive, Kaneohe, HI 96744, ☎ 888/590-7948, 808/261-0580; e-mail Oahuexpd@lava.net; www.rawspace.net/O`ahuexpd This outdoor guide company promotes eco-tourism through hiking, camping, kayaking, snorkeling and diving expeditions. Contact them for details.

**Discovering Hidden Hawai`i Tours,** 1440 Kapiolani Blvd., Suite 108-279, Honolulu, HI 96814, ☎ 808/946-0432. This operator offers a wide range of half-day and full-day narrated tours to all of O`ahu's major sites and attractions. Tour stops include beaches, rain forests, panoramic lookouts, pineapple fields, historic sites, Pearl Harbor, Punchbowl National Cemetery and much more. Contact them for details.

E Noa Tours, 1141 Waimanu Street, Honolulu, HI 96814, ☎ 800/824-8804, 808/591-2561. This operator offers several half-day and full-day Circle-Island tours with stops at major attractions like Bishop Museum, Chinatown, Hanauma Bay, Diamond Head Crater, Pali Lookout, Aloha Tower Marketplace, Pearl Harbor, Polynesian Cultural Center, Temple Valley, Waimea Valley and Adventure Park, North Shore beaches, Blow Hole and Sandy Beach, and the Windward Coast.

Top Gun Tours, PO Box 25204, Honolulu, HI 96825, ☎ 808/396-8112. This operator specializes in "Home of the Brave" military base tours of Hawai`i. There is a basic half-day tour that includes stops at Pearl Harbor Visitors Center and Museum and the USS Arizona Memorial, Hickam Air Force Base, Wheeler Army Base, Schofield Army Barracks, Punchbowl National Cemetery and other downtown Honolulu historic sites.

Polynesian Adventure Tours, 1049 Kikowaena Place, Honolulu, HI 96819, ☎ 808/833-3000. A wide range of guided half-day and full-day

O`ahu

Punchbowl Memorial Cemetery.

Circle-Island tours to all of O`ahu's major sites and attractions. Take in the Windward Coast and North Shore beaches, Pearl Harbor, USS Arizona Memorial, Polynesian Cultural Center village tour and luau show, mountain rain forests, downtown historic sites, shopping, panoramic lookouts, pineapple fields and more.

Hawaiian Isle Adventures, Honolulu, ☎ 808/261-2786. Specializing in unique adventure excursions to O`ahu's least crowded and most beautiful beaches for snorkeling, boogie boarding, beach exploring and sunning. There are also rain forest and waterfall hikes mixed with Hawaiian history, culture and legends and visits to historic sites like the royal mausoleum, Nuuanu Pali Lookout, Ulupo Heiau and Holona Blowhole.

**Roberts Hawai`i Tours,** 680 Iwilei Road, Suite 700, Honolulu, HI 96817, ☎ 808/523-7750. A variety of half-day and full-day Circle-Island tours, including all of O`ahu's major sites and attractions. Call for details.

**Trans Hawaiian O`ahu,** 720 Iwilei Road, Suite 101, Honolulu, HI 96817, ☎ 808/566-7300. Half-day and full-day Circle-Island tours to O`ahu's major visitor attractions. Call for details.

Adventures

O`ahu's Best Adventures

O`ahu and Honolulu offer exciting adventure activities, from casual to challenging and limited only by your own interests. The following are some of the best adventures on O`ahu.

- Take a Waikiki Beach and Pearl Harbor Cruise to the **Arizona Monument**; or visit the Arizona Monument via the National Park Service visitors center.

- Climb up **Diamond Head Mountain** for a great view of Honolulu.

- Take the **Haunted Honolulu Midnight Tour** and chill out with stories of Hawaiian ghosts and the supernatural.

- Take the **Hawaiian Culture & History Tour** of old Hawaiian archaeological sites around O`ahu.

- Do the **Maunawili Ridge Trail** hike on the Windward Coast.

- Take the **Iolani Palace** tour and learn about the history of Hawai`i's royal monarchy.

- Take a self-guided walking tour of **historic Honolulu**.

- **Ride a catamaran along Waikiki Beach** to Diamond Head.

- Visit the **Bishop Museum** and learn about Hawai`i's cultural heritage, social and natural history.

- See **Waimea Valley and Adventure Park** and take a wild ATV ride through jungled hills.

- Enjoy a Hawaiian **luau** and Polynesian music and dance program.

- Take a submarine ride along O`ahu's coral reefs or a snorkel and scuba dive excursion to see colorful marinelife.

O`ahu

■ On Foot

Honolulu and the island of O'ahu have many fine hiking trails along isolated beaches, through valleys and along mountain rain forest ridges. The trails provide panoramas of city, coastline and mountains. They are maintained by the state Division of Forestry and Wildlife under the Na Ala Hele Trail and Access Program.

Trail Safety Rules

- Stay on marked trails; hike with a companion.
- Tell someone your plans.
- Abide by posted warnings.
- Use common sense.
- Wear appropriate shoes and clothing.
- Take plenty of water and food.
- Do not drink stream water due to harmful bacteria.

The following is a partial listing of the many hiking trails around O'ahu.

Waikiki Area

Waikiki from Diamond Head.

DON'T MISS **Diamond Head State Park Hiking Trail** is a relatively easy .7-mile trail beginning inside Mount Leahi (Diamond Head) and leading to its upper ridge summit. It's a 1½-hour round-trip. Allow time at the top to enjoy the views. There are two long staircases and a 300-foot tunnel leading to 360° panoramic views of O'ahu's interior mountains, suburban areas, Waikiki Beach, downtown Honolulu and coastal areas. There are old World War II bunkers and gun emplacements at the summit. Access the trail by entering Diamond Head Crater from Monsarrat Avenue. First part of the trail is steep, with several switchbacks and then a gradual rise to the steps. Good hiking shoes recommended.

Manoa Cliffs Trail is one of several tropical jungle trails in the area and is 3.4 miles long. This moderate trail follows the contours of the Manoa Valley and goes around Tantalus Crater to Pauoa Valley. The trailhead is off Round Top Drive in Manoa Valley above the University of Hawai`i. Take McCully Street to Wilder Avenue and turn left, then take a right onto Makiki Street. Proceed on Makiki until it becomes Round Top Drive. The area gets frequent rain showers and the trail is often muddy and slippery.

Manoa Falls Trail.

Manoa Falls Trail lies just behind Waikiki in the Manoa Valley above the University of Hawai`i. This moderate .8-mile trail passes through the lush tropical vegetation of Manoa Valley and crosses the stream, finally leading to the base of small but picturesque Manoa Falls. Access the trail by taking Manoa Road all the way to the entrance of Lyon Arboretum. At the sharp left bend in the road, proceed straight on the dirt road and park.

Kanealole Trail is .7 mile long. From Nehoa and Makiki Streets proceed toward the mountains and turn left on Makiki Heights Drive. Go .5 mile to sharp left bend in road. There, proceed through iron gate past Makiki Forest Recreation Area sign and park on right. Trail begins behind parking lot and proceeds up Makiki Valley. The trail intersects Makiki Valley Trail; go left to Nahuina Trail/Tantalus Drive or take two rights back to parking lot.

Makiki Valley Trail is 1.1 miles long and is accessed about halfway up Tantalus Drive. Look for trailhead sign on right. Park in small corner lot. Trail goes into Makiki Valley for 1.1 miles to Round Top Drive, intersecting several other trails along the way.

Moleka Trail is .7 mile and is accessed at 4005 Round Top Drive. Park in small lot on left. On upper side of road is Manoa Cliffs trailhead. This

O`ahu

route follows contours of upper east edge of Makiki Valley, traversing a bamboo grove with panoramic views of Honolulu.

**Nu`uanu Trail** is 1½ miles long and is accessed on Tantalus Drive, past the Nahuina trailhead sign. Look for Manoa Cliff trailhead sign on left. Proceed on foot to just below first switchback where a connector trail meets Pauoa Flats Trail. Nu`uanu Trail intersection is on left, just after the Pauoa Flats Trail.

Kolowalu Trail is one mile long and is accessed on East Manoa Road above the University of Hawai`i in Manoa Valley. Proceed on East Manoa Road to Woodlawn Drive. Turn left and go .75 mile to sharp right. Proceed to Alani Lane to limited parking area. Walk past cable gate to Forestry and Wildlife picnic shelter. Trail climbs a very steep finger ridge to Wa`ahila Ridge.

Central O`ahu

DON'T MISS **Historic Downtown Honolulu** is a leisurely one-mile stroll that will take about an hour. This walk covers Honolulu's most important historic buildings and sites near the downtown commercial center. The **Mission Houses Museum** at King and Kawaiahao Streets is a good place to start. The museum provides a glimpse of early missionary life in Hawai`i from the 1820s on. The nearby **Missionary's Cemetery** holds the remains of many of the early missionaries and their families. The **Kawaiahao Church** here, built in 1842, was one of the first permanent churches and was constructed of coral stone blocks. Visitors can walk through this historic church. In front of the church is **King Lunalilo's Tomb**. He died in 1874 after a short one-year reign as monarch. Across King Street is **Honolulu Hale**, or city hall. The building has a beautiful open courtyard and stairways designed after a 13th-century Italian palace.

Back along King Street is the attractive **Ali`iolani Hale**, or Judiciary Building, with a handsome statue of King Kamehameha the Great in front. The building was built as a home for King Kamehameha V, but he didn't like it and turned it into an administrative office building instead. The statue of Kamehameha the Great is a duplicate of the one at North Kohala on the Big Island and one in Statuary Hall in the national capitol at Washington, DC.

Directly across King Street is **Iolani Palace**, the only royal palace on US soil. The palace is open for tours daily. It was built by King Kalakaua in 1879 and was the home of Hawaiian monarchs until Queen Lili`uokalani was deposed in 1893. Next to the palace is **Iolani Barracks**, which housed the royal house guards. The Coronation Pavilion/Bandstand is on the front lawn of the palace. Behind the palace is the modernistic State Capitol Building of Hawai`i, with reflecting pools and stylish decor.

On the Beretania Street side of the Capitol is a statue of **Father Damien**, the Belgian priest who ministered to the abandoned lepers at Kalaupapa on Moloka`i in the 1870s-80s. Across Beretania Street from the Capitol is **Washington Place**, a beautiful old estate that is now the official home of the Governor of Hawai`i. It was built in 1846 by John Dominis, a Boston merchant. His son later married High Chiefess Lydia Kamakaleha Kapalakea, who became Queen Lili`uokalani in 1891 and was deposed when the monarchy was overthrown in 1893. She later lived at Washington Place until her death in 1917.

Manana Trail is six miles long. Go inland toward the mountains on Waimano Home Road in Pearl City and turn left onto Komo Mai Drive to Pacific Palisades. Go to the end of Komo Mai Drive. Proceed on foot through the pedestrian passageway to water tank at end of road. The trail starts straight ahead on ridge, winding up to the Ko`olau Mountain Range summit.

Waimano Trail is 7.2 miles long. From the junction of Waimano Home Road and Kamehameha Highway 99 in Pearl City, go inland two miles to Waimano Home grounds. Two trail routes are on the left of the chain link fence. The Lower Valley Route follows an old jeep road to the valley floor and along a stream. About .5 mile from the end of old road, a side trail climbs the valley. The Upper Valley Route goes along the main road outside a chain link fence for .5 mile. The trail turns left and follows a ditch and tunnels to the east branch of Waimano Valley. It climbs over a ridge along the stream to an old abandoned dam. The trail continues to the right, making several switchbacks to the summit. The trail passes through the Ewa Forest Reserve.

Windward O`ahu

DON'T MISS **Nu`uanu Pali State Wayside** is about six miles above downtown Honolulu on the Pali Highway 61, which crosses the Ko`olau Mountains to Kailua on the windward coast. There is ample parking at the site. It's just a short walk to the incredible vista of the 1,200-foot pali lookout, which provides an expansive view of the windward coast and mountains, including the Waimanalo, Kailua and Kane`ohe areas. Interpretive signs relate the story of the invasion of Kamehameha the Great from the Big Island about 1795.

DID YOU KNOW?

Kamehameha's invading forces battled the defending O`ahu warriors, chasing them up into the Nu`uanu Valley and forcing some 400 warriors over the pali to their deaths. This victory consolidated Kamehameha's hold on O`ahu and eventually led to the unification of all the islands of Hawai`i under one kingdom. **Caution:** the winds are usually so strong here that you can literally lean into the wind without falling over.

DON'T MISS **Maunawili Trail** is a moderate to difficult nine-mile trail that takes you into some fairly untouched areas of O`ahu's windward eastern side. Begin from the Pali Highway 61 side, hike about an hour in and then turn back. Otherwise you will end up in Waimanalo far down on the southeast coast of O`ahu. Take Pali Highway to Nu`uanu Pali State Wayside and follow Old Pali Road at right of lookout to the trailhead. There is also trail access just past (east) the Pali Tunnels at a scenic pullout on a sharp turn heading down to Kailua. The trail has some steep rises but is mostly

Along the Maunawili Valley Trail.

level walking through rain forest and some open grassy areas. There are a few streams to cross. Beautiful views of east O`ahu coastal areas, mountains, ridges, sheer cliffs and valleys below. Good hiking shoes recommended. Take water and snacks.

**Kailuwa`a Falls** is in Sacred Falls State Park on the northeast coast, one mile north of Hau`ula town on the Kamehameha Highway 83. This is a moderate 4½-mile round-trip hike to the base of the 80-foot-high Sacred Falls and swimming hole. The trail begins on an old cane haul road and crosses the Kaluanui stream twice as it goes into the narrow valley. The canyon is rich in lore of the legendary demigod, Kamapua`a.

Danger! This canyon is susceptible to flash floods and falling rocks and is closed during rainy periods.

**Hau`ula Trail System** consists of three separate trails. From Kamehameha Highway 83 at Hau`ula, turn onto the northern access of Hau`ula Homestead Road across from Hau`ula Beach Park. Go .2 mile to a left bend in road. Trails begin straight ahead; park on gravel. Proceed along gravel road and turn left at the Forest Reserve cable. **Hau`ula Loop** is 2½ miles. The trail begins inland and where it branches off, take the right trail up the adjoining ridge. It crosses Waipilopilo Gulch to the next ridge overlooking Kaipapa`u Valley, returning across the gulch to rejoin the start of trail. **Ma`akua Gulch** is three miles. Follow the dirt road to the end. The trail continues inland and enters the canyon of Ma`akua Gulch, crosses a stream several times and leads to a waterfall and small pool. **Ma`akua Ridge** is 2½ miles. Follow the dirt road past Hau`ula Loop Trail intersection. The trail takes off left and crosses the gulch, switching back up Ma`akua Ridge and forming a loop. Go in either direction.

O`ahu

North Shore

**Ka`ena Point Natural Area Reserve** is the westernmost point of O`ahu Island and is the site of one of the last intact sand dune ecosystems in the Hawaiian Islands.

DID YOU KNOW?

A wild place of crashing surf on windswept beaches, this was known to ancient Hawaiians as "leina a ka`uhane," or "leaping place of souls," where it was believed the spirits of the dead were reunited with their ancestors.

The moderate five-mile round-trip walk, two-four hours, is along rough rocky shoreline with mostly level walking. Ka`ena Point is usually hot and sunny so take water, snacks and dress appropriately. Native animals found at Ka`ena include the Hawaiian monk seal and Laysan albatross. Native plants like the beach naupaka, `ilima papa, hinahina and pohinahina and nehe grow here as well. Ka`ena Point is reached from Waianae to the south via the Farrington Highway 93. Drive to road's end at Makua-Ka`ena Point State Park parking area and follow the trail signs 2½ miles to the point. From the east, take Highway 930 past Waialua and Mokuleia and park where the paved road ends, a mile beyond Camp Erdman. From there, it is 2½ miles to the point.

Mokuleia Trail is 2½ miles long and is accessed by going on Kuaokala-Mokuleia Access Road to a paved road. Turn left to the forest reserve gate. Just before the gate, take a road right to the end, where Mokuleia Trail begins. The trail goes through Mokuleia Forest Reserve and Pahole Natural Area Reserve.

Kealia Trail is 2.3 miles long. From North Shore, take Farrington Highway 930 past Camp Mokuleia, turn left into third Dillingham Airfield entrance. Proceed straight .4 mile to parking area at tower. Walk the gravel road toward pali (cliffs) through a gate in fence. The trail climbs up a hill on left. From the bottom, the trail switchbacks above the airfield. At one-mile, the trail crests at pali and becomes a dirt road running upward along the ridge connecting to Kuaokala Access Road. From the Waianae Coast, reach the trail by proceeding along Kuaokala Access Road from Ka`ena Point Satellite Tracking Station. Kealia Trail is 2.8 miles from the parking area on left.

Hiking Resources

The outfitters in this section have half- and full-day guided hiking adventures. Rates begin at $50 for half-day and $65 for full-day excursions, lunch and hiking gear included.

The State of Hawai`i has an excellent O`ahu Recreation Map which details hiking trails all over the island. For a free map and complete information on hiking trails, contact: **Department of Land and Natural Resources**, State of Hawai`i, Division of Forestry & Wildlife, 1151 Punchbowl St., Room 130, Honolulu, HI 96813, ☎ 808/587-0166.

For guided hikes and excursions on O`ahu, contact: **The Sierra Club of Hawai`i, O`ahu Group,** PO Box 2577, Honolulu, HI 96803, ☎ 808/538-6616 or 732-4489; e-mail david.frankel@sfsierra.sierraclub.org; www./urlinc.com/hisierra. This group conducts regular walks, hikes and excursions to areas around O`ahu. Visitors may be able to join their activities. Call, write or e-mail them for information.

Hawai`i Trail & Mountain Club, ☎ 808/488-1161.

Hike Hawai`i,** 91-261 Hanapouli Circle W., Ewa Beach, HI 96706, ☎ 808/683-3967; e-mail hikehi@hgea.org. This outfitter specializes in small group hikes to some of the best places O`ahu has to offer. These informative, educational hikes help you experience nature in Hawai`i while learning about its unique flora, fauna, history and culture. Choose from a variety of hikes suitable for the novice hiker, with distances ranging from three to six miles. **Mountain and **Rain Forest** hikes are half- or full-day, depending on weather conditions, distance to be traveled and guest preference. Hikes traverse steep mountain ridges with views along the windward coast to upland forest areas alive with native Hawaiian birds and plants and lush valley views. **Coastal** hikes are full-day five-mile roundtrips to the unique Ka`ena Point area, where you will see unique coastal plants, explore tide pools, observe sea birds and even seasonal whales in offshore areas. Hikes include snack or lunch, water, raingear, day packs and hotel transportation. Trips are personally guided and narrated by Hawaiian naturalist and educator, Reece Olayvar.

Golf Courses

O`ahu has many fine public and privately operated golf courses, some of them having hosted PGA championship tournaments. Most courses require advance assigned tee times, so plan accordingly. Greens fees at resort courses vary widely, from $60-125 and up. Check on availability of daily specials and seasonal rates. Public courses are usually less expensive to play but can be quite busy.

- **Ala Wai Golf Course,** 404 Kapahulu Avenue, ☎ 808/296-2000, is a municipal course of the City and County of Honolulu just behind Waikiki and across the Ala Wai Canal.

- **Ted Makalena Golf Course,** Waipio Point Access Road, ☎ 808/296-7888, is a municipal course of the City and County of Honolulu in the Waipahu area.

- **West Loch Golf Course,** 91-1126 Okupe Street, ☎ 808/296-5624, is a municipal course of the City and County of Honolulu on the west side of Pearl Harbor.

- **Pali Golf Course,** 45-050 Kamehameha Highway, Kailua, ☎ 808/296-7254, is a municipal course of the City and County of Honolulu on the windward east side of O`ahu.

- **Waialae Country Club,** 4997 Kahala Drive, Kahala area, ☎ 808/734-2151, is one of Hawai`i's best-known private courses and home to the PGA Hawaiian Open for many years. Call to see if you can get a guest tee time.

- **Makaha Valley Country Club,** 84-627 Makaha Valley Road, Waianae Coast, ☎ 808/695-9578, is open to the public and has two championship 18-hole layouts.

- **Olomana Golf Links,** 41-1801 Kalanianaole Highway, Hawai`i Kai, ☎ 808/259-7926, is a semi-private course open to the public.

- **Ko Olina Golf Club,** 3733 Aliinui Drive, off Farrington Highway 93 past Ewa and Makakilo, ☎ 808/676-5300, is a resort course open to the public; three championship 18-hole layouts.

- **Hawai`i Kai Golf Course,** 8902 Kalanianaole Highway, Hawai`i Kai, ☎ 808/395-2358, is a private course open to the public.

- **Hawai`i Prince Golf Club,** 91-1200 Ft. Weaver Road, ☎ 808/944-4567 is a semi-private club open to the public and has 27-holes of championship links.

- **Hawai`i Country Club,** Kunia Road, ☎ 808/621-5654, is a semi-private par-72 layout.

- **Koʻolau Golf Course,** 45-550 Kionaole Road, ☎ 808/236-4653, is a semi-private course with an 18-hole championship layout.

- **Mililani Golf Club,** 95-176 Kuahelani Avenue, ☎ 808/623-2222, is a semi-private course with an 18-hole championship spread located in central Oʻahu.

- **Pearl Country Club,** 98-535 Kaonohi, ☎ 808/487-3802, is a beautiful semi-private 18-hole course overlooking Pearl Harbor and is open to the public.

Tennis Courts

Several hotels and condos maintain tennis courts for guest use. The **City & County of Honolulu** also maintains many tennis courts throughout the city and the island. Facilities include some lighted courts and are located in public parks around Oʻahu. For details, contact: **Parks and Recreation Department**, City & County of Honolulu, 558 S. King St. City Hall Annex, Honolulu, HI 96813, ☎ 808/971-7150.

Private courts charge from $10 and up per hour. Other tennis courts include:

- **Hawaiʻi Pacific Tennis Association,** 2615 S. King St., ☎ 808/955-6696.

- **Kailua Racquet Club,** 629 Oneawa, Kailua, ☎ 808/263-4444.

- **Maunalua Bay Club,** 5275 Kalanianaole Highway, ☎ 808/377-3509.

- **The Oʻahu Club,** 6800 Hawaiʻi Kai Drive, ☎ 808/395-3300.

Shopping

Honolulu's shopping ranges from small specialty shops in Waikiki to outlying suburban malls and factory outlet centers. Visitors won't be disappointed. Most of the shopping centers and plazas in the Waikiki and metro Honolulu areas are accessible by the Waikiki Trolley or The-Bus city rapid transit system. Check with your hotel desk or with the shopping centers directly as business hours may vary.

Waikiki

Ala Moana Center, 1450 Ala Moana Boulevard, Waikiki, ☎ 808/946-2811. This has some 180 shops of all sorts, a huge food court, restau-

Chinatown Market, Honolulu.

rants, departments stores like Nordstrom's, Liberty House, Sears, etc. It's the place to shop in Honolulu.

International Market Place, 2330 Kalakaua Avenue, in the heart of Waikiki, ☎ 808/528-2236. This is an open-air bazaar with numerous small kiosks and shops plus an international food court. It has a colorful lively carnival-like atmosphere.

King's Village, 31 Kaiulani Avenue, between Prince Edward and Koa Streets, ☎ 808/944-6855. This complex has a turn-of-the-century atmosphere with royal guards, cobblestone paths and a clock tower amid the gift and specialty shops.

Royal Hawaiian Shopping Center, 2201 Kalakaua Avenue, Waikiki, ☎ 808/922-0588. Centrally located in the heart of Waikiki, this is a complex of some 160 shops, restaurants and lounges with nightly entertainment.

Waikiki Shopping Plaza, 2250 Kalakaua Avenue, Waikiki, ☎ 808/923-1191. Also in the heart of Waikiki, with some 50 shops and restaurants.

Metro Honolulu

Aloha Tower Marketplace, 1 Aloha Tower Drive, Honolulu Harbor off Ala Moana Blvd., ☎ 808/528-5700. A waterfront complex surrounding the famed Aloha Tower, long a Honolulu landmark for the early day cruise liners. There are 120 shops and restaurants of all kinds. Free trolley from Waikiki hotels.

Chinatown Cultural Plaza, 100 N. Beretania St., ☎ 808/521-4934. This modern complex in old Chinatown has some 70 shops and Chinese restaurants or food outlets.

The Dole Cannery, 650 Iwilei Road, ☎ 808/531-2886. Built on the site of an old pineapple cannery, there are 24 shops in the complex.

Maunakea Market Place, 1120 Maunakea St., Chinatown, ☎ 808/524-3409. A colorful marketplace in the heart of old Chinatown with 70 shops and stalls.

Restaurant Row, 500 Ala Moana Blvd., ☎ 808/538-1441. This modern complex has 33 restaurants, theaters, stores and nightclubs.

The Ward Warehouse and Ward Centre, 1050-1200 Ala Moana Blvd., ☎ 808/591-8411. Two separate complexes with over 100 shops and restaurants.

Central O`ahu

Mililani Shopping Center, 95-221 Kipapa Drive and 95-390 Kuahelani Avenue, Mililani, ☎ 808/523-5644. Some 60 shops and food outlets.

The Town Center of Mililani, 95-1249 Mehe`ula Parkway, Mililani, ☎ 808/625-5233. An urban mall with 80 shops and food outlets.

Aloha Flea Market, Aloha Stadium, off Moanalua Road #78 and the H-1 freeway near Pearl City, ☎ 808/486-1529. Hawai`i's largest flea market and open-air bazaar with vendors selling everything from new clothes to housewares, antiques, produce and more. It's a lively carnival atmosphere.

Windward O`ahu

Kahuku Sugar Mill, 56-565 Kamehameha Highway 83, ☎ 808/293-8747. This old sugar mill features 15 specialty and gift shops plus food outlets.

Windward Mall, 46-056 Kamehameha Highway 83, Kane`ohe, ☎ 808/235-1143. A traditional urban mall with large department stores, a wide range of shops and a food court.

Windward City Shopping Center, 45-480 Kane`ohe Bay Drive, Kane`ohe, ☎ 808/236-2527. This small center has 15 shops.

Southeast O`ahu

Koko Marina, Kalanianaole Highway and Lunalilo Home Road, ☎ 808/395-4737. A waterfront complex with some 60 restaurants, ocean sports and shops.

Kahala Mall, 4211 Waialae Avenue, Kahala, ☎ 808/732-7736. An urban mall with 80 shops, restaurants, food court and a theater complex.

Leeward O`ahu

Pearlridge Center, 98-1005 Moanalua Road, Pearl City, ☎ 808/488-0981. A traditional urban mall with more than 170 shops, food outlets, restaurants, theaters and more.

Pearl City Shopping Center, 850 Kamehameha Highway 99, Pearl City, ☎ 808/523-5644. There are 45 shops and food outlets.

O`ahu

Iolani Palace.

Pearl Kai Center, 98-199 Kamehameha Highway 99, ☎ 808/942-7100. This mall has 46 shops and food outlets.

Waikele Center, 94-790 Lumiaina St., Waipahu, ☎ 808/676-5656. Honolulu's factory outlet center with 76 stores of all sorts.

Wai`anae Mall, 86-120 Farrington Highway 93, ☎ 808/696-2690. Neighborhood mall with 41 shops and food outlets.

Hawaiian Arts & Crafts

Imua Shop Polynesia, 56-931 Kamehameha Highway, Laie, ☎ 808/293-5055.

Island Crafts Etc., 908 Bannister, #205, Kalihi, ☎ 808/841-1963.

Island's Best Inc., Ala Moana Center, Ala Moana Blvd., ☎ 808/949-5345.

Keali`i Kukui Nut Company, 94-296 Pupuole, Waipahu, ☎ 808/678-6500.

Kwilts 'n Koa, 1126-12th. Avenue, #101, Kaimuki, ☎ 808/735-2300.

Little Hawaiian Craft Shop, 2233 Kalakaua Avenue, #3028, Waikiki, ☎ 808/926-2662.

Products of Hawai`i Too, 2424 Kalakaua Avenue, Waikiki, ☎ 808/923-3399.

USS Arizona Memorial.

O`ahu

Quilts Hawai`i, 2338 S. King St., Punahou, ☎ 808/942-3195.

South Seas Mercantile & Trading Co., 720 Iwilei Road, Suite 201, Alakea, ☎ 808/537-9590.

Museums/Historic Sites

O`ahu has a number of interesting historical and cultural museums that are worth exploring. A visit to any of these museums will provide a better understanding of Hawai`i's unique history, cultural heritage and social-economic development from its pre-western contact days to the modern era.

DON'T MISS **Bishop Museum,** 1525 Bernice Street, ☎ 808/847-3511. Hawai`i's renowned cultural and natural history museum; galleries showcase Pacific, Hawaiian and natural history with changing exhibits and displays.

DON'T MISS **Iolani Palace,** King and Richards Streets next to Capitol Building, ☎ 808/538-1471/522-0832. The only royal palace in the US and a revered site. Hawai`i's last reigning monarch, Queen Liliu`okalani, was imprisoned here after American businessmen overthrew the monarchy in 1893. Frequent daily tours are offered; reservations required.

Mission Houses Museum, 553 S. King St., ☎ 808/531-0481. These historic buildings include the oldest original wood-frame western-style house still standing in Hawai`i. Buildings capture the lifestyle of early missionaries.

National Memorial Cemetery of the Pacific (Punchbowl), 2177 Puowaina Drive, ☎ 808/566-1430. A handsome memorial to America's war dead overlooks thousands of graves of military veterans and their wives and children in a beautiful volcanic crater setting above Honolulu. Thousands of names of those missing in action are inscribed on large monuments; exhibits and displays detail the many famous battles and operations of the Pacific war.

 DON'T MISS **Queen Emma Summer Palace,** 2913 Pali Highway, ☎ 808/595-3167. Located in the Nu`uanu Valley, this old home holds rare artifacts and personal memorabilia of Hawai`i's royalty; daily tours.

 DON'T MISS *USS Arizona* **Memorial,** 1 Arizona Memorial Drive, Pearl Harbor, ☎ 808/422-0561, 422-2771. One of Hawai`i's best known monuments, a "Shrine of Democracy" memorial built over the sunken hull of the battleship *USS Arizona,* sunk December 7, 1941. It is a tomb to 1,177 sailors and marines. The film and boat tour out to the memorial takes a minimum of three hours.

 DON'T MISS *USS Bowfin* **Submarine Museum and Park,** 11 Arizona Memorial Drive, Pearl Harbor, ☎ 808/423-1341. Tour a real World War II-era attack submarine and learn about life in the deep.

USS Missouri, the famed World War II battleship, on whose deck Japan surrendered, thus ending the war, is docked at Pearl Harbor and is being established as a historical museum; anticipated opening is January, 1999. For the latest information, call the *USS Missouri* Memorial Association at ☎ 808/545-2263. Information and tour reservations are available through Atlantis Adventures of Honolulu, toll free at ☎ 877-644-4896 (877-MIGHTYMO). Standard and deluxe coach tours from Waikiki hotels range from $29-49 per person; general admission to the Battleship Missouri Museum is $12 per person.

**Hawai`i Maritime Center,** Pier 7, Honolulu Harbor, near Aloha Tower just off Ala Moana Blvd., ☎ 808/536-6373. Displays and exhibits cover Hawai`i's maritime history from the arrival of the first Polynesians to the 1800s whaling days and the modern era of cruise passenger ships.

US Army Museum of Hawai`i, Fort DeRussy, Kalia Road, Waikiki, ☎ 808/955-9552. Displays and exhibits on early Hawaiian war artifacts and World War II.

Honolulu Academy of Arts, 900 S. Beretania St., ☎ 808/532-8700. Honolulu's fine art museum, with exhibits of Asian art, Japanese prints, Italian Renaissance paintings, American and European paintings, decorative and ceramic art, contemporary art and graphic arts plus theater features.

**Hawai`i's Plantation Village,** 94-695 Waipahu St., Waipahu, ☎ 808/677-0110. This outdoor museum features a collection of authentic restored and replica buildings from Hawai`i's sugarcane plantation era. Walking tours through the old town with historical narration provide a closeup view of plantation life, cultural and social history.

Hawaiian Railway Society, PO Box 1208, Ewa Station, 91-1001 Renton Road, Ewa Beach, HI 96706, ☎ 808/681-5461. Railroad buffs and adventurers will enjoy a ride along the historic track of the O`ahu Railway and Land Company. Take a ride on open-air cars through the Ewa plains and old sugarcane fields west of Pearl Harbor and Honolulu; listen to the story of railroading in early Hawai`i; see many old locomotives and train cars on the station grounds and the restored 1900 Dillingham Parlor Car.

**Japanese Cultural Center of Hawai`i,** 2454 South Beretania St., Honolulu, HI 96826, ☎ 808/945-7633. This unique historical gallery features an ongoing display, "Okage Sama De," the story of the Japanese in Hawai`i from the arrival of the first group of immigrant plantation laborers in 1868 to the later influences of Japanese culture on Hawai`i today.

25th Infantry Division Tropic Lightning Museum, Schofield Army Barracks, Wahiawa, central O`ahu, located at the end of Macomb Road, Building 360, Carter Hall. This small military museum traces the history of Schofield Barracks from its establishment in the early 1900s as a US Army base through the activation of the famed "Tropic Lightning" division; displays and exhibits from World Wars I & II, Korea and Vietnam; tanks, artillery, plus a P-39 airplane and helicopters on display at the main entrance of Wheeler Airfield nearby.

The North Shore Surf and Cultural Museum, North Shore Marketplace, 66-250 Kamehameha Highway, Haleiwa, ☎ 808/637-8888. One of O`ahu's newest museums and the only one in Hawai`i dedicated to Hawai`i's fabled "Sport of the Kings." The museum's exhibits celebrate the history and cult of surfing in the islands, where the sport was

O`ahu

born. There are surfboards hanging from the ceiling, photos, posters, paintings, trophies and other memorabilia. A huge weathered redwood board was made in the 1930s for one of Waikiki Beach's famous beach-boys, Turkey Love. And a pair of signature boards belonged to big wave surfer, Mark Foo, who drowned surfing in California a few years ago.

■ On Wheels

 Many of the hiking trails around O'ahu maintained by the Division of Forestry and Wildlife in the Na Ala Hele Trail and Access Program also allow mountain bikers. Exceptions are the 14 separate trails of the Tantalus Trail System of the Makiki and Manoa Valleys behind the Waikiki area, and Mokuleia Trail on the North Shore. There are also several interesting bike rides along more established roadways of Honolulu and O'ahu.

 Honolulu public transit's **TheBus** has some buses equipped with bicycle racks that can carry two bicycles. Bikers can put their bikes on the racks, board TheBus and pay regular fare to any point around O'ahu. For schedule and route information, call ☎ 808/848-5555.

Waikiki

Kolowalu Trail is one mile long. Proceed to Manoa Valley on East Manoa Road to Woodlawn Drive. Turn left and ride .75 mile to a sharp right and then to Alani Lane. Go past the gate to a picnic shelter. The trail climbs a steep, narrow finger ridge to Wa'ahila Ridge.

Wa'ahila Trail is 2.4 miles long; on Waialae Avenue. Go inland on St. Louis Drive to Ruth Place where an access road enters Wa'ahila State Park. Go through the parking lot to a jeep road leading to powerline. Trailhead is near the powerline.

Pu'upia Trail is .75 mile long. Use same access as for Kolowalu Trail above. The trail climbs up a valley on the left side of picnic shelter to a ridge; continue up the ridge on left to Pu'upia summit.

Diamond Head Crater Loop is four miles long. Start at end of Waikiki Beach at Kalakaua Avenue and Kapahulu, heading toward Diamond Head. The road passes by Honolulu Zoo and through Kapiolani Park. Hanging to the right, pick up Diamond Head Road, which continues south around the crater. The road passes by Diamond

Head Lighthouse and overlook before looping back on a gradual climb around the east and north sides of the crater. The road also passes by Kapiolani Community College before reaching residential neighborhoods and Monsarrat Avenue, which leads back to the start at the end of Waikiki Beach.

 DON'T MISS **Tantalus Drive Loop** is five-six miles long. From Waikiki, take Kalakaua Avenue inland to Beretania, turn right to Punahou Street and left to Nehoa. Turn left onto Nehoa then to Tantalus or Round Top Drive. The route makes a loop up and around the mountain ridge between Manoa and Makiki Valleys and residential neighborhoods. This is a steep, narrow, winding road with great views of Honolulu and Waikiki.

Ala Wai Bike Paths is a four-mile round-trip following established bike paths. Start at corner of Ala Wai Blvd. and Kapahulu Avenue behind Waikiki. Take the Kapahulu Bike Path .5 mile inland to Date Street Bike Path, going north .5 mile. This path loops around Ala Wai Golf Course and turns into McCully Bikeway Promenade, continuing north for one mile. Nice views of golf course, Ala Wai Canal, Waikiki and interior mountains. Return the same way or turn left off McCully Bikeway onto McCully Street down to Kalakaua Avenue and turn right back to Waikiki area.

Central O`ahu

Manana Trail is six miles long. Go inland at Pearl City on Waimano Home Road, turn left on Komo Mai Drive to Pacific Palisades; go to end of Komo Mai Drive. Pass through walkers' passageway to water tank at road's end. Trail starts straight ahead on ridge, climbing six miles to Ko`olau Mountains summit.

Waimano Trail is 7.2 miles long. At Pearl City junction of Waimano Home Road and Kamehameha Highway 99, go inland two miles to Waimano Home grounds. Two routes are on left of chain link fence. Lower Valley Route is accessed by old jeep road, which follows a stream to valley floor. About .5 mile from end of old road, a side trail climbs valley. Upper Valley Route is accessed by going along main road outside chain link fence for .5 mile. The trail turns left and follows ditch and tunnels to east branch of Waimano Valley. It crosses over ridge along stream to an old dam and turns right, following several switchbacks to summit.

Aiea Loop Trail is a five-mile round-trip. From Honolulu, take H-1 freeway westbound to Aiea; take exit 13A. Go on Moanalua Road, turn right at Aiea Shopping Center and follow Aiea Heights Drive past gated

O`ahu

entrance to Keaiwa Heiau State Recreational Park. The trailhead is at the right near the restrooms. There are nice views of the Ko`olau Mountains and lush surrounding valleys and Keaiwa Heiau, an ancient Hawaiian temple. You also pass by the crash site of a World War II-era C-47 cargo airplane.

Windward O`ahu

Hawai`iloa Ridge is two miles long. Off Kalanianaole Highway 72 past Aina Haina; turn left at Puuikena Drive. Pass through security gate, sign liability waiver. Go 1½ miles to parking lot; trail begins on ridge. Trail follows ridge to summit through dryland forest turning to wetter ohia/koa mix. This is a rough difficult trail.

Kuli`ou`ou Valley is .6 mile long; off Kalanianaole Highway 72 past Niu Valley and before Maunalua Beach Park. Valley Trail starts on right at hunter check-in station past Board of Water Supply gate and follows contours above right of valley stream bed. Trail ends near head of valley.

Kuli`ou`ou Ridge is 2½ miles long. Access is same as for above trail; trailhead begins about .2 mile on Kuli`ou`ou Valley Trail and proceeds right, passing a picnic shelter. Trail follows ridge and ends at summit. This is a difficult trail.

**Makapu`u Point Trail** is three miles long. On the southeast tip of O`ahu just off Kalanianaole Highway 72 two miles past Sandy Beach, rounding the bend toward Waimanalo and the windward side. Pass through locked gate and follow paved road. This is a dry exposed area, warm and windy with nice coastal views. There are lookout areas. Entrance is blocked to the scenic old Makapu`u Lighthouse but it's visible on the pali bluff from a distance.

Kualoa Ranch, PO Box 650, Kamehameha Highway 83, Ka`a`awa, HI 96730, ☎ 808/237-7321. This outfitter offers mountain biking adventures deep into the tropical rain forest of the beautiful Ka`a`awa Valley. See majestic Ko`olau Mountain Range, coastal views overlooking Kane`ohe Bay and Chinaman's Hat Island.

DID YOU KNOW?

The Ka`a`awa Valley was the site of the 1996 World Cup Finals of Mountain Biking. Numerous films and TV programs have been shot here as well, including scenes in *Jurassic Park*.

North Shore

Kaunala Trail is 2½ miles long. Off Kamehameha Highway 83, past Waimea Bay, go inland on Pupukea Road to end. At Boy Scout camp parking lot, go through to Forest Reserve gate. About .5 mile from gate is a grove of paperbark trees and trail is on left. Trail runs through Pupukea Forest Reserve to jeep road leading to Camp Paumalu. A loop route goes right from the jeep road to military access road. Turn right at this intersection.

Leeward O`ahu

Kealia Trail is 2.3 miles long. From satellite tracking station on Waianae Coast, go along Kuaokala Access Road. Kealia Trail is 2.8 miles from parking area. From North Shore, take Farrington Highway past Camp Mokuleia, turn left at third entrance to Dillingham Airfield, go to parking area near tower. Follow gravel road toward pali (cliffs) through fence gate; trail climbs hill on left. Trail switchbacks above airfield and crests on the pali one mile up, where trail becomes dirt road. Follow upward on ridge where it connects with Kuaokala Access Road, which leads to Yokohama Bay on Waianae Coast.

**Ka`ena Point Natural Area Reserve** is reached from the south from Waianae via the Farrington Highway 93. Drive to road's end at Makua-Ka`ena Point State Park parking area and follow the trail signs 2½ miles to the point. From the east, take Highway 930 past Waialua and Mokuleia and park where the paved road ends, a mile beyond Camp Erdman. From there, it is 2½ miles to the point. It's a five-mile trip all the way around the point or backtracking the way you came in. This is the westernmost point of O`ahu Island and site of one of the last intact sand dune ecosystems in the Hawaiian Islands. It's a wild place of crashing surf on windswept beaches. The trail follows along rough rocky shoreline, usually hot and sunny, so take water and snacks. Lots of native Hawaiian beach plants and occasional monk seals, albatross and whales offshore.

Biking Resources

For additional information and maps of bicycle routes around Honolulu and O`ahu, contact: **State Bicycle/Pedestrian Coordinator**, ☎ 808/587-7433 or **City & County of Honolulu Bicycle Coordinator**, ☎ 808/527-5044.

You can also check the Web sites of the following bicycling

groups and organizations for more information:
Hawai`i Bicycling League, PO Box 4403, Honolulu, HI
96812, ☎ 808/735-5756 or 735-6679; e-mail bicycle@pixi.com;
http://cycling.org:80/org/id/248.html.
Hawai`i Bike Classified, www.aloha.net:80/~paalaa/.
Koolau Pedalers, PO Box 290, 25 Kaneohe Bay Drive, #106,
Kailua, HI 96734, ☎ 808/843-2012 or 808/259-7752; e-mail
KPedal@msn.com; www.lava.net/~gg/kp/.

■ On Water

O`ahu's Best Beaches

Conditions on all beaches vary daily. Not all beaches have lifeguards all the time. Check with lifeguards before entering the water, ask about conditions. Read and heed any warning signs posted about currents, surf, rocks, jellyfish, other hazards.

Ala Moana Beach Park, located across from Ala Moana Shopping Center on north edge of Waikiki. Lots of picnic facilities, soft sand and clear waters; popular with local folks.

DON'T

MISS

Waikiki Beach, a magnet for visitors, one of the world's most famous beaches, with Diamond Head crater in the background.

Waimea Bay, 60 minutes from Waikiki near Haleiwa, North Shore. Nice sandy beach, but surf is huge in winter. Skilled surfers only; summer brings calm.

Hanauma Bay, 20 minutes from Waikiki in southeast O`ahu. Super snorkeling to feed tame fish – a picturesque ancient volcano crater open to sea on one side.

Sandy Beach, 30 minutes from Waikiki in southeast O`ahu. Boogie boarding and body surfing, but strong currents and large waves.

**Makapu`u Beach,** 35 minutes from Waikiki in southeast O`ahu below the lighthouse. Boogie boarding, body surfing, swimming on calmer days.

Waimanalo Beach, 40 minutes from Waikiki, two miles past Sea Life Park, east O`ahu. Usually gentle surf here to learn body surfing, boogie boarding; picnicking too.

Lanikai Beach, 50 minutes from Waikiki, east O`ahu. Good for windsurfing and boogie boarding.

Kailua Beach, 50 minutes from Waikiki, east O`ahu. The place to learn windsurfing on O`ahu; nice sand, gentle surf. This beach was listed in the annual "Top 10 Best Beaches" national survey conducted by the University of Maryland; it was one of six Hawai`i beaches so honored.

Kualoa Beach, 35 minutes from Waikiki via the Pali Highway. Safe snorkeling, nice sand, good view of Chinaman's Hat Island.

Sunset Beach, 60 minutes from Waikiki, North Shore. Known for super sunsets, nice sand, the site for World Cup of Surfing competition; rough surf in winter, usually calm in summer.

Ehukai Beach, 60 minutes from Waikiki, North Shore. Wide sandy stretch, site of famous "Banzai Pipeline" where waves curl in a hollow tube and surfers disappear, then shoot out in surfing's ultimate thrill; huge winter surf, usually calm in summer.

Haleiwa Beach Park, 55 minutes from Waikiki just past Haleiwa town, North Shore. Sandy beach, picnic tables, playgrounds.

O`ahu

Hanauma Bay Beach.

Catamaran off Waikiki Beach.

Makaha, located on O`ahu's leeward west side a few miles past Waianae on Farrington Highway 93. Nice sandy beach, good winter surf, calm in summer.

Yokohama Bay, located at end of Farrington Highway 93 in leeward O`ahu near northwest tip of island. Good sandy beach, uncrowded.

Cruises, Sailing & Submarines

Several operators offer a wide range of cruises and sailing adventures. One-hour catamaran sails are $15 per person. Pearl Harbor Historic Cruises are $20-25 per person. Popular sunset dinner cruises begin at $45-50 per person. Submarine rides begin at $50-60 per person. Half-day scenic coastal cruises begin at $25-50 per person with continental breakfast and/or lunch included. Round-trip bus transportation from Waikiki hotels is usually included in fare.

Navatek I, 2270 Kalakaua Ave., Waikiki, ☎ 800/852-4183, ☎ 808/848-6360. This high-tech cruise ship uses the twin-hull SWATH design to provide a smooth ride. Daily cruises along East O`ahu's famed Gold Coast, Waikiki to Koko Head.

DON'T *The Star of Honolulu,* 350 Ward Ave., Honolulu, HI 96814, ☎ 800/334-6191, 808/593-2493. This luxury cruise boat offers a range of Pearl Harbor and O`ahu coastal cruises with dinner **MISS** and entertainment packages.

Honolulu Sailing Co., 47-335 Lulani, ☎ 800/829-0114, 808/239-3900. This charter outfitter has yachts available for sailing/snorkeling trips, overnight cruises, whale watching and even weddings at sea.

Leahi Catamaran, ☎ 808/922-5665, on the beach at the Sheraton Waikiki Hotel. This fast 45-foot racing catamaran specializes in one-hour cruises from Waikiki to Diamond Head; sunset cocktail cruises too.

Dream Cruises, ☎ 800/400-7300, 808/592-5200, offers a special "Pacific Splash" cruise for snorkeling and swimming and a giant water slide and water trampoline for jumping into the water; other cruises include whale watching and Pearl Harbor coastal cruise.

Banana Boat Riders, PO Box 8984, Honolulu, HI 96830-0984, ☎ 888/922-5588, 808/922-5588. This operator offers ocean rafting adventures in a 32-foot rigid inflatable raft boat that skims along the Waikiki and leeward O`ahu coasts; sunset cocktail and dinner excursions also available.

Nautilus, ☎ 800/548-6262, 808/591-9199. This semi-submersible boat has underwater wrap-around windows for viewing the teeming marine life of O`ahu's coral reefs.

Voyager, ☎ 808/592-7850. This yellow submarine is a high-tech craft capable of diving to over 300 feet to view Hawai`i's fascinating underwater world. Large viewing ports let all guests see the marine life.

Atlantis, ☎ 808/973-9811. This is the original passenger submarine designed for exploring the colorful reefs, marine life and shipwrecks along O`ahu's coast; large viewports for all guests.

A Reef Adventure, ☎ 808/395-6133. This operator rents Wildthing Reef Explorer motor boats, inflatable boats with clear bottoms for viewing reef marinelife.

Scuba Diving & Snorkeling

Several outfitters offer scuba dive and snorkel adventures. One- and two-tank scuba dives begin at about $65 per person. Snorkel cruises begin at $60 per person, equipment included. Call operators for latest information.

Aloha Dive Shop, Koko Marina, Hawai`i Kai, ☎ 808/395-5922. This outfitter offers PADI certification dives and excursions to reefs off Koko Head Crater along O`ahu's south coast.

All Hawai`i Cruises, Inc. 1860 Ala Moana Blvd. #414, Honolulu, HI 96815, ☎ 800/262-8789, ☎ 808/942-5077. Daily sailings on the calm wa-

ters of beautiful Kane'ohe Bay for snorkeling, swimming, picnics and relaxing cruising along O'ahu's windward coast.

Paradise Divers, 2375 Ala Wai Blvd., Waikiki Sand Villa Hotel,
Waikiki, ☎ 808/921-3230. PADI instruction, tours and equipment rentals.

Paradise Snorkel Adventures, 2426 Kuhio Avenue, Continental
Surf Hotel, Waikiki, ☎ 808/923-7766. Rents a full line of snorkel gear
and water sports equipment.

Dan's Dive Shop, 660 Ala Moana Blvd., Waikiki, ☎ 808/536-
6181. Scuba dives to O'ahu's most popular dive sites.

Aquanautics Marine Services, ☎ 808/395-0725. Scuba and snorkel
dives to plane wrecks, sunken ships, barges, an army tank, sea caves,
reefs, Hanauma Bay and more; all-inclusive.

Flippers Scuba, 61-180 Iliohu Place, Haleiwa, HI 96712, ☎ 800/578-
3992, 808/637-7946; e-mail scuba@poi.net; www.poi.net/~scuba. PADI
certification programs and boat dive adventures to O'ahu's beautiful
Windward Coast and North Shore dive spots.

Snorkel Bob's, 700 Kapahulu Avenue, Waikiki, ☎ 808/735-7944. A full
line of snorkel rentals plus a large selection of water sports equipment.

Clark's Divemaster Tours, ☎ 808/923-5595. PADI instruction and
dive tours to O'ahu's best dive sites.

Ocean Works, ☎ 808/926-3483. Half-day catamaran snorkel cruises
plus three-hour scuba diving reef adventures; PADI instruction.

Kayaking, Parasailing & Jet Skiing

Several operators offer kayak, parasailing and jet ski adventures. Day-
long kayaking tours begin at $40 per person. Parasailing adventures
rise to 300-foot altitude along Waikiki Beach and rates are $40 per
person. Jet ski adventures begin at $60 per hour.

Go Bananas Kayaks, 799 Kapahulu Avenue, Kapahulu, ☎ 808/737-
9514. Kayaks, canoes, roof rack rentals and related equipment.

Kailua Sailboards & Kayaks, Inc., 130 Kailua Road, Kailua,
☎ 808/262-2555. On Kailua beach, they have kayak and related equipment rentals.

Twogood Kayaks Hawai'i, Inc., 171 Hamakua Drive, Kailua,
☎ 808/262-5656. Kayaking equipment rentals.

Jetcraft & Water Sports, Haleiwa Boat Harbor, Haleiwa, North Shore, ☎ 808/637-8006. Jet ski and water sports equipment rentals.

Jetski Waikiki, ☎ 808/949-8952, between Hilton Hawaiian Village and Outrigger Reef Hotel. Jet ski rentals plus wide selection of water sports and beach equipment.

Paradise Jet Ski, 3466 Waialae Avenue, Honolulu, ☎ 808/734-0717. Kawasaki jet skis for rent.

Aloha Parasail, ☎ 808/521-2446. Parasail along scenic Waikiki Beach and Ala Moana coastline.

Get Wet Hawai`i, ☎ 808/395-7255. Parasail along Waikiki Beach and Honolulu coastlines.

Waikiki Parasail, ☎ 808/735-6474. Parasail 300 feet above the Waikiki and Ala Moana coastlines.

Surfing & Windsurfing

Kailua Sailboard Co., 130 Kailua Road, Kailua Bay, ☎ 808/262-2555. Windsurfing lessons and equipment rentals.

North Shore Eco-surf Tours, PO Box 1174, Haleiwa, HI 96712, ☎ 808/638-9503. Surf lesson packages and equipment rentals plus guided tours to famed surf sites.

North Shore Windsurfing School, 59-452 Makana Road, Haleiwa, ☎ 808/638-8198. Full range of windsurfing instruction available.

Hawaiian Water Sports, Honolulu, ☎ 808/255-4352. Windsurfing and surfing lessons, equipment rentals.

Surf 'n' Sea, 62-595 Kamehameha Highway, Haleiwa, HI 96712, ☎ 808/637-9887. Surfing and windsurfing lessons for all levels and ages, water sports equipment rentals, surf excursions, etc.

Hans Hedemann Surfing School, ☎ 808/591-7778. This surf school is run by professional world tour surfing instructors; for all levels and ages.

Fishing - Deep Sea Charters

Try your luck on a high seas expedition in search of Hawaiian big game fish like Pacific marlin, yellowfin tuna, mahimahi, ono or even a shark. Charter boat rates begin at $85-100 per person for half-day, $125 and up per person for full day.

Blue Nun, ☎ 808/596-2443, Kewalo Basin off Ala Moana Blvd. Half/full-day charters, shared or private; equipment included.

ELO Sportfishing, ☎ 808/947-5208, Kewalo Basin off Ala Moana Blvd. 38-foot Bertram boat, half/full-day charters; equipment included.

Kona Sportfishing, ☎ 808/536-7472, Kewalo Basin off Ala Moana Blvd. Luxury 61-foot cabin cruiser, half/full-day charters, all amenities and equipment included.

Kuu Huapala, ☎ 808/596-0918, PO Box 6040, Honolulu, HI 96818, Kewalo Basin off Ala Moana Blvd. This 55-foot custom fishing yacht has half/full-day charters for all Hawaiian big game fish.

Magic, ☎ 808/596-2998, Kewalo Basin off Ala Moana Blvd. 50-foot Pacifica yacht with all amenities; half/full day charters.

Maggie Joe, ☎ 808/591-8888, Kewalo Basin off Ala Moana Blvd. Half/full-day charters, all amenities and equipment included.

Sea Verse, ☎ 808/591-8840, Kewalo Basin off Ala Moana Blvd. Half/full-day charters, deep water trolling, bottom fishing or reef fishing.

Pacific Blue **Sport Fishing,** ☎ 808/396-4401, 60 Nawiliwili, Kewalo Basin. This Bertram Sportfisher has half/full day charters for marlin, tuna, mahimahi and ono.

Ilima V **Charter Fishing,** ☎ 808/596-2087, Kewalo Basin off Ala Moana Blvd. This 42-foot Hatteras has all amenities for a half/full day of charter fishing for Hawaiian big game fish.

Kahuna Kai, ☎ 808/235-6236, 44-553 Kane`ohe Bay Drive, Kane`ohe, HI 96744, Kewalo Basin off Ala Moana Blvd. This 50-foot luxury boat has half/full-day charters for all Hawaiian big game fish.

■ In the Air

Scenic Flightseeing/Helicopter Tours

Several operators offer air tours of O`ahu. Standard one-hour island air tour over tropical rain forests, valleys, waterfalls, beaches and coastline begins at $65-75 per person.

Eco Air Tours Hawai`i, 99 Mokuea Place, Honolulu International Airport, ☎ 808/839-1499. Charters and custom air tours to all islands.

Paragon Air, Honolulu International Airport, ☎ 800/428-1231, ☎ 808/244-3356. This Maui airline offers custom charters to any destination in the islands.

Big Island Air, Honolulu International Airport, ☎ 800/303-8868, 808/329-4868. This Big Island carrier offers custom air charters and tours to all Hawaiian Islands.

Hawaiian Odyssey Helicopters, 120 Kapalulu Place, ☎ 808/833-4354. Tours and aerial photo shoots of O`ahu, including Ko`olau and Waianae Mountains, Diamond Head, beaches and interior areas.

Makani Kai Helicopters, 120 Kapalulu Place, ☎ 808/834-5813. Flightseeing tours and charters to O`ahu scenic places like beaches, Pearl Harbor, Diamond Head, Ko`olau Mountains and more.

Rainbow Pacific Helicopters, 110 Kalalulu Place, ☎ 808/834-1111. Scenic air tours of O`ahu sites like Diamond Head and coastal beaches, mountains and valleys.

Offshore Helicopters, 100 Iolana Place, ☎ 808/838-0007. Special air tours to O`ahu sites like beaches, Ko`olau Mountains, Pearl Harbor, interior valleys and more.

Stearman Bi-plane Rides, Dillingham Airfield, Farrington Highway 930, North Shore, ☎ 808/637-4461. Enjoy the thrill of an open-cockpit flight in a 1941-vintage Stearman N2S bi-plane. Cruise over O`ahu's beautiful north shore and experience a historical tour of the route flown by Japanese pilots as they attacked Pearl Harbor on December 7, 1941. Also exciting aerial acrobatics including loops and rolls.

Hang Gliding, Glider Planes, Sky Diving

A few operators offer hang gliding, skydiving and glider airplane adventures. Glider airplane rides begin at $60 per person. Hang-gliding adventures begin with a tandem instructional jump at $150 per person; the full hang-gliding instructional program of several hours is $1,000 per person and enables you to solo. Skydiving adventures begin with a tandem instructional jump at $195-275 per person.

North Shore Hang/Para Gliding, PO Box 640, Waialua, HI 96791, ☎ 808/637-3178. This outfitter offers all equipment for both hang-gliding and para-gliding, with instruction and excursions.

 DON'T MISS **The Original Glider Rides,** Dillingham Airfield, Farrington Highway, Mokuleia, HI 96791, ☎ 808/677-3404. This is a "wings of the wind" airplane ride soaring along the spectacular North Shore in a bubble-topped sailplane glider; operated by Honolulu Soaring Club.

Pacific International Skydiving Center, Dillingham Airfield, 68-760 Farrington Highway, Mokuleia, HI 96791, ☎ 808/637-7472. Tandem skydiving with an experienced instructor. Catch your thrills with a free fall from 12,500 feet.

Skydive Hawai`i, Dillingham Airfield, 68-760 Farrington Highway, Mokuleia, HI 96791, ☎ 808/637-9700. Single or tandem jumps with instructors. Soar two miles above the North Shore and Koolau Mountains before bailing out.

■ On Horseback

Trail ride outfitters offer rides through O`ahu's lush tropical countryside. Standard one-hour rides begin at $35 per person; two-hour rides begin at $45-50 per person.

**Correa Trails Hawai`i,** 41-050 Kalanianaole Highway 72, ☎ 808/259-9005. Horseback riding in the beautiful Ko`olau Mountain Range in Waimanalo with spectacular mountain and ocean views.

Happy Trails Hawai`i, ☎ 808/638-7433. This outfitter is located on the North Shore and provides adventurous trail rides with panoramic mountain and ocean coastal views.

Kualoa Ranch & Activity Club, PO Box 650, Kamehameha Highway 83, Ka`a`awa, HI 96730, ☎ 808/237-7321. This outfitter on O`ahu's beautiful windward east side offers trail rides deep into the lush tropical Ka`a`awa Valley. See Ko`olau Mountain Range, film location of *Jurassic Park* and views of Kane`ohe Bay and Chinaman's Hat Island on the Waimanalo Coast.

■ Eco/Cultural Activities

These activities have admission fees subject to frequent change. Call ahead and ask about current fees and rates and any available discounts.

Sea Life Park, 41-202 Kalanianaole Highway 72, Makapu`u Point, Waimanalo, HI 96795, ☎ 800/767-8046, 808/259-7933. This is Hawai`i's premier marinelife park. There are aquarium displays with Hawaiian marinelife, fish, seals, dolphins, sharks, waterbirds, turtles and more. Trained seals and dolphins provide entertaining performances. Free shuttle from Waikiki hotels.

DON'T
MISS
Waimea Valley and Adventure Park, 59-864 Kamehameha Highway 83, Haleiwa, HI 96712, across from Waimea Bay Beach Park, ☎ 800/767-8046, 808/638-8511. An outdoor eco-cultural center on the North Shore providing a glimpse of

the old Hawaiian lifestyle. Stroll through the grounds and see a Hawaiian village, visit an ancient heiau (temple), see agricultural terraces and Hawaiian farming methods, stroll botanical gardens and rain forest, watch and participate in arts and crafts demos, learn the hula and play Hawaiian games; they also offer adventure activities such as a downhill mountain bike cruise, snorkel dive, kayaking a mountain stream, horseback trail rides and exciting 4WD ATV (all-terrain vehicle) rides through the rain forest gulches and surrounding mountain and ridge trails.

Byodo-In Temple, 47-200 Kahekili Highway 83, Temple Valley, ☎ 808/239-8811. At the base of the majestic Ko`olau Mountains, there are several acres of beautiful landscaped gardens and ponds and an exact replica of the ancient temple at Uji, Japan. The temple houses a nine-foot- tall gold Buddha, the largest sculpted in 900 years. A three-ton brass bell rings out messages of calm and peace. This is a very picturesque, serene and colorful place.

Kualoa Activity Club & Secret Island, PO Box 650, Kamehameha Highway 83, Ka`a`awa, HI 96730, ☎ 808/237-7321. Part of Kualoa Ranch, they offer day excursions to Secret Island on Kane`ohe Bay. Snorkel in crystal waters on the coral reefs, see myriad marinelife, paddle an outrigger canoe or kayak out to Chinaman's Hat (Mokoli`i Island), stroll a deserted beach, play volleyball, enjoy a beachside BBQ lunch and relax on a hammock under the palm trees.

Dole Pineapple Plantation, 64-1550 Kamehameha Highway 99, three miles north of Wahiawa, ☎ 808/621-8408. On the way to the North Shore, the plantation is set among rolling hills covered with pineapple fields; stroll the Pineapple Garden, learn about Hawai`i's pineapple history and see the many varieties of pineapple from around the world. Enjoy a sample of fresh chilled pineapple or a pineapple ice cream sundae and browse the gift shop.

DON'T MISS **Polynesian Cultural Center,** Kamehameha Highway 83, Laie, Windward Coast, ☎ 800/367-7060, 808/293-3333; www.polynesia.com/. This is one of Hawai`i's top attractions, operated by the Mormon Church to provide scholarships to Brigham Young University-Hawai`i Campus for students from the island nations of Polynesia. The center features replica islands and villages of Fiji, Hawai`i, New Zealand, Marquesas, Samoa, Tonga and Tahiti. Various cultural shows and displays include a spectacular evening Polynesian dinner show performance.

DON'T **Kodak Hula Show,** 2805 Monsarrat Avenue, in Kapiolani Park at the Waikiki Shell, Waikiki, for information ☎ 808/591- 2211. One of Honolulu's longest-running free shows. It's been **MISS** delighting and entertaining visitors to Hawai`i for some 60 years and is one of the best free shows anywhere in Honolulu. Sponsored by the Eastman Kodak Company, it happens Tuesday and Thursday only, 10-11:15 a.m. It's a chance to experience some of Hawai`i's colorful hula dance and music. Bring your camera!

Waikiki Aquarium, 2777 Kalakaua Avenue, lower end of Waikiki across from Queen Kapiolani Park, ☎ 808/923-9741. The recently renovated aquarium features 64 exhibits containing some 1,900 colorful marine animals. There are also a theater, mahimahi hatchery, and endangered Hawaiian monk seals on display.

Honolulu Zoo, on Kalakaua Avenue between Kapahulu and Monsarrat Avenues, ☎ 808/971-7171. This 42-acre zoo offers a children's zoo, elephant encounter, simulated African savanna, primate exhibit, reptile house, aviary and many unique species from the world's eco-systems, including giraffe, lions, gazelles, kudu, wart hogs and much more.

**Hawai`i Nature Center,** 2131 Makiki Heights Drive, ☎ 808/955-0100. Self-guided and guided group hikes on O`ahu's nature trails to promote understanding and appreciation of Hawai`i's unique environment. Hikes and terrain vary depending on custom programs chosen. Programs are available for the physically challenged.

Lyon Arboretum, 3860 Manoa Road, ☎ 808/988-7378. This 193½-acre arboretum is filled with native Hawaiian and exotic tropical plant species; self-guided and guided tours available.

Honolulu Botanical Gardens. Four separate gardens are maintained by the City and County of Honolulu: **Foster,** 50 N. Vineyard Blvd., downtown Honolulu, ☎ 808/522-7065; **Ho`omaluhia,** 45-680 Luluku Road, Kane`ohe, ☎ 808/233-7323; **Koko Crater,** off Kealahou Street behind Sandy Beach next to Koko Crater Stables, ☎ 808/522-7060; **Wahiawa,** 1396 California Avenue, ☎ 808/621-7321. Stroll through the different environments to view tropical plants and trees, orchid gardens, cacti, palm trees and more.

DON'T **Honolulu Time Walks,** 2634 S. King St. #3, Honolulu, HI 96826, ☎ 808/943-0371. One of Honolulu's most unusual tours, this is highly recommended. Take one if you dare! Dr. **MISS** Glen Grant, noted Hawai`i educator, acclaimed author of ghost stories and folklorist, conducts "Haunted Honolulu Tours," providing insight into Hawai`i's supernatural and occult. These spooky, scary tours are based upon true accounts of supernatural events and experiences with spirits. If you like adventure at midnight and enjoy being scared out of your wits, this is for you. Guaranteed chicken-skin! This is not for the faint-of-heart!

Tour of the Stars, 92-1204 Umena St., Makakilo, Kapolei, HI 96707, ☎ 808/672-NOVA. This is operated by Ray Young at his private residence and star-gazing observatory. An enthusiastic amateur astronomer, he built his own private observatory complete with telescope and computer. He locates and tracks planets, stars and constellations, providing a running narration during the typical 90-minute observatory tour. Tours are by appointment only and limited to groups of 10.

Lodging

Honolulu and O`ahu offer lodging to fit every taste and budget, from first class hotels and vacation condominiums to budget hotels and bed and breakfasts. The hotels are centered in the Waikiki Beach area just south of downtown Honolulu. Rates below are for a standard double-occupancy room.

Accommodations Price Scale	
$	less than $100 per night
$$	$100-199 per night
$$$	$200-299 per night
$$$$	$300 and up per night

Bed & Breakfasts

All Islands Bed and Breakfast-O`ahu, 823 Kainui Dr., Kailua, HI 96734-2025, ☎ 800/542-0344, 808/263-2342; http://planet-Hawaii.com/all-island.

Bed & Breakfast Honolulu, 3242 Kaohinani Dr., Honolulu, HI 96817-1020, ☎ 800/288-4666, 808/595-7533; e-mail BnBsHI@aloha.net; www.travelsource.com/bnb/allhi.html.

Waikiki Beach

Aston Honolulu Prince Hotel, 415 Nahua St., Waikiki, ☎ 800/922-7866, 808/922-1616; www.aston-hotels.com. Aston has several other hotels in Waikiki as well as on all the neighbor islands. This budget hotel is centrally located in Waikiki just a couple of blocks from the beach. Suites have complete kitchens. $

Inn on the Park, 1920 Ala Moana Blvd., Waikiki, Castle Resorts ☎ 800/367-5004, 808/946-8355; www.castle-group.com. This economy hotel is near the entrance to the Waikiki area, close to shopping centers and restaurants. Pool, sun deck plus swimming, golf and tennis nearby; all hotel amenities. $

Aston Waikiki Beachside Hotel, 2452 Kalakaua Avenue, Waikiki, ☎ 800/922-7866, 808/931-2100; www.aston-hotels.com. This moderate hotel is right on Waikiki's strip, just across from the beach. Near all activities, Honolulu Zoo, Kapiolani Park and more. $$

Kuhio Village Resort, 2463 Kuhio Avenue, Waikiki, Castle Resorts, ☎ 800/367-5004, 808/926-0641; www.castle-group.com. This small 119-room hotel is in the center of Waikiki, two blocks from the beach. Some rooms have full-service kitchenettes; all hotel amenities and services available. $

Aston at the Waikiki Banyan, 201 Ohua Avenue, Waikiki, ☎ 800/922-7866, 808/922-0555; www.aston-hotels.com. This is a large well-furnished family-style condo. Units have full kitchens and amenities. Near the beach and all Waikiki activities. $$

Pacific Marina Inn, 2628 Waiwai Loop, Honolulu, Castle Resorts, ☎ 800/367-5004, 808/836-1131; www.castle-group.com. This budget hotel is just off Nimitz Highway near the end of Honolulu International Airport. Pool, sun deck, lounge, restaurant. Near Keehi Lagoon Park tennis and picnic areas. Good location from which to explore outlying areas of Honolulu and O`ahu. $

Aston Waikiki Terrace Hotel, 2045 Kalakaua Avenue, Waikiki, ☎ 800/922-7866, 800/445-8811, 808/955-6000; www.aston-hotels.com. This moderate-class hotel is on Waikiki's strip at the entrance to the resort area, three blocks from the beach. This is a full-service hotel with restaurant, pool, sun deck, fitness center and more. Easy walking distance to attractions. $$

Aston Waikiki Circle Hotel, 2464 Kalakaua Avenue, Waikiki, ☎ 800/922-7866, 808/923-1571; www.aston-hotels.com. This hotel has a central Waikiki location across from the beach and features full services and amenities. Rooms have private Lana`is with ocean or mountain views. Convenient to all Waikiki attractions. $$

Halekulani Hotel, 2199 Kalia Road, Waikiki, ☎ 800/367-2343, 808/923-2311; www.halekulani.com. This is one of Waikiki's old-time classic hotels, though it is now a modern highrise. Everything from services to location (right on the beach) to dining is first class. If your ideal adventure is soaking up the ambiance of a luxury hotel, you won't go wrong here. $$$$

Hawaiiana Hotel, 260 Beachwalk, Waikiki, ☎ 800/535-0085, 808/923-3811. A low-rise two- and three-story building complex nestled in a tropical garden setting just a half-block from Waikiki Beach. Studio and 1BR suites have kitchenettes; Kona coffee and juice served poolside each morning. Shops, restaurants, the entertainment of Waikiki are just steps away. This is a nice budget-category hotel. $$

Manoa Valley Inn, 2001 Vancouver Drive, Manoa, ☎ 800/535-0085, 808/947-6019. A historic country inn on a lush half-acre property near the University of Hawai`i campus in the scenic Manoa Valley. This is a quiet getaway above the hustle and bustle of Waikiki. It's still just minutes from Waikiki, downtown Honolulu and all area attractions. This comfortable country inn provides complimentary continental breakfast and an evening wine service for guests' enjoyment. $$

Waikiki Grand Hotel, 134 Kapahulu Avenue, Waikiki, ☎ 800/535-0085, 808/923-1511. This moderate-category hotel has a great location on the Diamond Head end of Waikiki, overlooking the white sands of Waikiki Beach and the cool, green expanse of 500-acre Kapiolani Park. Rooms have a/c, refrigerators, and some have kitchenettes plus private Lana`is and either city or ocean views. The hotel is close to shops, restaurants and Waikiki's noted entertainment, plus the Honolulu Zoo, Waikiki Aquarium and Honolulu Shell outdoor concert theater. $$

Hilton Hawaiian Village, 2005 Kalia Road, Waikiki, ☎ 800/HILTONS, 808/949-4321; www.hilton.com. One of Waikiki's largest resort hotels with over 2,000 rooms. A huge, sprawling complex of highrises right on the beach, it's also a very tasteful, elegant hotel with a great location at the top, or north end, of the Waikiki area. $$

Holiday Inn Waikiki, 1830 Ala Moana Blvd., Waikiki, ☎ 800/HOLIDAY, 808/955-1111; www.holiday-inn.com. This 200-room hotel has a good location atop the Waikiki area, convenient to all attractions, dining and shopping. Pool, restaurant, gift shop on grounds. This is a good budget hotel in Waikiki. $$

Hyatt Regency Waikiki, 2424 Kalakaua Avenue, Waikiki, ☎ 800/233-1234, 808/923-1234. A luxury-class twin tower hotel with over 1,200 rooms. Centrally located in the heart of Waikiki, just across the street from the beach. The hotel has restaurants, lounges, guest parking, pool and all hotel services and amenities. Convenient to all attractions. $$$

Outrigger Reef on the Beach, 2169 Kalia Road, Waikiki, ☎ 800/OUTRIGGER, 808/923-3111; e-mail reservations@outrigger.com; www.outrigger.com. Outrigger has several Waikiki hotels as well as hotels on all the neighbor islands. This hotel has an excellent location at the top of Waikiki Beach; rooms are spacious and very well appointed. Full services and amenities, near to all attractions. $$

Outrigger Waikiki on the Beach, 2335 Kalakaua Avenue, Waikiki, ☎ 800/OUTRIGGER, 808/923-0711; e-mail reservations@outrigger.com; www.outrigger.com. This hotel is located right on Waikiki Beach and provides full services and amenities. Convenient location to all Waikiki attractions. $$

Queen Kapiolani Hotel, 150 Kapahulu Avenue, Waikiki, Castle Resorts, ☎ 800/367-5004, 808/922-1941; www.castle-group.com. This is a conveniently located hotel at the south end of Waikiki and overlooks the 108-acre Kapiolani Park and famous Diamond Head mountain. It's also a short stroll to Honolulu Zoo, Waikiki Aquarium, Kodak Hula Show and the heart of Waikiki. Full hotel amenities and services, restaurants, lounges. $$

Outrigger Islander Waikiki, 270 Lewers Street, Waikiki, ☎ 800/OUTRIGGER, 808/924-7666; e-mail reservations@outrigger.com; www.outrigger.com. This is a newly renovated moderate hotel two blocks from the beach in the heart of Waikiki, next to Royal Hawaiian Shopping Center and near to all attractions. $$

Outrigger Royal Islander, 2164 Kalia Road, Waikiki, ☎ 800/OUTRIGGER, 808/922-1961; e-mail reservations@outrigger.com; www.outrigger.com. This is a small boutique budget hotel just a short walk to the beach. Convenient location at the top of Waikiki area close to all attractions. $

Waikiki Hana Hotel, 2424 Koa Avenue, Waikiki, Castle Resorts ☎ 800/367-5004, 808/926-8841; www.castle-group.com. This small 73-room budget hotel is right in the heart of Waikiki's excitement. Near the International Marketplace, nightlife, restaurants, and Waikiki Beach is just one block away. Variety of restaurants and activities all nearby. $

Outrigger Coral Seas, 250 Lewers Street, Waikiki, ☎ 800/OUTRIGGER, 808/923-3881; e-mail reservations@outrigger.com; www.outrigger.com. This budget hotel has units with kitchenettes. Centrally located to all Waikiki attractions and just a short walk to the beach. $

Royal Hawaiian Hotel, 2259 Kalakaua Avenue, Waikiki, ☎ 800/325-3535, 808/923-7311. This is Waikiki's famed "Pink Palace of the Pacific" and has been welcoming guests since 1927. The hotel has a prime beachfront location in the heart of Waikiki. This elegant first-class hotel on the beach allows guests to step back in time and enjoy luxury on a grand scale, at a price of course. $$$$

Sheraton Princess Kaiulani Hotel, 120 Kaiulani Avenue, Waikiki, ☎ 800/782-9488, 808/922-5811. This deluxe 1,150-room hotel has a great central location right in the heart of Waikiki and is a short stroll from the beach. It has pool, bar, restaurant and full amenities. $$

Sheraton Waikiki Hotel, 2255 Kalakaua Avenue, Waikiki, ☎ 800/325-3535, 808/922-4422. This sprawling 1,700-room beachfront luxury hotel has a great location right on Waikiki Beach and fantastic views of the beach and Diamond Head mountain. The hotel provides full amenities; located right in the heart of Waikiki. $$$

Sheraton Moana Surfrider Hotel, 2365 Kalakaua Avenue, Waikiki, ☎ 800/325-3535, 808/922-3111. This 790-room hotel is the designated "First Lady of Waikiki" and has been in business since 1901. It's a historic place and still retains the charm and elegance of a long past era when things were slower and travel more romantic. Located on the beach in the heart of Waikiki. $$$

Camping

 Camping is allowed at certain parks maintained by the City and County of Honolulu and State of Hawai`i parks on O`ahu. No-fee permits are required far in advance of intended camping dates. Maximum length of stay at any public campground is five days; no camping is allowed on Wednesdays and Thursdays. That's to allow for maintenance and cleaning of campground/park areas. Another reason for this is to discourage extended or "permanent" camping by homeless individuals or those who would otherwise be inclined to live on the beach.

Officials caution campers on using the beach park campgrounds on the Leeward Coast, notably Kahe, Nanakuli, Lualualei and Kea`au Parks. Honolulu, being a large urban area, has its share of social ills. The Leeward Coast area is no different. It's an economically depressed area and during the last few years there have been incidents directed at campers. It'd be a good idea to check with the city and county parks office for the latest information; see below. If you plan on using any of these camgrounds, it would be best not to camp alone. Check with other campers on the situation and camp near them. Also keep in mind that the quality of public campground facilities is frequently affected by vandalism and lack of proper maintenance.

For more information on camping, contact: **Department of Parks and Recreation**, City & County of Honolulu, Permits, 650 S. King St., Honolulu, HI 96813, ☎ 808/523-4525; and **Department of Land & Natural Resources**, State of Hawai`i, Camping Permits, PO Box 621, Honolulu, HI 96809, ☎ 808/587-0300.

City Camping Sites

Bellows Field Beach Park, 41-043 Kalanianaole Highway #72, Waimanalo, Windward Coast. This park is located within Bellows Air Force Station. It's a large park in an ironwood forest along a nice sandy beach. Backdrop of steep cliffs and views of offshore islands. Sandy ocean bottom slopes gradually to deeper water. There are 50 campsites scattered among the trees; lots of shade. Picnic tables, rest rooms, outdoor showers, drinking water. Easy access to good swimming, fishing, beachcombing.

**Hau`ula Beach Park**, 54-135 Kamehameha Highway #83, Hau`ula, Windward Coast. This is a small park squeezed between the beach and highway. Campground area is very near the highway and has some shade trees. Tent camping; rest rooms, picnic tables drinking water. Shallow water makes for safe swimming but bottom is rocky in places; good snorkeling and fishing.

**Ho`omaluhia Botanical Garden**, 45-680 Luluku Road, Kane`ohe, Windward Coast. This beautiful 400-acre park at the base of the scenic Ko`olau Pali on the Windward Coast is the only botanical garden in the state that allows camping. Campgrounds are set amidst spacious green lawns, soaring green cliffs and exotic tropical plants, an incredible campground by any measure. There is lots of peace and quiet here, far removed from O`ahu's traffic and hustle and bustle. Five separate camping areas have rest rooms, cold showers, picnic tables, outdoor grills and water. Visitor center has exhibits, displays and info. Hiking and exploring the botanical gardens here are the main activities; easy access to Windward Coast attractions.

Kahe Point Beach Park, 92-301 Farrington Highway #93, Ewa Beach, Leeward Coast. There is an open, grassy campground area at this beach park. Beach is rocky with cliff area but access to ocean is via a sandy cove. Tent camping; rest rooms, outdoor showers, picnic tables, covered pavilion, drinking water. Good swimming, snorkeling and fishing on calm days; heavy surf and strong currents exist in winter months.

Kaiaka Bay Beach Park, 66-449 Haleiwa Road, Haleiwa, North Shore. This campground is located on flat grassy peninsula with a rocky foreshore but an adjoining sandy beach. There are just seven campsites, each with a picnic table. Ironwood trees provide some shade in the area; also has rest rooms, showers and drinking water. Good swimming and snorkeling in the sandy beach area.

Kea`au Beach Park, 83-431 Farrington Highway #93, Waianae, Leeward Coast. This is a grassy park area with scattered shade trees and palms very close to the highway. Shore is rocky with some sandy beach and the Waianae Mountains are in background. Tent camping; rest rooms, outdoor showers, picnic tables.

Lualualei Beach Park, 86-221 Farrington Highway #93, Waianae, Leeward Coast. This grassy and sandy park has palm trees scattered about and limited shade trees; close to the highway. Beachfront is rocky cliff and raised coral reef areas offshore. Tent camping; rest rooms, picnic tables, outdoor showers and drinking water.

Mokuleia Beach Park, 68-919 Ka`ena Point Road, Waialua, North Shore. This is one of O`ahu's most isolated and remote beaches. The beach is sandy but offshore water has lots of rocks. Tent camping; rest rooms, outdoor showers, picnic tables, drinking water. Rocks and offshore reefs make for good fishing and snorkeling, but there are high surf hazards and dangerous currents in winter months.

O`ahu

Nanakuli Beach Park, 89-269 Farrington Highway #93, Nanakuli, Leeward Coast. This curving sandy beach park has grassy camp sites and some shade trees. Tent camping; rest rooms, outdoor showers, picnic tables, drinking water; park also has playground, baseball field and basketball court. Good swimming, but heavy surf and currents in winter months; good fishing and snorkeling on calm days.

Swanzy Beach Park, 51-369 Kamehameha Highway #83, Ka`a`awa, Windward Coast. This is a grassy field with limited shade trees next to the ocean. There is a nice mountain-view background. But it is very close to the busy highway. Tent camping only; rest rooms, outdoor showers, picnic tables, drinking water, also playground, baseball field and basketball court. Beach is small with some rocks; fair swimming and snorkeling, good fishing.

Waimanalo Bay Beach Park, 41-043 Alo`ilo`i St., Waimanalo, Windward Coast. This campground is on a beautiful 3½-mile stretch of golden sandy beach, one of O`ahu's nicest. There is a background view of steep cliffs and views of offshore Rabbit Island and the Mokolua Islands. Campground located behind treeline along the beach. Tent camping only; each tent site has picnic table, grill and trash can; central rest room with showers. Good swimming, fishing, body and board surfing.

Waimanalo Beach Park, 41-741 Kalanianaole Highway #72, Waimanalo, Windward Coast. One of the best beaches on O`ahu. It's a long crescent backed by a stand of ironwood trees. Nice grassy campground with scattered shade trees. Tent camping; picnic tables, covered pavilion, rest rooms, outdoor showers and drinking water. Beach has gentle sloping sandy bottom, good swimming, beachcombing, fishing.

State Camping Sites

Kahana Valley State Park, 52-222 Kamehameha Highway #83, Kahana, Windward Coast. This is a sandy beach with a mountain background. Lots of shade trees and coconut grove across the road. Tent camping; rest rooms, picnic tables, drinking water. Good beach swimming and fishing; easy access to Kahana Valley hiking trails and fresh water pools for swimming.

Keaiwa Heiau State Recreation Area, end of Aiea Heights Drive, Aiea Heights, Aiea, behind Pearl Harbor, central O`ahu. There are 385 acres of upland forest with cool, breezy environment. Tent camping only in two camping areas; scattered picnic tables, enclosed rest rooms and cold showers, outdoor grills, a covered pavilion and drinking water. Easy access to hiking trails and historic heiau (temple) site.

Malaekahana Beach Park, off Kamehameha Highway #83, Malaekahana Beach, north of Laie town, northwest coast of O`ahu. This campground is situated in a sheltered forest grove behind a nice stretch of sandy beach. Nice grassy areas with lots of shade trees. There are sweeping coastal and mountain views. Campsites have picnic tables, rest rooms, showers and drinking water; campers bring own portable stoves/grills. The beach is usually safe for swimming. Good snorkeling around offshore Moku`auia Island which is also a seabird sanctuary.

Sand Island State Recreation Area, end of Sand Island Access Road, off Nimitz Highway #92, Sand Island, Honolulu Harbor. This is a spacious 102-acre waterfront park directly on the ocean. Behind it is a large industrial area of docks, warehouses and industrial shops. However, the park is an oasis of grass lawns and some shade trees. Tent camping only. There are open and covered picnic tables but no central pavilion. Rest rooms, cold showers, drinking water available. Nice beach, but the offshore bottom is rocky; good shoreline fishing.

Dining

Honolulu and the Island of O`ahu have numerous restaurants of all types, from inexpensive to moderate to upscale fine dining. There are also a number of operators who offer full Hawaiian-style beach luaus and sunset dinner cruises. The cosmopolitan nature of the city is reflected in its diverse range of island eateries. Honolulu is a veritable gourmet's delight with a wide range of cuisines. There are simple diners serving excellent local-style plate lunches featuring ethnic foods. And there are fine dining restaurants serving the creative, popular and trendy Hawaiian Regional Cuisine and exotic Asian and Pacific fare. Sampling the wonderful local ethnic cuisine of Hawai`i is one adventure all visitors to Honolulu will enjoy. The following section lists only a few of the many options. The restaurant price ranges, as in the other island sections of this book, are based on the average dinner meal, exclusive of tax, alcoholic beverages and desserts.

Dining Price Scale	
$	under $10 per person
$$	$10-25 per person
$$$	$25 and up per person

■ Luaus

Polynesian Revue, ☎ 808/931-4660, Sheraton Princess Kaiulani Hotel, Waikiki, offers two complete dinner/show packages: "King David Kalakaua-A Musical Legacy" and "Drums of the Islands." Each dinner show includes a full Asian/Pacific buffet dinner with salad bar, entrée bar and dessert bar. Colorful show features culture and pageantry of the islands in song and dance. $$$

Germaine's Luau, ☎ 800/367-5655, 808/949-6626, offers a private beachside luau in the Ewa area west of Pearl Harbor about 35 minutes from Waikiki; hotel pickups provided. This is a real backyard family-style luau with authentic Hawaiian roast pig and all the extras. A full Pacific Island song and dance program included. $$$

Paradise Cove Luau, ☎ 800/775-2683, 808/973-LUAU. These private luau grounds are at Paradise Cove at Ko Olina Resort, 27 miles from Waikiki in the Ewa area west of Pearl Harbor. Enjoy an evening of Hawaiian entertainment, luau buffet dinner of special island foods, village activities and more. $$$

The Royal Luau, ☎ 808/931-7194, on the beach at the Royal Hawaiian Hotel, Waikiki. This is one of Waikiki's most elaborate beachside luaus, complete with island-style entertainment program of music and hula and a sumptuous island buffet. $$$

**Ali`i Luau,** Polynesian Cultural Center, Laie, North Shore, ☎ 800/367-7060, 808/293-3333. This dinner/show is performed by students at Brigham Young University-Hawai`i campus. The center and the luau dinner/show is among O`ahu's largest visitor attractions. It's a fantastic show in comfortable surroundings, with traditional luau food. $$$

■ Dinner Cruises

The Star of Honolulu, Paradise Cruises, ☎ 800/334-6191, 808/593-2493. This elegant small ship is state-of-the-art and provides an evening to remember with cruises along Waikiki and Honolulu to Diamond Head. Full dinner and live island entertainment. Various dinner/show packages available. $$$

Starlet Dinner Cruise, Paradise Cruises, ☎ 800/334-6191, 808/983-7827. This luxury yacht offers a full island-style steak and fish dinner along with Polynesian revue show. $$$

Dream Cruises, ☎ 808/592-5200, offers a special "Sunset Grill Dinner" cruise along Waikiki to Diamond Head or "Island Grill Dinner Dance

Cruise" with the lights of Waikiki and Honolulu as a background. Enjoy a full grill meal of seafood kabobs, mahimahi, shrimp, teriyaki beef kabobs, chicken breast, salad bar, dessert and more. Dance under the stars. $$$

Ali`i Kai, 680 Iwilei Road, Honolulu, HI 96817, ☎ 808/524-6694, 800-831-5541. This Polynesian-style catamaran offers a sunset dinner cruise with choice of lower deck regular buffet meal or upper deck deluxe gourmet dinner; includes a show. $$$

Kulamanu, 181 Ala Moana Blvd., Pier 7-A, Honolulu, HI 96813, ☎ 808/537-1122, 800-367-5000, Windjammer Cruises, has nightly cruises and choice of Luau at Sea, Captain's Buffet or the Admiral's Table; includes Polynesian show. $$$

■ Restaurants

Waikiki Beach

Golden Dragon, 2005 Kalia Road in the Hilton Hawaiian Village, ☎ 808/949-4321. This is an elegant dining room filled with attractive Chinese decor. There is an extensive Chinese menu. Nice service and atmosphere. $$$

Orchids, 2199 Kalia Road, Halekulani Hotel, ☎ 808/923-2311. This is the hotel's signature seaside dining room. The menu is regional American with broiler and rotisserie specials. $$$

Hee Hing Restaurant, 449 Kapahulu Avenue, ☎ 808/735-5544. This busy Chinese restaurant provides a lengthy menu of Chinese cuisine specialties. Try the dim sum dumplings, duck and fresh fish. $$

Hanohano Room, 2255 Kalakaua Avenue, Sheraton Waikiki Hotel, ☎ 808/922-4422. A very elegant rooftop dining room some 30 stories above Waikiki Beach. The sunsets and views are fabulous and the food is excellent, with attentive service. $$$

Sarento's Top of the I, 1777 Ala Moana, Ilikai Hotel, ☎ 808/955-5559. The menu here is authentic Italian, with selections ranging from pizzettes to cioppino, steaks to seafood. Everything is excellent, as are the panoramic views from this lovely rooftop dining room. Fine food with attentive service in a very romantic and special setting. $$$

Sam Choy's Diamond Head Restaurant, 449 Kapahulu Avenue, ☎ 808/732-8645. Sam's is a leader of the Hawaiian Regional Cuisine trend but adds his own twist. His servings are colorful and gargantuan

O`ahu

in size. Try the seafood laulau, osso bucco or any of the fresh island seafood dishes. You'll be challenged to eat it all. $$$

Sergio's, 445 Nohonani Street, Ilima Hotel, ☎ 808/926-3388. The menu here is authentic Italian, with an emphasis on fresh ingredients, generous servings and colorful presentation. Fine dining in a romantic setting. $$

Spaghetti! Spaghetti!, Royal Hawaiian Shopping Center, 2201 Kalakaua Avenue, ☎ 808/922-7724. Nothing fancy in decor about this place but it provides a buffet table of pasta and salad. The food is adequate and reasonably priced, but don't expect five-star food. This is a good place for families and groups to eat inexpensively in Waikiki. $$

Surf Room, 2259 Kalakaua Avenue, The Royal Hawaiian Hotel, ☎ 808/931-7194. Fine dining doesn't get much better than at this elegant oceanside hotel dining room. The menu is traditional American with some contemporary Hawaiian Regional Cuisine. There are lavish breakfast and lunch buffets daily, a magnificent royal seafood buffet on Friday night, and a sumptuous champagne Sunday brunch. Attentive service, nice ambiance, right on Waikiki Beach. $$$

Top of Waikiki, 2270 Kalakaua Avenue, Waikiki Business Plaza, ☎ 808/923-1191. This is a revolving restaurant perched atop a highrise and offers spectacular sunset dining high above colorful lights of Waikiki. Lovely panoramic views go well with the continental dinner menu. $$$

Metro Honolulu

Akasaka Marina, Koko Marina Shopping Center, Hawai`i Kai, ☎ 808/396-4474. The menu here is Japanese, with choices including teriyaki beef, chicken katsu, seafood, noodle dishes, sushi and more. $$

Alan Wong's Restaurant, 1857 S. King Street, ☎ 808/949-2526. Alan Wong is one of the Hawaiian Regional Cuisine chefs noted for his creative Asian-Pacific flair using local produce. The food is colorful, flavorful and innovative. $$$

Assagio Restaurant, 7192 Kalanianaole Highway, Hawai`i Kai Shopping Center, ☎ 808/396-0756. A small, cozy Italian eatery offering a menu with several excellent pasta and Italian specials daily, plus antipasto, soups and salads. Menu selections include pepper steak, osso buco, several veal dishes, scampi, calamari and fresh fish, several chicken dishes. The lengthy list of house specials, includes baked stuffed eggplant, cheese ravioli, Sicilian chicken, rigatoni and lasagna. The dining room has subdued lighting and white table cloths with a nice view overlooking Hawai`i Kai Marina. $$

Columbia Inn, 645 Kapiolani Boulevard, ☎ 808/596-0757. An old-fashioned neighborhood coffee shop with good plate meals, sandwiches, soups and fresh pie for dessert. $

3660 On the Rise, 3660 Waialae Avenue, ☎ 808/737-1177. This is another of Honolulu's rising stars, featuring a menu of creative Hawaiian Regional Cuisine. The dishes are innovative, colorful and almost certain to please any palate. Tables are a bit crowded here but the food is worth the slight inconvenience. $$$

Indigo, 1121 Nu`uanu Avenue, ☎ 808/521-2900. Located in the old Chinatown section of downtown Honolulu, this is one of Honolulu's leading-edge restaurants, featuring innovative Euro-Chinese cuisine. The lengthy menu features many dishes combining the flavors, ingredients and essence of traditional European and Chinese cookery. Sample and enjoy such entrées as wokked hot sour Pacific fish pagoda, Asian style bouillabaise, Mongolian lamb chops, miso grilled salmon with cucumber salad, lilikoi glazed baby back ribs, charred pesto crusted ahi tuna and many more creative dishes; appetizers, soups, salads and incredible desserts as well. It's well worth a visit. $$

Rainbow Drive In, 3308 Kanaina Avenue, ☎ 808/737-0177. This is one of Honolulu's old standard plate lunch shops. The menu lists a number of local favorite plate lunch items, with the most popular item being the fried chicken and gravy. $

Kapahulu Poi Shop, 3110 Winam Avenue, ☎ 808/737-8014. If you like traditional Hawaiian food such as laulau, smoked pork, lomi salmon, chicken luau, fresh poi and haupia pudding, look no further. Get the Hawaiian special plate lunch, a mini-luau in one box. Excellent Hawaiian food. $

Ono Hawaiian Foods, 726 Kapahulu Avenue, ☎ 808/737-2275. This is one of Kapahulu's old time plate lunch shops. Everything is good here, but do try the Hawaiian plate, a sampler of traditional authentic Hawaiian luau cuisine. $

Masu's Massive Plate Lunch, 1808 Liliha Street, ☎ 808/524-4260. The name says it all. The local-style plate lunches, daily special and local favorite selections, are indeed massive and good on top of that. There's enough for two on one plate, unless you're really hungry. $

Roy's Restaurant, 6600 Kalanianaole Highway, ☎ 808/396-7697. This is famed chef Roy Yamaguchi's original Honolulu outlet. He began his

O`ahu

expanding fine dining restaurant chain with this dining room. His Hawaiian Regional Cuisine is the main attraction. Good food in a busy open-kitchen atmosphere that can get a bit noisy at times. $$$

Salerno, 1960 Kapiolani Boulevard, ☎ 808/942-5273. The menu here is authentic Italian, with a variety of pasta, seafood and specialty dishes. Good food in a pleasant atmosphere, although it does get a bit crowded especially on weekends. $$

Yum Yum Tree, Kahala Mall Shopping Center, ☎ 808/733-3544. This shopping mall coffee shop serves up good family-style plate meals, sandwiches, burgers, soups, salads and more. They have several other Honolulu locations as well. $

Palomino Restaurant, 55 Merchant St., Harbor Court Building, ☎ 808/528-2400. This upscale dining room has a classy Mediterranean ambiance and seats 200. Classical contemporary art decor. Lots of fine woodwork, marblework, flowers and plants and original art. The menu features Mediterranean cuisine, including dishes with Italian, French, Spanish and Moroccan accents. There is a variety of soups and salads, plus entrées like spit-roasted garlic chicken and lamb shanks, rotisserie pork loin, fresh seafood and fish, paella, pizza and a number of pasta dishes. At meal's end, the waiter gives each guest a card with a proverb or message. If your car was parked by a valet, you'll find after-dinner mints on the dashboard when you pick it up. $$$

Tai Pan on the Boulevard, 1680 Kapiolani Blvd., near Ala Moana Center, ☎ 808/943-1888. This restaurant features the trendy new Euro/Asian cuisine, which combines ingredients and flavors of traditional Asian/Chinese and European cuisines, in this case French. The menu has creative appetizers like crab and taro cake cilantro, stonecrab claws with shrimp mousse. Salads include misoyaki grilled black cod with spinach and endive, Caesar salad with tea-smoked duck; entrées range from braised squab with herb crab stuffing, to French lamb curry stew, rosemary crusted pork loin, crispy island chicken with Pinot-Noir, to the intriguing peppered frog legs with linguini. There are equally tempting dessert offerings. The accent is on freshness of produce and entrée products with unique combinations and cookery methods. $$

Sushi King, 2700 S. King Street, Moiliili area, ☎ 808/947-2836. This busy restaurant features an incredible variety of sushi, from light California-style, New York-style, Washington-style to nigiri, makimono, futomaki and more. In addition, the menu has several types of fish, shrimp, calamari, sashimi (raw fish), broiled fresh water eel, squid legs, cherry stone clams, plus chicken, beef and tonkatsu. Dining here is definitely a culinary adventure. $$

Sam Choy's Breakfast, Lunch & Crab, 580 N. Nimitz Highway, ☎ 808/545-7979. This is celebrity chef Sam Choy's second Honolulu restaurant. The specialty here is fresh seafood with creative local-style preparations. This is a combination family diner, brew pub, oyster bar and crabhouse operation in a casual atmosphere. If you like seafood, you'll find lots of adventurous dining here. $$

North Shore/Windward O`ahu

**Ko`olau Ranch House,** 46-077 Kamehameha Highway, Kaneohe Bay Shopping Center, Kane`ohe, ☎ 808/247-3900. This family dining room offers homestyle cooking and American and Oriental cuisine, but the specialty is their famous "Ko`olau pulehu T-bone steak." Pulehu-style is essentially charcoal-broiled with Hawaiian salt; very tasty! $$

Smokin' Bob Barr-B-Q and Authentic Mexican Food, 46-132A Kahuhipa, Kane`ohe, ☎ 808/247-8811. The menu features lots of BBQ-style chicken, beef, pork and ribs, done Texas-style and kiawe-smoked. They serve lunch and dinner and provide take outs. $

Crouching Lion Inn, 51-666 Kamehameha Highway, Ka`a`awa, ☎ 808/237-8511. This oceanside location has great water views of the windward coast and a menu featuring many local-style favorites, including seafood, beef, chicken and more. $$

Palm Terrace, Turtle Bay Hilton, 57-091 Kamehameha Highway, Kahuku, ☎ 808/293-8811. This resort dining room offers casual dining with oceanfront views. There is a nightly buffet of local-style and international cuisine. $$

Pikake Pavilion, Waimea Valley and Adventure Park, Waimea Valley, 59-864 Kamehameha Highway, Haleiwa, ☎ 808/638-8531. This airy, open dining room offers nice views of surrounding Waimea Valley, along with its daily sumptuous lunch buffet featuring international and local cuisine. $$

The Proud Peacock Restaurant, Waimea Valley and Adventure Park, Waimea Valley, 59-864 Kamehameha Highway, Haleiwa, ☎ 808/638-8531. A garden setting overlooking the famed North Shore in the background and the lush and lovely Waimea Valley in the foreground. Diners will enjoy selections from a continental menu of prime rib, steaks, pastas, seafood and more. $$

O`ahu

Helemano Plantation Country Inn Restaurant, 64-1510 Kamehameha Highway, Wahiawa, ☎ 808/622-3929. This country dining room offers a daily buffet as well as an à la carte menu of salads, sandwiches and daily specials. $

Sea Lion Café, Sea Life Park, 41-202 Kalanianaole Highway, Waimanalo, ☎ 808/259-9911. This cafeteria-style eatery offers a variety of American, Japanese and local Hawaiian favorites. $

Chart House at Haiku Gardens, 46-336 Haiku Road, Kane`ohe, ☎ 808/247-6671. This dining room provides comfortable and relaxing open-air dining with a great view of lush botanical gardens. Enjoy an extensive menu of continental selections, including steaks, prime rib, seafood, pastas, salad bar and more. $$

Café Haleiwa, 66-460 Kamehameha Highway, Haleiwa, ☎ 808/637-5516. A surfers' hangout in this North Shore surfing center. It's a small, simple country café. The menu features traditional breakfast items and sandwiches, burgers and local favorites on the lunch menu. Lots of surf memorabilia on the walls. $

Lana`i

The Pineapple Island

Geography

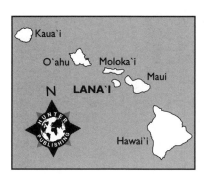

L ana`i, once known as the Pineapple Island, although pineapple is no longer grown there commercially, has a land area of 140 square miles. It is the sixth largest of the Hawaiian Islands and has 47 miles of generally rugged, rocky coastline with some isolated sandy beach areas. Lana`i is part of the County of Maui and has a population of about 3,000. Its only town and settlement is Lana`i City. The island is 18 miles across at its widest point. It rises from sea level to the highest point at Lana`ihale, 3,370 feet, at the eastern end of the island. The island is marked by broad flat plains and plateaus that were formerly used by the pineapple plantation until its demise in the '80s. The north and east sides of the island have dry deep gulches and ravines running far inland. Lana`i is probably as old as its nearest neighbors, Maui and Moloka`i. That would put its age at one to two million years, based on studies of those islands' underlying lava flows.

Climate

Lana`i's average temperature range is 70-75° and its annual rainfall is about 30 inches, mostly in the higher elevations. The lower plains, plateaus and gulches tend to be much drier and warmer the year around.

Garden of the Gods, Lana`i.

History

DID YOU KNOW?

Legend has it that Lana`i was once an evil place, overrun with demons. For nearly 1,000 years after Polynesians settled Hawai`i, Lana`i remained uninhabited. It wasn't until sometime after 1400 that the evil spirits were driven out by Kaulalaau, exiled son of a West Maui king, and Hawaiians finally came to live on Lana`i.

In 1779, Captain James Cook cruised the islands and took note of the many Hawaiians who lived by fishing and raising taro on the south shore of Lana`i. Their numbers soon decreased, however, as a result of the internecine wars among the chiefs and kings. The first missionaries arrived in 1835 and found farmers and fishermen the primary residents.

Over the years, Lana`i has gone through different stages of development under several different owners. At various times it was a thriving sheep and cattle ranch, a sugarcane plantation and then a pineapple plantation for many years. Because it is such a small island and lacks the resources others have, it has been perceived by some as an inhospitable place. But in the early 1990s two magnificent resorts were built by Castle & Cooke to attract world travelers and tourism may loom large in its future. Before long this small, isolated island may have a new nickname to replace the no-longer-apt "Pineapple Island."

Information Sources

**Hawai`i Visitors and Convention Bureau,** Waikiki Business Plaza, 2270 Kalakaua Avenue, 8th. Fl., Honolulu, HI 96815, ☎ 800/GOHawai`i, 808/923-1811; www.visit.Hawaii.org/.

**Destination Lana`i,** PO Box 700, Lana`i City, HI 96763, ☎ 800/947-4774, 808/565-7600.

**The Lana`i Company,** PO Box 310, Lana`i City, HI 96763, ☎ 808/565-8200.

References

Alford, John. *Mountain Biking the Hawaiian Islands: Mauka to Makai,* Ohana Publishing, Honolulu, HI. 1997.

Clark, John. *Beaches of Maui County,* University of Hawai`i Press, Honolulu, HI. 1994.

Early, Dona, and Stilson, Christie. *Maui and Lana`i: A Paradise Family Guide,* Prima Publishing, Rocklin, CA. 1996.

Koch, Tom. *Six Islands on Two Wheels,* Bess Press, Honolulu, HI. 1990.

Malinowski, Judy and Mel. *Snorkel Hawai`i: Maui and Lana`i,* Indigo Publications, 1996.

Olsen, Brad. *Extreme Adventures Hawai`i,* Hunter Publishing, Edison, NJ. 1998.

Smith, Rodney. *Hawai`i: A Walker's Guide,* Hunter Publishing, Edison, NJ. 1997.

Zurick, David. *Hawai`i, Naturally,* Wilderness Press, Berkeley, CA. 1990.

Getting There

■ Airline Service

Currently, there are only two airlines providing regular scheduled flights to Lana`i from Honolulu and Maui. Call them for details.

- **Island Air,** US, ☎ 800/323-3345, Canada, ☎ 800/235-0936, Hawai`i, ☎ 800/652-6541, Lana`i, ☎ 808/565-6744; e-mail aloha@alohaair.com; www.alohaair.com/. This subsidiary of Aloha Airlines operates daily shuttle flights to Lana`i from Honolulu and Kahului, Maui.

- **Hawaiian Air,** US and Canada, ☎ 800/367-5320, Lana`i ☎ 808/565-7281; www.Hawaiianair.com/.

■ Ferry Service

- **Expeditions,** PO Box 10, Lahaina, HI 96767-0010, ☎ 808/661-3756. This ferryboat company provides shuttle service between Lahaina Harbor on Maui and Manele Bay Harbor on Lana`i, with several daily departures; it's a one-hour trip between islands. Rates: $25 one way.

Getting Around

Resort guests have access to shuttle buses that link Manele Bay Hotel with the Lodge at Koele, the airport and stops in town and along the way. Inquire with your hotel concierge desk. Depending on your lodging arrangements, you may be met at the airport and transported to where you'll stay.

Lana`i is unique among the Hawaiian Islands in many respects. For one thing, it has only about 25 miles of paved road. The rest of the roads are Lana`i's famous red dirt. And since Lana`i doesn't get too much rain in the lower elevation plains, most of these roads are usually dry and dusty. But when it rains, the roads can be a mess. The mountain Munro Trail is known to be difficult after a rain, so those going offroad must be aware of this and check on the local road conditions first.

Whether you're exploring Lana`i by bike, car, on foot or otherwise, a good map would be helpful. The *Map of Moloka`i and Lana`i,* by James Bier, published by the University of Hawai`i Press, is an excellent detailed full color topographic map of the two islands. It's a very useful resource to navigating your way and finding the special attractions and sights on each island. Look for the latest edition in shops around the islands.

The airport is about 3½ miles southwest of Lana`i City in the Palawai Basin, a wide open dry plain formerly used for pineapple plantation fields. Lana`i City, where most of the island's 3,000 souls live, is located almost exactly in the middle of this irregular lima-bean-shaped island. To the east are the hills and summit of Lana`ihale – at 3,370 feet, the island's highest point. Dry, sloping gulches and valleys from the higher interior taper down to the coastline all around the island.

Lana`i City has a fortuitous location at the 1,700-foot elevation level near the foothills of the island's main mountain. This keeps the town's climate delightfully cool and breezy compared to the surrounding dry, dusty and hot plains, where the pineapples used to grow. The town is

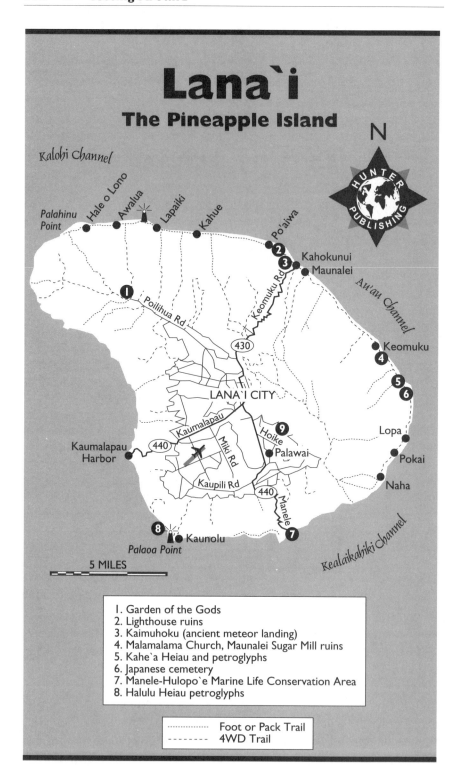

Lana`i
The Pineapple Island

N

HUNTER PUBLISHING

Kalohi Channel

Palahinu Point

Hale o Lono

Awalua

Lapaiki

Kahue

Po'aiwa

2

3

Kahokunui
Maunalei

Au'au Channel

Keomuku Rd

430

1

Poilihua Rd

Keomuku

4

5

6

LANA`I CITY

Kaumalapau

9

Hoike

Lopa

Kaumalapau Harbor

440

Miki Rd

Palawai

Pokai

Kaupili Rd

440

Naha

Manele

8

7

Kaunolu

Palaoa Point

Kealaikahiki Channel

5 MILES

1. Garden of the Gods
2. Lighthouse ruins
3. Kaimuhoku (ancient meteor landing)
4. Malamalama Church, Maunalei Sugar Mill ruins
5. Kahe`a Heiau and petroglyphs
6. Japanese cemetery
7. Manele-Hulopo`e Marine Life Conservation Area
8. Halulu Heiau petroglyphs

```
............. Foot or Pack Trail
- - - - - - - 4WD Trail
```

marked by towering Norfolk Island pine trees planted years ago. In the afternoon when the tradewinds pick up, it's not unusual for banks of clouds and light mists to come blowing through the town and the towering pine trees. This gives the town a cool, quasi-alpine atmosphere.

From town, it is about 7½ miles south to the Manele Bay Hotel, Challenge at Manele Golf Course and Hulopo'e Beach Park. The Lodge at Koele sits just at the northeast edge of town, along with the Experience at Koele Golf Course. From just past the Lodge at Koele, the Keomuku Road #430 descends 8½ miles downslope to the northeast coast, Shipwreck Beach and other sites along the Keomuku coastal road. The Polihua Road extends west just past the Lodge at Koele for 6½ miles. This is nothing more than a dirt road running through old pineapple fields now used for cattle grazing. The road passes through the Kanepu`u Dryland Forest Reserve and the Garden of the Gods, with its artsy rock formations and wind-eroded hillsides, before descending on a very rugged 4WD road to Polihua Beach on the northwest coast.

The Kaumalapau Highway 440 is the road that runs about eight miles from town to the airport and continues downslope to Kaumalapau Harbor, where the supply barges from Honolulu land Lana`i's weekly shipment of goods and groceries. It's not much of a scenic drive but it does provide a view of the island's west coast area.

You won't find a lot of traffic on Lana`i and what traffic there is will be moving slow. So drive with caution. The roads won't allow fast driving, except perhaps for a stretch across the Palawai Basin from Manele Bay or the airport. But Lana`i is so small, there's no need to hurry.

Lana`i is about as rural and laid-back as Moloka`i, maybe more so. And, like Moloka`i, it doesn't have even one traffic light as yet. So take your time and enjoy this delightful little corner of Hawai`i, a place with one foot still in the past.

■ Car Rentals & Car Service

Rental cars and Jeeps are expensive on Lana`i, much higher than other areas of Hawai`i. But a rental car or Jeep may be your best bet if you intend to see some of the backroad areas or sights on Lana`i. If you plan to

Lana`i City

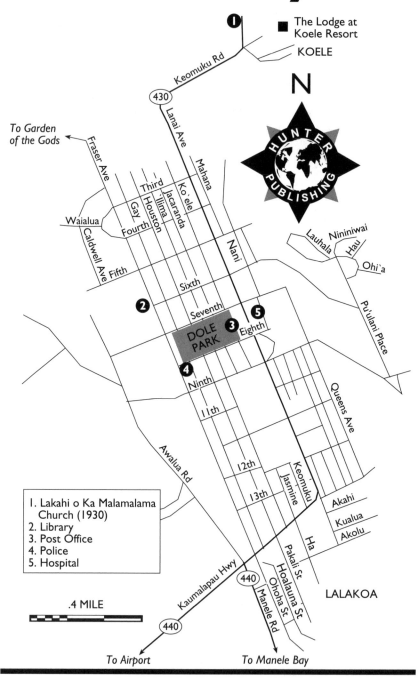

The Lodge at
Koele Resort

KOELE

N

HUNTER PUBLISHING

To Garden of the Gods

Keomuku Rd

430

Lanai Ave

Fraser Ave

Waialua

Caldwell Ave

Gay

Third

Fourth

Fifth

Houston

Jacaranda

`Ilima

Ko`ele

Mahana

Nani

Sixth

Seventh

DOLE PARK

Eighth

Ninth

11th

12th

13th

Awalua Rd

Jasmine

Keomuku

Pakali St

Ha

Kaumalapau Hwy

440

Manele Rd

Ohoha St

Hoalauna St

440

Lauhala

Nininiwai

Hau

Ohi`a

Pu`ulani Place

Queens Ave

Akahi

Kualua

Akolu

LALAKOA

1. Lakahi o Ka Malamalama
   Church (1930)
2. Library
3. Post Office
4. Police
5. Hospital

.4 MILE

To Airport

To Manele Bay

stay at either of the two major resorts and not venture much beyond them, you probably won't need your own vehicle. You could rely on the resort shuttles or book a tour to see the Lana`i sights. But if you like the freedom and independence of having your own wheels, explore at your leisure and discover the treasures of Lana`i's famed Munro Trail across the highest peaks, Shipwreck Beach and the unique Garden of the Gods area of west Lana`i. Typical daily rental rates are: Jeep Wrangler $119; compact 4-door $60; minivan $129; large van $175.

■ **Lana`i City Service** (a Dollar Rent A Car outlet), 1036 Lana`i Avenue, PO Box 370, Lana`i City, HI 96763, ☎ 800/JEEP-808 or 808/565-7227. This operator specializes in renting 4x4 Jeep Wranglers to explore Lana`i's backcountry mountain and coastal offroad areas. They also have compact 4-door cars, mini-vans and deluxe 15-passenger vans for large groups. Rentals include airport and/or hotel transport/pickup, personal briefing on Lana`i attractions, sites, operation of the Jeep 4x4 and a Jeep Safari guidebook on Lana`i.

■ **Rabaca's Limousine Service,** PO Box 304, Lana`i City, HI 96763, ☎ 808/565-6670. This operator provides airport/hotel shuttle service as well as custom-designed tours on Lana`i.

Lana`i

Exploring a back road on Lana`i's west end.

■ Bicycle-Moped Rentals & Tours

If you want a biking adventure on Lana`i, you'll find the island well adapted to it. The low traffic roads lend themselves well to casual exploration, whether along the high mountain ridge Munro Trail and through the forest or a downhill trek to Shipwreck Beach and along the northeast shore to historic sites, or even exploring the incredible rock formations of the Garden of the Gods on the island's west end.

- **Lana`i City Service,** 1036 Lana`i Avenue, PO Box 370, Lana`i City, HI 96763, ☎ 800/JEEP-808 or 808/565-7227. In addition to their rental cars, Jeeps and vans, they also have bicycle rentals and mopeds by the day or week; call for current rates.

- **Chris' Adventures,** PO Box 869, Kula, HI 96790, ☎ 808/871-BIKE; www.lmg.com:80/maui/hykebyke.htm. This outfitter offers day trips to Lana`i from Maui via ferry boat. Bikers then tackle the daunting and beautiful Munro Trail, which follows the island's highest mountain ridges and forests for scenic views of valley, gorge and coastline. This is a day-long trek for experienced riders only. Rates begin at about $110 per person.

Touring Lana`i

The following operators can provide island tours on Lana`i to the major sights and attractions, plus other adventure activities as well. Call them for details. Standard hiking adventures begin at $69 per person. Standard kayaking adventures begin at $89 per person. Half-day guided van tours of Lana`i begin at $75 per person.

**Lana`i Adventure Company,** PO Box 1394, Lana`i City, HI 96763, ☎ 888/TREKLanai (873-5526), 808/565-9485. This outfitter specializes in sea kayaking, snorkeling and hiking excursions around Lana`i. Enjoy the clear waters surrounding Lana`i and see dolphins, sea turtles and reef fish in their natural environment. Hike and explore Lana`i's rolling hills and valleys, cool mountain highlands, dryland gulches and windswept coastlands. Discover something of the old culture and lifestyle of Lana`i long ago.

**Lana`i City Service,** PO Box 370, Lana`i City, HI 96763, ☎ 800/JEEP-808, 808/565-7227. This operator offers fully guided 4x4 van tours of

Lana`i. This is a comfortable air-conditioned van tour to some of the best sites on the island, such as the Munro Trail and Shipwreck Beach. Includes continental breakfast on the mountain slopes of the Munro Trail and time to beachcomb the remote coastal beaches of the north side of Lana`i. Tours are half-day, but custom tours can be arranged.

Adventures

Lana`i's Best Adventures

- Take a bike ride or 4WD trek on the **Munro Trail**.
- Take a bike ride or 4WD trek to the **Garden of the Gods**.
- Explore **Shipwreck Beach** and the other historic sites along the North Coast.
- Explore the tiny town of **Lana`i City** on foot, discovering its small shops and local eateries.
- Enjoy a day at **Hulupo`e Bay Beach Park**.
- Play **golf** at either of the two marvelous resort courses on Lana`i or the town public course.
- Take a **snorkel or scuba dive cruise** around Lana`i.
- Tour Lana`i's main points of interest in a **guided van or 4WD Jeep**.
- Enjoy a **horseback trail ride** through Lana`i's western side.
- Experience a **gourmet meal** at either the **Manele Bay Hotel** or the **Lodge at Koele** fine dining rooms.

■ On Foot

There are many backcountry 4x4 vehicle roads, hunters' trails and foot trails across the island that are suitable for day hiking. Check with the hotel concierge or The Lana`i Company for details on other roads and trails not listed here. The Lana`i Company, PO Box 310, Lana`i City, HI 96763, ☎ 808/565-8200, runs most hotels and lodging on the island and oversees the visitor industry.

Koloiki Ridge Hike is a three-hour, five-mile round-trip beginning behind The Lodge at Ko`ele. Pick up a brochure/map of the hike from the hotel concierge. The trail heads uphill from the golf course clubhouse, winding along the ridge above Kaiholena Valley. Follow the trail markers. As the trail ascends, it passes the golf course fairways and leads to the "Cathedral of Pines," a tall stand of Norfolk Island pine trees. The trail continues on into Hulopo`e Valley and links up with the mountain ridge Munro Trail, a well-traveled cross-island backroad. Turn right onto the Munro Trail heading to Kukui Gulch. The Munro Trail can be very muddy and slippery in wet weather. It passes through a thick patch of yellow ginger on the opposite side of the road from Kukui Gulch. The next marker is at an area of colorful eroded bare hills. Just past this point is a stand of large sisal plants, resembling desert agave plants. Around a sharp curve there is a straight stretch of road. About 50 yards past the curve, take a left turn. Watch for a trail marker. The trail here heads through a tunnel of low thicket branches that leads to Koloiki Ridge. Out of the trees, the trail opens to stunning vistas of rugged east Lana`i, including Naio Gulch and Maunalei Valley. Continue on to a stand of Norfolk Island pines at trail's end on Koloiki Ridge. This area is brushed with cooling tradewinds and a view making the hike well worth it. Return to The Lodge at Ko`ele the same way.

DON'T MISS **Munro Trail** (see *On Wheels* section below) is a 10½-mile backcountry 4x4 vehicle trail that is also used for biking and hiking. The road crosses the highest mountain ridges and peaks on Lana`i and provides some of the most spectacular vistas on the island. This is not an easy hike and can be muddy and slippery in wet weather. The trail runs from a mile west of The Lodge at Ko`ele on Highway 430, the Keomuku Road, to about 4½ miles east of Lana`i City on Highway 440, the Manele Road. The road follows the mountain ridges to Lana`ihale, the island's highest point at 3,370-foot elevation. On a clear day, there are steep gulches and valleys to see, views of Palawai Basin and the old pineapple plantation fields, dense forest areas and swirling misty clouds. At the higher elevations, the cooling tradewinds can be quite gusty. The eastern end of the road passes through old pineapple fields before linking with the Manele Road and this is one of Lana`i's famous dusty red dirt roads. You might see Axis deer, wild turkeys and other game animals and birds along the way. Take lots of water and snacks.

DON'T MISS **Polihua Beach Trail,** five-mile round-trip, is at the west end of the island and begins after passing through the Garden of the Gods area, 6½ miles west of The Lodge at Ko`ele. The Garden of the Gods is a colorful area of wind-eroded rock formations and exposed cliffsides. The trail down to the beach becomes very narrow and rugged at a point past the open eroded rock formations. The trail terminates at a small sandy beach on this windswept northwest tip of the island. There is a large area of shifting sand dunes formed over the ages by the relentless wind. The beach is a seasonal nesting ground for the protected Hawaiian sea turtles. This is a warm, dry, sunny area so take lots of water and sunscreen.

Golf & Tennis

Both of Lana`i's resort hotels have tennis courts for guest use. There is also a public court at the school in Lana`i City.

Cavendish Golf Course is a public nine-hole, par-36 short course at the edge of town and in front of the nearby Lodge at Koele. The course is free to residents and resort guests. Others who use it are expected to leave a donation for maintaining the course. For information, ☎ 808/565-8200.

DON'T MISS **The Experience at Koele** is a cool 18-hole golf layout in the high country behind Lana`i City at 2,000-foot elevation. The fairways meander across hilly terrain among dense stands of forest and brushlands. They are marked by deep ravines with stands of pine, koa and eucalyptus trees. Cool gusty tradewinds blow clouds of mist through the course. The course is also marked by a number of ponds and flowing streams. It was designed by golf professional Greg Norman and is one of Hawai`i's classic courses. It has received wide acclaim. For reservations and information: The Experience at Koele, PO Box 310, Lana`i City, HI 96763, ☎ 800/321-4666, 808/565-4653. Greens fees are $125.

The Challenge at Manele is a beautiful oceanside golf layout of 18 holes extending from behind Hulopo`e Bay and the Manele Bay Hotel to Kaluakoi Point and Huawai Bay. The course was sculpted from natural lava fields and rocky outcroppings. Golf legend Jack Nicklaus designed the course. Three holes use the Pacific Ocean as a water hazard, making for a thrilling challenge. From most any point on the course, there are expansive vistas of ocean, beach, bay and blue sky. This course has also received wide acclaim. For reservations and information: The Challenge at Manele, PO Box 310, Lana`i City, HI 96763, ☎ 800/321-4666, 808/565-2222. Greens fees are $125.

Shopping

Lana`i's town center surrounds Dole Park right in the heart of town. The park has magnificent towering Norfolk Island pines planted many years ago. The town location upcountry gives it a generally comfortable climate with cooling breezes. The handful of shops and stores around Dole Park on Seventh and Eighth Streets make for interesting small-town browsing and exploring. A shopping venture will also give you a glimpse into the lifestyle of a very small, quite isolated rural community in modern Hawai`i.

Richard's Shopping Center, ☎ 565-6407, is a general store with groceries, clothing and more.

Dis N' Dat Shop, ☎ 565-6061, is a general sundry store with a little of everything and some unique gifts.

Akamai Trading, ☎ 565-6587, sells sundries, with snacks, small gifts and souvenirs.

Pine Isle Market, ☎ 565-6488, is a general store with groceries, liquor, sundries.

Lana`i Family Store, ☎ 565-6485, carries clothing, accessories.

Maria M's Boutique, ☎ 565-9577, carries clothing for women and children.

**Heart of Lana`i,** ☎ 565-6678, is a gift shop with made-on-Lana`i arts and crafts, products and gifts.

Lana`i Art Program, ☎ 565-7503, carries locally made arts and gifts.

Hunting

Adventurers can enjoy hunting on Lana`i for its famed Axis deer and Mouflon sheep as well as game birds like wild turkey, pheasant, partridge and quail. Non-resident license is required; fee is $100. For details, contact:

**The Lana`i Company Game Management Office**, PO Box 700, Lana`i, HI 96763, ☎ 808/565-8202. The Lana`i Company, which oversees all operations on the island, has hunting packages available only for Axis deer. These guided hunts include permit and guide fee and are $750 per person; state hunting license fee of $100 is extra. Contact the game management office for details. All hunting must be arranged well in advance.

Department of Lands and Natural Resources, Game Management-Lana`i, ☎ 808/565-6688 or Forestry and Wildlife Division Information, no charge to calling party, ask for ENTERPRISE-6315. All other hunting on Lana`i for deer, sheep and game birds is seasonal and must be arranged in advance. Contact either number above for details and information; they can assist with arranging guides and licenses.

■ On Wheels

Lana`i has some fantastic backcountry roads that are a biker's delight. These country roads and trails will give you a view of Lana`i that few other visitors see, especially those who stay only at the island's resorts. Be sure to take along plenty of water, food, sunscreen and a hat for warm open sunny areas.

Munro Trail is a 10½-mile 4x4 vehicle trail that can also be a biker's ultimate challenge on Lana`i (see *On Foot* hiking section above). This is one of Lana`i's best land adventures. The route passes over Lana`ihale, the highest mountain peak on the island. It follows the mountain ridges through high country forestlands and provides spectacular views of valleys, gulches and distant coastal areas. The trail is named after George Munro, manager of the Lana`i Ranch Company, who began a reforestation program for Lana`i in the 1930s. The narrow, winding and rugged road can be rutted, muddy and impassable during wet weather. It's also a chance to see the backside of Lana`i. Few visitors take this road.

**Manele Bay Hotel-Lana`i City via Manele Road** is a 7½-mile ride in either direction. This ride along a fine paved highway passes through the wide open spaces of the Palawai Basin, the old pineapple fields of the island. It is a warm, dry region buffeted by gusty trade winds. From the hotel to Lana`i City west is a steep winding ride the first 3.2 miles, leveling off at the flatlands of the basin. There is a gradual rise to Lana`i City in the distance for the final few miles. The town sits at the foot of the mountains and thus has a much cooler and breezier climate than the dry coastal areas. If you're riding back to the Manele Bay Hotel, it's mostly downhill.

**Lana`i City-Garden of the Gods** is a delightful country ride on one of Lana`i famous red dirt roads. Be prepared to get dusty! This is a 13-mile round-trip from The Lodge at Ko`ele at the west edge of town to the Garden of the Gods. The route begins at the tennis courts and horse stables and extends out through cattle pastures. It is a mostly flat country ride with only some slight, gradual climbs. If it's been wet, the road can be muddy and have ruts in places. The road continues on for over four miles to Kanepu`u Preserve, a dryland forest preserve of endangered native Hawaiian plants and trees maintained by The Nature Conservancy. Stop here to explore the preserve, watch for wild turkeys, pheasant, partridge, quail, and maybe even an Axis deer or two. The road continues another 1.7 miles before entering the Garden of the Gods area. This area is marked by unique and colorful rock formations and exposed cliffs, eroded by the strong tradewinds that scour the area. The early morning or late afternoon sun provides special lighting for nature photographers. Take lots of water and snacks.

Keomuku Road/Highway 430 is Lana`i's ultimate "downhill coast." This is an 8½-mile downhill ride on a paved but winding road to the remote north shore of the island. The road runs west from The Lodge at Ko`ele and turns north not far out. After a short stretch of flat road, as the saying goes, "its all downhill from here." The route winds along the ridge between Naio and Halulu Gulches. There are nice views of this north side of Lana`i, distant gulches and ravines, coastal areas, the reef and ocean. As you approach the road's end near the coast, to the left up the coast, the old World War II cargo ship stranded on the reef is visible. Thus the name given to "Shipwreck Beach." At the end of the road, you can go right to the site of old Keomuku Village and other historic sites further down the coast. But this is a rugged coastal road. You can also turn left and follow the coastal road to near Shipwreck Beach. You'll have to walk a mile or more to get really near the ship itself. And, unless you want to bike back up the hill you just came down on, you'd better have arranged a pickup to haul you and your bike back to the top.

■ On Water

Beaches

Hulopo`e Bay Beach Park is on the south coast just opposite the Manele Bay boat landing and anchorage, below the Manele Bay Hotel. This is a wide, golden beach with great body boarding, surfing and good for swimming. But beware of

DON'T

MISS

strong undertows in heavy surf conditions. Hulopo`e is a marine reserve and the snorkeling is also excellent, with lots of marinelife to be seen. This beach is listed in the annual "Top 10 Best Beaches" national survey conducted by the University of Maryland. Hulopo`e was rated the #1 beach in the US in that survey for 1997. Five other Hawai`i beaches made the top 10 listing.

DON'T MISS **Shipwreck Beach**, near Kaiolohia Bay on the north shore near the end of Highway 430. The coast track running from road's end is for 4WD vehicles and passes long stretches of beach and rocky coastline. The beach gets its name from the large World War II-era liberty ship sitting high on the reef. This stretch of beach is good for exploring and sunning. Not recommended for swimming or snorkeling due to the strong currents throughout the area.

Hulupo`e Beach.

Club Lana`i is on the east coast seven-eight fairly rough bouncy 4WD miles along the coast from the end of Highway 430; this beach area is where ferries shuttle day visitors over from Maui for a day of relaxation and fun.

Lopa Beach is a couple of miles past Keomoku Village on the east coast trail and is a nice picnic site and beach area, good for sunbathing only; no swimming. Lopa has a gulch going inland and is noted as a summer south swell surfing area. It is the location of one of four ancient fishponds in the area.

Polihua Beach is on the far northwest tip of Lana`i and is accessible by a rugged 4WD trail leading downslope from the Garden of the Gods area. This is not a swimming beach, however, as it is often windy and rough surf is common. The area is marked by a long stretch of sand dunes and blowing sand can be extreme at times. The beach is noted for the sea turtles that nest here. In Hawaiian, poli means "cove or bay" and hua means "eggs." Thus, Polihua is a place where turtles lay their eggs. This is a scenic, windswept area remote from just about everything else on Lana`i.

Cruises & Ferry Boat

**Club Lana`i**, 355 Hukilike St., #211, Kahului, HI 96732, ☎ 800/531-5262 or 808/871-1144; e-mail clbLana`i@maui.net; www.maui.net/~clbLanai. This operator offers cruises from Maui to Lana`i and day trips to their pri-

Main Street, Lana`i City.

vate Club Lana`i Resort on the remote and isolated east shore of Lana`i. Enjoy snorkeling, diving, dolphin and whale watching, a day of ocean cruising across the Au`au Channel between Maui and Lana`i, plus beachcombing, a beach picnic, sunbathing and just relaxing in the sun. Rates begin at $80-90 per person.

Expeditions, PO Box 10, Lahaina, HI 96767-0010, ☎ 808/661-3756. This ferry provides shuttle service between Lahaina Harbor on Maui and Manele Bay Harbor on Lana`i, with several daily departures; it's a one-hour trip between islands. Rates are $25 one way.

Scuba Diving, Snorkeling & Kayaking

Ocean kayaking and snorkeling adventures begin at $89 per person. Cruises to Lana`i from Maui range from $129 to $162.

Trilogy, PO Box 1119, Lahaina, HI 96767-1119, ☎ 800/874-2666. This outfitter operates daily half-day snorkeling and scuba diving excursions on its luxury sailing catamarans; full PADI diving instruction and certification programs; snorkel and dive along Lana`i's famed southern coast marine reserves, protected bays and coves.

**Lana`i Adventure Company,** PO Box 1394, Lana`i City, HI 96763, ☎ 888/TREKLanai (873-5526), 808/565-9485. This outfitter specializes in sea kayaking, snorkeling and other adventures on and around Lana`i. Explore the clear waters surrounding Lana`i and enjoy sea turtles, dolphins and myriad marinelife and reef fish in their natural environment. Snorkel and dive in pristine waters, explore underwater caves, the dazzling color of tropical coral reefs and remote isolated beaches and coastal areas of Lana`i.

Fishing - Deep Sea Charters

**Spinning Dolphin Charters of Lana`i,** ☎ 808/565-6613; or visit any hotel concierge desk on Lana`i. This outfitter operates a 28-foot Omega Sportfisher boat using the latest in light and heavy tackle and equipment; go after marlin, ahi tuna, mahimahi, barracuda and more; half- and full-day charters available, beverages included.

■ In the Air

Scenic Flightseeing & Helicopter Tours

To arrange scenic flights of Lana`i by plane or helicopter, see *Scenic Flightseeing & Helicopter Tours* in the Maui section of this book.

■ On Horseback

The Lodge at Koele Stables provides trail rides through the open pasture lands, old pineapple plantation fields and the mountain foothills of western Lana`i. For details, see the concierge desk or call the Lodge at Koele, ☎ 808/565-7300.

■ Eco/Cultural Activities

If you're renting a 4x4 offroad vehicle, you might want to explore some of Lana`i harder to reach historic and cultural sites. Lana`i has several old Hawaiian heiau (temples) and village ruins scattered along its coastal areas. Most are reached only by rugged backcountry roads, which require an off-road 4x4 vehicle.

DON'T MISS **Garden of the Gods** is a windswept plateau area at the west end of Lana`i. It's reached via the hardpacked red dirt Polihua Road, 6.4 miles, leading off from the Lodge at Koele stables and tennis courts. The route passes through old pineapple fields now converted to cattle grazing. The road eventually comes to the Kanepu`u Forest Reserve, an area of rare native Hawaiian plants and dryland forest maintained by The Nature Conservancy of

Hawai`i. There are some 48 native species found in the preserve, including the endangered Lana`i sandalwood, rare Hawaiian gardenia and local cousins of olive and persimmon. Just past the forest reserve, the road goes straight to enter the Garden of the Gods or branches left and downslope to remote Ka`ena Iki Point, site of Ka`ena Heiau, one of Lana`i's largest old Hawaiian temple ruins. As you enter the Garden of the Gods you pass a large stone entry marker sign. The area has numerous interesting rock formations and exposed colorful cliffsides that have been weathered and buffeted by the relentless winds scouring the area. It's a lunar-like landscape. The exposed hillsides and rock formations reveal the very earthy tones of red, rust, russet, yellow and brown. In the early morning or late afternoon sunlight, the place takes on an etheral presence, somewhat befitting its rather lofty name. From this area, the rough jeep trail heads downslope to Polihua Beach noted for its small beach and large sand dunes.

Honopu Bay, on the leeward west coast, is a rocky fishing ground frequented by local fishermen. It's subject to rough seas despite being on the lee side of the island. There is a seabird sanctuary here as well as the islets of Nanahoa. According to Hawaiian legend, they were once a man named Nanahoa and his wife, who were turned into stone pillars for violating a taboo (kapu).

Kaunolu Bay is on the southwestern tip of the island. This is the location of a deserted early Hawaiian village, once a thriving fishing community. Kaunolu is also the site of a heiau (temple) and place of refuge called "Halulu," which was still in use between 1778 and 1810. Official archaeological work may be underway in this area. If so, do not disturb any workings underway.

Keomoku Village is on the windward northeast coast of the island. Keomoku is marked by the presence of an old church along this isolated area of the island. The Maunalei Sugar Company in the 1890s began an extensive effort to raise sugar along the coast. However, the company failed. In the early 20th century, the Gay family utilized Keomoku as the coastal headquarters for their cattle and sheep ranch. But by 1954 all ranch operations had ceased and the remaining Keomoku population moved up to Lana`i City.

**Lana`ihale,** a 3,370-foot overlook on the Munro Trail, means "House of Lana`i" in Hawaiian. This is the highest mountain peak on the island.

Luahiwa Petroglyphs are on the way to the Palawai Basin, central Lana`i. These early rock carvings and drawings are incribed on 34 boulders on a steep slope overlooking the Palawai Basin. The rock drawings are a mixture of ancient and historic styles. The petroglyphs are fragile and should not be disturbed or damaged in any way. Visit and enjoy them and leave them for those who follow.

East Coast Trail. From Highway 430 on the way to Shipwreck Beach, turn right to head south along the east coast. This rugged coastal 4x4 vehicle trail meanders some 13 miles along the coast past beaches, old village ruins, heiau (temples) and churches, fishponds and even an old Japanese cemetery at Halepalaoa Landing near Club Lana`i. Halepalaoa was the site of the wharf used for shipping sugarcane to Maui in the old days. The trail continues to Naha, site of an ancient fishpond seen clearly on the reef at low tide. No swimming here, as currents and surf can be very dangerous. The road ends at Naha and return is back the same way to Highway 430.

DID YOU KNOW?

Pu`upehe is a rock islet off the southwest point of Manele Bay. According to Hawaiian legend, a man named Makekehau hid his wife, Pehe, here in a sea cave where she later drowned in high surf. Makekehau, with the help of the gods, was able to scale the cliff with Pehe's body and bury her on the summit of this sea tower. Hence, the name Pu`upehe, "Pehe's hill" – or, as some refer to it, "Sweetheart Rock."

**The Lana`i Art Program,** PO Box 701, Lana`i City, HI 96763, ☎ 808/565-7503, is located on Seventh Street in Lana`i City just opposite Dole Park in the center of town. This is a cluster of four converted older buildings housing a gallery and studio space, pottery barn, woodworking shop and a photographic darkroom. The Lana`i Art Program offers ongoing fine arts and crafts classes in a wide range of mediums, including silk painting, watercolors, printmaking, ceramics, photography and woodworking, to name just a few. This is a haven for visitors seeking a different experience while on Lana`i. Explore and discover your hidden artistic talents while working in a totally different environment.

Lodging

Lana`i offers varied but limited lodging options, from a couple of bed and breakfasts to a moderate country-style hotel or a pair of luxury resort hotels. The rates below are for a standard double-occupancy room.

Accommodations Price Scale	
$	less than $100 per night
$$	$100-199 per night
$$$	$200-299 per night
$$$$	$300 and up per night

Bed & Breakfast Hawai`i-Lana`i, PO Box 449, Kapa`a, HI 96746, ☎ 800/733-1632, 808/822-7771; e-mail bandb@aloha.net; www.planet-Hawaii.com/bandb. $

Dreams Come True, 547 Twelfth St., PO Box 525, Lana`i City, HI 96763, ☎ 800/566-6961, 808/565-6961; e-mail hunters@aloha.net; www.go-native.com/. This bed and breakfast operation is in an older

The Hotel Lana`i.

The Lodge at Koele.

home, five minutes walk from the center of Lana`i City. There is also a separate guest cottage. 4WD vehicle rental available. $

**Hotel Lana`i,** PO Box 520, Lana`i City, HI 96763, ☎ 808/565-7211. This is the old pineapple plantation executive clubhouse and dates from 1923. The 10 modest guest rooms have baths and are neat but simply furnished. Located in the cool upland center of town. $$

The Lodge at Koele, PO Box 310, Lana`i City, HI 96763, ☎ 800/321-4666, ☎ 808/565-7300. This is a 102-room luxury country lodge on the edge of Lana`i City. The cool upcountry location next to the golf course provides rustic charm, for a price. $$$$

The Manele Bay Hotel, PO Box 310, Lana`i City, HI 96763, ☎ 800/321-4666, 808/565-7700. This is a 250-room luxury beachside resort with a surrounding golf course and all resort amenities. $$$$

Hale O`Lana`i, 405 Lana`i Avenue, Lana`i City, HI 96763, ☎ 808/247-3637; e-mail hibeach@lava.net; www.hotspots.Hawaii.com/beachrent1.html. This is a private home listing service with vacation homes for rent. $$

Okamoto Realty, PO Box 552, Lana`i City, HI 96763, reservations, ☎ 808/565-7519. This rental agency has fully equipped vacation homes, cottages and executive residences for rent by day, week or month. Contact them for details.

Lana`i

Camping

The only campgrounds on Lana`i are at Hulopo`e Bay Beach Park on the southern coast. Camping permits are required in advance. Contact: **The Lana`i Company**, PO Box 310, Lana`i City, HI 96763, ☎ 808/565-8200.

Dining

Lana`i, being such a small island, offers only a handful of dining options. But there are interesting choices, from a surprisingly good local-style plate lunch to a resort dining room gourmet meal. The restaurant price ranges, as in the other island sections of this book are based on the average dinner meal, exclusive of tax, alcoholic beverages and desserts.

Dining Price Scale
$ . . . . under $10 per person
$$ . . . . $10-25 per person
$$$ . . . . $25 and up per person

Henry Clay's Rotisserie, in the Hotel Lana`i, Lana`i City, ☎ 808/565-6450. This is the old hotel's dining room and the menu features spit-roasted meats, seafood, fresh island fish, pasta specials, pizza and more. $$

Blue Ginger Café, 409 Seventh, Lana`i City, ☎ 808/565-6363. The menu here is plate lunches and dinner specials like pork adobo, fried fish, sweet/sour shrimp, teri beef and chicken, chicken enchiladas, burgers, sandwiches and daily fresh baked pastries. Good food in simple surroundings. $

Tanigawa's, 407 Seventh, Lana`i City, ☎ 808/565-6537. The menu at this simple country café features saimin, won ton, beef stew, teri beef and chicken, sandwiches and other local favorites. $

Pele's Other Garden, 811 Houston, Lana`i City, ☎ 808/565-9628. The fast food menu at this small eatery features snack items like sandwiches, burgers, pizza and more. $

**Lana`i City Service Snack Shop,** 1036 Lana`i Avenue, Lana`i City, ☎ 808/565-7227. This snack counter offers breakfast and lunch items like omelettes, fried rice, sandwiches and burgers. $

The Formal Dining Room, Lodge at Koele, Lana`i City, ☎ 808/565-7300. American cuisine accented with Hawaiian produce. Entrées include lamb shank with polenta, roast chicken and bean stew, grilled mahimahi and other creative fare. $$$

The Terrace, Lodge at Koele, Lana`i City, ☎ 808/565-7300. American country cooking using local Hawai`i produce. $$$

**Hulopo`e Court,** The Manele Bay Hotel, ☎ 808/565-7700. This lovely dining room with dramatic ocean views offers innovative Hawai`i Regional Cuisine using local Hawaiian produce. $$$

Ihilani, The Manele Bay Hotel, ☎ 808/565-7700. This elegant resort dining room features French Mediterranean cuisine. It's one of the few resort dining rooms remaining in Hawai`i where dinner jackets for men are recommended. $$$

Lana`i

Maui
The Valley Isle

Geography

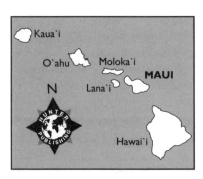

Maui, the Valley Isle, has a land mass area of 728.8 square miles and is the second largest of the Hawaiian Islands. It has a population of about 104,000. The County of Maui is comprised of the Islands of Maui, Lana`i, Moloka`i and the uninhabited Island of Koho`olawe. The county seat of Maui is Wailuku. Two volcanoes rose from the sea to form Maui. Mauna Kahalawai, the area known as West Maui, is the oldest. Its highest point is 5,788-foot Pu`u Kukui. The dominating dormant volcano of Mt. Haleakala makes up the entire southeast portion of the island and rises 10,023 feet above the sea. The island has some 120 miles of coastline ranging from rocky seacliffs to lava fields and long stretches of golden beaches. The age of the island, based on comparison of its structural lava flows, ranges from 800,000 to 1.3 million years.

Climate

Average temperatures range from 71-77° in most areas. Rainfall varies with the different sectors and elevations of the island. The winter, from November to March, brings heavier rains and cooler temperatures overall.

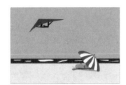

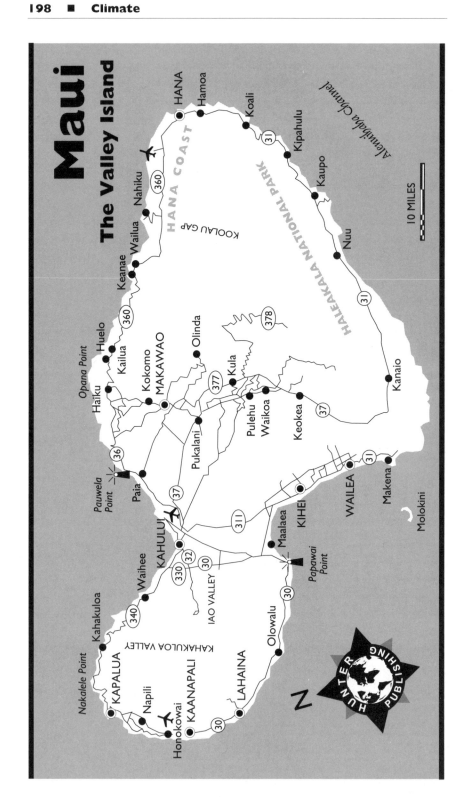

Maui
The Valley Island

HANA
Hamoa
Koali
Kipahulu
Kaupo
Nuu
Kanaio

HANA COAST
KOOLAU GAP
HALEAKALA NATIONAL PARK

Alenuihaha Channel

10 MILES

31

HANA

360

Nahiku
Wailua
Keanae

360
Huelo
Haiku
Opana Point
Kailua
Kokomo
MAKAWAO
Olinda

378

377
Kula
Pulehu
Waikoa
Keokea
37

Pukalani

31
WAILEA
Makena
Molokini

311
Maalaea
KIHEI

Papawai
Point

36
Pauwela
Point
Paia

37

KAHULUI
Waihee
32
330
30
IAO VALLEY

340
Kahakuloa
Nakalele Point
KAPALUA
Napili
KAANAPALI
Honokowai
LAHAINA
30
Olowalu
30

KAHAKULOA VALLEY

N

HUNTER PUBLISHING

History

Maui was probably first settled by the Polynesians between 500 and 1000 AD. It was an autonomous kingdom for generations. Its people lived the traditional Hawaiian communal lifestyle and were controlled by the ruling ali`i (kings and chiefs). Kamehameha the Great of the Island of Hawai`i invaded Maui and subdued the forces of King Kalanikupule in 1795 at the bloody battle of Iao Valley. This was Kamehameha's first step in his goal to conquer all the islands. He later conquered Moloka`i and O`ahu in battle and, in 1810, Kaua`i acceded to his rule, thus uniting all the islands under one kingdom. Kamehameha later made Lahaina the capital of the Hawaiian Kingdom.

American missionaries and whaling seamen arrived on Maui after 1820. Maui was soon caught up in a struggle between these opposing forces. Both sides had considerable impact on the social and moral fabric of the community. The end of the whaling era came with the discovery of oil in Pennsylvania in 1859. But the sugarcane and pineapple industries continued to grow on Maui and with this growth came a demand for cheap contract labor, imported mostly from Asia. By the late 1800s, there were numerous Chinese, Japanese, Filipinos and others working on Maui's plantations. The island evolved through the 1900s into a peaceful, rural, agricultural area of great charm and rustic beauty. It was only after World War II, statehood and the development of the modern tourism industry that Maui became widely known as a top visitor destination.

Information Sources

Maui Visitors Bureau, 1727 Wili Pa Loop, Wailuku, HI 96793, ☎ 800/525-MAUI, 808/244-3530; www.visit.Hawaii.org/.

Ka`anapali Beach Resort Association, 2530 Kekaa Drive, Lahaina, HI 96761, ☎ 800/245-9229, 808/661-3271.

Kapalua Resort, 800 Kapalua Drive, Kapalua, HI 96761, ☎ 800/KA-PALUA, ☎ 808/669-0244; www.kapaluamaui.com.

Wailea Destination Association, 3750 Wailea Alanui, Kihei, HI 96753, ☎ 800/78-ALOHA, 808/879-4258.

Information Office, County of Maui, 200 High Street, Wailuku, HI 96793, ☎ 808/243-7587.

Department of Parks and Recreation, Camping Permits, County of Maui, 1580-C Ka`ahumanu Avenue, Wailuku, HI 96793, ☎ 808/243-7230.

Department of Land and Natural Resources, Division of State Parks-Camping Permits, 54 S. High Street, Room 101, Wailuku, HI 96793, ☎ 808/984-8109.

Haleakala National Park, Camping Permits/Information, PO Box 369, Makawao, HI 96768, ☎ 808/572-9306.

Maui Chamber of Commerce, 250 Alamaha, Suite N16A, Kahului, HI 96732, ☎ 808/871-7711.

Maui Net, www.maui.net/. Web page covering Maui for the visitor; details and links to other sites.

National Weather Service, daily forecasts for Maui, ☎ 808/877-5111; marine forecast, ☎ 808/877-3477; recreational areas of Maui, ☎ 808/871-5054.

References

Alford, John. *Mountain Biking the Hawaiian Islands: Mauka to Makai,* Ohana Publishing, Honolulu, HI. 1997.

Carter, Frances. *Hawai`i on Foot,* Bess Press, Inc., Honolulu, HI. 1990.

Clark, John. *Beaches of Maui County,* University of Hawai`i Press, Honolulu, HI. 1994.

Early, Dona, and Stilson, Christie. *Maui and Lana`i: A Paradise Family Guide,* Prima Publishing, Rocklin, CA. 1996.

Koch, Tom. *Six Islands on Two Wheels,* Bess Press, Honolulu, HI. 1990.

Morey, Kathy. *Maui Trails: Walks, Strolls and Treks on the Valley Isle,* Wilderness Press, Berkeley, CA. 1996.

Olsen, Brad. *Extreme Adventures Hawai`i,* Hunter Publishing, Edison, NJ. 1998.

Smith, Robert. *Hiking Maui, The Valley Isle,* Hawaiian Outdoor Adventures Publications, Maui, HI. 1997.

Stone, Robert. *Day Hikes on Maui,* Day Hike Books, Red Lodge, MT. 1997.

Smith, Rodney. *Hawai`i: A Walker's Guide,* Hunter Publishing, Edison, NJ. 1997.

Zurick, David. *Hawai`i, Naturally,* Wilderness Press, Berkeley, CA. 1990.

Getting There

■ Inter-Island Air Service

These airlines provide numerous daily scheduled flights between Maui, Honolulu and other destinations in the Hawaiian Islands. Flights operate from Kahului Airport, as well as Hana Airport and West Maui's Kapalua Airport.

- **Aloha Airlines,** US, ☎ 800/367-5250, Canada, ☎ 800/235-0936, on Maui, ☎ 808/244-9071; e-mail aloha@alohaair.com; www.alohaair.com/.

- **Island Air,** US, ☎ 800/323-3345, Canada, ☎ 800/235-0936, within Hawai`i, ☎ 800/652-6541; e-mail aloha@alohaair.com; www.alohaair.com/. This subsidiary of Aloha Airlines operates shuttle flights to Kahului, Hana and Kapalua Airports from Honolulu and other points in Hawai`i.

■ **Hawaiian Airlines,** US and Canada, ☎ 800/367-5320, on Maui, ☎ 808/871-6132; www.Hawaiianair.com/.

■ US Mainland & Maui

These airlines operate regularly scheduled and special seasonal flights between Maui's Kahalui Airport and the US mainland. Some airlines also operate flights to Honolulu with connecting inter-island flights to Maui.

■ **Hawaiian Airlines,** US and Canada, ☎ 800/367-5320, on Maui, ☎ 808/871-6132; www.Hawaiianair.com.

■ **American Airlines,** US and Canada, ☎ 800/433-7300, on Maui, ☎ 808/244-5522; www.americanair.com/.

■ **Delta Airlines,** US, ☎ 800/221-1212; delta-air.com/.

■ **America West Airlines,** US, ☎ 800/235-9292; www.americawest.com/.

■ **United Airlines,** US, ☎ 800/241-6522; www.ual.com.

■ **Pleasant Hawaiian Holidays,** US, ☎ 800/242-9244, on Maui, ☎ 808/879-4467 or 661-9318; www.pleasantholidays.com. This tour operator specializes in air/room packages and regularly scheduled flights direct to Maui or via Honolulu.

■ Cruise Ships

The last few years have seen an increase in international cruise ships making port calls in the Hawaiian Islands. So, once again, it is possible to sail to the islands on a luxurious ocean liner. Several cruise lines now regularly route their ships on a seasonal basis into Honolulu as well as the neighbor islands of Kaua`i, Maui and the Big Island of Hawai`i at Kona and Hilo. Schedules vary, as do itineraries. For details, it is recommended that you check with a travel agent or cruise tour reservation specialist.

Among the ships that have made Hawai`i port calls on regular sailings recently from North America and other points are: **Princess Cruise Lines'** *Island Princess, Sea Princess* and *Golden Princess* (☎ 800-PRINCESS/774-6237); **Royal Viking Lines'** *Sagafjord* and *Royal Vi-*

king Sun (☎ 800-426-0821); **Holland America Lines'** *Statendam, Rotterdam* and *Maasdam* (☎ 800-426-0327); **Cunard Lines'** *Queen Elizabeth II* (☎ 800-221-4770); **Royal Caribbean Lines'** *Legend of the Seas* (☎ 800-327-6700); and **Carnival Cruise Lines'** *MS Tropicale* (☎ 800-327-9501).

In addition, within the Hawaiian Islands, American Hawai`i Cruises offers exclusive inter-island cruises between Honolulu and the neighbor islands aboard the *SS Independence*. There are three-day and week-long packages. The ship spends a day in each port at Kaua`i, Maui and the Big Island's Kona and Hilo. There are shore excursions and tours available from dockside at each port. For details and information, contact your travel agent or: **American Hawai`i Cruises**, 550 Kearny St., San Francisco, CA 94108, ☎ 800/765-7000.

Getting Around

Most inter-island flights arrive at Kahului Airport, some arrive at West Maui's Kapalua Airport and others at Hana Airport on the east coast. From Kahului Airport to West Maui's resorts it is 27 miles to Lahaina, 28 miles to Ka`anapali Resort, 37 miles to the Napili area and 38 miles to Kapalua Resort, all via the Honoapiilani Highway 30, which follows the coastline of West Maui from Ma`alaea. From Kahului Airport to the South Maui resorts, it is 13 miles to Ma`alaea via the Kuihelani Highway 380. It's nine miles to Kihei, 12 miles to the Wailea area, and 19 miles to Makena Resort via the Mokulele Highway #311. If you're heading upcountry from Kahului Airport, it is 10 miles to Pukalani and about 15 miles to the Kula area via the Haleakala Highway #37. If you're heading further east to the Hana area, it is a slow, winding 53-mile drive to Hana via the Hana Highway #36. The drive will take you two-three hours. The Hana Airport is very near to Hana town.

You'll find Maui's highway system generally in excellent condition. However, expect traffic to be heavy on this small island. Because Maui is such a popular visitor destination year-round, all roads tend to be busy. Be aware of heavy trucks and tour buses as well. As on the other

Maui

islands, it is difficult to get lost. Heading in most directions, there is only one main road which usually follows the coast, either to West Maui, South Maui, East Maui, or upcountry to Haleakala and the mountain communities.

> With a good map – one from the car rental agency will do just fine – you'll be able to navigate your way around pretty well. A good map available at Maui bookstores and other shops is the latest edition of the full color topographic *Map of Maui* by James Bier, published by the University of Hawai`i Press.

■ Bus/Taxi Airport Transportation

There are several bus/taxi operators providing airport/hotel shuttle transportation from all of Maui's resort areas. Check with any of the companies below for information and reservations; it's best to make reservations as far in advance as possible.

- **A Sun Transportation,** PO Box 1094, Kihei, HI 96753, ☎ 808/879-1610.

- **Airport Shuttle,** 70 Kapunakea St., Lahaina, HI 96761, ☎ 808/661-6667.

- **Airport Taxi,** Kahului, ☎ 808/877-0907.

- **Airporter Shuttle,** Kahului, ☎ 808/871-7595.

- **Alanui Cab,** Kihei, ☎ 808/874-4895.

- **Kapalua Executive Transportation Services,** Kapalua, ☎ 808/669-2300.

- **Lei-Aloha Shuttle & Tours,** Kihei, ☎ 808/879-6001.

- **Makena-Kihei Taxi,** PO Box 1469, Kihei, HI 96753, ☎ 808/879-3000.

- **Speedi Shuttle,** Kihei, ☎ 808/875-8070.

- **Super Shuttle,** Kapalua, ☎ 808/669-2300.

- **Yellow Cab of Maui,** PO Box 1637, Kihei, HI 96753, ☎ 808/877-7000.

- **Roberts Hawai`i Tours,** ☎ 800/831-5541, on Maui, ☎ 808/871-6226.

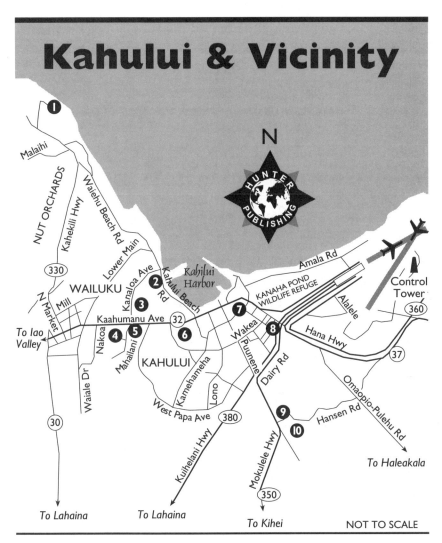

Kahului & Vicinity

N

To Iao Valley

To Lahaina

To Lahaina

To Kihei

To Haleakala

NOT TO SCALE

1. Waiehu Golf Course
2. Maui Arts & Cultural Center
3. Maui Zoo
4. Maui Memorial Hospital
5. Police
6. Kaahumanu Shopping Center
7. Maui Mall
8. Maui Coffee Roasters
9. A & B Sugar Museum
10. Puunene Sugar Mill

Maui

▪ Limousine Service

Maui has several limousine services providing airport shuttles, custom-designed tours, golf outings, restaurant and night club packages, scenic excursions and more. They have a range of deluxe limousines ranging from Cadillacs to super stretch Lincolns and luxury vans. If you'd like to have a private limo adventure on Maui, any of the following can provide all the information necessary.

- **Arthur's Limousine Service,** 283 Lalo, Kahului, HI 96732, ☎ 808/871-5555.

- **Bob & Sons Limousine Service,** PO Box 6143, Kahului, HI 96732, ☎ 808/877-7800.

- **Coastline Limousine,** Makawao, Maui, ☎ 808/572-1152.

- **Esquire Limousine Service,** PO Box 1094, Kihei, HI 96753, ☎ 808/879-1610.

- **Kapalua Executive Limousine,** Kapalua, Maui, ☎ 808/669-2300.

- **Limousines Hawai`i,** Kihei, Maui, ☎ 808/874-5466.

- **Rocky's Limousine Service,** 87 S. Puunene Avenue, Kahului, HI 96732, ☎ 808/877-7511.

- **Star Maui Limousine,** Kihei, Maui, ☎ 808/875-6900.

- **Town & Country Limousine Service,** Makawao, Maui, ☎ 808/572-3400.

- **Wailea Limousine Service,** Kihei/Wailea, Maui, ☎ 808/875-4114, West Maui, ☎ 808/661-4114; e-mail ylealimo@maui.net

■ Car & Truck Rentals

Having your own rental car on Maui will give you freedom and flexibility to plan your own adventure schedule. Maui has all the major national car rental agencies and a few local ones. Those agencies with outlets at Kahului Airport include Alamo, Andres Rent a Car, Avis, Budget, Dollar, Hertz, National, Regency; some agencies have additional counters at hotels around Maui.

- **AA Aloha Cars R Us,** ☎ 800/655-7989, 938 S. Kihei Road, Kihei, ☎ 808/879-7989.

- **AA Paradise Network,** ☎ 800/942-2242, on Maui, ☎ 808/579-8277.

- **AA Rent A Dent,** 1135 Makawao Avenue, Makawao, ☎ 808/573-1722.

- **Adventures Rent a Jeep,** 190 Papa Place, Kahului, ☎ 808/877-6626; superpages.gte.net.

- **Alamo Rent a Car,** ☎ 800/327-9633, on Maui ☎ 808/871-6235.

- **Andres Rent a Car,** Kahului Airport, ☎ 808/877-5378.

- **Avis Rent a Car,** ☎ 800/321-3712, on Maui, ☎ 808/871-7575.

- **Budget Rent a Car,** ☎ 800/527-0700, on Maui, ☎ 808/244-4721.

- **Dollar Rent a Car,** ☎ 800/800-4000, on Maui, ☎ 808/877-6526.

- **Enterprise Rent a Car,** ☎ 800/325-8007, on Maui at 335 East Wakea Avenue, Kahului, ☎ 808/871-1511.

- **Ferrari Rentals II,** 70 Kapunakea, Lahaina, ☎ 808/667-2277. Cruise Maui in a Ferrari or other exotic car.

- **Hertz Rent a Car,** ☎ 800/654-3011, on Maui, ☎ 808/877-5167.

- **Island Riders Inc.,** 126 Hinau St., Lahaina, ☎ 808/661-9966; 1794 S. Kihei Road, Kihei, ☎ 808/874-0311. Cruise the sights in a Ferrari, Viper, Porsche, Cobra, Corvette, BMW or other exotic car.

- **Kihei Rent a Car,** 1819 S. Kihei Road, Kihei, ☎ 808/879-7257; e-mail krac@maui.net; www.maui.net/~krac

- **Maui Windsurfing Vans,** 180 E. Wakea Avenue, Kahului, ☎ 808/877-0090; rent a van to carry your windsurfing boards and equipment.

- **National Car Rental,** ☎ 800/227-7368, on Maui, ☎ 808/871-8851.

- **Regency Rent a Car,** located at Kahalui Airport, ☎ 808/871-6147.

- **Thrifty Car Rental,** ☎ 800/367-2277, on Maui at 542 Keolani Place, Kahului, ☎ 808/871-2860.

- **The Toy Store,** 70 Kapunakea St., Lahaina, ☎ 808/661-1212. Drive away in a Ferrari, Viper, Corvette, Lamborghini, Porsche, Miata, Mercedes, Lotus, BMW or other exotic.

Maui

- **Wheels R Us,** 150 Lahainaluna Road, Lahaina, ☎ 808/667-7751.

- **Word of Mouth Rent a Used Car,** 150 Hana Highway, Kahului, ☎ 808/877-2436.

■ Motorcycle & Moped Rentals

If your idea of an adventure on Maui is riding a Harley Hogg or a modest moped, any of the following motorcycle-moped rental shops can get you on wheels and on the road in no time. Just give them a call.

- **A & B Moped Rental,** 3481 Lower Honoapiilani Road, Napili, ☎ 808/669-0027.

- **Island Riders Inc.,** 126 Hinau St., Lahaina/Kahana, ☎ 808/661-9966, ☎ 1794 S. Kihei Road, Kihei/Wailea, ☎ 808/874-0311. They rent a full line of Harley-Davidsons, along with exotic cars.

- **Kukui Activity Center,** 1819 S. Kihei Road, Kihei, ☎ 808/875-1151. A full line of moped rentals.

- **Maui Island Dual Sport,** Napili/Kapalua, Maui, ☎ 808/669-7785; MDSPORT@maui.net. They rent Suzuki motorcycles by the day or week.

- **Mavrik Motorcycles Maui,** North Ka`anapali, Honoapiilani Highway at Halawai Drive, ☎ 808/661-3099; Kahului, Dairy Road at Alamaha Street next to Dairy Road Shell, ☎ 808/871-7118. Harley-Davidson rentals by the day or week.

- **The Toy Store,** 70 Kapunakea, Lahaina, ☎ 808/661-1212; e-mail toystore@maui.net; www.maui.net/-toystore. This operator has Harley-Davidsons and Kawasaki motorcycle rentals by the day or week.

- **Wheels R Us Inc.,** 75 Kaahumanu, Kahului, ☎ 808/871-6858; 150 Lahainaluna Road, Lahaina, ☎ 808/667-7751.

■ Bicycle Rentals

If you want to take the time to savor Maui's delights and beautiful scenery from the back of a bike, any of the following rental shops will be able to get you going in a hurry. Give them a call, grab your day pack and be on your way.

- **A & B Rentals,** 3481 Lower Honoapiilani Road, Napili, ☎ 808/669-0027.

- **Extreme Sports Maui,** 397 Dairy Road, Kahului, ☎ 808/871-7954.

- **Haleakala Bike Company,** 810 Haiku Road, Haiku, ☎ 808/572-2200.

- **Hawai`i Sail & Sport,** 101 N. Kihei Road, Kihei, ☎ 808/879-0178.

- **The Island Biker,** 415 Dairy Road, Kahului, ☎ 808/877-7744.

- **Kukui Activity Center,** 1819 S. Kihei Road, Kihei, ☎ 808/875-1151.

- **Snorkels N' More,** 3600 Lower Honoapiilani Road, Napili, ☎ 808/665-0804.

- **South Maui Bicycles,** 1993 S. Kihei Road, Kihei, ☎ 808/874-0068.

- **West Maui Cycles,** 193 Lahainaluna Road, Lahaina, ☎ 808/661-9005; 4310 Honoapiilani Road, Napili, ☎ 808/669-1169.

Touring Maui

Exploring and discovering the beauty, history and culture of Maui is an adventure by itself. And there are a number of fascinating ways to enjoy touring this beautiful island, with each area of the island having its own highlights and attractions.

■ Central Maui

Kahului Airport is just east of **Kahului** town, which is on the island's north-central shore, an isthmus connecting the larger mountain land-masses of east and West Maui. **Wailuku**, the county seat of Maui County, lies at the foot of the West Maui mountains just a couple of miles upslope from Kahului and the harbor front area. Kahului is a newer residential community with more development than its upslope neighbor. Kahului has shopping centers, service stations, supermarkets, fast food outlets, theaters and just about everything else. Wailuku has more

Upcountry Maui

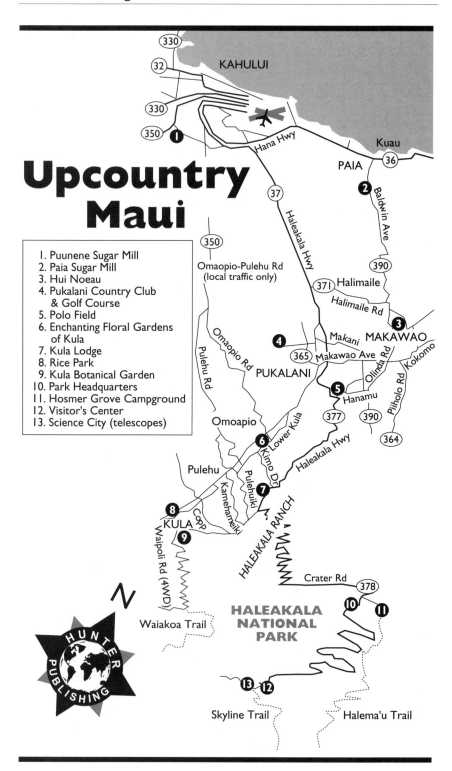

1. Puunene Sugar Mill
2. Paia Sugar Mill
3. Hui Noeau
4. Pukalani Country Club
   & Golf Course
5. Polo Field
6. Enchanting Floral Gardens
   of Kula
7. Kula Lodge
8. Rice Park
9. Kula Botanical Garden
10. Park Headquarters
11. Hosmer Grove Campground
12. Visitor's Center
13. Science City (telescopes)

KAHULUI

Kuau

PAIA

Hana Hwy

Omaopio-Pulehu Rd
(local traffic only)

Halimaile

Halimaile Rd

MAKAWAO

Makani

Makawao Ave

PUKALANI

Hanamu

Omaopio

Lower Kula

Kimo Dr

Pulehu

Kaneheameiki

Pulehuiki

KULA

Copp

Waipoli Rd (4WD)

HALEAKALA RANCH

Crater Rd

Waiakoa Trail

HALEAKALA NATIONAL PARK

Skyline Trail

Halema'u Trail

HUNTER PUBLISHING

of an air of a historic old plantation town with a number of older buildings. In fact, Wailuku had a working sugar mill right off Lower Main Street until it closed just a few years ago. Wailuku has filled in the gaps with a few trendy restaurants and specialty shops thrown in for good measure. Main Street above Wailuku passes by the historic **Ka`ahumanu Church** and **Bailey House Museum**, winding its way up the Iao Valley to **Kepaniwai Park Heritage Garden** and **Iao Valley State Park**. There are nature trails to stroll through lush green gulches surrounded by sheer cliffs and the famous **Iao Needle**. Just south of Wailuku at Waikapu is the **Maui Tropical Plantation and Country Store**. From Kahului and Wailuku, roads branch out in all directions, leading to East Maui and the Hana Highway, upcountry to Makawao, Kula and Haleakala, south to the Kihei, Wailea and Makena resorts, or west around the pali (cliffs) to West Maui's Lahaina, Ka`anapali, Napili, and Kapalua resorts.

■ Upcountry Maui

The **Haleakala Highway 37** runs from Kahului through the upcountry towns of Pukalani and Makawao and, as the Kula Highway, continues on through the beautiful farm and ranch country of Kula and Keokea on its way to Ulupalakua. The **Haleakala Highway 377** is a loop road branching off from #37 at Pukalani and reconnecting at Kula. It passes through rolling and sloping upcountry ranchlands. From #377, the **Haleakala Crater Road 378** branches off and winds upslope to the Haleakala summit. This road provides some grand views of the crater and the countryside of Central Maui and the West Maui mountains. The summit drive is suitable for standard rental cars. **Haleakala National Park** offers a number of crater sights, with sunrise views over the crater especially popular. There are also many short hikes and walks, day hikes and overnight backpacking adventures within the park. The "**Science City**" complex at the summit has a US Air Force satellite tracking station, a University of Hawai`i lunar and solar observatory and FAA facilities. Near the end of the Kula Highway 37, just past the Ulupalakua Ranch, is the **Tedeschi Winery**, which specializes in vintage pineapple and red wines. The road past Ulupalakua around the southern flank of Haleakala is narrow and rough – not recommended for standard rental cars. Other areas worth exploring are **Paia, Haiku** and **Makawao**, east of Kahului and below Pukalani. These old plantation towns have interesting shops and restaurants – plus the drive through backcountry Maui's pineapple plantations is an experience many visitors miss.

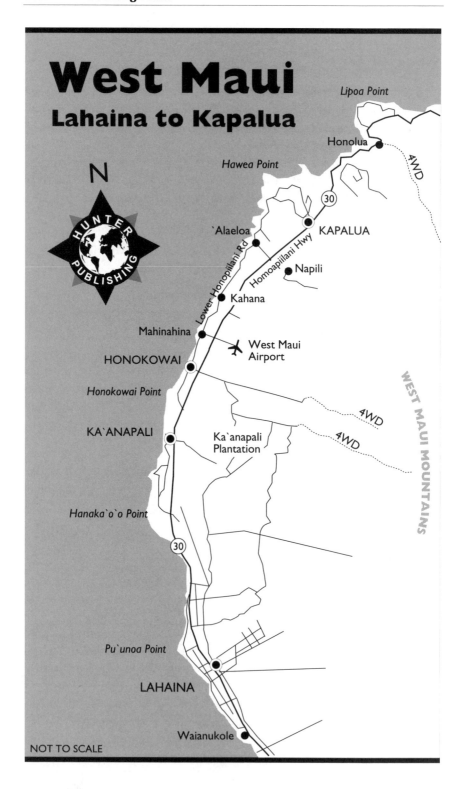

Lahaina

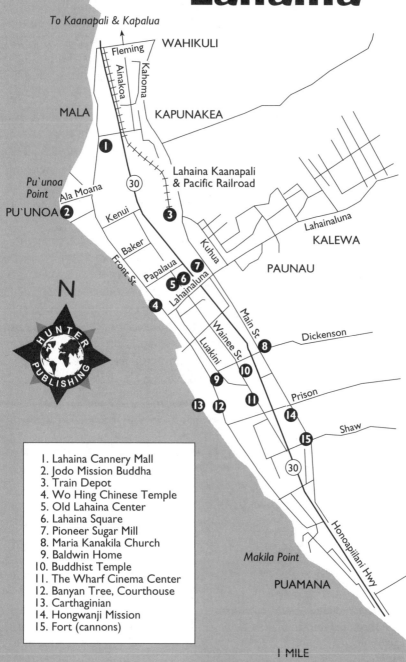

To Kaanapali & Kapalua

WAHIKULI

Fleming

Ainakoa

Kahoma

MALA

KAPUNAKEA

Pu`unoa Point

Ala Moana

PU`UNOA ②

Kenui

30

Lahaina Kaanapali & Pacific Railroad

③

Lahainaluna

KALEWA

Baker

Front St

Papalaua

Kuhua

PAUNAU

N

⑦

⑤ ⑥

④ Lahainaluna

Wainee St

Main St

Luakini

Dickenson

⑧

⑨

⑩

⑪

Prison

⑬ ⑫

⑭

Shaw

⑮

30

Makila Point

Honoapiilani Hwy

PUAMANA

① Lahaina Cannery Mall
2. Jodo Mission Buddha
3. Train Depot
4. Wo Hing Chinese Temple
5. Old Lahaina Center
6. Lahaina Square
7. Pioneer Sugar Mill
8. Maria Kanakila Church
9. Baldwin Home
10. Buddhist Temple
11. The Wharf Cinema Center
12. Banyan Tree, Courthouse
13. Carthaginian
14. Hongwanji Mission
15. Fort (cannons)

Maui

1 MILE

■ West Maui

The **Honoapi`ilani Highway 30** runs from Wailuku and Ma`alaea around the pali (cliffs) to West Maui's resorts of **Lahaina, Ka`anapali, Honokowai, Napili** and **Kapalua**. The road continues past Kapalua to **Honokohau** and **Kahakuloa**, following a rugged coastline and equally rough backcountry road returning to Wailuku. This last section of the road is usually off-limits to standard rental cars but is suitable for 4WD vehicles.

It is possible to do a loop drive around West Maui. Maui's modern resort industry began at **Ka`anapali Beach**. This was the island's first comprehensive planned resort community and it is still a wonderful place to vacation. Beaches, condos, hotels, golf courses, tennis courts, swimming pools, shopping, restaurants, and more make up the corridor and coast of West Maui from Lahaina to Kapalua. The center of all this is **Lahaina**, the old whaling port and early capital of the Hawaiian Islands. The town, nestled along Front Street and the harbor area is a historic place with a number of attractions dating from the early 1800s – its whaling and early missionary heyday. This is where some of the first Christian missionaries from America took up residence, converting the Hawaiians and battling the wretched whaling seamen who wallowed in drink and debauchery when in port at Lahaina. The whaling and nautical theme is still evident everywhere in town. The Lahaina Harbor is still busy with visitors shuttling back and forth across the Au`au Channel to Lana`i, while others embark on fishing charters or go for a sail.

Fields of sugarcane and pineapple cover the lower slopes of the West Maui mountains, adding a rural charm to a modern resort community spread out along its entire coastal length. Railroad buffs will enjoy the sugarcane train ride from Lahaina through the backside of the Ka`anapali resort area. The **Lahaina-Ka`anapali & Pacific Railroad** steam trains used to haul cane to the mill in an earlier era, but now take visitors on fun rides through the countryside.

■ East Maui

The **Hana Highway 36 heads east from Kahului through the coastal town of Pa`ia. The highway has been rated one of the most scenic highways in America by publications over the years. The drive along the rugged coast through the lush rain forest is slow, but it's certainly worthwhile. The distance from Kahului to Hana is only 53 miles, but allow two-three hours to give yourself time to enjoy the sights. There are

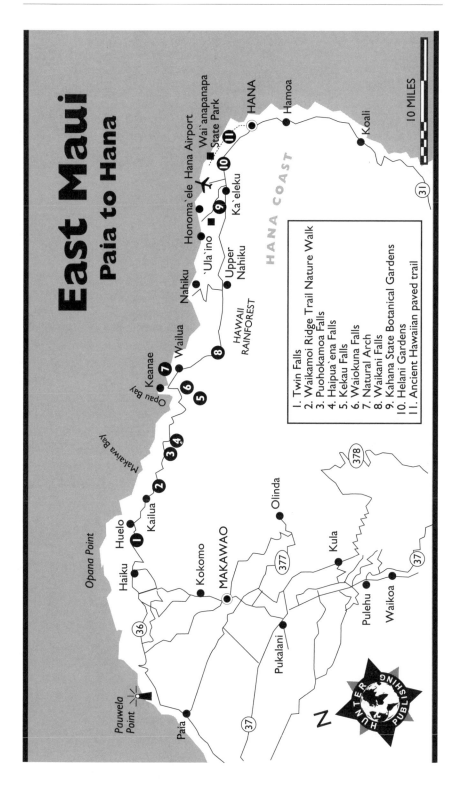

East Maui
Paia to Hana

1. Twin Falls
2. Waikamoi Ridge Trail Nature Walk
3. Puohokamoa Falls
4. Haipua`ena Falls
5. Kekau Falls
6. Waiokuna Falls
7. Natural Arch
8. Waikani Falls
9. Kahana State Botanical Gardens
10. Helani Gardens
11. Ancient Hawaiian paved trail

HANA COAST

HAWAII RAINFOREST

Maui

To Kahului Airport

MAALAEA (30)   Kealia Pond   (350)

Honoapiilani Hwy

To Lahaina

North Kihei Road   *Mokulele Hwy*

(31)

South Maui

Uwapo St

Maalaea to Makena

Ohukai

Waipuilani

East Lipoa

Welakahau

N

KIHEI

South Kihei Rd →   *Kanakanui*

Maui Vista   *Kauhale*   *Piilani Hwy*

Maui Hill   *Kapiliii*   (31)

Wailea Ekahi   *Kalaiwaa*   *Mapu*

Wailea Point   WAILEA
Polo Beach   *Wailea Ekolu*

Old Makena Rd   *Wailea Alanui Dr*   MAKENA

NOT TO SCALE

Ulua Beach, Wailea, South Maui.

56 bridges to cross and too many winding turns to count on this road. The best thing to do would be to allow a full day to enjoy a picnic and attractions in the Hana area. Better yet, plan an overnight stay or longer. Plan to stop at such places as the **Waikamoi Ridge Trail Nature Walk, Kaumahina State Wayside Park, Wailua Valley Lookout** over the taro fields, the village of **Keanae, Hana Town** and **Hana Bay**, the famous **Hasegawa General Store, Wai`anapanapa State Park, Oheo Gulch** and its **Seven Pools**, and **Charles Lindbergh's Grave at Palapala Ho`omau Church** at Kipahulu.

■ South Maui

The **Mokulele Highway 35** heads south out of Kahului through the old sugar town of Pu`unene and past the old mill. It continues across the isthmus of Central Maui to **Ma`alaea Bay**, where it follows the coast south through the resorts of **Kihei, Wailea** and **Makena**. Somewhat like the resorts of West Maui, this South Maui area is one long corridor of vacation condos, hotels, golf courses, tennis courts, shopping centers, service stations, supermarkets, restaurants of all kinds and much more. There are some terrific beaches all along this coast and many nice parks to enjoy. If your sort of adventure is settling into a comfortable condo or hotel with all the amenities and first-class service, you'll certainly find it in South Maui.

Maui

■ Land Tours/Operators

The following operators offer a variety of half-day and full-day coach and van tours to all of Maui's major attractions, including beaches, historic Lahaina town, shopping, upcountry Kula and Makawao, Haleakala and the ranch country, pineapple fields, East Maui and Hana and more. Contact operators directly for details. Standard Haleakala sunrise tour is $50 per person. Full-day tours to Haleakala and Central Maui historic and cultural sites is $55 per person. Full-day tours to Hana and East Maui areas range from $45 to $100 per person (deluxe tour includes lunch and snacks).

Polynesian Adventure Tours, 400H Hana Highway, Kahului, HI 96732, ☎ 808/877-4242. Offers a variety of half-day and full-day tours to Maui's major sights and attractions, including Haleakala sunrise tours, Iao Valley and Central Maui, the Hana Coast and rain forest.

Akina Aloha Tours, PO Box 933, Kihei, HI 96753, ☎ 808/879-2828. A range of custom tours to all of Maui's major sights and attractions.

Roberts Hawai`i Tours, ☎ 800/831-5541, on Maui ☎ 808/871-6226. Half-day and full-day tours to Maui's major sights and attractions.

Ekahi Tours, 532 Keolani Place, Kahului, HI 96732, ☎ 808/877-9775. Mini-van tours to all of Maui's major attractions.

Temptations Tours, Kula, Maui, ☎ 808/877-8888. Luxury limo-van tours for small groups of six-eight to Maui's top attractions.

Trans Hawaiian Maui, Kaonawai Place, Kahului, HI 96732, ☎ 808/877-7308. Coach and van tours to all of Maui's top attractions.

Adventures

Maui's Best Adventures

Maui offers challenging adventures that will make your visit a memorable experience. Following are the top dozen adventures.

- Take the downhill bike cruise on Haleakala after viewing the sunrise over the crater.

- Drive and picnic along the scenic **Hana Highway**.
- Hike the **Manienie Ridge Trail** above Kapalua in West Maui.
- Take a snorkel cruise to **Molokini Island marine preserve**.
- Do the **Waikamoi Ridge hike** in East Maui.
- Take a **sailboat ride or fishing charter** from Lahaina.
- Do a self-guided walking tour of **historic Lahaina town**.
- Walk through **Iao Valley Park** to the **Iao Needle** lookout.
- Bike or take a 4WD ride on the scenic **Honokohau Road** from Kapalua to Wailuku.
- Do the **summit road drive to Haleakala**.
- Hike any of the several high-country forest trails at **Poli Poli Springs State Park** above Kula.
- Visit **Hosmer Grove Park** at Haleakala National Park and take the nature trail hike.

■ On Foot

Maui has many hiking trails through the ecosystems of the island. Trails are located in state forest reserves and parks, county parks and national parks. You can hike on your own or take one of the guided hikes with an outfitter listed below.

Central Maui

Iao Valley is an easy 1½-mile nature walk that allows hikers to experience the dark, cool environment of a lowland Hawaiian rain forest while following trails beneath a canopy of towering kukui (candlenut) trees. Learn about Hawaiian plants and natural history of the area. Hikes are for young and old alike; walking shoes and rain gear recommended. Guided hikes are conducted through Iao Valley by Hawai`i Nature Center of Maui, 875 Iao Valley Road at the gate to Iao Valley State Park, ☎ 808/244-6500.

Waihee Ridge Trail. From Wailuku, take the Kahekili Highway 33 through the town of Waihee to three miles beyond. Turn left at a sign for Camp Maluhia, Boy Scouts of America. Up the road about .8 mile take a sharp right. Then on the left is the trailhead and gate. Hikers head .2

mile uphill through a pasture to the Forest Reserve boundary gate and the beginning of the ridge trail. The trail is 2½ miles long and follows the ridge crest to 2,600 feet elevation. There are numerous vantage points along the way with nice views of the coastline, Wailuku, Waihee Stream and valley, as well as verdant slopes and cliffs of the surrounding mountains. Many native plants are seen along this trail. Hikers should have good shoes for muddy trails, and bring water and food.

South Maui

Hoapili Trail. A jeep or pickup is best for this rough road. Take the Kihei Highway 31 just past Makena State Park where pavement ends and dirt road continues to Makena village. Another five miles of rough road goes through Ahihi-Kinau Natural Area Reserve at La Perouse Bay. The trail follows Maui's southern coastline from La Perouse Bay east 5½ miles to Kanaio Beach.

DID YOU KNOW?

The Hoapili Trail is the old Hawaiian "King's Highway" and runs through barren, rough and very dry lava flows. The trail follows a path of smooth stepping stones laid out in ancient times so that the kings and their retinues could travel around the island to collect taxes and tribute from the people in outlying districts.

The vegetation is sparse, consisting mostly of scattered kiawe trees and other hardy dryland plants. There are a number of secluded coves and small pocket beaches along the coastline here. The trail eventually turns inland and ends at a small cove where the old King's Highway leaves protected state land.

Upcountry Maui

Kula & Kahikinui Forest Reserve Trails. Access to these trails is via Highway 37 to the second junction with Highway 377, just before the 14-mile marker. Turn left on #377 for .3 mile, then right onto Waipoli Road, which becomes Polipoli Road as it climbs through cattle pastures and mountain terrain to enter the forest reserve at the 6,400-foot level. The paved road narrows and becomes a dirt road with some rough spots. The trail system begins at road's end at **Polipoli State Park,** 6,200 feet elevation.

There are 10 trails to choose from, all offering routes through the forest reserve, with varied terrain and scenic mountain and valley views. **Redwood Trail** is 1.7 miles; **Tie Trail** is a short .5 mile; **Plum Trail** is 1.7 miles, passing through ash and redwood forest and lots of plum fruit trees along the way; **Haleakala Ridge Trail** is 1.6 miles through alternating rough lava cinders, scrub brush, grassy swales, and pine forest; **Polipoli Trail** is .6 mile, traversing dense stands of cypress, cedars and pines; **Boundary Trail** is four miles, with lots of switchbacks through gulches, native forest and planted pine and cedar forest; **Waiohuli Trail** is 1.4 miles through young pine forest and open scrub and grasslands; **Upper Waiakoa Trail** is seven miles through scrub vegetation and increasingly barren rocky lands; **Waiakoa Loop Trail** is three miles and passes through native scrub and grasslands with some pine forest and nice views in all directions; **Skyline Trail** is 6½ miles of barren, rugged terrain, with several cinder cones and craters along the way and vegetation almost non-existent.

Haleakala National Park has several interesting hikes, including some down into Haleakala Crater. These hikes are accessible via Haleakala Highway 378, a winding road leading to the 10,023-foot summit. **Leleiwi Overlook** is an easy .25-mile walk with views down into Haleakala Crater and good vantage points for panoramic photography. **White Hill** is an easy .5-mile rocky trail to the top of a volcanic cin-

Haleakala Crater.

The East Maui coast, near Hana.

der cone, with good views of surrounding volcanic landscape. **Halemau`u to Valley Rim** is a moderate 2.2-mile hike allowing hikers to experience several ecosystems while hiking through native shrubland to a tradewind-exposed cliff overlooking the high cloud forest below. **Hosmer Grove Nature Trail** is an easy .5-mile nature walk loop. Trails are in good condition, passing through dense forest and open grass and shrublands. Trees and plants are marked. **Sliding Sands Trail** is an easy hike with panoramic views of cinder cones and lava flows for .7 mile, allowing hikers to feel the solitude and quiet of the crater. Continuing on the same trail to Ka Lu`u o ka O`o, a distance of five miles, provides images of the multi-colored cinder cones, ever-changing clouds and rare silversword plants of this unique crater ecosystem. This is a moderate half-day hike. **Halemau`u to Silversword Loop** is a full-day hike of 10 miles. Hikers journey through shrubland, down steep switchbacks and across a rough lava flow on the crater floor to a field of silversword plants. **Sliding Sands to Halemau`u Trailhead** is another full day hike of 11 miles. Hikers traverse the crater floor and see the many moods of Haleakala as it changes during the day. An additional hiking challenge is the **Kaupo Gap Trail**, which leads on east out of the crater and downslope through upland forest to the village of Kaupo on the east coast. This trail of seveneight miles would require a ride arranged to meet you at Kaupo. Permits are required to camp overnight in Haleakala. Three hikers' cabins, Kapalaoa, Holua, and Paliku, are available by reservation. Contact: **Haleakala National Park**, PO Box 369, Makawao, HI 96768, ☎ 808/572-9306.

East Maui

DON'T

MISS

Waikamoi Ridge Trail. On Hana Highway 360, drive 3½ miles past Kailua Village going west toward Keanae. Look for a parking area with picnic shelters above the road. This .8-mile nature trail climbs a forested slope to a lookout and picnic site. The trail passes through lush forest of bamboo, native species and planted trees. A return loop follows the ridge to an overlook and then back to the start. The trail is in good condition but can be muddy and slippery.

Kaeleku Ulaino Road. On the Hana Highway 360, go to Kaeleku, a junction on the main road just past the rodeo arena and .5 mile before the Hana Airport Road. This is a rough three-mile old roadway leading from Hana Highway to the coastline at the site of the old village of Ulaino. The first two miles pass through ranch pasture before entering a very lush kukui and hala (pandanus) forest growing in the rough lava terrain. The trail ends at a scenic, rocky cove with good snorkeling. A stream

Central Maui vista to West Maui Mountains.

forms a large shallow pool backed up by a rocky bar along the shore. It's often rainy and humid here; good hiking boots are highly recommended. Remote and secluded location.

Hana-Waianapanapa Coastal Trail. Access is by a gravel road leading past a cemetery to Kainalimu Bay just northwest of Hana Bay in town. This three-mile trail follows the coastline and the old Hawaiian "King's Highway" from just north of Hana Bay to beyond Waianapanapa State Park. Parts of the old trail are still visible as smooth stepping stones set into the rugged lava and cinders. This is a rugged, scenic coastline with black lava points jutting into the deep blue ocean and frothing surf pounding the shore. Beach vegetation includes hala (pandanus) and naupaka shrub. Inland are views of the Hana Forest Reserve at a distance. The state park and facilities are about two miles down the trail. There is usually a strong ocean breeze blowing on the coast. Good hiking boots recommended for this hike.

West Maui

The **Lahaina Pali Trail** is an historic trail, probably part of the old Hawaiian "Alaloa" (the long road) that once circled Maui. The Lahaina Pali Trail was first built as a horse and foot trail about 200 years ago. The five-mile trail goes up and over the pali (sea cliffs) of the southern shore of West Maui between Ma`alaea and the Ukumehame area on the Lahaina side. The warm, dry and breezy trail traverses scrubland, kiawe

Maui

forest and deep gulches. The old trail was replaced with a narrow winding road built by prison laborers around 1900. The modern Honoapi`ilani Highway replaced that old road in 1951. The Lahaina Pali Trail offers magnificent views of Ma`alaea Bay, Molokini, Kaho`olawe, the West Maui coast and Haleakala. Take lots of water and snacks; allow four-five hours one-way and arrange a ride pickup at the opposite end of the trail. For a detailed trail booklet, contact: **Na Ala Hele-Maui**, Division of Forestry and Wildlife, DLNR, 54 South High St., Room 101, Wailuku, HI 96793, ☎ 808/871-2521.

The Kapalua Nature Society offers a series of weekly guided hikes into remote wilderness areas of the West Maui Mountains behind the Kapalua Resort area. The **Manualei Arboretum & Pu`u Ka`eo Ridge Nature Walk** is a moderate 1.75-mile, half-day hike starting at the 1,200-foot level to the summit of Pu`u Ka`eo Ridge (1,635-foot elevation). Along the way, the guide provides insight into the native and introduced vegetation, natural history and Hawaiian culture of the area. There are great views of the surrounding ridges and interior mountain peaks, distant waterfalls and streams. Rare and endangered Hawaiian birdlife is also evident in the area. Trails are generally good, with some steep rough spots and heavy underbrush vegetation.

DON'T MISS The **Manienie Ridge Hike** is somewhat longer at four miles and four-six hours duration, depending on conditions. The trail begins at 851-foot elevation and rises to 1,255-foot elevation, traversing a mostly gentle to moderate slope with some steep slopes and heavy underbrush. There are nice panoramic views of the surrounding mountain peaks, ridges and upland forest areas. For information on these guided hikes at Kapalua, contact: **Kapalua Nature Society**, 800 Kapalua Drive, Kapalua, HI 96761, ☎ 800/KAPALUA or 808/669-0244.

Hiking Resources

Several outfitters offer hikes of varied duration and difficulty. Rates range from $45 to $75 for one- to four-hour hikes, $88 to $115 for full-day excursions. Check with outfitters for details.

Crater Bound, PO Box 265, Kula, HI 96790, ☎ 808/878-1743, is a hiking, camping and van tour outfitter offering a variety of tours and three different hikes: three-mile, eight-mile and 12-mile treks into Haleakala Crater, including exploring a lava tube. They also offer unique Maui Mule Rides into Haleakala Crater, with two- and six-hour rides available.

Mango Mitch Ecotours, PO Box 2511, Wailuku, HI 96793, ☎ 808/875-9106; e-mail mangopik@maui.net. This outfitter offers guided hiking, snorkeling and cultural adventures to Maui's marine sanctuaries, hidden valleys, secluded beaches, old Hawaiian ruins, lush tropical rain forest and Haleakala Crater. Excursions from 3½-hours to overnight campouts.

Hana Cave Tour, offered by Island Spelunkers, ☎ 808/248-7808, is a 1½-hour hike into the subterranean passages of an extinct lava tube.

Hike Maui, PO Box 330969, Kahului, HI 96732, ☎ 808/879-5270. This outfitter offers guided hikes to all areas of Maui.

The Nature Conservancy of Hawai`i, PO Box 1716, Makawao, HI 96768, ☎ 808/572-7849. An environmental group offering monthly guided hikes to Waikamoi Preserve and different areas of Maui.

Paths in Paradise, PO Box 667, Makawao, HI 96768, ☎ 808/573-0094; e-mail corvusco@maui.net; www.maui.net/~corvusco/paths.html. This outfitter offers a range of half- and full-day hikes exploring the unique natural history and culture of Hawai`i.

Sierra Club, Hawai`i Chapter, Maui Group, PO Box 2000, Kahului, HI 96732, ☎ 808/878-2664 or 879-7039. This group has regular outings, walks, hikes and excursions around Maui. Visitors may be able to join their activities. Call or write for information.

Golf Courses

Maui has fabulous championship resort courses, some of which regularly host major PGA tournaments. There are exciting public links as well. Seasonal greens fees at the resort courses range from $60 to $140; fees at the public courses are generally much less. Call the course for details.

■ **Ka`anapali Resort** has a North Course and South Course, both equally beautiful and challenging; annual Ka`anapali Classic Senior PGA Tourney is held here, ☎ 800/665-4742, 808/661-3691.

Wailea Golf Course.

■ **Kapalua Resort** has three courses, Bay Course, Village Course, and Plantation Course; annual Lincoln-Mercury Kapalua International Tournament is held here, ☎ 808/669-8044.

■ **Makena Resort** features a North Course and South Course, both with stunning ocean and mountain vistas, ☎ 808/879-3344.

■ **Wailea Resort** boasts three courses, Blue Course, Gold Course, and Emerald Course, that have been acclaimed by the golf media, ☎ 808/875-5111.

■ **Waiehu Golf Course,** in Wailuku, has oceanside and mountain fairways, ☎ 808/243-7400.

■ **Pukalani Country Club,** in Pukalani. This upcountry course has views of ocean, mountains and Central Maui, ☎ 808/572-1314.

■ **Silversword Golf Club,** in Kihei, has nice ocean views from most greens, ☎ 808/874-0777.

■ **Sandalwood Course,** in Waikapu, offers good views of the ocean and Haleakala, ☎ 808/242-4653.

Tennis Courts

There are several public and private tennis courts and complexes on Maui. Many hotels and condos have their own courts. Private courts open to the public charge use fees. Some courts operated by Maui County are lighted. Hourly private court use fees are generally in the range of $8-15.

- **Kapalua Tennis Club,** Kapalua, reservations, ☎ 808/669-5677.

- **Makena Tennis Club,** 5415 Makena Alanui, Makena, ☎ 808/879-8777.

- **Royal Lahaina Tennis Ranch,** Ka`anapali Resort, ☎ 808/661-3611.

- **Wailea Tennis Club,** 131 Wailea Ike Place, Wailea, ☎ 808/879-1958.

Maui County maintains free tennis courts at Hali`imaile, Hana, Kahului (Maui Community College, Kahului Community Center, War Memorial Complex), Wailuku, Kihei, Lahaina, Makawao, and Pukalani. Contact: **Department of Parks and Recreation**, Maui County, 200 S. High St., Wailuku, HI 96793, ☎ 808/243-7230

Shopping

If your definition of an adventure is a shopping spree at a mall or cozy complex of fashion designer boutiques and specialty shops, Maui is the place to be. You'll find everything from local arts and crafts to the finest of European designer fashions.

Whalers Village Fine Shops and Restaurants, 2435 Ka`anapali Parkway, Ka`anapali Resort, Maui, HI 96761, ☎ 808/661-4567. Located right on Ka`anapali Beach, it combines elegant shopping and dining with an ocean view.

The Wharf Cinema Center, 658 Front Street, Lahaina, HI 96761, ☎ 808/661-8748. This centrally located complex is across from the Banyan Tree in the heart of historic Lahaina. There are over 50 shops and a dozen restaurants plus a tri-plex theater with the latest hit movies.

Pioneer Inn Shops, in the historic Pioneer Inn Building on the Harbor Front, old Lahaina town, has a number of interesting shops, boutiques and activity counters to meet your needs.

Lahaina Cannery Mall, 1221 Honoapi`ilani Highway, Lahaina, HI 96761, ☎ 808/661-5304. Located just north of Lahaina town on the site of an old pineapple cannery, this mall has many specialty fashion, accessories, jewelry and gift shops, plus food outlets and a Safeway grocery store.

Wailea Shopping Village, 3750 Wailea Alanui, Kihei, HI 96753, ☎ 808/879-4474. This resort center features a number of outstanding resort wear fashion shops, jewelry shops, arts and crafts galleries, gift shops and more.

Makawao Town, in upcountry Maui, has interesting restaurants, arts and crafts boutiques featuring the work of Maui artisans, paniolo (cowboy) apparel shops and specialty gift shops along its busy main street.

**Ka`ahumanu Center,** 275 Ka`ahumanu Avenue, Kahului, HI 96732, ☎ 808/877-3369. This is Maui's largest shopping mall and has over 100 stores and shops, restaurants and a theater complex. The food court has varied choices of cuisine.

Wailuku's Old Town doesn't have the glitz the newer malls have but some interesting and funky shops can be found on Market and Vineyard Streets in the old uptown area, along with a few good restaurants.

Hasegawa General Store, Hana, ☎ 808/248-8231. This country general store has a little bit of everything, from groceries to fish hooks and hardware. Pick up a Hana souvenir tee shirt here.

Hawaiian Arts & Crafts

Hawaiiana Arts & Crafts, 658 Front St., Lahaina, ☎ 808/661-9077.

Memory Lane, 130 N. Market, Wailuku, ☎ 808/244-4196.

Tiare's Specialties, 277 Wili Ko Place, #225, Lahaina, ☎ 667-5638.

RT Unlimited, 3620 Baldwin Avenue, #204, Makawao, ☎ 808/573-0119.

Everything In This Store Is Made In Hawai`i, Lahaina Center, 900 Front St., Lahaina, ☎ 808/661-5883.

Products of Hawai`i Too, Pioneer Inn Hotel, Front Street, Lahaina, ☎ 808/661-5008.

Sugar Cane Gifts, 957 Limahama Place, Lahaina, ☎ 808/661-3325.

Totally Hawaiian Gift Gallery, Lahaina Cannery Mall, Lahaina, ☎ 808/667-2558.

Makani Hou Gifts, 375 W. Kulaha Road, Haiku, ☎ 808/575-2384.

Maui Creations, Ka`ahumanu Center, Kahului, ☎ 808/871-8470.

Museums/Historic Sites

Maui's museums capture the culture, color, history and heritage of Maui's early Hawaiian population through the missionary days of the early 1800s, and Maui's history as a whaling fleet center, to the rise of the sugar industry and its impact on the development of Maui's multi-cultural population.

Alexander and Baldwin Sugar Museum, located at 3957 Hansen Road, Pu`unene, Highway 35 between Kahului and Kihei. The museum is easily located by the tall smoke stacks of the sugar mill next door. The museum itself is in a historic early 1900s plantation home that belonged to the plantation superintendent. The museum traces the history of the sugar industry on Maui, with lots of exhibits, memorabilia and displays.

Bailey House Museum, 2375-A Main St., Wailuku, HI 96793, ☎ 808/244-3326, is operated by the Maui Historical Society. The museum has the largest collection of pre-Western contact Hawaiian artifacts in Maui; a gift shop also has many local arts and crafts.

Baldwin Missionary Home, Front Street across from Pioneer Inn, Lahaina, ☎ 808/661-3262, is operated by the Lahaina Restoration Foundation. The home was built in 1834-35 for the Reverend Dwight Baldwin and family who lived in the home until 1871. The Baldwins were one of Maui's first missionary families and the home is still maintained much as it was in those days.

Whale Center of the Pacific, located in Whalers Village Shopping Center, Ka`anapali Resort, ☎ 808/661-5992. This museum features a full skeleton of a humpback whale. There are interactive displays, memorabilia, artifacts and research exhibits on the natural history of whales.

■ On Wheels

Maui Bike Trails

One of Maui's more challenging bike adventures is the **Honokohau to Wailuku Route** via Highway 340 around the north shore of the West Maui Mountains. This is a fairly difficult 38-mile ride. The rough and winding road is unimproved in some areas, with a lot of steep hilly sections and hairpin curves. It follows the north shore coast and does give bikers some wonderful panoramic vistas of rugged coastline and the West Maui Mountains. There are no services along the entire route from roughly Kapalua to Waihee town just outside Wailuku. This is a ride for experienced mountain bikers only. Take along food and plenty of water, as it can be a dry, very warm ride. The ride can also be done in reverse, traveling from Wailuku to Honokohau and on to Lahaina.

DON'T MISS The **Kahului to Hana Route** via the famed Hana Highway 360 is about 60 miles long. This stretch of highway has long been noted as one of America's most scenic highways. But be aware that it is a very narrow winding road. It's a moderate ride through the open sugarcane lands of Central Maui, past the beaches and upland pineapple fields of the Paia and Haiku areas and gradually entering the tropical rain forest region of East Maui. The road narrows considerably but is paved all the way to Hana. It follows the winding coastline, into and out of gulches. The road has 56 very narrow bridges and numerous sharp hairpin turns. It crosses many streams and waterfalls, passing the Hawaiian villages of Keanae and Wailua with their picturesque taro patches, and several scenic overlooks. Bikers will revel in the sights and will probably want to take some of the side trips along the way. Allow a whole day to reach Hana and plan on staying overnight or longer. See *Lodging* section for places to stay in Hana. There are additional side trips from Hana to places like Kipahulu Valley area of Haleakala National Park and its noted "Pools of Oheo." The grave of the famed aviator, Charles Lindbergh, is also at Kipahulu in the grounds of Kipahulu Hawaiian Church. But there are so many other attractions in the Hana area, you'll need to stay a while to check them all out. This is Maui's most scenic ride.

The **Honoapi`ilani Highway 30** runs from Wailuku to West Maui and the Lahaina area around the southern pali (sea cliffs). The route begins in Wailuku and heads south out of town through sugarcane fields. By mid-day, gusty tradewinds can whip through this area. The 6½-mile route leads to Ma`alaea Bay after passing through the small settlement of Waikapu and past the Maui Tropical Plantation, a sizeable visitor attraction with fruit orchards and flower gardens. Ma`alaea Harbor anchors a large fleet of fishing and cruise boats and is busy during the winter whale watching season. The road bends west as it passes Ma`alaea and turns around the pali toward Lahaina, 15 miles away. The road climbs to about 500 feet and there are overlooks on Ma`alaea Bay toward South Maui, Kaho`olawe and beyond to Haleakala. The road is nicely paved with fairly good shoulders for bikers.

This is a very busy highway, the major link between east and West Maui, so caution is advised at all times.

The road traverses one short tunnel through the rock and gradually drops back to sea level. Entering the West Maui side, it passes by several fine beach areas and the old settlement of Olowalu. Nearer Lahaina are two nice state beach parks, Launiupoko and Puamana. The Honoapi`ilani Highway continues a few miles further north of Lahaina through the resort areas of Ka`anapali, Honokowai, Kahana, Napili and to Kapalua.

Several outfitters offer bike rides, safaris and excursions. Rates for the popular downhill Haleakala ride from summit to Kula and the sea run from $48 to $87. Other rides range from $95 to $115 depending on length and itinerary. Some outfitters offer other morning Maui bike rides ranging from $76 to $110 and evening rides from $49 to $69. Check with the outfitters for details.

 DON'T MISS Perhaps Maui's greatest bicycle adventure is the famous downhill **"Summit to the Sea"** ride from the summit of Mount Haleakala (House of the Sun) all the way to the beach at Paia town, a distance of 38 miles. On this ride, bikers have only 400 yards of real pedaling and coast the rest of the way. Super views from the summit of Haleakala and on the way downhill of the West Maui Mountains, panoramic views of Central Maui and of upcountry ranchlands. Several bike tour outfitters offer this cruise, including bike and all equipment, as well as variations of it with sidetrips to other upcountry Maui attractions and sites.

Maui Downhill Bicycle Safaris, 199 Dairy Road, Kahului, HI 96732, ☎ 808/871-2155. Downhill safari rides from 22 to 38 miles long.

Aloha Bicycle Tours, ☎ 800/749-1564, ☎ 808/249-0911; www.maui.net/~bikemaui/. A full downhill bike tour from Haleakala summit through scenic upcountry Kula, taking in a number of area attractions along the way.

Chris' Adventures, PO Box 869, Kula, HI 96790, ☎ 808/871-2453; www.lmg.com:80/maui/hykebyke.htm. Offers 22-mile, 34-mile and 46-mile rides down Haleakala and surrounding countryside. The 46-mile ride explores the wild and remote backside of Haleakala and is suited for really adventurous and experienced bikers.

Maui

Haleakala Bike Co., 810 Haiku Road, Haiku, HI 96708, ☎ 808/572-2200. Downhill Haleakala cruises and other bike adventures.

Mountain Riders Bike Tours, 220 Lalo, Bay 5, Wailuku, HI 96793, ☎ 808/242-9739. Specializes in 38-mile downhill cruises from the summit of Haleakala to the Pacific Ocean.

Upcountry Cycles, 81 Makawao Avenue, Pukalani Square, Pukalani, HI 96768, ☎ 808/573-2888. Bike cruises down Haleakala, through scenic Kula and to area attractions.

Maui Mountain Biking, for general information on biking on Maui and other interesting links; e-mail tomg@maui.net; www.maui.net/~tomg/mauimtb.html.

Biking Resources

The Bike Shop, 425 Koloa, Triangle Square, Kahului, HI 96732, ☎ 808/877-5848, 877-5876. This is a full-service retail bike shop with bikes, equipment and repair service.

South Maui Bicycles, 1993 S. Kihei Road, Kihei, HI 96753, ☎ 808/874-0068. This is a retail bike shop carrying a wide range of bikes, clothing, accessories, parts, equipment, etc. and repairs.

West Maui Cycles, 193 Lahainaluna Road, Lahaina, HI 96761, ☎ 808/661-9005, and 4310 Lower Honoapiilani Road, Kahana, ☎ 808/669-1169. This shop's two locations carry a variety of bikes, equipment, parts and accessories, and they feature a service shop and rentals.

Island Biker, 415 Dairy Road, Kahului, HI 96732, ☎ 808/877-7744. A full line of mountain bike rentals, clothing, accessories, equipment, a service shop and visitor information.

Maui Sports & Cycle, 1215 S. Kihei Road, Kihei, HI 96753, ☎ 808/875-8448, and in Dolphin Plaza at 2395 S. Kihei Road, Kihei, HI 96753, ☎ 808/875-2882. The two locations have a full line of rental mountain bikes, equipment, accessories, plus parts and service.

■ On Water

Beaches

Maui has fine sandy beaches for enjoying the entire range of beach activities from swimming and sunning, to surfing and windsurfing, fishing and tidepool exploring – or just relaxing. Most of the better beaches are on the western shores of the island in the Kihei to Makena area and the Lahaina to Kapalua areas. Some of the parks have picnic tables or pavilions, BBQ facilities and more. Conditions at the parks vary and are weather-dependent. Check surf conditions with lifeguards, hotel activity desks, surf shops. Read and heed all posted warning signs. A partial listing of the more popular parks is provided here.

South Shore

Kamaole Beach Parks I, II, III. These three parks are next to each other on South Kihei Road; swim, boogie board, surf and windsurf.

Mokapu & Ulua Beaches are between the Aston Wailea Beach Resort and Stouffer Wailea Beach Resort; beautiful golden sand for swimming and snorkeling.

Wailea Beach fronts the Grand Hyatt Wailea and Four Seasons Wailea resorts. This beach is a beautiful wide crescent of golden sand. There is good swimming and snorkeling around the rocky outcrops on south end; good windsurfing. This beach was listed in the annual "Top 10 Best Beaches" national survey conducted by the University of Maryland, one of six Hawai`i beaches so honored.

Big Beach at Makena, past the Makena Prince Hotel and golf course, is a two-mile stretch of beautiful white sand, one of Maui's best; no facilities.

Maluaka Beach, next to Keawalai Church and in front of the Maui Prince Hotel, has good swimming, snorkeling, boogie boarding.

Ka`anapali Beach.

Maui

West Maui

Ka`anapali Beach runs along the resort area of the same name from just opposite the Lahaina Civic Center north to the area of Honokowai; lovely stretches of golden sand; swimming, snorkeling, surfing and boogie boarding.

Launiupoko Beach Park three miles south of Lahaina on Highway 30; good swimming, snorkeling, picnic area.

Fleming Beach Park on Lower Honoapi`ilani Highway, Kapalua; good swimming, snorkeling, surfing and boogie boarding; picnics.

Moluleia and Honolua Bay is located one mile north of Fleming Beach on Lower Honoapi`ilani Highway; parking is along the road, with a trail leading down to beaches. Good swimming, surfing, boogie boarding and snorkeling; no facilities.

Central Maui

Kanaha Beach, near Maui Airport, Kahului, is good for boogie boarding, surfing and windsurfing.

Spreckelsville Beach, just off the Hana Highway 36 on the east side of Maui Airport, is good for boogie boarding, surfing and windsurfing.

Baldwin Beach, just west of Paia town off the Hana Highway 36, is good for swimming, boogie boarding, surfing, windsurfing, picnics.

Ho`okipa Beach, east of Paia town a couple of miles off Hana Highway 36, is good for windsurfing.

DID YOU KNOW?

Ho`okipa Beach is known as the "Windsurfing Capital of Maui."

East Maui

Waianapanapa State Park, just north of Hana. The beach is mostly rocky here but good for picnics and exploring.

Hana Beach Park, at Hana Bay in town, is good for swimming, snorkeling, picnics.

Hamoa Beach is in Hana. Look for sign just past Hasegawa Store. Park along road, follow steps down to the beach. Good for boogie boarding and surfing. This is a long white sand beach in a nice tropical setting. Grounds and facilities are maintained by the Hotel Hana Maui.

Hamoa Beach was listed in the annual "Top 10 Best Beaches" national survey conducted by the University of Maryland, one of six Hawai`i beaches so honored.

Kayaking & Rafting

Several outfitters offer ocean kayaking and inflatable raft adventures. Rates range from $59 for a two-three-hour guided ocean kayak excursion to $69-89 for four- to six-hour excursions. Inflatable ocean raft excursions range from $38 to $69 per person.

South Pacific Kayaks & Outfitters, 2439 S. Kihei Road, Kihei, HI 96753, ☎ 800/77-OCEAN, 808/875-4848; www.mauikayak.com. Paddling and snorkeling excursions along the La Perouse and Ahihi Lava flows of South Maui; snorkel, picnic and hike plus seasonal whale watching.

Big Kahuna Kayak, ☎ 808/875-6395; www.maui.net./~paddle/. This outfitter has a variety of excursions to kayak, dive, snorkel and whale watch in season. Their motto, "Beginners & families our specialty, catering to the cowardly & uncoordinated." Sounds like my kind of outfit.

Blue Water Rafting, PO Box 1865, Kihei, HI 96753, ☎ 808/879-RAFT. This operator uses six- and 24-passenger rafts and does two- to five-hour or longer trips along the Kanaio Coast of South Maui and to Molokini for snorkeling at the marine reserve.

**Hawai`i Ocean Rafting,** PO Box 381, Lahaina, HI 96767, ☎ 808/667-2191. They operate half- and full-day snorkel cruises to the island of Lana`i plus special seasonal two-hour whale watching trips.

Ultimate Rafting, ☎ 808/667-5678, e-mail ecoraft@maui.net. This operator uses a large inflatable raft for wildlife and snorkeling cruises to Lana`i.

Ocean Riders Rafting, ☎ 800/221-3586, Mala Wharf, Lahaina. This adventure rafting company specializes in full-day circumnavigations of Lana`i for marine life, scenery and more.

Cruises, Sailing & Whale Watching

Several boat operators offer cruises and whale watching adventures. Rates for a half-day cruise generally range from $40-60 per person. Ferry boat rides from Lahaina to Lana`i are $25 one way. Check with operators for seasonal and daily special rates.

Maui

Reefdancer, ☎ 808/667-2133, Lahaina Harbor. A semi-submersible cruise boat. The underwater cabin has wraparound windows for viewing the coral reefs and marinelife. One-hour cruises are featured.

Expeditions, PO Box 10, Lahaina, HI 96767, ☎ 808/661-3756. This is the Lahaina-Lana`i ferry, offering frequent departures between Lahaina Harbor on Maui and Manele Harbor on Lana`i. Excursion packages on Lana`i available.

Silent Lady, Ma`alaea Harbor, ☎ 808/875-1112. A 64-foot luxury schooner with full amenities aboard. It offers sailing and snorkeling cruises to Molokini, coral reefs and sunset party cruises.

Zip Purr, Ka`anapali Beach, ☎ 808/667-2299. This large, comfortable catamaran offers six-hour sailings to Lana`i for snorkeling and sunset cocktail cruises off Ka`anapali Beach.

Four Winds, Ma`alaea Harbor, ☎ 808/879-8188. A catamaran cruiser offering morning and afternoon snorkel cruises to Molokini. The boat has all amenities plus glass bottom for non-snorkelers.

Lavengro, Ma`alaea Harbor, ☎ 808/879-8188. This twin-master sailer offers sailing, snorkeling and sport fishing excursions.

Trilogy, 180 Lahainaluna Road, Lahaina, ☎ 800/874-2666, 808/661-4743. Trips to Lana`i plus half-day snorkel sails to Molokini marine preserve.

America II, Lahaina Harbor, Lahaina, ☎ 808/667-2195. This sleek racing yacht was an America's Cup challenger in 1987. Daily trips include a morning snorkel and/or whale watching sail, an afternoon tradewind sail, a sunset sail and a starlight sail.

Pacific Whale Foundation Eco-Adventures, 101 N. Kihei Road, #21, Kihei, HI 96753, ☎ 808/879-8811. One of Hawai`i's best whale watch cruises. Whale sightings are best in winter when humpbacks migrate to Hawai`i waters. Eco-sensitive cruises, with departures from Lahaina and Ma`alaea.

Pride of Maui, ☎ 808/875-0955. This operator specializes in seasonal whale watching adventures; cruises are coordinated by Whales Alive, Earth Island Institute and Free Willy Foundation.

Scuba Diving & Snorkeling

Scuba and snorkeling outfitters provide dive and snorkel cruises and excursions to the Molokini Islet marine sanctuary and other sites around Maui. Typical half-day snorkel cruises include snacks, lunch and use of snorkel equipment. Rates range from $40 to $70 per person. Introductory beach scuba one-tank dives begin at about $50. Deep ocean two-tank dives are $80 and up. Contact outfitters for details and latest rates.

Seafire, ☎ 808/879-2201, Ma`alaea Harbor. This powerboat operator offers two daily trips to Molokini and its famous marine sanctuary to see reef fish and green sea turtles; snorkeling equipment provided.

Maui Diamond II, ☎ 808/879-9119, Ma`alaea Harbor. This is a 36-foot power boat with all amenities offering daily scuba and snorkeling trips to Molokini marine sanctuary. Snacks, lunch, equipment included.

Lahaina Princess, ☎ 808/661-8397, Lahaina Harbor. This large cruising yacht has daily trips to Molokini for scuba diving and snorkeling and Olowalu Turtle Reef; includes all equipment, instruction, snacks and lunch.

Maui Diving, ☎ 800/959-8319, 808/667-0633, Lahaina. This operator takes trips to Molokini and Lana`i for scuba diving and snorkeling, plus special Maui beach dives. All equipment, food and beverages included.

Ocean Activities Center, ☎ 808/879-4485, Ma`alaea Harbor. This cruise company operates *Maka Kai* and *Wailea Kai*, both power catamarans. Daily trips to Molokini for snorkeling the marine sanctuary to see reef fish, green sea turtles and more. All snorkel gear, instruction, food and beverages provided.

Hawaiian Rafting Adventures, 1223 Front St., Lahaina, ☎ 808/661-7333. This is a full-service PADI dive center with dive trips to Maui's most exotic dive sites; all equipment included.

Maui Bubbles, ☎ 808/879-5070. This scuba diving outfitter offers PADI instruction, beach, boat and night dives.

Parasailing, Paragliding & Jet Skiing

Outfitters offer parasailing at heights ranging from 400-800 ft. Rates are $28-52 per person. Jet ski adventures are $65 per hour per person.

UFO Parasail, ☎ 800/FLY-4UFO, 808/661-7UFO, Ka`anapali Beach.

Parasail Ka`anapali, ☎ 808/669-6555, Mala Wharf, Lahaina.

West Maui Parasail, ☎ 808/661-4060, Lahaina Harbor.

Pacific Jet Sports, ☎ 808/667-2066, south end of Ka`anapali Beach at Hanakao`o Beach Park.

Proflyght Hawai`i Paragliding, ☎ 808/87-GLIDE, is a unique Maui activity offering spectacular flights off Haleakala Crater. Experience incredible views and thrills high above Maui and soar with the birds by gliding in a parachute/glider.

Surfing & Windsurfing

These surf school operators offer instruction programs for beginners, intermediates and experts. Instructional rates generally begin at $45-55 per hour.

Goofy Foot Surf School, PO Box 11813, Lahaina, HI 96761, ☎ 808/244-WAVE. They offer all levels of surf instruction from beginners to advanced.

Maui Surfing School, PO Box 424, Pu`unene, HI 96784, ☎ 808/875-0625. Located at Lahaina Harbor. Surfing lessons for all levels and ages.

Big Kahuna Surf School, ☎ 808/875-6395. They help you learn to surf in one lesson.

Al West's Windsurfing West, 415 Dairy Road, Kahului, HI 96732, ☎ 808/871-8733. Surf instruction for all ages and levels.

Second Wind School, 111 Hana Highway, Kahului, HI 96732, ☎ 808/877-7467. Beginner classes of two hours to advanced levels.

Nancy Emerson School of Surfing, Lahaina and Kihei, ☎ 808/244-SURF. They specialize in instruction to "Learn to Surf in One Lesson."

Fishing - Deep Sea Charters, Freshwater

Maui is a great place to try your luck with deep sea fishing or a trip to a remote forest stream to test your skill with wily trout. Anyway you go, angling on Maui is a first-rate adventure. Most charter boats take a minimum of four persons, maximum six. Standard charter boat rates per person are: four hours/$95, six hours/$110, eight hours/$135.

Absolute Sportfishing, Ka`anapali Beach, Lahaina, ☎ 808/669-1449. A 31-foot Bertram Sportfisher with half/full-day charters for mahimahi, marlin, yellowfin tuna (ahi) and other popular Hawaiian gamefish.

Lucky Strike Charters, PO Box 1502, Lahaina, HI 96767, Lahaina Harbor, ☎ 808/661-4606. Deep sea trolling and light tackle bottom fishing for all game fish.

Marlin Mischief, Lahaina Harbor, Lahaina, ☎ 808/662-FISH. Offering a 47-foot Buddy Davis Yacht with all amenities.

Lahaina Charter Boats, Lahaina Harbor, Lahaina, ☎ 808/667-6672. Half/full-day charters for fishing the calm blue waters surrounding Maui.

Rascal Charters, Ma`alaea Harbor, Ma`alaea, ☎ 808/874-8633. A 31-foot Bertram Sportfisher with heavy and light tackle trolling and bottom fishing for all Hawaiian game fish.

Carol Ann Charters, Ma`alaea Harbor, Ma`alaea, ☎ 808/877-2181. A 33-foot Bertram Sportfisher offering half/full-day charters; all amenities for comfortable adventure.

Hawaiian Shoreline Fishing Adventures, ☎ 808/573-0169. Light tackle rod & reel shore fishing, ancient Hawaiian net throwing and overnight camping and fishing along Maui's secluded coastlines.

Trout Fishing Maui, 1449 Front St., Lahaina, HI 96761, ☎ 808/667-2118. A private trout farm in the lush tropical rain forest beyond Kapalua. It's a nicely landscaped setting with five ponds full of huge, hungry rainbow trout. Adventure includes transportation from West Maui hotels, all fishing tackle, guaranteed fish, and fresh BBQ trout lunch.

■ In the Air

Scenic Flightseeing & Helicopter Tours

 There are a few air tour and helicopter lines on Maui offering a variety of flightseeing adventure tours to Haleakala National Park, East Maui, West Maui and coastal areas of the island. Typical helicopter rates per person: West Maui 20-30-minute air tour, $69-79; East Maui-Hana-Haleakala one-hour air tour, $89-119; Circle Island one-hour air tour, $129-169 and up.

Air Maui, Kahului Heliport, Kahului, ☎ 808/877-7005. Aerial adventures, taking in all the scenic splendors of Maui.

Blue Hawaiian Helicopters, Kahului Heliport, Kahului, ☎ 800/745-BLUE, 808/871-8844; http://maui.net/~blue/bluehaw/blue.html. Flightseeing adventures all around Maui.

Sunshine Helicopters, 107 Kahului Heliport, Kahului, ☎ 800/544-2520, 808/871-0722; www.sunshinehelicopters.com. Air adventures to the incredible "Wall of Tears," one of the wettest spots in West Maui's mountains, where 17 waterfalls stream over the sheer cliffs. It's an awesome sight. Other Maui air tours available.

Maui

Hawai`i Helicopters, 106 Kahului Heliport, Kahului, ☎ 808/873-7703; www.Hawaiiheli.com. Three flightseeing adventures from 45-60 minutes each to East Maui and Haleakala, the Valley Isle Deluxe, and Hana Heli-Trek over Hana's famous winding highway.

Biplane Barnstormers, Maui Airport, Kahului, ☎ 808/878-2860. This air tour outfit flies a new production version of a WACO Classic Biplane, a old-fashioned open-cockpit double-winger that will give you a flying experience like no other. Aerial adventures around Maui from 30-60 minutes long.

Alexair Helicopters, Kahului Heliport, Kahului, ☎ 808/871-0792. Flightseeing adventures from 30-80 minutes long and covering East Maui, West Maui, Haleakala and mountain valleys.

■ On Horseback

Trail Rides

 Horseback riding outfitters have rides available in different areas of Maui. The typical two-hour trail ride is $50-60 per person. Other rides and excursions, such as rides into Haleakala Crater, range from $130 and up. Check with outfitters for details.

The Maui Mule Ride, PO Box 265, Kula, HI 96790, ☎ 808/878-1743, offers two- and six-hour mule rides down into Haleakala Crater to see the stark beauty of Maui's volcano.

Pony Express Tours, PO Box 535, Kula, HI 96790, ☎ 808/667-2200, offers a variety of one- to two-hour rides across the scenic uplands of Haleakala Ranch and half/full-day rides down into the awesome scenery of Haleakala Crater.

Thompson Ranch Riding Stables, off Kula Highway 37, Kula, ☎ 808/878-1910. Trail rides across the upland ranch country of Kula on the slopes of Haleakala.

Mendes Ranch & Trail Rides, PO Box 150, Wailuku, HI 96753, ☎ 808/871-5222. Trail rides through lush tropical valleys and upland cattle ranch country of West Maui; great views of North Shore and Waihee Valley.

Adventures on Horseback, PO Box 1419, Makawao, HI 96768, ☎ 808/242-7445 or 808/572-6211. Horseback adventures through East Maui's rolling hill country and lush tropical forestlands to cascading streams and Haiku Falls, hidden deep in the forested slopes of Haleakala.

Ohe`o Stables, 25 minutes past Hana in Kipahulu on Highway 31, ☎ 808/667-2222. Trail rides through the Kipahulu district of Haleakala National Park.

Makena Stables, Makena, South Maui, ☎ 808/879-0244. Riding excursions into the high rangelands of Ulupalakua Ranch on the west side of Haleakala Mountain.

■ Eco/Cultural Activities

 Lahaina-Ka`anapali & Pacific Railroad, PO Box 816, Lahaina, HI 96767-0816, ☎ 808/661-0089. This is an original 1890 railroad that used to haul sugarcane to the Lahaina mill. The train has been reconstructed and now carries passengers on a route from Lahaina along the coast through the sugarcane fields and the Ka`anapali Resort area. It's a pleasant scenic one-hour round-trip. Depart from either the Lahaina station or Ka`anapali station. Rates are about $20 per person.

Kepaniwai Park Heritage Garden, located on the way up to the Iao Valley State Park above Wailuku town, is a tropical floral garden. The park has pavilions, monuments and garden plots honoring the ethnic

Iao Needle, Iao Valley.

The Carthaginian, an early whaling ship, Lahaina Harbor.

and cultural groups that have contributed to Hawai`i's development and modern cross-cultural community. These include the Hawaiians, Japanese, Chinese, Portuguese, Filipinos and Koreans. There are picnic tables and BBQ grills. A pleasant park for lunch, strolling and relaxing after a visit to Iao Valley State Park.

 DON'T MISS Iao Valley State Park is directly above Wailuku town on Main Street. This is a lovely tropical garden park surrounded by sheer cliffs and steep mountain walls, with a patchwork of walking trails crossing splashing streams. The 2,250-foot Iao Needle is a big attraction. The Needle is a lava rock pinnacle covered in lush tropical vegetation rising from the ridgeline. The trails offer good vantage points for photographers.

Maui Tropical Plantation and Country Store, Honoapi`ilani Highway 30 between Wailuku and Ma`alaea, ☎ 808/244-7643. This is one of Maui's top attractions, even though it's a pretty touristy sort of place. There are several acres of tropical fruit and flower gardens, with orchards including sugarcane, pineapples, guava, papaya and other exotics. A tram ride carries visitors through the fields for fresh samples of tropical fruits. A large country store has all sorts of Hawaiian food products, snacks, macadamia nuts, coffee, chocolates and more. There is a tropical plant nursery and café for buffet and menu meals. They also feature a Hawaiian Country Barbecue dinner show.

 DON'T MISS Poli Poli Springs Recreational Area is on the slopes of Haleakala above Kula at 6,200-foot elevation. Take Highway 377 past Kula and turn left on Waipoli Road. Waipoli becomes Poli Poli Road and climbs steeply up the mountain where the pavement ends and dirt road begins. The road is rough in some spots and it is 10 miles to the park. The park has many hiking trails, plus picnic tables, restrooms and water. This is a beautiful forest reserve with many introduced trees. Great place to lose the crowds and enjoy the peace and beauty of upcountry Maui.

The Pioneer Inn.

DON'T MISS **Hosmer Grove** is on the Haleakala Highway 378 about halfway to the summit at the 6,000-foot level. This national park campground has tent camping facilities. It also has one of Maui's best upcountry nature trails through an incredible forest of giant eucalyptus, redwoods, fir, ash and other introduced tree species. The nature trail is .5 mile and about 30 minutes long. Lots of birdlife in the forest.

The area along Front Street in **Old Lahaina Town** has much of historical interest. The **Pioneer Inn** on the harbor front dates from 1901 and originally catered to inter-island travelers who came by ferryboat. The **Lahaina Courthouse** dates from 1859 and is home to the Lahaina Visitors Center and Lahaina Art Society.

The Banyan Tree behind the courthouse spreads out its roots and branches over a 200-foot area. This massive tree dates from 1873. **Lahaina Harbor** in front of the Pioneer Inn is home to Maui's fishing fleet and recreational cruise boats plus the old sailing brig, *Carthaginian.* The ship serves as an exhibit tied to Lahaina's whaling era of the early 1800s. **Wo Hing Temple** on Front Street is an early Chinese fraternal society building dating to the early 20th century when the Chee Kung Tong Society had over 100 local members. It's now a museum.

US Seamen's Hospital, also on Front Street, housed ill sailors in the mid-1800s and is now a cable TV station. **Hale Pa`ahao** (The Old

Prison) is on Prison Street a short way from Front Street. The prison was built for the rowdy whaling sailors who spent time in port in Lahaina doing things for which sailors are noted.

The rest of Lahaina has other historical sites and buildings worth a casual exploration on foot. **Lahaina Jodo Mission** is on Ala Moana Street near Mala Wharf. The Buddhist church complex has a magnificent statue of Buddha and a colorful pagoda temple. The Buddha statue was dedicated in 1968 to commemorate the centennial anniversary of Japanese immigration to Hawai`i.

Lodging

 Maui has hotel, condominium and bed & breakfast accommodations to suit every budget. The rates below are for a standard double-occupancy room.

Accommodations Price Scale

$	less than $100 per night
$$	$100-199 per night
$$$	$200-299 per night
$$$$	$300 and up per night

Bed & Breakfasts

Maui has a number of bed and breakfasts throughout the island. Check with the following booking services for reservations and full information.

All Islands Bed and Breakfast-Maui, 823 Kainui Drive, Kailua, HI 96734-2025, ☎ 800/542-0344, 808/263-2342; http://planet-Hawaii.com/all-island.

**Bed & Breakfast Hawai`i-Maui,** PO Box 449, Kapa`a, HI 96746, ☎ 800/733-1632, 808/822-7771; e-mail bandb@aloha.net; www.planet-Hawaii.com/bandb.

Central Maui - Wailuku and Kahului

Maui Beach Hotel, 170 Ka`ahumanu Avenue, Kahului, Castle Resorts ☎ 800/367-5004, 808/877-0051. This is a conveniently located 152-room hotel right on the main street of Kahului town and adjacent to Ka`ahumanu Shopping Center. It's a basic tourist-class hotel, with modest rooms at a modest rate. A good choice for Central Maui. $

Maui Seaside, 100 Ka`ahumanu Avenue, Kahului, ☎ 800/367-7000, 808/922-1228. This hotel is next door to the Maui Beach Hotel so enjoys the same benefits of a convenient location in Kahului town and close to shopping, dining, etc. The rooms are simply furnished; good choice for budget travelers and groups. $

Maui Palms Hotel, 170A Kaahumanu Avenue, Kahului, HI 96732; Castle Resorts ☎ 800/367-5004, 808/877-0071; www.castle-group.com. This small 44-room budget hotel is located on the shores of Kahului Bay (next to the other two hotels listed above). Convenient location in town for shopping, dining and other Maui attractions and for exploring upcountry and East Maui. Pool on grounds, tennis and golf nearby, plus swimming and windsurfing beaches. Strictly for budget travelers. $

West Maui - Lahaina, Ka`anapali to Kapalua

West Maui has some of Maui's longest established hotels, resorts and vacation condos. The West Maui coastline, stretching from Lahaina, the old capital, to Ka`anapali, Honokowai, Kahana, Napili to Kapalua, is filled with first-class and luxury hotels, condominiums, private residences, shopping centers, restaurants, golf courses, tennis court complexes, pools and some of Maui's finest beaches. The Ka`anapali Resort area, first developed in the 1960s, was one of the first major comprehensive resorts developed in the islands. Today, it is still a prime destination and has expanded all the way up the coast to the luxurious Kapalua area.

Aloha Lani Inn, 13 Kauaula Road, Lahaina, ☎ 800/57-ALOHA, 808/661-8040; e-mail tony@maui.net; www.maui.net/~tony/index.html. This is a casual guest home just off Front Street within walking distance of Lahaina town. It is across from the beach, close to Lahaina activities, restaurants, shopping. Kitchen and laundry available. $

Plantation Inn, 174 Lahainaluna Road, Lahaina, ☎ 800/433-6815, 808/667-9225; e-mail inn@maui.net; www.maui.net/~inn. This 18-room hotel, located in the heart of old Lahaina town, has the feel of an elegant Victorian inn. There are tasteful furnishings, antiques and modern conveniences; very comfortable and cozy. It also has fine dining at Gerard's Restaurant. $$

Maui

Lahaina Inn, 127 Lahainaluna Road, Lahaina, ☎ 800/669-3444, 808/661-0577. This 13-room hotel has a history dating back to the '30s as an old family general store. The restored facility evokes the early days, with antiques, early furnishings and decorative accents. Centrally located in the heart of Lahaina, adjacent to David Paul's Lahaina Grill for fine dining. $

**Ka`anapali Beach Hotel,** 2525 Ka`anapali Parkway, Ka`anapali, ☎ 800/262-8450, 808/661-0011; e-mail mauikbh@aloha.net. This hotel, one of Ka`anapali's oldest, is also its most Hawaiian in atmosphere. The hotel and staff reflect a sense of Hawaiiana in services and activities. Rooms have an island decor, a/c, fridges and more. This is an excellent location right on Ka`anapali Beach. $$

The Westin Maui, 2365 Ka`anapali Parkway, Ka`anapali, ☎ 800/WESTIN1, ☎ 808/667-2525. This is a deluxe 760-room hotel right on the beach. There is a large water/pool recreation complex, health spa, restaurants, lounges, shops and full resort services and amenities. Located in the heart of Ka`anapali Resort and convenient to shopping, golf, activities and dining. $$$

Hyatt Regency Maui, 200 Nohea Kai Drive, Lahaina, HI 96761, ☎ 800/233-1234, 808/661-1234; www.travelweb.com/hyatt.html. A luxury 808-room hotel right on Ka`anapali Beach with convenient location to all resort attractions and activities. It has all the comforts, amenities and services expected in a first-class beach resort. There are restaurants, lounges, health spa, pool, shops, plus easy access to golf and tennis. $$$

Maui Marriott, 100 Nohea Kai Drive, Lahaina, HI 96761, ☎ 800/763-1333, 808/667-1200. This 720-room luxury hotel is right on the beach in Ka`anapali Resort. There are restaurants, lounges, shops, pool, beach activities center, easy access to golf and tennis and all resort services and amenities. $$$

**Aston Ka`anapali Shores,** 100 Ka`anapali Shores Place, Honokowai, ☎ 800/922-7866, 808/667-2211; www.aston-hotels.com. This luxury vacation condo has studio and 1/2BR units available. Units are fully furnished with kitchens and have private lanais. The beachside complex just north of Lahaina town has tennis courts, pools, spa-sauna, fitness center, and more. This is a great setting for adventurous family groups. $$

Outrigger Napili Shores, 5315 Lower Honoapi`ilani, Napili, ☎ 800/OUTRIGGER, 808/669-8061; e-mail reservations@outrigger.com; www.outrigger.com. This is a smaller condo complex on the beach at Napili Bay. There are studio and 1BR units with full kitchens; pool and barbecue picnic area on grounds. $$

**Aston Maui Ka`anapali Villas,** 2805 Honoapi`ilani Highway, Ka`anapali, ☎ 800/922-7866, 808/667-7791; www.aston-hotels.com. This condo has an oceanfront garden setting right on famed Ka`anapali Beach. The complex offers hotel rooms, spacious studios and 1BR suites with full kitchens. There is a pool, activities desk, sundries shop on grounds and tennis courts and golf nearby. $$

`Outrigger Maui Eldorado,** 2661 Keka`a Drive, Ka`anapali, ☎ 800/OUTRIGGER, 808/661-0021; e-mail reservations@outrigger.com; www.outrigger.com. This luxurious condo complex is on the fairway of the famous Ka`anapali Resort golf course very near to the beach. There are spacious and well-appointed studios and 1/2BR units with full kitchens. The complex has three swimming pools and beachfront cabanas for gatherings. Short walk to shopping and dining at Whaler's Village. $$

**Aston Mahana at Ka`anapali,** 110 Ka`anapali Shores Place, Honokowai, ☎ 800/922-7866, 808/661-8751; www.aston-hotels.com. This large complex is right on Ka`anapali Beach and every suite has a panoramic view of the Pacific Ocean. There are studio and 1/2BR units with a/c, full kitchen and large Lana`i. There is a beachfront pool, tennis court, sauna and more. $$

**Outrigger Ka`anapali Royal,** 2560 Keka`a Drive, Ka`anapali, ☎ 800/OUTRIGGER, 808/879-2205; e-mail reservations@outrigger.com; www.outrigger.com. These nicely furnished 1/2BR condo suites are right on the fairway of famed Ka`anapali Resort golf course. Units have garden/fairway views plus full kitchen. Complex has pool, barbecue and tennis courts. $$

Maui Park, 3626 Lower Honoapi`ilani Highway, Honokowai, Aston Resorts ☎ 800/922-7866, or Castle Resorts ☎ 800/367-5004, 808/669-6622; www.aston-hotels.com. This budget level condo is in Honokowai. Studio and 1/2BR units have a/c, full kitchens and private Lana`is with garden views. The complex has a pool, spa, barbecue area and laundry facilities. $$

Kapalua Bay Hotel, One Bay Drive, Kapalua, ☎ 800/367-8000, 808/669-5656. This is a luxurious, relatively small hotel (194 rooms) in the upscale Kapalua Resort area. All rooms have a/c, fridges, and are casually elegant. The hotel has all resort amenities, including pool, water activities, tennis, golf at the Kapalua Course. Lots of tropical gardens, pools and waterfalls. $$$

The Kapalua Villas, One Bay Drive, Kapalua, ☎ 800/367-8000, 808/669-5656. These luxury-class condo units are very large and roomy, with bright light decor and lots of room to move around. Units are exceptionally well-furnished, have TV, a/c, full kitchens and Lana`is. These are wonderful for families or groups. $$$

The Ritz-Carlton Kapalua, One Ritz Carlton Drive, Kapalua, ☎ 800/241-3333, 808/669-6200; e-mail mauiritz@maui.net; www.maui.net/~mauiritz/. This resort hotel is Kapalua's largest at 548 luxury rooms and has a tropical garden setting. It offers all the amenities and services expected at a first-class resort, including fitness center/spa, tennis, golf, restaurants, lounges and nearby Kapalua Beach. $$$

South Coast - Ma`alaea, Kihei to Makena

Maui's south-facing coast stretching from Ma`alaea to Kihei, Wailea and Makena covers miles of beautiful sunny beach, with numerous hotels and vacation condominiums, plus shopping, restaurants and activities. These beachside resort communities were developed during Maui's boom years from the 1970s through the 1980s.

Lauloa, 100 Hauoli, Ma`alaea, ☎ 800/367-6084. This is a small 47-unit complex of 2BR suites. Spacious airy rooms have nice ocean views of Ma`alaea Harbor area. $$

Makani A Kai, 300 Hauoli, Ma`alaea, ☎ 800/367-6084. This is a beachside condo next to a long stretch of Ma`alaea beach at the end of the Ma`alaea area. 1/2BR units have ocean views. Laundry facilities, pool and barbecue on site. $$

The Palms at Wailea, 3200 Wailea Alanui Drive, Wailea, ☎ 800/OUTRIGGER, 808/879-5800; e-mail reservations@outrigger.com; www.outrigger.com. This is a deluxe resort condo in well known Wailea Resort. Suites are luxuriously furnished with all amenities included. Near to golf, tennis and beach. $$

Maui Hill, 2881 S. Kihei Road, Kihei, ☎ 800/922-7866, 808/879-6321. This is a quiet, exclusive hideaway near the Wailea Resort. The 1/2/3BR units have a/c and all have ocean views, full kitchens and private Lana`is plus tennis, pool and spa. $$

Kamaole Sands, 2695 S. Kihei Road, Kihei, Castle Resorts ☎ 800/367-5004, 808/874-8700; www.castle-group.com. This complex is located on 15 acres of tropically landscaped grounds just across the road from Kamaole Beach. The spacious 1/2BR units have full kitchens and private lanais. There are tennis courts, pool, spa, barbecue area and guest services desk on site. $$

Aston at the Maui Banyan, 2575 S. Kihei Road, Kihei, ☎ 800/922-7866, 808/875-0004; www.aston-hotels.com. This deluxe condo complex is just across the road from popular Kamaole Beach Park. The 1/2/3BR units have full kitchens, private Lana`is, in-unit laundry. There are also two pools, spas, tennis court and barbecue area with golf nearby. $$

Aston Maui Lu Resort, 575 S. Kihei Road, Kihei, ☎ 800/922-7866, 808/879-5881; www.aston-hotels.com. This is one of Kihei's oldest hotels and has a decidedly old Hawai`i feel. Located on 28 acres of lush tropical grounds. Rooms are a/c with garden or ocean views; across the road from the beach. All hotel amenities and services available. $$

Maui Coast Hotel, 2259 S. Kihei Road, Kihei, ☎ 800/426-0670, 08/874-6284. One of Kihei's newer hotels, it has 260 rooms and suites. Across the road from Kamaole Beach, it has all the standard hotel amenities – pool, spa, restaurant, tennis courts, and laundry facilities. Central location close to shopping, activities, dining, etc. $$

Maui Vista, 2191 S. Kihei Road, Kihei, ☎ 800/922-7866, 808/879-7966. A quiet location just across from Kamaole Beach. The studio and 1/2BR units are spacious and well furnished with complete kitchens, in-room laundry and private lanais. There are three pools, six tennis courts and lots of barbecue facilities on grounds. Good value. $$

Maui Oceanfront Inn, 2980 S. Kihei Road, Kihei, HI 96753; Castle Resorts ☎ 800/367-5004, 808/879-7744; www.castle-group.com. This 85-room hotel is at the end of the Kihei area, right on white-sand Keawakapu Beach, with excellent swimming and water sports. Full hotel services and amenities, golf, tennis and shopping nearby in addition to other attractions and activities. $

Aston Wailea Resort, 3700 Wailea Alanui, Wailea, ☎ 800/922-7866, 808/879-1922; www.aston-hotels.com. This is a sprawling 516-room oceanfront property flanked by two fine beaches, Ulua Beach and Wailea Beach. The hotel has a large open-air lobby, shops, artwork throughout the public areas, restaurants, two pools and all the usual hotel amenities and services. $$$

Renaissance Wailea Beach Resort, 3550 Wailea Alanui, Wailea, ☎ 800/992-4532, 808/879-4900. This 347-room deluxe resort hotel is one of Wailea Resort's older but nicely kept properties. Rooms are luxuriously appointed with all the amenities, including fridge, a/c, mini-bar and private lanai. The hotel has all services and recreational activities available. The grounds are adjacent to Ulua Beach and filled with dense tropical foliage. $$$

Maui Prince Hotel, 5400 Makena Alanui, Makena, ☎ 800/321-6284, 808/874-1111; www.westin.com. The Makena Resort area is at the far end of Maui's south coast and the Maui Prince is its flagship hotel. This is a luxury 310-room hotel with a distinct classy elegance. There are lovely central courtyard grounds with fish ponds and waterfalls. Rooms are well furnished and have all amenities. The hotel has pools, golf, tennis and Maluaka Beach fronting the property. $$$

Upcountry - Makawao to Kula

Staying in upcountry Maui is an opportunity to enjoy the country ambiance of small towns and ranch country, plus a decidedly cooler climate than the beachside resorts. Enjoy good views across Central Maui to the West Maui mountains. Explore country towns and discover interesting shops and restaurants.

Ahinahina Farm Vacation Bungalows, 210 Ahinahina Place, Kula, HI 96790, ☎ 808/878-3927, ext. 5. This upcountry bed and breakfast operation has a studio and 2BR cottage unit available. The studio sleeps two, while the cottage sleeps four. Units have private bath, TV, private deck. $

Banyan Tree House, 3265 Baldwin Avenue, Makawao, HI 96768, ☎ 808/572-9021. This is an upcountry bed and breakfast in Makawao. Bedrooms have private bath, while a studio cottage has kitchen and open lanai. Full breakfast included. $

Hale Kokomo, 2719 Kokomo Road, Haiku, ☎ 808/572-5270. A 1920s-era Victorian B&B located between Haiku and Makawao towns at the 1,500-foot elevation, just minutes from famed Ho`okipa Beach and Paia town. Surrounded by tropical gardens of ginger, jasmine, banana, avocado and coconut trees. There are four guest rooms. $

Kula Lodge, RR1, Box 474, Kula, ☎ 800/233-1535, 808/878-2517. This country lodge is located 5½ miles past Pukalani town on the Haleakala Highway. The lodge is at the 3,200-foot level and there are five mountain chalet cabins. A good location to enjoy the cool mountain climate of upcountry Maui. Restaurant on site. $$

Kula Hula Inn, 112 Ho`opalua Drive, Makawao, HI 96768, 888/HU-LAINN, ☎ 808/572-9351; e-mail kulahula@maui.net; www.maui.net/~kulahula/. Located upcountry in the Kula area near Makawao town, this is a delightful B&B at a 2,300-foot elevation, with super views of the ocean and West Maui. Enjoy warm sunny days and cool nights. Convenient to all Maui attractions, beaches, town and excursions. $

Kula View B&B, PO Box 322, Kula, HI 96790, ☎ 808/878-6736. This country B&B is on the slopes of Haleakala. Guest room has private bath, deck and entrance. $

Silver Cloud Upcountry Guest Ranch, RR2, Box 201, Kula, HI 96790, ☎ 800/532-1111, 808/878-6101; e-mail slvcld@mau.net; www.maui.net/~slvcld. This small ranch is at the 2,800-foot level of Haleakala. Guests choose from main house suites, Paniolo Bunkhouse studios or the private Lana`i Cottage. The units all have private bath and other amenities, some with kitchen and lanai. $

East Maui - Hana

Enjoy the tropical rain forest splendor of Maui's rugged and lush east coast area and historic Hana town. This quiet laid-back area of remote villages and settlements also provides many adventure activities, from hiking and biking to historic site visits and driving the beautiful Hana Highway.

Hana Alii Holidays, PO Box 536, Hana, HI 96713, ☎ 800/548-0478, 808/248-7742; e-mail duke@maui.net; www.maui.net/~duke/hanaAlii-Holidays.html. Studio and 1BR condos, as well as cottages or homes available. Units overlook Hana Bay, are near to Hamoa Beach or have scenic hillside country views. $

Hana Plantation Houses, PO Box 249, Hana, HI 96713, ☎ 800/228-HANA, 808/923-0772; e-mail hana@kestrok.com; www.kestrok.com/~hana/Hana.html. Vacation homes ranging from a two-story plantation-style house to a solar-powered home near town. Units sleep up to four. $$

Heavenly Hana Inn, PO Box 790, Hana, HI 96713, ☎ 808/248-8442. A Japanese-style inn with 2BR suites. Rooms have Japanese furo bath, Lana`i and other amenities. $$

Hotel Hana-Maui, PO Box 8, Hana, ☎ 800/321-HANA, ☎ 808/248-8211. Hana's world famous secluded and sophisticated luxury hotel. This 93-room hotel is in the middle of Hana town. Rooms are modest yet elegant, with no a/c or TV. The hotel also has a number of oceanview plantation-style cottages at Kaihalulu Bay. Emphasis is on privacy, personalized service and Aloha. Hotel has full services and amenities. $$$$

Camping

■ County Camp Sites

 There are campgrounds on Maui operated by the County of Maui, State of Hawai`i and the national park service. Permits are required for the county and state park campgrounds, but not for the federal campgrounds.

Baldwin Park at Paia town is operated and maintained by the County of Maui. Facilities include restrooms, showers and space for tent camping.

Kanaha Park at Kahului is operated and maintained by the County of Maui. Camping space and restrooms available.

Permits and camping fees ($3 per person per day) through **Department of Parks and Recreation**, County of Maui-Permits Office, 1580-C Ka`ahumanu Avenue, Wailuku, HI 96793, ☎ 808/243-7230.

■ State Camp Sites

There are two state parks on Maui where camping is allowed. A no-fee permit is required. Contact **Division of State Parks**, 54 South High Street, Wailuku, HI 96793, ☎ 808/984-8109.

Polipoli State Park is located in a wooded area at the 6,200-foot elevation level on the west slope of Haleakala Crater. Facilities include restrooms and picnic tables; 4WD vehicle recommended for upper portion of road.

Waianapanapa State Park is on a scenic rocky coastline in East Maui near the small town of Hana, 55 miles from Kahului. Facilities include restrooms, picnic tables, outdoor showers and BBQ grills; campers must have tent or camper van. There are also a dozen self-contained fully-furnished housekeeping cabins with beginning rental rates of $45 per night for up to four people.

■ National Park Camp Sites

No permits or fees required to camp in federal campgrounds within Haleakala National Park. Three hikers' cabins located in Haleakala Crater require advance reservations and minimal per person use fees. For information, contact **Haleakala National Park**, PO Box 360, Makawao, HI 96768, ☎ 808/572-9306.

Hosmer Grove is at the 7,000-foot elevation on Haleakala off the summit highway. Facilities include space for tent camping, restrooms, BBQ grills, water and picnic tables. Nice nature hike through forest area and open grassland.

Ohe`o-Seven Pools is 15 miles beyond Waianapanapa State Park on the Hana Highway in the Kipahulu area. Facilities include campgrounds, portable restrooms, picnic tables, BBQ grills; campers provide own drinking water.

Dining

Maui has a veritable cornucopia of eateries. There are inexpensive family restaurants and diners serving local-style favorite cuisine and plate lunches. And there are also first-class fine dining rooms in resorts featuring exotic Asian/Pacific and the popular Hawaiian Regional Cuisine. If anything, Maui has too many dining choices. The following are just a few of the options. The restaurant price ranges, as in the other island sections of this book, are based on the average dinner meal, exclusive of tax, alcoholic beverages and desserts.

Dining Price Scale
$ . . . . under $10 per person
$$ . . . . $10-25 per person
$$$ . . . . $25 and up per person

■ Luaus

Legends of Makena, Maui Prince Hotel, Makena Resort, ☎ 808/875-5888. This legendary dinner show takes place on the hotel grounds and features table-service with a full Hawaiian feast of laulau, kalua pig, island fish, poi, fresh fruits and much more. Sunday evenings only, 5:30 p.m. $$$

Wailea's Finest Luau, Aston Wailea Resort, Wailea, ☎ 808/879-1922. This dinner show features an open tropical cocktail bar, torchlighting ceremony, hula show and more on lovely oceanfront grounds. Includes a full island buffet of traditional luau foods and delicacies. Call for times. $$$

Old Lahaina Luau, Old Lahaina Café & Luau, 505 Front Street, Lahaina, ☎ 808/667-1998. This oceanfront café also puts on a traditional nightly Hawaiian luau complete with lei greeting, hula and song and a full buffet luau feast. $$$

Drums of the Pacific Luau, Hyatt Regency Maui, Ka`anapali Beach, ☎ 808/667-4727. This is an exciting Polynesian revue featuring songs and dances of the Pacific Islands and a spread of authentic Hawaiian luau foods. $$$

Marriott Luau, Maui Marriott Hotel, Ka`anapali Beach, ☎ 808/661-LUAU. This luau dinner show takes place beachside and features a full buffet with traditional Hawaiian foods and a Polynesian music and dance program. $$$

■ Dinner Cruises

Taste of Maui Dinner Cruise, sponsored by Pacific Whale Foundation, ☎ 808/879-8811, offered on the 50-foot catamaran *Manute`a*. Enjoy a four-course gourmet island dinner accompanied by live Hawaiian music. $$$

Sunset Odyssey Dinner Cruise, ☎ 808/661-8787, offered on the high tech SWATH (small waterplane area twin hull) *Navatek II,* which delivers the smoothest ride possible regardless of ocean conditions. Enjoy a full island style dinner and Hawaiian entertainment. $$$

Maui's Finest Sunset Dinner Cruise, ☎ 808/667-6165, aboard the 118-foot luxury yacht, *Maui Princess*, is a romantic cruise on Lahaina's calm waters. Spectacular views from the open-air dining deck. Air-conditioned main deck and lounge, island-style dinner and live entertainment. $$$

■ Restaurants

Central Maui - Wailuku and Kahului

Chum's, 1900 Main Street, Wailuku, ☎ 808/244-1000, is one of Maui's venerable family-style cafés noted for local-style favorites such as chicken katsu, beef tomato, pork cutlet and mahimahi stir fry. $

Cupie's Drive In, 134 W. Kamehameha Avenue, Kahului, ☎ 808/877-3055, is one of Maui's oldest and most popular plate lunch eateries. This lunch counter, originally a drive-in, features such items as hamburger steak, beef teriyaki, kalbi short ribs, chili with hot dog, saimin noodles and chow fun noodles. $

Picnics, 30 Baldwin Avenue, Paia town, ☎ 808/579-8021. This country town eatery has a lengthy menu of sandwiches, burgers, salads and plate lunch specials like herb roasted chicken, teriyaki beef and chicken, fish and chips and fresh grilled fish. They specialize in take-out picnic baskets for excursions to the Hana Coast or Upcountry Maui. $

Norm's Café, 740 Lower Main St., Wailuku, ☎ 808/242-1667, is a funky local-style café with plain decor – nothing fancy here. The lunch-dinner menu features local favorites like chop steak, beef tomato, roast pork, fried chicken, beef stew, chicken curry, tripe stew, fried corn beef and onions, fried rice, burgers, sandwiches and salads. $

Nazo's Restaurant, 1063 Lower Main St., Wailuku, ☎ 808/244-0529. This family-operated local-style café features Filipino, Hawaiian and Oriental specials like chicken papaya, pork adobo, pork and squash, chicken luau stew, pig feet soup, Hawaiian plate, teriyaki steak, chicken katsu, ahi tuna, liver and onions, plus noodles and sandwiches. $

Fujiya's, 133 Market Street, Wailuku, ☎ 808/244-0206, has some of Maui's best Japanese food. The menu includes choices like tempura, teriyaki, chicken katsu, pork tofu, miso butterfish, ahi or salmon. They also have a variety of fresh-made sushi. $

Sam Sato's, 1750 Wili Pa Loop, Wailuku, ☎ 808/244-7124. This is a local-style noodle eatery famous for their saimin and Maui-style chow fun noodles. The menu also has daily specials plus standards like teriyaki beef, stew and hamburger steak. The fresh baked peach, apple and coconut turnovers and traditional Japanese pie crust manju are excellent. A great lunch stop. $

Chart House, 500 N. Pu`unene Avenue, Kahului, ☎ 808/877-2476. If you want great steaks and seafood, this is the place. They have an extensive American menu of steaks, prime rib, fresh island fish, lobster, crab, prawns and salmon. $$

Saeng's Thai Cuisine, 2119 Vineyard, Wailuku, ☎ 808/244-1567. This is among the best of Maui's Thai restaurants with a pleasant clean atmosphere and lots of decorative plants. The menu is authentic Thai hot and spicy cuisine, including everything from curry chicken to ginger beef, garlic shrimp or spring rolls. They also have a Lahaina outlet. $$

Goldie's Store, 1951 Vineyard Street, Wailuku, ☎ 808/242-5519. This small operation serves up Maui's best local Filipino food. The menu has choices like pork & peas, chicken papaya, pork adobo, menudo and pin-acbet, plus desserts. There are several daily specials. $

Mama's Fish House, Highway 36 east, past Paia town, ☎ 808/579-8488. The menu here emphasi zes fresh island seafood. An old-fashioned by-the-sea restaurant. This is one of Maui's best seafood dining rooms and has been very popular over the years. $$$

Koho Grill and Bar, 275 Ka`ahumanu Avenue, Ka`ahumanu Center, Kahului, ☎ 808/877-5588. This is a good family dining place with a menu of sandwiches, burgers, some local-style favorites and Mexican fare as well. $

West Maui - Lahaina, Ka`anapali to Kapalua

Roy's Kahana Bar and Grill, 4405 Honoapi`ilani Highway, Kahana Gateway Center, ☎ 808/669-6999. This is the West Maui outlet of noted Roy's chain. Chef Roy Yamaguchi's restaurants are known for creative Hawaiian Regional Cuisine using local products. The menu changes nightly but includes dishes like blackened ahi tuna, banana pork loin, Mongolian rack of lamb and lemon grass chicken. Roy's is always busy, so reservations are suggested. $$$

Roy's Nicolina, 4405 Honoapi`ilani Highway, Kahana Gateway Center, ☎ 808/669-5000. This sister restaurant is next door to Roy's Kahana Bar and Grill. The menu is similar to Roy's but has different nightly specials and unique flatbreads. $$$

The Rusty Harpoon, Whalers Village at Ka`anapali Resort, ☎ 808/661-3123. This American-continental restaurant has a menu of sandwiches, burgers, entrées, pizza and appetizers. Popular with the tourist crowd. $$

BJ's Chicago Pizzeria, 730 Front St., Lahaina, ☎ 808/661-0700. This mainland chain introduced their special version of pizza to Maui and it's proven quite popular. Among the best are deep-dish, thick crust pizzas smothered in a variety of cheeses and fresh creative local-style toppings. The menu also features creative appetizers, sandwiches, pasta and salads. $

Lahaina Treehouse Restaurant, Lahaina Market Place on Front Street, Lahaina, ☎ 808/661-3235. There's been a treehouse restaurant here for years and it's a unique dining spot. The menu features sandwiches, burgers, pizza and creative dishes served with special pastries, breads and other bakery products. $$

Avalon, 844 Front Street, Lahaina, ☎ 808/667-5559. This restaurant is noted for its fine Hawaiian Regional Cuisine as done by Chef Mark Ellman, one of Hawai`i's culinary leaders. Emphasis is on fresh produce, meats and seafood prepared and served in a creative, tantalizing style. This is a casual yet elegant dining room with a '40s Hawaiian theme. $$$

Gerard's Restaurant, 174 Lahainaluna Road, in the Plantation Inn, Lahaina, ☎ 808/661-8939. This popular French cuisine restaurant offers a menu of local seafood and special selections done with a creative French/Hawaiian flair. Casual indoor or outdoor dining available. $$$

Longhi's, 888 Front Street, Lahaina, ☎ 808/667-2288. Long a Maui favorite, Longhi's has a menu of continental-Italian specials from creative pastas to exotics like prawns amaretto, Venetian shrimp or Italian lamb chops and chicken. Fabulous desserts complete the menu. $$$

Chez Paul, Highway 30 at Olowalu, ☎ 808/661-3843. This small classy dining room has a reputation for fine French food. Specials include poached fish, scampi, lobster and duck, a variety of superb appetizers and creative soups and salads plus exotic desserts. $$$

David Paul's Lahaina Grill, 127 Lahainaluna Road, Lahaina, ☎ 808/667-5117. This elegant restaurant features New American cuisine with southwestern accents. Creative entrées in an ever-changing menu include Maui onion seared ahi, Kona coffee roasted lamb, kalua duck and macadamia smoked salmon. Great food in a lavish setting. $$$

Hula Grill, in Whalers Village Shopping Center, Ka`anapali Resort, ☎ 808/667-6636. This is another of the famed Hawaiian Regional Cuisine restaurants, this one operated by Chef Peter Merriman. Everything from appetizers, salads and soups to entrées are creative and original with an emphasis on Hawaiian and Asian/Pacific flavors. This is a relaxing oceanfront dining room. $$$

Anuenue Room, The Ritz-Carlton Hotel, Kapalua, ☎ 808/669-6200. There are lots of hotel fine dining rooms in West Maui but this one is really nice. The cuisine is Hawaiian continental done with a French flair. The fine food is complemented by expert service and a plush comfortable ambiance. $$$

South Coast - Ma`alaea, Kihei to Makena

Aroma D'Italia Ristorante, 1993 S. Kihei Road, Kihei, ☎ 808/879-0133. This small authentic Italian café is a real find. Clean, bright and cheery, the food is equally zesty and satisfying. The menu features daily specials plus pasta selections, ravioli, spaghetti, lasagna, veal, chicken, shrimp and salads. $$

Maui

Alexander's Fish, Chicken & Ribs, 1913 S. Kihei Road, Kihei, ☎ 808/874-0788. The menu features lots of local seafood selections in a funky fast-food atmosphere across from the beach. Items include mahimahi, ono, ahi, shrimp and calamari, plus chicken and ribs. $

Maui Tacos, Kamaole Beach Center, 2411 S. Kihei Road, Kihei, ☎ 808/879-5005, other outlets at Napili, Lahaina and Kahului. The menu offers enchiladas, hard and soft tacos, quesadillas, burritos and more with an open salsa bar to spice your own. $

Chuck's Steak House, Kihei Town Center, Kihei, ☎ 808/879-4489. There is an extensive menu of steaks and prime rib plus Korean kalbi ribs and seafood items like cajun mahimahi, shrimp, fresh fish, appetizers and a great salad bar. $$

Lana`i Terrace, Aston Wailea Resort, Wailea, ☎ 808/879-1922. This hotel dining room offers an international menu and special themed buffet dinners several nights weekly. The food is excellent with views overlooking the property and ocean. $$$

Tony Roma's, 1819 S. Kihei Road, Kihei, ☎ 808/875-6188. This mainland chain features BBQ ribs plus combos with chicken, shrimp, fish and steak. Some local-style items like teriyaki beef and chicken, shrimp skewers, sandwiches. Nice family restaurant. $$

A Pacific Café-Maui, 1279 S. Kihei Road, Kihei, ☎ 808/879-0069. This is the Maui outlet for noted Chef Jean-Marie Josselin. He also has a restaurant on Kaua`i. The menu features fresh island products and creative Hawaiian Regional Cuisine. Entrées range from grilled steaks, chops and island fish to delicate roast duck, and seared scallops, mahimahi or beef tenderloin. Many terrific appetizers and desserts round out the menu. $$$

Buzz's Wharf, Ma`alaea Harbor, Highway 30, Ma`alaea, ☎ 808/244-5426. Buzz's has been around a long time. The steak and seafood menu has items like oriental fried shrimp, scallops Provencal, New York steak, prime rib, chicken pineapple, fresh fish. Try the Maui onion soup. There are nice views of Ma`alaea boat harbor. $$

Hula Moons, Aston Wailea Resort, Wailea, ☎ 808/879-1922. This Hawaiian-themed restaurant offers a seafood and American menu with choices like lemongrass chicken, lilikoi (passionfruit) duckling, garlic shrimp, mahimahi tempura and many more creative dishes, plus sandwiches and salads. It has a pleasant poolside location. $$

Waterfront, in Milowai Condo, Ma`alaea, ☎ 808/244-9028. If you like fresh seafood, it doesn't get much better than here. This family-owned restaurant features fresh island seafood with a variety of unique preparations. They get their fish right from Ma`alaea harbor boats. The menu also has veal, chicken and an occasional wild game selection for variety. $$

Upcountry - Makawao to Kula

Grandma's Maui Coffee, Highway 37 at Keokea, ☎ 808/878-2140. This small country coffee house offers fresh brewed Maui coffees plus homemade pastries, sandwiches and light lunch fare. $

Upcountry Café, Highway 37, Pukalani, ☎ 808/572-2395. This is a bright, clean country style café. The menu is local favorites including beef and chicken teriyaki, mahimahi, chicken curry, hamburgers, sandwiches and daily specials. $

Casanova Italian Restaurant, 1188 Makawao Avenue, Makawao, ☎ 808/572-0220. The menu includes a variety of breakfast selections and lunch-dinner sandwiches, salads, baked fish, filet mignon, veal chop, seafood, pastas and pizza. $$

Kula Lodge, on Haleakala Highway 377, five miles past Pukalani, ☎ 808/878-1535. They have a breakfast menu and continental-international fare featuring local products. Featured entrées include raspberry duckling, rack of lamb, seafood pasta, shrimp and crab. Enjoy a scenic view of Maui's splendor and mountain sunsets next to a cheery fireplace. $$

**Hali`imaile General Store,** Hali`imaile Road, Hali`imaile, ☎ 808/572-2666. This old pineapple plantation village store has won wide acclaim for its creative Hawaiian regional and continental-inspired cuisine. The seasonal menu features local products with fresh innovations in preparation and cookery. Entrées might range from Hawaiian blackened chicken to Hunan lamb or duck to coconut seafood curry and BBQ salmon. The menu also features creative appetizers and desserts. $$$

Makawao Steak House, 3612 Baldwin, Makawao, ☎ 808/572-8711. This upcountry steak house features New York steak, prime rib, fresh island fish, pork chops, chicken, scampi and pasta dishes plus interesting appetizers, soups (try the Portuguese bean soup) and salads. $$

East Maui - Hana

Hana Ranch Restaurant, Hana town, ☎ 808/248-8255. They feature a daily buffet lunch and a dinner menu of BBQ ribs, steaks, teriyaki chicken, prawns, pasta, seafood and pizza. $$

Maui

Hotel Hana Maui Dining Room, Hotel Hana Maui, ☎ 808/248-8211. This exclusive fine dining room features a continental menu. Selected entrées include prime rib, steaks, Thai chicken, pork, pastas and fresh island fish, also appetizers, salads. $$$

Hana Gardenland Café, Hana Highway, ☎ 808/248-7340. This small eatery is part of the nursery operation. They have breakfast items plus sandwiches, soups, salads, light lunch and other snacks. $

Tutu's, at the pavilion, Hana Bay, is a small lunch and snack counter offering sandwiches, local-style plate lunch fare, ice cream and cold drinks. $

Moloka`i

The Friendly Island

Geography

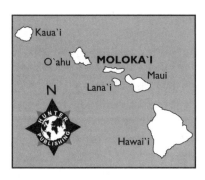

Moloka`i, the Friendly Isle, has a land mass area of 261 square miles and is the fifth largest of the Hawaiian Islands. It has a population of about 6,000. Moloka`i is part of the County of Maui and its main population center is the small port town of Kaunakakai. The island has 88 miles of coastline ranging from some of the highest seacliffs in the world (over 3,000 feet) on the north shore to sandy beaches and placid coral reef lagoons on the south shore. The island is rectangular in shape, 38 miles long by 10 miles wide. The highest point is Kamakou at 4,970 feet on the island's eastern end. The age of Moloka`i, as measured by a comparison of its structural lava flows, ranges from 1.3 to 1.8 million years.

Climate

The average temperature range is 70-75° around the island. Rainfall averages 30 inches annually on the lush, windward, eastern end to only a few inches on the dry, windy, leeward end of the island.

History

The Friendly Isle of Moloka`i was once known as the Lonely Isle due to the power of its kahuna (priests), who were feared throughout the islands for their supposedly supernatural powers. Generally, warring island kings gave Moloka`i a wide berth. Persecuted natives and those seeking protection often fled there for refuge. The nobility of Moloka`i was as princely as any in Hawai`i.

Kamehameha the Great journeyed to Moloka`i in 1790 to arrange for the hand of his queen, the high chiefess Keopuolani. In 1795, Kamehameha conquered the island in his westward offensive toward O`ahu. It was from Moloka`i that Kamehameha launched his final assault on O`ahu, which culminated in the unification of the islands under one kingdom.

Moloka`i, being small and relatively insignificant, fell into relative obscurity. It wasn't until the 1860s that Moloka`i once again became important. This was when the government of Hawai`i established a Hansen's Disease (leprosy) treatment settlement at Kalaupapa on the isolated northern peninsula of Makanalua. Actually, it was more like a penal colony, as the unfortunate victims of the disease were unceremoniously dragged from their homes and families all over the islands and shipped off to Kalaupapa. Once there, the "patients" were never allowed to leave. Kalaupapa became a hell-hole of despair and hopelessness for those who contracted the feared disease and were sent there to live out their days. It was onto this scene that Father Damien de Veuster, a Belgian priest, happened in 1873. The good priest chose to go to Kalaupapa and minister to the sick and dying lepers. For the next several years he did so until he himself caught the horrible disfiguring disease and died. Father Damien is one of the true heroes of Hawai`i. Today, the old settlement is known as the Kalaupapa National Historical Park.

Information Sources

Hawai`i Visitors and Convention Bureau, Waikiki Business Plaza, 2270 Kalakaua Avenue, 8th. Fl., Honolulu, HI 96815, ☎ 800/GOHawaii, 808/923-1811; www.visit.Hawaii.org/.

Moloka`i Visitors Association, PO Box 960, Kaunakakai, HI 96748, ☎ 800/800-6367, 808/553-3876 or 553-5221; e-mail mva@Molokai-Hawaii.com; http://Molokai-Hawaii.com/.

Avatar Public Relations, 2587 La`i Road, Honolulu, HI 96816, ☎ 808/732-5278, fax 808/737-4278; e-mail: avatar@hi.net.

Halawa Valley lookout, east end of Moloka`i.

References

Alford, John. **Mountain Biking the Hawaiian Islands: Mauka to Makai,** Ohana Publishing, Honolulu, HI. 1997.

Brocker, James. **A Portrait of Moloka`i,** Moloka`i Island Creations. 1995.

Brocker, James. **The Lands of Father Damien,** Moloka`i Island Creations. 1998.

Clark, John. **Beaches of Maui County,** University of Hawai`i Press, Honolulu, HI. 1994.

Englebert, Omer, Crawford, Benjamin T. **Damien, Hero of Moloka`i,** Pauline Books & Media, 1994.

Kepler, Angela K. and Cameron B. **A Majestic Moloka`i: A Nature Lover's Guide,** Mutual Publishing, Honolulu, HI. 1992.

Koch, Tom. *Six Islands on Two Wheels,* Bess Press, Honolulu, HI. 1990.

Olsen, Brad. *Extreme Adventures Hawai`i,* Hunter Publishing, Edison, NJ. 1998.

Smith, Rodney. *Hawai`i: A Walker's Guide,* Hunter Publishing, Edison, NJ. 1997.

Zurick, David. *Hawai`i, Naturally,* Wilderness Press, Berkeley, CA. 1990.

Getting There

■ Airline Service

- **Island Air,** ☎ 800/323-3345, in Hawai`i, ☎ 800/652-6541; e-mail aloha@alohaair.com; www.alohaair.com/. This subsidiary of Aloha Airlines operates several daily flights to Moloka`i from Honolulu or Kahului and Hana on Maui.

- **Hawaiian Airlines,** US and Canada, ☎ 800/367-5320, on Moloka`i, ☎ 808/553-3644; www.Hawaiianair.com/. There are daily flights from Honolulu to Moloka`i and connecting flights to the other neighbor islands.

- **Moloka`i Air Shuttle/Kalaupapa Air Shuttle,** 99 Mokuea Place, Honolulu, HI 96819, ☎ 808/567-6847, 808/545-4988; this airline specializes in air tours of Moloka`i's North Shore and Kalaupapa; they also have flights to O`ahu and Lana`i.

- **Polynesian Airways,** 471 Aowena Place, Honolulu, HI 96819, ☎ 808/836-3838, and on Moloka`i, ☎ 808/567-6647; daily flights, charters and air tours between Honolulu and Moloka`i.

Getting Around

Moloka`i Airport is near the middle of this elongated island. From the airport it is eight miles east to Kaunakakai town; Maunaloa Village and Moloka`i Ranch are about 12 miles west; Kaluakoi Resort on the far west end of the island is 15 miles; the beautiful Halawa Valley on the far eastern end is 36 miles; Pala`au State Park and Kalaupapa Lookout is nine miles northeast of the airport.

Most of the lodgings and accommodations are located in two places. The first major concentration of hotels and condos is at Kaluakoi Resort on the far west end of Moloka`i. Located here are the Kaluakoi Hotel, Ke Nani Kai Condo, Kaluakoi Villas, and Paniolo Hale Resort Condo. Most of the other major lodgings are spread out along the southern coast just east of Kaunakakai town. These include the venerable Pau Hana Inn, Moloka`i Shores Condo, Hotel Moloka`i, and Wavecrest Condo. Bed and breakfasts are found in residential areas around Moloka`i.

Whether you're exploring by bike, car, or on foot, a good map will be helpful. The *Map of Moloka`i and Lana`i,* by James Bier, published by the University of Hawai`i Press, is an excellent full color topographic map. Look for the latest edition in shops around the islands.

There is basically one road on Moloka`i. It goes from the east end of the island at Halawa Valley through Kaunakai town, past the airport and continues west to Maunaloa Village, ending at Kaluakoi Resort on the far west end. There is a short branch road north to the Kalaupapa Lookout, but that's about it. So, navigating around the island will be a breeze. The road east from Halawa Valley runs through the rain forest hills and gulches of the east end and becomes an enjoyable drive along a beautiful coast of beaches and fishponds. At Kaunakai, the road bends inland past the airport and heads west through drier, warmer open farmlands and plains with a gradual climb uphill. From the Maunaloa area, the road passes through cattle pastures, remnants of the old pineapple plantation fields, and descends through open arid rolling countryside to the golden beaches of Kaluakoi.

Moloka`i

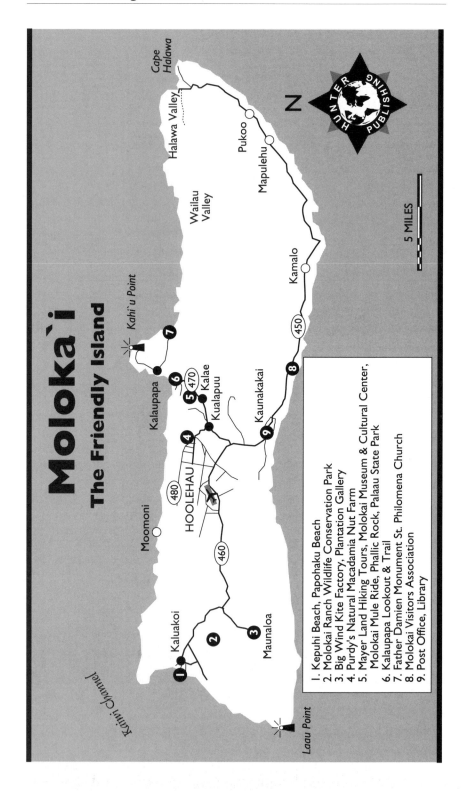

Moloka'i
The Friendly Island

1. Kepuhi Beach, Papohaku Beach
2. Molokai Ranch Wildlife Conservation Park
3. Big Wind Kite Factory, Plantation Gallery
4. Purdy's Natural Macadamia Nut Farm
5. Mayer Land Hiking Tours, Molokai Museum & Cultural Center, Molokai Mule Ride, Phallic Rock, Palaau State Park
6. Kalaupapa Lookout & Trail
7. Father Damien Monument St. Philomena Church
8. Molokai Visitors Association
9. Post Office, Library

Since Moloka`i is small and traffic is generally light and slow, it won't take you long to get to your lodging. Do drive slowly; there is no need to rush anywhere on this small rural island. Take the time to enjoy the sights along the way. Remember Moloka`i doesn't even have a traffic signal anywhere on the island. It's a very special sort of place.

■ Car Rentals & Car Service

Your best option for freedom and independence on Moloka`i is renting your own car. Car rental rates are a bit higher here generally than elsewhere in the Hawaiian Islands. But, with your own car, you can explore the island pretty thoroughly in a couple of days. There are just two car rental agencies at present on Moloka`i and one airport shuttle service.

- **Budget Rent a Car,** Moloka`i Airport, PO Box 217, Ho`olehua, HI 96729, ☎ 800/527-0700, 808/567-6877.

- **Dollar Rent a Car,** Moloka`i Airport, PO Box 346, Ho`olehua, HI 96729, ☎ 800/367-7006, 808/567-6156.

- **Kukui Tours & Limousine,** PO Box 1985, Kaunakakai, HI 96748, ☎ 808/553-5133. This operator provides island-wide scenic tours, as well as special custom tour and airport transportation packages.

■ Bicycle Rentals

If you didn't bring your own bike to Moloka`i, there is one shop that rents bikes and equipment. Biking Moloka`i is a relaxing and enjoyable experience. There is little traffic, the roads are quite good generally and Moloka`i is just a great place to explore at a leisurely pace on a bike.

- **Moloka`i Bicycle,** PO Box 379, Kaunakakai, HI 96748, ☎ 800/709-BIKE, 808/553-3931. This shop has a full line of bike rentals, accessories and equipment; also ideas and suggestions on seeing Moloka`i via quiet uncrowded roads.

Moloka`i

Touring Moloka`i

Any of the following can provide details on sightseeing tours of Moloka`i's major attractions. Call them for details. Standard two-hour scenic tours begin at $36 per person; standard four-hour tours begin at $49 per person. Backroad rain forest adventures begin at $53 per person. Tour packages to **Kalaupapa National Historic Park** include airfare from Moloka`i Airport ($50 per person) and a four-hour guided tour ($22 per person, adults only).

Kukui Tours & Limousine, PO Box 1985, Kaunakakai, HI 96748, ☎ 808/553-5133. Island-wide scenic tours as well as special custom tour and airport transportation packages.

**Moloka`i Off-Road Tours & Taxi,** PO Box 747, Kaunakakai, HI 96748, ☎ 808/553-3369 or ☎ 808/552-2218. Specializes in "A Rain Forest Adventure," exploring Moloka`i's backroads and unique rain forest environment of eucalyptus, cypress and pine trees, plus over 500 different species of native Hawaiian plants. Pass through climates ranging from hot to mountain cool, dry desert to humid and rainy; view magnificent panoramas of verdant sea cliffs, waterfalls and offshore islands.

**Moloka`i Style Services,** Box 1, Kaunakakai, Moloka`i, HI 96748, ☎ 808/553-9090. This local family-operated service arranges all necessary transportation, accommodations and activities with one phone call. They can book every kind of adventure activity from whale watching, diving, snorkeling and fishing cruises to hiking, biking, hunting and off-road 4WD mountain tours of backcountry Moloka`i. Owned and operated by the Camara Ohana (family), who know their island better than anyone else.

**Damien Moloka`i Tours,** Box 1, Kalaupapa, Moloka`i, HI 96742, ☎ 808/567-6171. Tours to the historic Makanalua Peninsula, site of the former Hansen's disease (leprosy) colony. Known today as Kalaupapa National Historical Park, it is a restricted area and all visits must be coordinated by Damien Moloka`i Tours. You can arrive and depart Kalaupapa via the popular mule ride down the cliff trail, by hiking on foot, or by air service via Moloka`i Air Shuttle or Paragon Air. Or you can travel by different means, provided arrangements are made in advance. There are four-hour ground tours of the settlement and historic sites, including a picnic lunch. The tour includes visits to Father Damien de Veuster's church (St. Philomena), gravesite, the old settlement of Kalawao and historic buildings.

Adventures

Moloka`i's Best Adventures

Moloka`i has enough exciting and unique adventures to make any visit a memorable one. The following are 10 of Moloka`i's best.

- Stay at the **Moloka`i Ranch** and take part in their adventure activities – hiking, biking, kayaking, horseback riding or cattle roundups.

- Take the famous **Moloka`i Mule Ride** down to Kalaupapa on the Makanalua Peninsula.

- Take the land tour at **Kalaupapa National Historical Park** and learn the story of Father Damien and the leper settlement there.

- Drive or bike along the **east Moloka`i coast** to Halawa Valley.

- Drive or bike and picnic at **Pala`au State Park** and the Kalaupapa Lookout.

- Drive or bike to **Kaluakoi Resort** in west Moloka`i with its beautiful beaches.

- Take a Nature Conservancy of Hawai`i wilderness walk through the **Mo`omomi Dunes** area or the mountain bog **Kamakou Preserve**.

- Explore the **Coffees of Hawai`i** plantation farm at Kualapu`u and learn all about coffee production.

- Visit the **Purdy Macadamia Nut Farm** on Lihipali Avenue behind the Moloka`i High School in Ho`olehua to learn about macadamia nut production on a working family farm.

- Visit downtown **Kaunakakai** and stroll the shops and stores; pick up a loaf of famous Moloka`i bread. Better yet, make a late night visit (10 p.m.) to Kanemitsu Bakery's backdoor to buy their fresh bread hot from the oven. Ono! (Delicious!)

Moloka`i

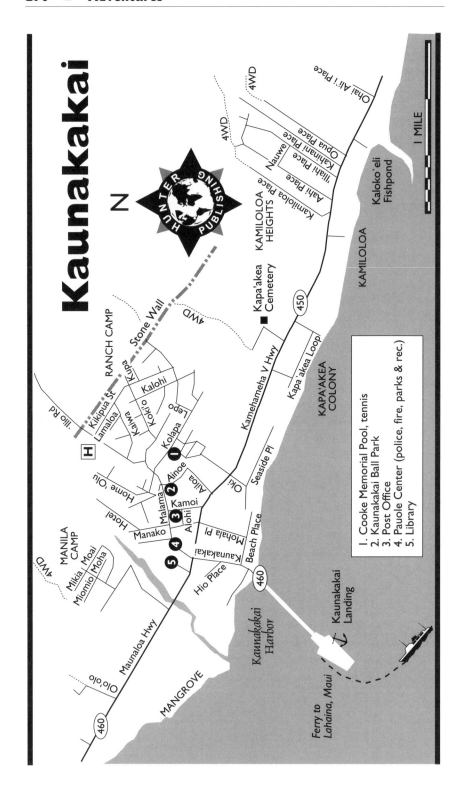

Kaunakakai

N

1. Cooke Memorial Pool, tennis
2. Kaunakakai Ball Park
3. Post Office
4. Pauole Center (police, fire, parks & rec.)
5. Library

1 MILE

■ On Foot

Moloka`i's best wilderness and backcountry hiking trails have controlled access by The Nature Conservancy environmental protection group. Visits must be arranged in advance and there are guided hikes on a regular basis. For information, contact **The Nature Conservancy**, Moloka`i Preserve, PO Box 220, Pueo Place, Kualapu`u, HI 96757, ☎ 808/553-5236, e-mail emisaki@tnc.org; or call the Honolulu office at ☎ 808/537-4508.

These trails are accessed only by 4WD vehicles via rugged backcountry mountain roads. **Kamakou Preserve** includes three separate trails. **Pelekunu Trail** is .4 mile and climbs to the rim of Pelekunu Valley, with spectacular views of a cloud forest, valleys and gulches. **Pepeopae Trail** is .6 mile and goes through the Pepeopae Bog via a boardwalk to keep hikers from disturbing the fragile native plant ecosystem. **Pu`u Kolekole Trail** is two miles long, beginning at the Pepeopae trailhead and leads through the cloud forest to the 3,951-foot summit of Pu`u Kolekole.

DON'T MISS **Mo`omomi Dunes** is on Moloka`i's northwestern coast. This area comprises three beaches, Kalani Beach, Kawa`aloa Beach and Mo`omomi Beach. This is a lonely, haunting and windswept place of crashing surf, gusty tradewinds and blowing sand. There are few wilder spots on Moloka`i. It is a dry, almost barren place where a few hardy native plants and seabirds hold on in a fragile ecosystem. Behind the coast, a large expanse of sand dunes called Keonelele is constantly being reshaped by the elements. It is an incredible place to wander and experience the wild elements of nature.

For a quiet relaxing adventure, pick any beach on Moloka`i's east coast along Highway 450, and walk the shoreline. The numerous old Hawaiian fishponds and reef lagoons, some of which have been and are being restored, are teeming with fish and seabirds. A quiet stroll along Moloka`i's uncrowded coastal areas can be an adventure in itself.

DON'T MISS **Moloka`i Ranch Trail System** covers the dry, rolling hill country of west Moloka`i and the ranch country. There are spectacular ocean coastal views, mountain views and open savannah-like country. Trails lead to historic sites such as old Hawaiian heiau (temple) ruins, village sites and caves. The ranch has guided and self-guided history and cultural hikes available. For information, contact: **Moloka`i Ranch Outfitters Center**,

Moloka`i

PO Box 259, Maunaloa, HI 96770, ☎ 800/254-8871, 808/552-2791; http://Moloka`i-ranch.com.

Halawa Valley once had an open trail network but parts of it have been closed indefinitely by private landowners due to liability problems. However, there have been recent reports that this may change and guided hikes may be restarted (or have been by the time this goes to press). If so, you will be able to hike once again all the way to the valley head and view the spectacular 500-foot Hipuapua Falls or the 250-foot Moa`ula Falls. The falls are visible from the highway lookout above the valley. For information on hiking Halawa Valley, contact **Moloka`i Visitors Association**, PO Box 960, Kaunakakai, HI 96748, in US and Canada, ☎ 800/800-6367 or 808/553-3876.

DON'T **MISS** **Kalaupapa Trail** is a four-mile round-trip up and down the 1,600-foot sea cliffs. This is an all-day adventure for strong hikers. The trail begins near Pala`au State Park close to the end of Highway 470, just above the Moloka`i Mule Ride barn. The rugged trail switchbacks down to Kalaupapa and the Makanalua Peninsula and the former leper colony settlement. This is the place where Father Damien de Veuster ministered to the lepers who were destined to live out their lives on this isolated peninsula. The colony existed from the late 1800s through the mid-1950s, when modern drugs were able to control the disease. The peninsula is now protected

Kalaupapa sea cliffs.

Mule riders along the beach, Kalaupapa Peninsula.

and preserved as Kalaupapa National Historical Park and includes a portion of the spectacular north shore cliffs, a National Natural Landmark. Permits are needed to traverse the trail and enter the settlement. Visitors can hike both ways, or hike in and fly out, hike in and ride a mule out or vice versa. It's most convenient to arrange a tour with **Damien Moloka`i Tours**, PO Box 1, Kalaupapa, HI 96742, ☎ 808/567-6171. As an alternative, contact **Moloka`i Mule Ride**, PO Box 200, Moloka`i, HI 96757-0200, ☎ 800/567-7550, 808/567-6088.

**Moloka`i Consulting & Associates, Inc.,** Lawrence Aki, PO Box 788, Kaunakakai, HI 96748, ☎ 808/553-9803, is a local company with interests in many areas. They can assist with individual and/or group visits to Moloka`i and help in arranging guided historical and cultural walks, hikes, cultural and history presentations, excursions and outings of various types to some of Moloka`i's most important areas, including Halawa Valley. Contact them for details.

Golf

Kaluakoi Golf Course, PO Box 26, Maunaloa, HI 96770, 888/552-2550, ☎ 808/552-2739. A par-72 layout at Kaluakoi Resort on Moloka`i's western end. The course has beautiful, expansive views of west Moloka`i and ocean fairways along Kepuhi and Papohaku Beaches. Rugged, open rangeland surrounds the course and deer, pheasant, turkey, quail and

Moloka`i

partridge roam the grounds. The course is subject to gusty tradewinds in the afternoons. Greens fees: $55-75.

Ironwood Hills Golf Course, PO Box 182, Kualapu`u, HI 96757, ☎ 808/567-6000. A delightful nine-hole golf course in Kalae on Highway 470 at the 1,200-foot elevation level on the way to Kalaupapa Lookout at the pali (cliffs). This mountain course provides a cool, breezy and enjoyable round of golf, perfect for a relaxing walk around the links. Greens fees: $10 for nine holes.

Shopping

DON'T **MISS** The Plantation Store, Coffees of Hawai`i, PO Box 160, Kualapu`u, Moloka`i, HI 96757, ☎ 808/567-9241. This country plantation store is near the junction of Highways 470 and 480 at Kualapu`u. Arts and crafts from over 30 Moloka`i artisans are featured, along with coffee plantation souvenirs, and the famous Malulani Estate Coffee and robust MuleSkinner Coffee; there is also an espresso bar, with snacks.

**Moloka`i Island Creations,** Ala Malama Street in Kaunakakai, ☎ 808/553-5926. This shop specializes in made-in-Hawai`i swimwear, tropical and Aloha-wear, general clothing and accessories, jewelry and unique gift items, Hawaiiana notecards, books.

Dudoit Imports, Ka Hua Center, Wharf Road in Kaunakakai, PO Box 138, Kualapu`u, HI 96757, ☎ 808/553-5011. Arts and crafts, collectibles, island coffees, teas, candies, plants, baskets, mats.

Imports Gift Shop, Ala Malama Street in Kaunakakai, ☎ 808/553-5734. Clothing, accessories, jewelry, surf gear, Hawaiiana, snacks, groceries.

**Moloka`i Surf,** Ala Malama Street in Kaunakakai, ☎ 808/553-5093. Look for the "Wear in There" sign. Moloka`i shirts, swimwear, surfwear, sportswear and surf accessories.

Take's Variety Store, Ala Malama Street in Kaunakakai, ☎ 808/553-5442. This small town variety store has just about everything.

Friendly Market Center, Ala Malama Street in Kaunakakai, ☎ 808/553-5595. A general grocery store right in town.

Misaki's, Ala Malama Street in Kaunakakai, ☎ 808/553-5505. Moloka`i's oldest grocery store right in the heart of town.

**Moloka`i Drug Store,** Kamoa Professional Plaza, Ala Malama Street in Kaunakakai, ☎ 808/553-5313, 808/553-5790. Moloka`i's only pharmacy and full-service drug store; good selection of Hawaiiana books.

Big Wind Kite Factory, in Maunaloa Town, west Moloka`i, ☎ 808/552-2364. This colorful shop specializes in handmade Hawaiian design, appliqued kites and windsocks for kids of all ages. Hula dancers, tropical fish kites and rainbow spinners are but a few of the many unique and colorful designs available, free flying lessons are included. Also an incredible array of imports, antiques, collectibles.

Hawaiian Arts & Crafts

**Basket Creations Moloka`i,** PO Box 1451, Kaunakakai, Moloka`i, HI 96748, ☎ 808/558-8202. This local artist will create special Aloha gift baskets of Moloka`i products, including famous Moloka`i bread, macadamia nuts, coffee, ready for shipping.

Carole Klein Jewelry Design, PO Box 610, Kaunakakai, HI 96748, ☎ 808/558-8569. This fine jewelry artist creates distinctive work in gold and silver; hand-crafted necklaces, earrings with Hawaiian themes and unique creations; custom orders.

Designs Pacifica, PO Box 1365, Kaunakakai, HI 96748, ☎ 808/553-5725. Watercolor artist Jule Patten creates papercast Hawaiian quilt designs, cards, clothing, glassware, floral and spirit paintings.

**H/S Pali & Sons of Moloka`i,** PO Box 154, Kualapu`u, HI 96757, ☎ 808/567-6769. This floral designer specializes in quality leis and floral arrangements; haku headband leis, akulikuli leis and any type of fresh or dry floral arrangement can be custom made.

**Moloka`i Emporium,** Puali Place, Kaunakakai. Browse through a variety of local made-on-Moloka`i arts and crafts, including opihi shell jewelry, puka shells, wood carvings and much more.

Artists of Moloka`i, PO Box 610, Kaunakakai, HI 96748, ☎ 808/553-3461. A network of local artisans creating contemporary and traditional Hawaiian art works, including jewelry, woodwork, painting, sculpture, quilts, photography and wearable art; studio visits and on-going exhibits.

Haku Designs, PO Box 900, Kaunakakai, HI 96748, ☎ 808/558-8419. Original silk-screened designs by Zennie Sawyer on Hawaiian-style garments, bags, shirts and dresses; nature-inspired designs, floral, ferns and tapas.

Hanaoka's Crafts & Furniture, PO Box 918, Kaunakakai, HI 96748, ☎ 808/553-3421. Beautiful woodwork bracelets, pendants, earrings, hairpicks, wall plaques made from koa, milo, monkey pod and mango woods.

Moloka`i

He Ki`i Kapa, PO Box 102, Kaunakakai, HI 96748, ☎ 808/553-5408 or 808/553-9989. This artist makes Hawaiian quilt pillow kits and hand-made Hawaiian quilts mounted in a frame.

Ida's Fine Lauhala, PO Box 5, Ho`olehua, HI 96729, ☎ 808/567-6662. Original pandanus (lauhala) hand-woven designs, bracelets, earrings, pendants, hair ornaments.

Tica's Creations, PO Box 235, Ho`olehua, HI 96729, ☎ 808/567-9406. Hand-made crafts like lauhala bracelets, earrings, ornaments, assorted haku and wili leis, fresh flower and ti-leaf leis and custom-made leis.

Moloka`i Kamani Kreations, PO Box 1355, Kaunakakai, HI 96748, ☎ 808/558-8405. Original one-of-a-kind art pieces like black-eyed Susy necklaces, kamani necklaces, earrings, warrior helmet designs, feather headbands, hair picks.

Pacific Frames, 287 Ilio Road, PO Box 1041, Kaunakakai, HI 96748, ☎ 808/553-5890. A custom picture framing and art workshop.

Plantation Gallery, PO Box 10, Maunaloa, HI 96770, ☎ 808/552-2364. On the main street of this small village, they carry works by Moloka`i's best artists and craftspeople, South Seas imports, and Hawaiiana.

Purdy's Natural Macadamia Nut Farm Giftshop, PO Box 84, off Highway 480 behind Moloka`i High School, Lihipali Avenue, Ho`olehua, HI 96729, ☎ 808/567-6601 or 808/567-6495. Their giftshop specializes in local Moloka`i-made arts and crafts.

Seaside Place Enterprises, Kamoi, Moloka`i, ☎ 808/553-4287, carries a collection of local Moloka`i arts and crafts.

Hunting

Hunting excursions for Moloka`i game begin at $150 for bow hunting and $250 for rifle hunting; non-resident hunting license is $100. Call outfitters for details.

**Ma`a Hawai`i-Moloka`i Action Adventures,** PO Box 1269 Kaunakakai, Moloka`i, HI 96748, ☎ 808/558-8184. Outfitter Walter Naki provides personal guided expeditions to hunt Axis deer, wild boar and Spanish goats plus gamebirds; fishing excursions also arranged. Rates for seasonal wild boar and goat hunting: $150 bow, $250 rifle. He takes no more than two hunters per day.

Moloka`i Ranch Hunts, PO Box 259, Maunaloa, HI 96770, ☎ 800/254-8871, 808/552-2791; http://Molokai-ranch.com. The ranch outfitters provide fully guided seasonal hunting expeditions on 2,400 acres of rolling ranchlands for Axis deer and gamebirds such as pheasant, quail, francolin and partridge.

The state non-resident hunting license fee is $95. The hunter has to get that himself. For hunting license info, contact: **Dept. of Land & Natural Resources**, Hunting Licenses, 1151 Punchbowl St., Honolulu, HI 96813; ☎ 808/587-3257.

■ On Wheels

 Moloka`i Airport is eight miles west of Kaunakakai town. Paved Highway 450 runs east along Moloka`i's east coast to Halawa Valley. Moloka`i's east end is lush, green and wet. Highway 460 runs west from Kaunakakai past the airport. It goes through west Moloka`i's midsection to Kaluakoi Resort on the far west coast and to the small village of Maunaloa, home to Moloka`i Ranch. The west end of Moloka`i is dry, breezy and usually warm. Highway 470 runs north and climbs to 1,600 feet elevation from near Kaunakakai through Kualapu`u to Pala`au State Park and the lookout to the Kalaupapa Peninsula. This north side of Moloka`i is usually breezy, cool and comfortable, with frequent cloudy mists rising up and over the towering sea cliffs of the north shore.

From Kaunakakai to Kaluakoi Resort's Papohaku Beach is a hot, dry ride of 23 miles. This is mostly a ride through rolling plains and hills of the west end's former pineapple fields. From the airport, the highway makes a gradual five-mile climb through farmlands, pastures and dry scrublands. The road branches off to the right, Kaluakoi Road, and leads downhill to the Kaluakoi Resort and its hotel, condos, and private homes, Kaluakoi Golf Course, Papohaku Beach, Po`olau Beach and Kepuhi Beach. There are hotel shops and a restaurant available. Highway 460 continues on a couple of more miles to the remote little village of Maunaloa, once home to a thriving pineapple plantation and community. The area is now owned by Moloka`i Ranch, which is developing an adventure-themed eco-cultural resort featuring upscale tent camping facilities. Maunaloa itself has been undergoing a transition, getting many new and renovated buildings along the main street. There are now gift shops, snack shops and general stores. The Moloka`i Ranch visitor program has given a new lease on life to this once-struggling community. The Moloka`i Ranch Outfitters Center in town can provide information on riding their ranch trail network, although it is usually reserved for guests. They also have a full range of other adventure activities available. As you ride through the countryside, you'll note the

Moloka`i

St. Joseph's Church.

old pineapple fields, which have been turned into cattle pastures. The ride back to town is downhill and flat, except for the climb up from Kaluakoi Resort to the highway.

From Kaunakakai to Halawa Valley and the East End is a scenic coastal ride on Kamehameha V Highway 450 of 36 miles. It rises into the hills of east Moloka`i, terminating at Halawa Valley. Riding east of town, there are several old Hawaiian fishponds enclosed with rock walls on the reef lagoons. There are also a number of historic sites, old Hawaiian heiau (temples) and burial caves along this stretch of coastline. Just 8½ miles east of Kaunakakai at Kamalo is St. Joseph's Church, built in 1876 by Father Damien DeVeuster of Belgium. This is the Father Damien who later went to minister to the outcast lepers at Kalaupapa and eventually contracted the fatal disease himself. He actually built several churches on Moloka`i during his many years on the island.

DID YOU KNOW?

A historic marker just down the road from St. Joseph's Church notes the spot where Ernest Smith and Emory Bronte crashed-landed in a kiawe thicket on the first transpacific flight from California in 1927, a historic event of the day.

Another of Father Damien's churches, Our Lady of Sorrows, built in 1874, is six miles further east at Kalua`aha and sits back off the road. The Kalua`aha Church here dates from 1844. A little further east at Puko`o is the Neighborhood Store and Snack Counter, a good place to pause for refreshments. Just past Waialua is Murpheys Beach County Park and behind the road the ruins of the old Moanui Sugar Mill. The Waialua Congregational Church here dates from 1855.

From Waialua, the road narrows considerably the last few miles as it winds along the indented and rugged coastline, gradually climbing inland and uphill. Offshore is the tiny islet of Moku Ho`oniki, which was used as a bombing target in World War II and is now a seabird sanctuary. As the road climbs toward Halawa Valley it passes through rolling ranchland pastures on Cape Halawa and Pu`u Hoku Ranch and Lodge. There are rustic accommodations available here but no grocery stores.

At the top of Halawa Valley is a nice lookout point with valley, beach and coastline views. The road descends sharply down the steep valley wall in a narrow winding route. Caution is advised on this stretch. The road ends at the beach and mouth of the valley. The valley has a network of trails and 4WD tracks, but most cross private lands. There used to be a two-mile trail to Hipuapua and Moa`ula Falls, visible at the head of the valley from the highway lookout. There have been recent reports that hiking into Halawa Valley may again be available. See the earlier section on hiking.

The ride back to town is mostly all downhill or flat except for the two-mile ride up from the valley.

DON'T **MISS** **Kaunakakai to Kalaupapa** is a definite uphill ride of about nine miles, climbing to 1,600 feet elevation and the ultimate overlook to Kalaupapa Peninsula on the island's north shore. This is an invigorating ride through the cool, breezy upcountry of Moloka`i. Take Highway 450 west from Kaunakakai to Highway 470, which goes north through Kualapu`u and Kalae to road's end at Pala`au State Park. Check out **Coffees of Hawai`i** plantation and store at Kualapu`u and the **Moloka`i Museum & Cultural Center** and **Meyer Sugar Mill** at Kalae. At Pala`au State Park, a short stroll through the breezy pine forest leads to the Kalaupapa Peninsula lookout. This provides a majestic panoramic view of the famed peninsula and Moloka`i's towering sea cliffs, rising to 3,000 feet in some areas. The state park also has an interesting rock formation called "**Phallic Rock**" for obvious reasons. The rock is associated with Hawaiian legends and fertility rites. Camping and picnicking is available at the state park. Also, just below the park is the **Moloka`i Mule Ride** and the **Kalaupapa Trail** down the pali (cliffs) begins nearby. Permits are required to hike the trail and enter the **Kalaupapa National Historical Park** and settlement below. Biking this trail is out of the question. Check with Moloka`i Mule Ride for details. The ride back to town is all downhill.

Moloka`i

Biking Resources

Bike rentals are available for about $20-25 daily; full-day bike adventures begin at about $140-169.

**Moloka`i Bicycle,** PO Box 379, Kaunakakai, HI 96748, ☎ 800/709-BIKE, 808/553-3931. Bike sales, rentals, accessories. They arrange tours to Moloka`i's quiet, uncrowded roads and attractions.

Moloka`i Ranch Outfitters Center, PO Box 259, Maunaloa, HI 96770, ☎ 800/254-8871, 808/552-2791; http://Molokairanch.com. The ranch provides luxury tent camping accommodations and outdoor activities, including biking through ranch country on a private network of trails to historic Hawaiian sites, scenic coastal routes and mountain trails with spectacular views.

Chris' Adventures, PO Box 869, Kula, HI 96790, ☎ 808/871-BIKE; www.lmg.com:80/maui/hykebyke.htm. This outfitter has day-long biking/hiking treks to Halawa Valley. Bike along beautiful coastal areas and ancient Hawaiian fishponds to Halawa Valley via Moloka`i's east coast. Check on availability of three-day bike adventures at special rates.

■ On Water

Beaches

Papohaku Beach Park, at Kaluakoi Resort, west Moloka`i.

Kepuhi Beach, at Kaluakoi Resort, west Moloka`i.

**Po`olau Beach,** off Kaluakoi and Pohakuloa Roads at Kaluakoi Resort, west Moloka`i.

Kioea Beach Park, next to Kapuaiwa Coconut Grove, Kaunakakai.

One Ali`i Beach Park, 2½ miles east of Kaunakakai on Highway 450.

**Kakahai`a Beach Park,** located five miles east of Kaunakakai on Highway 450 and next to Kakahai`a National Wildlife Refuge, a seabird preserve.

Murphey's Beach Park, located near Waialua about 18 miles east of Kaunakakai on Highway 450.

Halawa Beach Park, located 36 miles east of Kaunakakai at the end of Highway 450 at Halawa Valley.

Sailing, Diving, Snorkeling, Kayaking

There are a few operators and outfitters for ocean activities on Moloka`i. Check with any of the following. Rates for a two-hour sunset sail begin at $30 per person. Rates for a half-day sail and whale watch cruise are $40 per person. A full day of sailing to Lana`i with swimming and snorkeling is $90 per person. Scuba dives begin at about $75 per person. Half-day kayak adventures begin at about $30-40 per person.

**Moloka`i Charters,** PO Box 1207, Kaunakakai, Moloka`i, HI 96748, ☎ 808/553-5852. Richard and Doris Reed's *Satan's Doll* is a 42-foot sloop available for half- and full-day sailing charters, whale watching in season and snorkeling cruises to Lana`i.

Bill Kapuni's Snorkel & Dive Adventures, Kaluakoi Hotel, ☎ 808/552-2555. Hawaiian Bill Kapuni knows Moloka`i well and has morning and afternoon PADI instruction and dive/snorkel tours to some of the best reefs on Moloka`i to see dense populations of sea turtles, rays and other marinelife; all equipment included.

**Ma`a Hawai`i-Moloka`i Action Adventures,** PO Box 1269 Kaunakakai, Moloka`i, HI 96748, ☎ 808/558-8184. Outfitter and guide, Walter Naki, has guided excursions for snorkeling, skindiving, spearfishing, reef trolling and kayaking to some of Moloka`i's best outdoor areas.

**Moloka`i Fish & Dive,** PO Box 576, Kaunakakai, Moloka`i, HI 96748, ☎ 808/553-5926. This shop is right on Kaunakakai's main street and has a large selection of snorkeling equipment, fishing and camping gear, boogie boards for rent in addition to clothing, accessories and much more.

Fishing Charters

Half-day charters begin at $150 per day; full-day charters are $275.

Alyce C, PO Box 825, Kaunakakai, Moloka`i, HI 96748, ☎ 808/558-8377. Captain Joe Reich's Custom 31-foot sportfisher has half- and full-day charters available for ahi tuna, mahimahi, ono, ulua and Pacific blue marlin; whale watching cruises and inter-island charters.

Moloka`i

■ In the Air

Scenic Flightseeing

Airtours to Kalaupapa Peninsula begin at $50 per person; check with the airlines on current fares to other areas from Moloka`i.

**Moloka`i Air Shuttle/Kalaupapa Air Shuttle,** 99 Mokuea Place, Honolulu, HI 96819, ☎ 808/567-6847, 808/545-4988. Air tours of Moloka`i's North Shore and Kalaupapa; they also have flights to O`ahu and Lana`i.

Paragon Air, ☎ 800/428-1231, 808/244-3356; www.maui.net~wings/index.htm. Charters and air tours of Moloka`i, including Kalaupapa and Damien Tours.

Polynesian Airways, 471 Aowena Place, Honolulu, HI 96819, ☎ 808/836-3838, and on Moloka`i, ☎ 808/567-6647. Daily flights, charters and air tours between Honolulu and Moloka`i.

■ On Horseback

Trail Rides, Mule Rides & Wagon Rides

The mule ride to Kalaupapa Peninsula is $135 per person; hike in/hike out packages are $40 per person; hike in/fly out packages are $72 per person. Horseback trail rides begin at $40 per person. Horse-drawn wagon rides are $35 per person.

**Moloka`i Mule Ride,** Box 200, Moloka`i, HI 95757-0200, ☎ 800/567-7550, 808/567-6088, mule barn, ☎ 808/567-9269; e-mail muleman@aloha.net; www.muleride.com/company.html. This is one of Hawai`i's most unusual adventures and surely Moloka`i's best. Ride a sure-footed gentle mule down some of the highest sea cliffs in the world to the isolated former leper colony at Kalaupapa. Explore the place where Father Damien de Veuster labored among the outcast lepers in the 1870s-80s until he died of the disease himself. The ride up and down the rugged 1,700-foot cliff trail provides spectacular views of Kalaupapa and Moloka`i's north coast. Ride includes a van tour of the Makanalua peninsula and lunch. This is an eight-hour tour.

Moloka`i Horse & Wagon Ride, PO Box 1528, Kaunakakai, HI 96748, ☎ 800/670-6965, 808/558-8132; e-mail wgnride@aloha.net; www.visit-Molokai.com/wgnride/. This is a family-operated activity, located at Mapulehu Mango Grove, about 15 miles east of Kaunakakai town. There are hour-long horse-drawn wagon tours featuring the history and culture of the area and a guided tour of Ili`ili`o`pa`e, one of Hawai`i's largest remaining ancient heiau (temples). BBQ lunch is beachside, with Hawaiian crafts and games. Separately arranged horseback trail rides are similar and include treks into the mountains for scenic views of neighboring Maui, Kaho`olawe and Lana`i.

■ Eco/Cultural Activities

For a long time, Moloka`i's economy was dependent on large pineapple plantations. But in the mid-1970s, Dole Pineapple Company closed its operations. Then in the early '80s Del Monte Pineapple did the same. This of course brought long economic hardship for many residents. But today, with the help of new technology and farming methods, aquaculture and diversified small-crop agriculture are making a comeback on Moloka`i. As you drive through the Kualapu`u and Ho`olehua areas, you'll see large groves of coffee trees, macadamia nuts and papaya, plus fields of sweet potatoes, mild onions and famous Moloka`i watermelons. You can visit some of the farms and orchards to sample their products. Some are listed below.

Moloka`i Museum & Cultural Center,** Highway 470 at the four-mile marker at Kalae, ☎ 808/567-6436. This museum provides a step back 100 years in time to early Moloka`i. At the authentic 1878 **R.W. Meyer

Kalaupapa Peninsula, site of former Hansen's Disease settlement.

Moloka`i

Sugar Mill you can see a mule-driven cane crusher, copper clarifiers, redwood evaporating pans and a colorful old steam engine, all still in operating condition. A museum gift shop carries arts and crafts by local artisans. The Cultural Center staff can arrange activities such as Hawaiiana archaeological lectures, historical field trips and hiking excursions.

**Coffees of Hawai`i,** Highways 470/480 in Kualapu`u, ☎ 800/709-BEAN, 808/567-9241; e-mail coffees@aloha.net. Nestled in the cool foothills of Kualapu`u, this plantation has over 450 acres of Hawaiian coffee groves in production. They grow some of Hawai`i's newest coffees, including "Malulani Estate" (heavenly aroma), a full-bodied low-acidic washed arabica rich in taste and flavor, and the original "Mule Skinner" brand, a natural dry and robust arabica dedicated to the mule skinners of Moloka`i. The coffee is entirely produced and processed at the plantation to ensure the freshest farm quality and standard. Visit this working plantation and enjoy a mule-drawn wagon tour through the fields, browse the Plantation Store for coffee products, souvenirs and Moloka`i crafts and sample an array of fresh-brewed coffees and snacks at the Espresso Bar.

Purdy's Natural Macadamia Nut Farm, PO Box 84, off Highway 480 behind Moloka`i High School on Lihipali Avenue, Ho`olehua, HI 96729, ☎ 808/567-6601 or 808/567-6495. Enjoy a free educational tour of this 70-year-old nut orchard planted by the original homesteader, the Purdy family. Sample the freshest macadamia nuts, cracked right from the shell. Nuts and island honey available for sale. The Purdy family also has a new island arts and crafts giftshop featuring locally made Hawaiian handcrafts.

**The Nature Conservancy of Hawai`i,** PO Box 220, Kualapu`u, HI 96757, ☎ 808/553-5236; e-mail emisaki@tnc.org. This environmental protection organization conducts monthly hiking excursions to Moloka`i's best natural areas, including Kamakou Preserve, Mo`omomi Sand Dunes, Pelekunu Valley.

Kapuaiwa Coconut Grove. A grove of more than 1,000 coconut palms planted in the 1860s by King Kamehameha V. It was established as a memorial to the thousand Hawaiian warriors who died in the great Battle of Kawela in the 1790s when Kamehameha the Great united the islands under one kingdom. The grove covers some 10 acres next to Kioea Beach Park just outside of Kaunakakai town.

Royal Coconut Grove at Kapuaiwa.

Lodging

 Moloka`i offers varied but limited lodging options ranging from bed and breakfast homes and budget hotels to vacation condos and an adventure ranch lodge. The rates below are for a standard double-occupancy room.

Accommodations Price Scale	
$	less than $100 per night
$$	$100-199 per night
$$$	$200-299 per night
$$$$	$300 and up per night

Bed & Breakfast Hawai`i-Moloka`i, PO Box 449, Kapa`a, HI 96746, ☎ 800/733-1632, 808/822-7771; e-mail bandb@aloha.net; www.planet-Hawaii.com/bandb. $

Bed & Breakfast Moloka`i, PO Box 295, Kaunakakai, HI 96748, ☎ 808/553-5048. A separate guest cottage with cooking facilities and private bath. $

Moloka`i

Condos Direct, PO Box 54, Maunaloa, HI 96770, ☎ 800/303-5703. These studio/1BR/2BR condo units are in west Moloka`i. $/$$

Honomuni House, HC 1, Box 700, Kaunakakai, HI 96748, ☎ 808/558-8383. A fully furnished, private cottage in lush garden setting; sleeps four. Complimentary seasonal tropical fruit available. $

Ha Hale Mala, PO Box 1582, Kaunakakai, HI 96748, ☎ 808/553-9009; e-mail 73124.1477@compuserve.com; http://Molokai.com/kahale-mala. A spacious two-story home with bed and breakfast guest rooms in the ground floor unit. Includes full kitchen, TV, bath, laundry. $

Kamalo Plantation B&B, HC 1, Box 300, Kaunakakai, HI 96748, ☎ 808/558-8236. A five-acre tropical paradise at the foot of Moloka`i's highest mountain; fully equipped country cottage and extra rooms in main house available. $

**Kumue`li Farms B&B,** PO Box 1829, Kaunakakai, HI 96848, ☎ 808/558-8284; e-mail dcurtis@aloha.net. A secluded eight-acre country tropical farm and garden oasis on Moloka`i's east end. The spacious, private guest quarters have spectacular views and an Olympic-length lap pool. $

**The Lodge at Pu`u O Hoku Ranch,** HC 01 Box 900, Kaunakakai, HI 96748, ☎ 808/558-8109. A rustic, remote and quiet retreat in the ranch and hill country on Moloka`i's east end. It's located on Highway 450 near the end of the road and Halawa Valley. This is a perfect getaway for business or inspirational retreats, with 11 guest rooms accommodating 22 people. Most rooms have private baths, some share. Full kitchen facilities are available. There is also a separate self-contained Country Cottage that can sleep up to six people. The nearest convenience store is a 30-minute drive to Wavecrest Condo. Kaunakakai town is a one-hour drive along the very scenic east Moloka`i coast. $

Intersource Realty, Inc., PO Box 212, Kaluakoi, HI 96770, ☎ 800/Moloka`i, ☎ 808/552-2991. Specializes in vacation rentals, from West MMoloka`i's most luxurious holiday homes to family-style oceanfront condo units. $/$$

**Moloka`i Ranch,** 100 Maunaloa Highway, Maunaloa, HI 96770, ☎ 800/254-8871, 808/552-2791; http://Molokai-ranch.com. This west Moloka`i working cattle ranch is a leader in Hawaiian eco/cultural tourism, with several upscale tent accommodation units as the guest rooms. The unique "tentalow" and yurt-style units are solar-powered and use eco-friendly facilities. These are comfortable and spacious units, making for a relaxing stay – camping with the conveniences. The units are located in various areas of the ranch, from the dry upland mountain slopes to beachside sites. Choose from Paniolo Camp, Kolo Camp, and Kaupoa Camp (a fourth camp was being developed at press time). There are over a hundred units available. Activities include hiking, mountain biking, ocean kayaking, whale watching cruises, fishing, snorkeling, horseback riding, cultural and history walks. Each camp also has a swimming pool. The all-inclusive rate packages include all meals and activities. Guests meet in a central dining pavilion at each camp for meals, featuring hearty Moloka`i-style country fare from freshly prepared breakfast specials, to gourmet picnic lunches and kiawe-broiled steaks, BBQ chicken or island fish for dinner entrées. This is a great family adventure and provides many opportunities to see the real Moloka`i. $$$

Kaluakoi Villas, 1131 Kaluakoi Road, Maunaloa, HI 96770; Castle Resorts ☎ 800/367-5004, 808/552-2721; www.castle-group.com. These moderate, simply-furnished family vacation condo units are located in the middle of the golf course and near the beach at Kaluakoi Resort in west Moloka`i. $$

Kaluakoi Hotel, PO Box 1977, Maunaloa, HI 96770, ☎ 888/552-2550, 808/552-2555; e-mail kaluakoi@juno.com; www.aloha.net/~kmkk. This Polynesian-style hotel is in west Moloka`i. Trade winds sweep the surrounding golf course, hills and golden beach fronting the hotel. All resort amenities available, minutes from town and airport. $$

Paniolo Hale Resort, PO Box 190, Lio Place, Maunaloa, HI 96770, ☎ 800/367-2984, 808/552-2731. These oceanfront units have country decor and easy access to Kaluakoi Resort golf course and attractions. $$

Ke Nani Kai, PO Box 289, Maunaloa, HI 96770, Marc Resorts Hawai`i ☎ 800/535-0085, 808/552-2761; e-mail marc@aloha.net: www.marcresorts.com. This complex is at the west end of Kaluakoi Resort and has spacious and well-appointed 1-2BR units. Each is fully equipped for a relaxing, carefree stay, with full kitchen, Lana`i, appliances, TV, plus pool, spa, BBQ area, tennis courts and the Kaluakoi Golf Club close by. $$

Wavecrest Resort, HC01 Box 541, Kaunakakai, HI 96748, Marc Resorts Hawai`i, ☎ 800/535-0085, 808/558-8103; e-mail marc@aloha.net; www.marcresorts.com. This clean, bright condo complex has an oceanfront location and all resort amenities. Easy access to explore east Moloka`i and near town. $$

**Moloka`i Shores**, Kamehameha Highway, Kaunakakai, HI 96748, Marc Resorts Hawai`i, ☎ 800/535-0085, 808/553-5954; e-mail marc@aloha.net; www.marcresorts.com. This oceanfront condo complex is just east of Kaunakakai town in a quiet on-the-beach location. Swimming pool, kayaks for beach use, easy access to east Moloka`i attractions. $$

**Hotel Moloka`i**, PO Box 546, Kaunakakai, HI 96748, ☎ 800/423-6656, 808/531-4004. This is a strictly budget accommodation on the beach in east Moloka`i five minutes from town. $

Pau Hana Inn, PO Box 546, Kaunakakai, HI 96748, ☎ 800/423-6656, 808/531-4004. This budget lodge is on the beach at the east edge of Kaunakakai town. Convenient to all attractions and activities. Good value for budget travelers or backpackers looking for a rest stop; restaurant and bar/lounge on premises. The bar can get a bit noisy as it's the only watering hole in town. But it's a good place to meet local folks. $

Swenson Real Estate, PO Box 1507, Kaunakakai, HI 96748, ☎ 800/553-3648, 808/553-3783; e-mail 76351.3644@compuserve. This realtor has a variety of vacation rentals available around Moloka`i. $

Camping

Moloka`i's only option for camping at the present time is at **Pala`au State Park** at the end of Highway 470 near the Kalaupapa Peninsula lookout. Campers will find lots of room to pitch a tent, along with picnic facilities and restrooms. This is a cool, breezy forested location, often with misty clouds and rain blowing up from the nearby cliffs, so appropriate clothing is required.

A no-fee camping permit is required. To obtain a permit in advance, contact: **Division of State Parks**, 54 South High Street, Wailuku, Maui, HI 96793, ☎ 808/984-8109.

Dining

Moloka`i, being the small place it is, doesn't have a wide range of dining options. The choices are limited and range from resort to rustic. The restaurant price ranges, as in the other island sections of this book are based on the average dinner meal, exclusive of tax, alcoholic beverages and desserts.

Dining Price Scale

$ . . . . under $10 per person

$$ . . . . $10-25 per person

$$$ . . . . $25 and up per person

Ohia Lodge, Kaluakoi Hotel, Maunaloa, ☎ 808/552-2555. This is Moloka`i's only major resort hotel dining room. The menu is continental, with some local Hawaiian favorites. It has a nice beachside location, open to the ocean breezes. $$

Banyan Tree Terrace Restaurant, Pau Hana Inn, Kaunakakai, ☎ 808/553-5342. This is a popular dining spot with the locals. The menu features prime rib as the house special, as well as steaks, seafood, island fish; breakfast served also. $$

Moloka`i Drive Inn, Kamehameha V Highway, Kaunakakai, ☎ 808/553-5655. The focus here is simple plate lunch and snack fare such as burgers, sandwiches, beef stew, chili, fried fish and chicken. $

Kanemitsu Bakery, Ala Malama Street, Kaunakakai, ☎ 808/553-5855. They serve breakfast and lunch with a varied menu; fresh pastries, donuts and baked goods are excellent. The big thing here is their famous fresh Moloka`i bread. $

**Moloka`i Pizza Café,** Wharf Road, Kaunakakai, ☎ 808/553-3288. This clean bright café has an Italian menu of pizza and pasta selections, plus sandwiches and daily specials in a clean, pleasant atmosphere. One of Moloka`i's nicest dining spots. $

**Kualapu`u Cookhouse,** in Kualapu`u off Highway 470, ☎ 808/567-6185. This rustic country café features prime rib as a house special, along with BBQ ribs, steaks, BBQ chicken and daily specials. Located amid groves of coffee trees between town and the airport. $$

Outpost Natural Food, off Ala Malama Street, behind Kalama's Service Station, Kaunakakai, ☎ 808/553-3377. Natural and health foods, fresh produce, beverages, plus a vegetarian lunch counter serving healthy salads, veggie sandwiches, daily lunch specials and tropical fruit smoothies. $

Kamoi Snack-N-Go Minimart, Kamoa Professional Plaza, Ala Malama Street, Kaunakakai, ☎ 808/553-3742. This convenience store has prepared foods and snacks to go, plus freshly made Hawaiian ice creams, candies, beverages. $

Moloka`i

Sundown Deli, on Kaunakakai's main street, ☎ 808/553-3713. This small lunch counter features a variety of sandwiches, salads, soups and special Moloka`i-style saimin noodles. $

Oviedo's Lunch Counter, on Kaunakakai's main street, ☎ 808/553-5014. This small diner lunch counter features excellent local-style Filipino food, including such things as pork adobo, pinacbet, pork and peas, chicken papaya, and other daily specials. $

Ike's Lunch Wagon, usually located in the heart of Kaunakakai town, this mobile caterer offers a variety of local-style favorite plate lunches such as luau stew, roast pork, shoyu chicken, island fish, beef stew, beef curry and many more. $

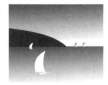

Hawai`i
The Big Island

Geography

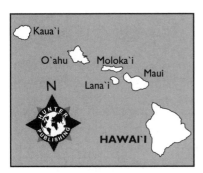

Hawai`i, the Big Island, has an area of 4,038 square miles and is the largest of all the Hawaiian Islands. In fact, it is larger than all the other islands combined. The population is 135,500. The County of Hawai`i is comprised solely of the Island of Hawai`i, with Hilo as the county seat. Hilo's population is 45,000.

Volcanoes

The island has some 266 miles of rugged coastline – lava fields, high seacliffs, rocky shores and limited stretches of sandy beach. It rises from sea level to the highest volcanic peaks in the islands, Mauna Kea at 13,796 feet and Mauna Loa at 13,677 feet. These two towering peaks dominate the island. Mauna Loa and adjacent Kilauea Volcano are among the world's most active volcanoes. Kilauea has been in an active phase since 1983, with almost continuous lava eruptions into the sea on the southern side of the island. The Island of Hawai`i is the youngest in the chain of islands. The ongoing eruptions of Kilauea, in fact, continue to add to the island's size with buildup of lava on the coastline. As measured by comparison of its structural lava flows, the age of Hawai`i is about 700,000 years, very young compared to the other Hawaiian Islands.

Climate

The Big Island's average temperatures range from 71-77°, with cooler climes of 57-63° in mountain areas, and 62-66° at Waimea at the 2,670-foot level.

Rainfall is highly variable around the island by elevation and location. Hilo, on the rainy windward side of the island, has long been recognized as the wettest population center in the US, with an average 128 inches of rainfall annually. In one recent year, Hilo had a record 211 inches of rainfall. Along the Kohala Coast on the leeward side, the climate is just the opposite and receives a scant 10 inches annually. Winter, from November through March, tends to be slightly wetter and cooler, but rainfall is equally distributed throughout the year. The heavy rainfall on the windward east coast is, of course, the reason for its lush tropical rain forest environment. And the lack of rainfall on the leeward west side is the reason for west Hawai`i's desert-like environment.

History

The Island of Hawai`i is believed to be the first island settled by the migrating Polynesians sometime around 500-700 AD. With its southerly location at the end of the Hawaiian chain and with its towering mountains visible from far at sea, the Big Island may well have been the first stop for the new settlers on their journeys from the Marquesas and islands of Polynesia far to the south.

■ Kamehameha & the Missionaries

The island is the birthplace of King Kamehameha the Great, who united the islands under one kingdom in 1795. It was from the Big Island that Kamehameha set out on his goal to unify the islands and put an end to the rampant civil wars of the day. Kamehameha ruled his realm from Kona until his final days. A year after his death in 1819, the first Christian missionaries from America arrived to introduce a new religion and new ways. The Big Island still has a number of preserved historic sites such as heiau (temples), village sites and other archaeological remains, where the history of the early Hawaiians can be seen first-hand.

Man on streets of Honolulu, 1851-53.

■ Sugar & Cattle

During the 1800s, development focused on sugarcane plantations and cattle ranching. These were, for a long time, the primary industries of the island. The sugar industry was active right up into the early 1990s, when the last mill and plantation finally closed. Sugar plantations covered the slopes from far up the mountains down to the seashore, from the far North Kohala District to the far southern Ka`u District. Cattle ranching was the mainstay in the Waimea area, home to the world famous Parker Ranch, and the upcountry Kona Coast area. Because the plantation industry required a large labor force, immigrant laborers were recruited for Big Island plantations, as they were for the other Hawaiian Islands. Chinese, Japanese, Koreans, Filipinos, Portuguese and Puerto Ricans were brought in to work on the plantations. For generations, these groups lived and worked together in the plantation and housing camps spread around the countryside. In the process, these ethnic groups melded together to form the modern multi-cultural community of today's Hawai`i.

Information Sources

Hawai`i Convention & Visitors Bureau-Big Island Chapter, 250 Keawe St., Hilo, HI 96720, ☎ 808/961-5797; and 75-5719W Alii Drive, Kailua-Kona, HI 96740, ☎ 808/329-7787; www.visit.Hawaii.org/.

Destination Hilo, PO Box 1391, 400 Hualani St. #20B, Hilo, HI 96721, ☎ 808/935-5294.

Destination Kona Coast, PO Box 2850, Kailua-Kona, HI 96745, ☎ 808/329-6748.

Kona-Kohala Resort Association, PO Box 5000, Kohala Coast, HI 96743-5000, ☎ 808/885-4915.

Hawai`i Island Chamber of Commerce, 202 Kamehameha Avenue, Hilo, HI 96720, ☎ 808/935-7178.

Kona-Kohala Chamber of Commerce, 75-5737 Kuakini Highway, Suite 207, Kailua-Kona, HI 96740, ☎ 808/329-1758.

Information Office-County of Hawai`i, 25 Aupuni St., Hilo, HI 96720, ☎ 808/961-8223.

Parks and Recreation Department-County of Hawai`i, Camping Reservations, 25 Aupuni St., Hilo, HI 96720, ☎ 808/961-8311.

Lands and Natural Resources Department-State of Hawai`i, State Parks Division, 75 Aupuni St., Hilo, HI 96720, ☎ 808/974-6200.

National Weather Service, Hilo International Airport, weather forecast Hilo area, ☎ 808/935-8555; Island of Hawai`i, ☎ 808/961-5582.

**Hawai`i Volcanoes National Park,** Superintendent, National Park Service, Hawai`i National Park, 96718; visitor information and current eruption information, ☎ 808/985-6000.

References

Alford, John. *Mountain Biking the Hawaiian Islands: Mauka to Makai,* Ohana Publishing, Honolulu, HI. 1997.

Carter, Frances. *Hawai`i on Foot,* Bess Press, Inc., Honolulu, HI. 1990.

Chisholm, Craig. *Hawai`i, The Big Island Hiking Trails,* The Fernglen Press, Lake Oswego, Oregon. 1994.

Clark, John. *Beaches of the Big Island,* University of Hawai`i Press, Honolulu, HI. 1985.

Koch, Tom. *Six Islands on Two Wheels: A Cycling Guide to Hawai`i,* Bess Press, Honolulu, HI. 1990.

Morey, Kathy. *Hawai`i Trails: Walks, Strolls and Treks on the Big Island,* Wilderness Press, Berkeley, CA. 1992.

Olsen, Brad. *Extreme Adventures Hawai`i,* Hunter Publishing, Edison, NJ. 1998.

Penisten, John. *Hawai`i-The Big Island: A Paradise Family Guide,* Prima Publishing, Rocklin, CA. 1996.

Smith, Robert. *Hiking Hawai`i-The Big Island,* Hawaiian Outdoor Adventures Publications, Maui, Hawai`i. 1991.

Smith, Rodney. *Hawai`i: A Walker's Guide,* Hunter Publishing, Edison, NJ. 1997.

Zurick, David. *Hawai`i, Naturally,* Wilderness Press, Berkeley, CA. 1990.

Getting There

■ Inter-Island Air Service

The following airlines provide regularly scheduled daily flights between the Big Island's two major airports, Kona International Airport and Hilo International Airport, as well as to other destinations within the Hawaiian Islands.

- **Aloha Airlines,** US, ☎ 800/367-5250, Canada, ☎ 800/235-0936, on Maui, ☎ 808/244-9071; e-mail aloha@alohaair.com; www.alohaair.com/.

- **Hawaiian Airlines,** US and Canada, ☎ 800/367-5320, on Maui, ☎ 808/871-6132; www.Hawaiianair.com/.

■ US Mainland & the Big Island

Currently, United Airlines is the only major US air carrier providing direct service from the mainland to Hawai`i through Kona International Airport on the Big Island. Other major carriers provide service to Maui,

Hawai`i

Kaua`i and Honolulu with connecting inter-island flights to the Big Island.

United Airlines, US, ☎ 800/241-6522; www.ual.com.

■ Cruise Ships

The last few years have seen an increase in international cruise ships making port calls in the Hawaiian Islands. So, once again, it is possible to sail to the islands on a luxurious ocean liner. Several cruise lines now regularly route their ships on a seasonal basis into Honolulu, as well as to the neighbor islands of Kaua`i, Maui and the Big Island of Hawai`i at Kona and Hilo. Schedules vary, as do itineraries. For details, check with a travel agent or cruise tour reservation specialist.

Among the ships that have made Hawai`i port calls on regular sailings recently from North America and other points are: **Princess Cruise Lines'** *Island Princess, Sea Princess* and *Golden Princess* (☎ 800-PRINCESS/774-6237); **Royal Viking Lines'** *Sagafjord* and *Royal Viking Sun* (☎ 800-426-0821); **Holland America Lines'** *Statendam, Rotterdam* and *Maasdam* (☎ 800-426-0327); **Cunard Lines'** *Queen Elizabeth II* (☎ 800-221-4770); **Royal Caribbean Lines'** *Legend of the Seas* (☎ 800-327-6700); and **Carnival Cruise Lines'** *MS Tropicale* (☎ 800-327-9501).

Hobie Cats on Hilo Bay.

In addition, within the Hawaiian Islands, American Hawai`i Cruises offers exclusive inter-island cruises between Honolulu and the neighbor islands aboard the *SS Independence*. There are three-day and week-long packages. The ship spends a day in each port at Kaua`i, Maui and the Big Island's Kona and Hilo. There are shore excursions and tours available from dockside at each port. For details and information, contact your travel agent or: **American Hawai`i Cruises**, 550 Kearny St., San Francisco, CA 94108, ☎ 800/765-7000.

Getting Around

You have two gateways into the Big Island, either Kona or Hilo International Airports. The two are almost directly opposite each other, with Hilo on the windward east coast and Kona on the leeward west coast. You can begin your exploration of the Big Island from either place. Both have equal access to the entire island via a generally well-maintained highway system. Some parts of the main circle-island highway may have narrow, winding sections, such as the south Kona area, which crosses old lava fields, and the Hamakua Coast area, which passes through several deep gulches along the coast. So don't expect to hit freeway speeds. But you want to take it slow in any case, taking the time to see some of the most magnificent scenery in the islands. Overall, the Big Island has an excellent highway system. And you can't get lost because all roads link to the main circle-island route and it's the only way around the island. The circle-island northern route is Highway 19 and the southern route is Highway 11.

📖 If you rent a car, the agency will provide a good map of the Big Island. But you may want to pick up a copy of the latest *Map of Hawai`i,* a full color detailed topographic map of the Big Island by James Bier and published by the University of Hawai`i Press. It's available in many island bookstores and shops. It provides great information on roads, highways and major attractions.

Depending upon your final destination on the Big Island, you'll be arriving at either Hilo International Airport or Kona International Air-

Hawai`i
The Big Island

N

Ale nuihaba Channel

Pacific Ocean

HUNTER PUBLISHING

Upolu Point Hawi Kapa`au
Makapala
270

Mahukona Waipi`o
250 WAIMEA 240 Honoka`a
KOHALA 19
19 Laupahoehoe
Puako Waimea/Kohala
Airport Ninole
Ka`upulehu 19 Mauna Kea Honomu
190 (13,796 ft)

Queen Ka`ahumanu Hwy
Hawaii Belt Rd
200
Keahole Papa'ikou
Airport Saddle Rd HILO
KAILUA-KONA Hilo Int'l
Holualoa Airport
Kurtistown Kea'au
Mauna Loa Mountain View 130 Kapoho
(13,680 ft) Pahoa 132
Napo`opo`o 137
Honaunau HAWAII VOLCANOES Opihikao
Ho`okena NATIONAL PARK *Volcano Rd* Kalapana

KOHALA COAST

Papa Pahala Apua
11 Point
Wai`ohinu  Punalu`u
11 Na'alehu

Pacific Ocean

South Point

20 MILES

port. And you'll need to make arrangements for local transportation to your hotel or lodging. The Hilo Airport is less than three miles from the Banyan Drive hotels. The Kona Airport is seven-14 miles from the hotels of the Kailua-Kona to Keauhou area. Kohala Coast resorts are spread out for 20-30 miles north of the Kona Airport. Taxis are numerous at both airports but they can be expensive. Check the taxi stands out in front of the baggage claim areas.

■ Bus/Taxi Service

There are local tour bus operators that provide airport/hotel transportation in both Hilo and Kona. Call in advance for reservations and pickup. Try: **Roberts Hawai`i**, ☎ 800/831-5541, Kona office, 808/329-1688, Hilo office, 808/966-5483; **Hawai`i Resorts Transportation Co.,** ☎ 808/775-7291; **Jack's Tours, Inc.,** Kona, ☎ 808/329-2555, Hilo, 808/961-6666.

Local buses provide transportation, but not between the airports and hotels. The **Alii Shuttle,** ☎ 808/775-7121, provides service along the entire length of Alii Drive from Kailua-Kona to Keauhou. The run takes 45 minutes in each direction and it stops enroute at all major hotels, condos and shopping centers in the resort district.

The County of Hawai`i operates the public mass transit **"Hele On"** bus system, which serves the entire Big Island. The buses provide point-to-point service between Hilo and Kona, with feeder routes to towns and villages around the island. Rates are very reasonable and bulk tickets can be purchased for multiple rides. It's an adventurous way to see the entire island at low cost. For bus schedules and information contact **Mass Transit Agency**, County of Hawai`i, 25 Aupuni St., Hilo, HI 96720, ☎ 808/961-8744.

- **C & C Taxi,** Kailua-Kona, ☎ 808/329-6388.

- **D & E Taxi,** Kailua-Kona, ☎ 808/329-4279.

- **Sprint Discount Taxi Shuttle,** Kailua-Kona, ☎ 808/329-6974.

- **Air Taxi & Tours,** Waikoloa, Hawai`i, ☎ 808/883-8262.

- **Kona Airport Taxi,** Kailua-Kona, ☎ 808/329-7779.

- **Marina Taxi,** Kailua-Kona, ☎ 808/329-2481.

- **Ace One Taxi,** Hilo, ☎ 808/8303.

- **Percy's Taxi,** Hilo, Hamakua, Volcano, ☎ 808/969-7060.

Hawai`i

- **Hilo Harry's Taxi,** Hilo, ☎ 808/935-7091.

- **A-1 Bob's Taxi,** Hilo, Puna, Volcano, Hamakua, ☎ 808/959-4800, 963-5470.

- **Alpha Star Taxi,** Waimea/Kona, ☎ 808/885-4771.

- **Island Cruise Taxi,** Waimea, ☎ 808/885-8687.

■ Limousine Service

If you want a real treat and don't mind splurging, you might want to check out hiring a limousine service to provide either airport/hotel transfer or even indulge in an around-the-island deluxe limousine tour. It all depends on how deep your pockets are. For information on limousine service, contact any of the following:

- **A Touch of Class,** Kona, ☎ 808/325-0775.

- **Aloha Aina Limousine,** PO Box 2087, Kailua-Kona, HI 96745, ☎ 808/334-0633.

- **Luana Limousine Service,** PO Box 2891, Kailua-Kona, HI 96745, ☎ 800/999-4001, 808/326-LIMO.

- **Meridian Hawaiian Resorts Transport,** Mauna Lani Bay Hotel and Bungalows, ☎ 808/885-7484.

- **Rocky's Limousine Service,** 74-5563 Kaiwi St., Suite 135, Kailua-Kona, HI 96740, ☎ 808/334-0342.

■ Car & Truck Rentals

A rental vehicle will probably be your best value for transportation on the Big Island. Having your own car allows you greater freedom to explore at your leisure and to pick your own adventures on the road. The Big Island has over 1,500 miles of paved county and state roads and highways, not to mention the secondary country roads and lanes. These roads pass through some of the liveliest and most diverse scenery in Hawai`i.

You can do a circle drive around the island, a total distance via the main routes of about 225 miles, in a day. That may not sound like much in mainland freeway distances, but because of some narrow, winding sections and gulches, driving full-circle around the island wouldn't allow you to fully enjoy all the sights and attractions along the way and is not advised. From Kona to Hilo via Waimea and the north route Highway 19 is a distance of about 100 miles. From Hilo to Kona via Volcano and the south route Highway 11 is about 125 miles.

The best approach would be to drive one way to Hilo or Kona, spend a day or two exploring the area along the way, and then return via the other route to complete a circuit of the island.

Most car rental agencies on the Big Island have airport outlets in both Hilo and Kona; some have rental desks in hotels and shopping centers.

- **Aloha Cars-R-Us, ☎** 800/655-7989.

- **AA Paradise Network,** US/Canada ☎ 800/942-2242

- **Alamo Rent a Car, ☎** 800/327-9633, Hilo, ☎ 808/961-3343, Kona, ☎ 808/329-8896.

- **Avis Rent a Car, ☎** 800/321-3712, Hilo, ☎ 808/935-1290, Kona, ☎ 808/327-3000.

- **Budget Rent a Car, ☎** 800/527-0700, Hilo, ☎ 808/935-6878, Kona, ☎ 808/329-8511.

- **Dollar Rent a Car, ☎** 800/800-4000, Hilo, ☎ 808/961-6059, Kona, ☎ 808/329-2744.

- **Harper Car & Truck Rentals Hawai`i,** 800-852-9993, Hilo, ☎ 808/969-1478, Kona, ☎ 808/329-6688.

- **Hertz Rent a Car, ☎** 800/654-3011, Hilo, ☎ 808/935-2896, Kona, ☎ 808/329-3566.

- **National Car Rental, ☎** 800/227-7368, Hilo, ☎ 808/935-0891, Kona, ☎ 808/329-1674.

You might want to consider renting an off-road 4WD vehicle like a Jeep, Geo Tracker or Toyota Forerunner. Not all rental agencies have them. A 4WD vehicle is required for certain routes considered "off-road" or "backcountry" like the Saddle Road between Mauna Kea and Mauna Loa, the Mauna Kea Summit Road, Waipio Valley Road and others. Keep in mind that your car rental insurance coverage may be voided if you take a regular rental car onto any of these roads. Inquire upon renting any car what the limitations are, if any.

Hawai`i

Be aware that car rental agencies on the Big Island may impose a "drop off charge" if you rent the car in one location and drop it off at another. Finally, keep in mind that even Hawai'i has its share of thieves. So never leave your vehicle unlocked at the beach, park, scenic site or parking lot. Secure your car and don't leave valuables or your keys in the car. Don't invite trouble.

■ Motorcycle & Moped Rentals

Contact any of the following to arrange motorcycle, moped or motor-scooter rentals by the day or week.

- **DJ's Rentals,** 75-5663A Palani Road, Kailua-Kona, across from the King Kamehameha Hotel, ☎ 808/329-1700; e-mail harleys@ilHawaii.net; http://HARLEYS.COM. They rent Harley-Davidsons, mopeds and scooters.

- **Kona Harley-Davidson,** 74-5616 Luhia, Kailua-Kona, ☎ 808/326-9887. Harley-Davidsons, Kawasakis and other motorcycles for rent.

- **T&K Motorcycles,** 471 Kalanianaole, Hilo, ☎ 808/969-4991. They rent Harley-Davidsons.

■ Bicycle Rentals

Check with any of the following bike shops to arrange bicycle rentals by the day or week.

- **B&L Bike & Sports,** 75-5699 Kopiko Place, Kailua-Kona, ☎ 808/329-3309.

- **C&S Cycle & Surf,** Highway 19, east edge of Waimea, ☎ 808/885-5005.

- **Dave's Bike & Triathlon Shop,** 74-5588M Pawai Place, Kailua-Kona, ☎ 808/329-4522.

- **Hawaiian Pedals,** Kona Inn Shopping Village, Alii Drive, Kailua-Kona, ☎ 808/329-2294.

- **Hilo Bike Hub,** 318 E. Kawili St., Hilo, ☎ 808/961-4452.

- **HP Bike Works,** 74-5599 Lukia St., Kailua-Kona, ☎ 808/326-2453.

- **Mauna Kea Mountain Bikes, Inc.,** PO Box 44672, Kamuela, ☎ 808/883-0130.

- **Mid Pacific Wheels,** 1133C Manono St., Hilo, ☎ 808/935-6211.

- **Red Sail Sports,** Hilton Waikoloa Village, ☎ 808/885-2876; Orchid at Mauna Lani, ☎ 808/885-2000.

Touring the Big Island

The Big Island presents a changing scene as one travels around the island. And since it is a rather "big island," it does take a while, probably the better part of a day just to drive it completely. But you shouldn't rush because there is an awful lot to see. The Big Island has the most varied terrain, climate and geophysical features of any of the islands. You can literally surf and swim on a tropical beach in the morning, then go snow skiing on Mauna Kea in the afternoon. So take your time and enjoy all that it has to offer.

■ The Kona Coast

Kailua-Kona town is the visitors center for the Kona Coast region. The town is located just about midway down the west coast and seven miles south of Kona International Airport at Keahole via the Queen Ka`ahumanu Highway 19. Kailua-Kona has a number of significant adventure activities and attractions. From Kona, there is easy access to the numerous Kona coffee farms and mills where you can sample a complimentary cup of Kona brew and learn about Kona's famed coffee industry. The small upcountry town of **Holualoa** on the old Mamalahoa Highway 180 is a colorful art colony with numerous art shops, studios and galleries in the old buildings lining the narrow, winding main street. There are also attractions like Kailua-Kona's **Hulihe`e Palace** on Alii Drive and **Ahuena Heiau**, fronting the Hotel King Kamehameha. Then there is **Kealakekua Bay** and **Captain Cook's Monument**, about 12 miles south, **Pu`uhonua O Honaunau National Historical Park**, 20 miles south, numerous old heiau (temples) and other historic sites and beaches along the Kona Coast. **Keauhou Bay, Kailua Bay** and **Honokohau Harbor** are busy boating centers for snorkel/dive cruises,

Hawai`i

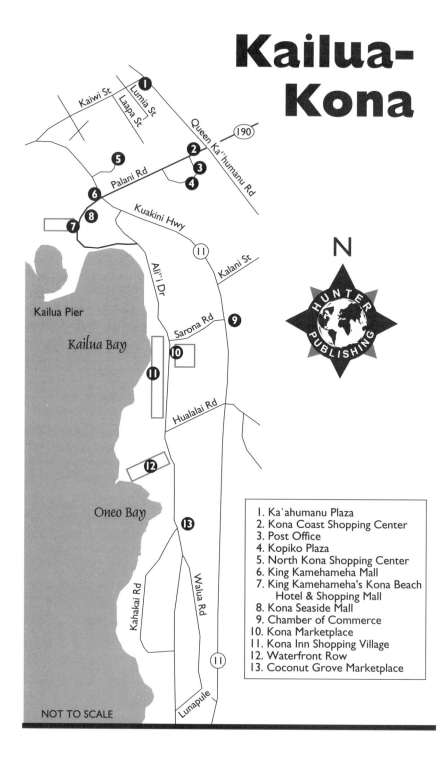

Kailua-Kona

Kaiwi St
Lumia St
Laapa St
Queen Ka'ahumanu Rd
190
Palani Rd
Kuakini Hwy
Ali'i Dr
Kalani St
Sarona Rd
Hualalai Rd
Kahakai Rd
Walua Rd
Lunapule

Kailua Pier

Kailua Bay

Oneo Bay

N

HUNTER PUBLISHING

NOT TO SCALE

1. Ka`ahumanu Plaza
2. Kona Coast Shopping Center
3. Post Office
4. Kopiko Plaza
5. North Kona Shopping Center
6. King Kamehameha Mall
7. King Kamehameha's Kona Beach
   Hotel & Shopping Mall
8. Kona Seaside Mall
9. Chamber of Commerce
10. Kona Marketplace
11. Kona Inn Shopping Village
12. Waterfront Row
13. Coconut Grove Marketplace

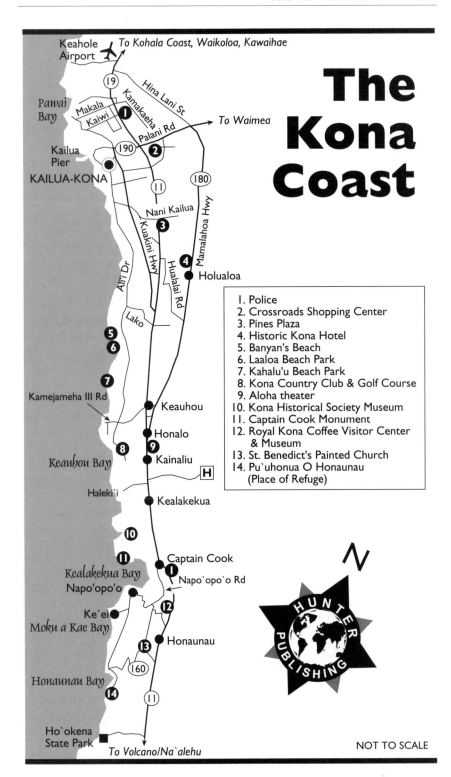

Keahole Airport

To Kohala Coast, Waikoloa, Kawaihae

The Kona Coast

19

Hina Lani St

Kamakaeha

Pawai Bay

Makala

Kaiwi

1

Palani Rd

To Waimea

190

2

Kailua Pier

KAILUA-KONA

11

180

Nani Kailua

3

Mamalahoa Hwy

Kuakini Hwy

Ali'i Dr

4

Hualalai Rd

Holualoa

Lako

5

6

7

Kamejameha III Rd

Keauhou

Honalo

8

9

Kainaliu

Keauhou Bay

H

Haleki'i

Kealakekua

10

11

Captain Cook

Kealakekua Bay

Napo'opo'o

Napo'opo'o Rd

Ke'ei

12

Moku a Kae Bay

13

Honaunau

Honaunau Bay

160

14

11

Ho'okena State Park

To Volcano/Na'alehu

1. Police
2. Crossroads Shopping Center
3. Pines Plaza
4. Historic Kona Hotel
5. Banyan's Beach
6. Laaloa Beach Park
7. Kahalu'u Beach Park
8. Kona Country Club & Golf Course
9. Aloha theater
10. Kona Historical Society Museum
11. Captain Cook Monument
12. Royal Kona Coffee Visitor Center & Museum
13. St. Benedict's Painted Church
14. Pu'uhonua O Honaunau (Place of Refuge)

N

HUNTER PUBLISHING

NOT TO SCALE

Hawai'i

sailing cruises, deep sea fishing charters, rafting and submarine excursions and parasailing adventures.

■ The Kohala Coast

Over the last few years, the Kohala Coast on the Big Island's northwest side has become Hawai'i's leading luxury resort destination. Spread along some 20 miles of spectacular warm, dry lava desert coastline north of Kailua-Kona are the magnificent resorts of **Kona Village** and **Four Seasons at Kaupulehu**, **Waikoloa**, **Mauna Lani** and **Mauna Kea**. These resorts and their individual hotel properties combine world-class luxury accommodations with vacation activities like golf, tennis, water sports, plus fine dining as well. Some of the Kohala Coast's best attractions are **Anaeho`omalu Beach Park** at Waikoloa, **Holoholokai Beach** and the **Puako Petroglyph Archaeological Preserve** at Mauna Lani Resort, **Hapuna Beach Park**, **Kauna`oa Beach** at Mauna Kea Resort, **Spencer Beach Park** and **Pu`ukohola Heiau National Historic Site** at Kawaihae. All of these sites are easily accessible from the Queen Ka`ahumanu Highway 19, which follows along the length of the Kohala Coast.

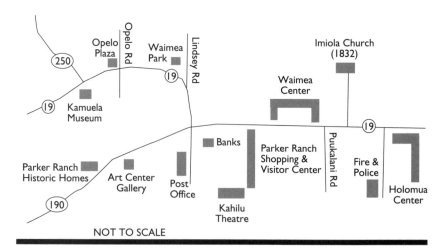

■ Waimea & Parker Ranch Country

Waimea (also known locally as Kamuela, its post office name) sits on the northern route, the **Hawai`i Belt Road** or **Mamalahoa Highway 19**, linking Hilo and Kona, and is about an hour drive from either one. This cool and breezy ranchland country is home to the famous Parker Ranch. Waimea is on a generally flat plateau or plain at the foot of the Kohala Mountains which lie to the north and dominate the northern tip and peninsula of the island. To the south of Waimea is an expansive view of the towering mass of **Mauna Kea**. It's a cozy little town with lots of places to explore and is noted for at least two of the Big Island's better restaurants, Merriman's and Edelweiss. The **Parker Ranch Visitors Center and Museum** is located at the Parker Ranch Shopping Center in town, while the historic ranch homes at **Pu`uopelu**, open to the public, are located on the west edge of town on Mamalahoa Highway 190. In Waimea, take a stroll through the shopping centers, browse the arts and crafts shops, or take a horseback trail ride across Parker Ranch country. Waimea also has a number of charming country-style bed and breakfast lodges that make for a pleasant stay in Hawai`i's ranch country.

Old Hawaiian fishponds at Anaeho`omalu Beach Park, Waikoloa, Kohala Coast.

Hawai`i

The Kohala Coast

To Hawi &
Kapa`au

Kohala Ranch Rd

(270)

Lapakahi State ■
Historic Park

To Waimea

Kawaihae ●

❶ (19)

1. Spencer Beach Park
2. Mauna Kea Beach Golf Course
3. Hapuna Golf Course
4. Heliport
5. Waikoloa Village Golf Club
6. Waikoloa Highlands Shopping Center
7. Royal Waikoloa & Waikoloa Beach
   Golf Courses
8. Makalei Hawaii Country Club &
   Golf Course
9. Old Airport Beach Park

❷ ❸ ❹

■ Hapuna Beach State Park

Puako ●

Waikoloa ❺❻
Village

❼❹

Anaeho`omalu Bay

Kiholo Bay

Queen Kaahumanu Hwy

N

HUNTER PUBLISHING

Ka`upulehu ●

Mamalahoa Hwy

❽

(19)

(190)

Kalaoa

Kona Coast State Park ■

Kona
Palisades

Keahole-Kona
Airport

Kaiminani Dr

Hina Lani St

(180)

To Holualoa

Pawai Bay ❾ ● (11)

KAILUA-KONA

Ali`i Dr

To Keauhou

■ North Kohala

The extreme northern tip of the Big Island comprises the North Kohala District. This is historic country, the birthplace and origin of Kamehameha the Great, the warrior king who conquered and united the Hawaiian Islands under one kingdom in the 1790s. Access the area via Kawaihae and the **Akoni Pule Highway 270** or via Waimea and the **Kohala Mountain Road 250**. The district's main towns are **Hawi**, where the two highways intersect, and **Kapa`au**, the district center.

Sugar was once the industry in North Kohala, but the mill closed in the early 1970s, forcing folks to either leave or turn to the Kohala Coast hotel industry for livelihoods. Many chose to stay and did the latter. The area is noted for a rural country charm and a quiet lifestyle. There's lots of history here and several worthwhile attractions. **Lapakahi State Park** is an old Hawaiian village site where visitors can do a self-guided walking tour. The **King Kamehameha statue** at Kapa`au and his birthplace near the **Molokini Luakini Heiau** at Upolu Point are also worth seeing.

The lush **Pololu Valley** is at the end of the road just past Kapa`au town and trails lead down to it and the beach. The **Kohala Mountain Road 250** with its beautiful views of rolling mountains, green pastures and distant coast is one of the Big Island's most scenic drives.

Kapa`au is the location of the **Kohala Mountain Kayak Company**, which runs what is the Big Island's most unusual eco/cultural adventure: a kayak ride through the upcountry irrigation ditch of the old Kohala Sugar Company. The ride goes through beautiful rain forest, pastures, hills and caves. It's definitely a one-of-a-kind Big Island experience.

■ Hilo & the Hamakua Coast

Hilo, the county seat and commercial center of Hawai`i County, is located on the lower end of the eastern coast of the Big Island. The town, the second largest community in the Hawaiian Islands, hugs the shoreline surrounding Hilo Bay and extends south and west upslope. Hilo International Airport is located on the eastern edge of town behind the Keaukaha area and coast.

Hawai`i

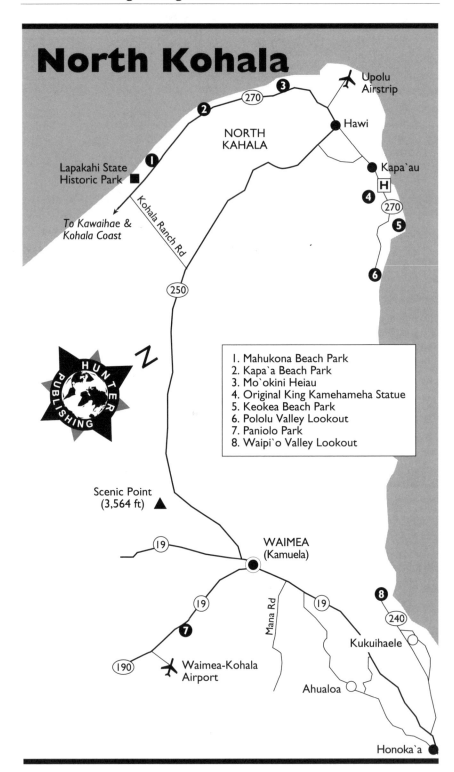

North Kohala

Upolu Airstrip

270 ❸

❷

NORTH KAHALA

Hawi

Lapakahi State Historic Park ■ ❶

Kapa`au

H

❹

270

To Kawaihae & Kohala Coast

Kohala Ranch Rd

❺

250

❻

N

1. Mahukona Beach Park
2. Kapa`a Beach Park
3. Mo`okini Heiau
4. Original King Kamehameha Statue
5. Keokea Beach Park
6. Pololu Valley Lookout
7. Paniolo Park
8. Waipi`o Valley Lookout

Scenic Point (3,564 ft) ▲

19

WAIMEA (Kamuela)

19

Mana Rd

19

❽

240

Kukuihaele

❼

190

Waimea-Kohala Airport

Ahualoa

Honoka`a

The Hamakua Coast extends for some 45 miles north of Hilo and the **Hawai`i Belt Road 19** follows the rugged rain forest coast up to Honoka`a and the Waipio Valley. The Hamakua Coast is a rugged scenic drive through former sugarcane plantation lands that have been abandoned and are gradually being overgrown with trees and exotic vegetation. The plantations all closed within the past three-five years after having been the sole industry and job provider for generations. The local population is still struggling to adjust. Along the Hamakua Coast, one passes through tiny rural settlements and quiet old plantation towns like **Pepe`ekeo, Honomu, Hakalau, Papa`aloa, Laupahoehoe** and **Pa`auilo**. The highway continues upslope from Honoka`a to Waimea and on down to the Kohala and Kona Coasts.

The Hamakua Coast has several interesting attractions, including Akaka Falls State Park and Nature Trail, the **World Botanical Gardens**, **Laupahoehoe Point Park and Overlook**, and the famous **Waipio Valley**. In and near Hilo there are anthurium and orchid farms and nurseries, **Rainbow Falls**, the morning **Suisan fish auction**, downtown Hilo shops, **Lyman Museum, Farmers' Market** and much more to discover.

■ Hawai`i Volcanoes National Park

South out of Hilo, the **Hawai`i Belt Road 11** leads to Hawai`i Volcanoes National Park about 25 miles upslope. The road passes through the small farming towns and communities of **Kea`au, Kurtistown, Mountain View** and **Glenwood** on its way to **Volcano**. There are a number of orchid and anthurium farms along the way and some are open to the public. Watch for signs. Hawai`i Volcanoes National Park is a big attraction. There are numerous adventure activities to enjoy in the park including hiking to the current eruption site (if active), crater walks, observatory museum, visitors center, camping, numerous hikes, picnicking, golf at **Volcano Country Club** or wine tasting at **Volcano Winery**.

■ Puna

At **Kea`au town, Highway 130** leads southeast to the **Puna District**, a sprawling area of semi-dry lavalands with large country residential subdivisions. The road passes through **Pahoa town**, reminiscent of a wild west town, complete with old wooden storefronts lining its narrow main street. Highway 130 continues south from Pahoa and terminates at the Kalapana and Kaimu areas on the coast. This is where lava flows

Hilo to Hawaii Volcanoes National Park

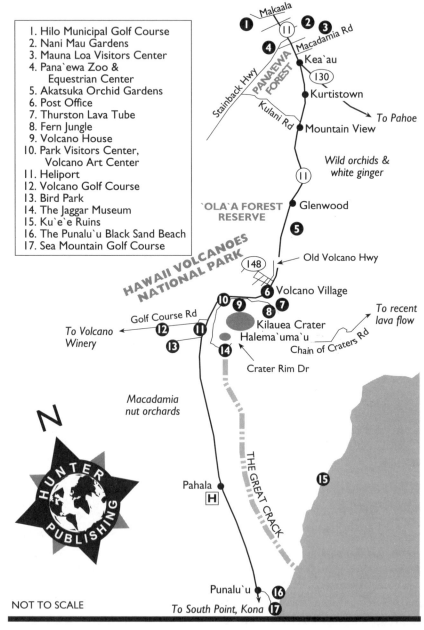

1. Hilo Municipal Golf Course
2. Nani Mau Gardens
3. Mauna Loa Visitors Center
4. Pana`ewa Zoo & Equestrian Center
5. Akatsuka Orchid Gardens
6. Post Office
7. Thurston Lava Tube
8. Fern Jungle
9. Volcano House
10. Park Visitors Center, Volcano Art Center
11. Heliport
12. Volcano Golf Course
13. Bird Park
14. The Jaggar Museum
15. Ku`e`e Ruins
16. The Punalu`u Black Sand Beach
17. Sea Mountain Golf Course

Makaala

Macadamia Rd

Kea`au

Stainback Hwy

PANAEWA FOREST

130

Kurtistown

Kulani Rd

Mountain View

To Pahoe

Wild orchids & white ginger

`OLA`A FOREST RESERVE

Glenwood

Old Volcano Hwy

148

HAWAII VOLCANOES NATIONAL PARK

Volcano Village

Golf Course Rd

To Volcano Winery

Kilauea Crater
Halema`uma`u

To recent lava flow

Chain of Craters Rd

Crater Rim Dr

Macadamia nut orchards

THE GREAT CRACK

Pahala
H

Punalu`u

To South Point, Kona

NOT TO SCALE

N

HUNTER PUBLISHING

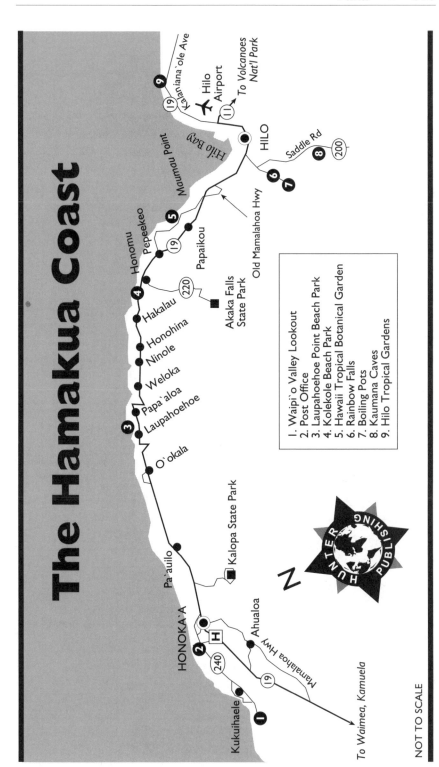

The Hamakua Coast

Kalaniana`ole Ave

To Volcanoes Nat'l Park

Hilo Airport

HILO

Hilo Bay

Maumau Point

Saddle Rd

Pepeekeo

Honomu

Papaikou

Old Mamalahoa Hwy

Akaka Falls State Park

Hakalau

Honohina

Ninole

Weloka

Papa`aloa

Laupahoehoe

O`okala

Kalopa State Park

Pa`auilo

HONOKA`A

Ahualoa

Mamalahoa Hwy

Kukuihaele

To Waimea, Kamuela

1. Waipi`o Valley Lookout
2. Post Office
3. Laupahoehoe Point Beach Park
4. Kolekole Beach Park
5. Hawaii Tropical Botanical Garden
6. Rainbow Falls
7. Boiling Pots
8. Kaumana Caves
9. Hilo Tropical Gardens

N

HUNTER PUBLISHING

NOT TO SCALE

Hawai`i

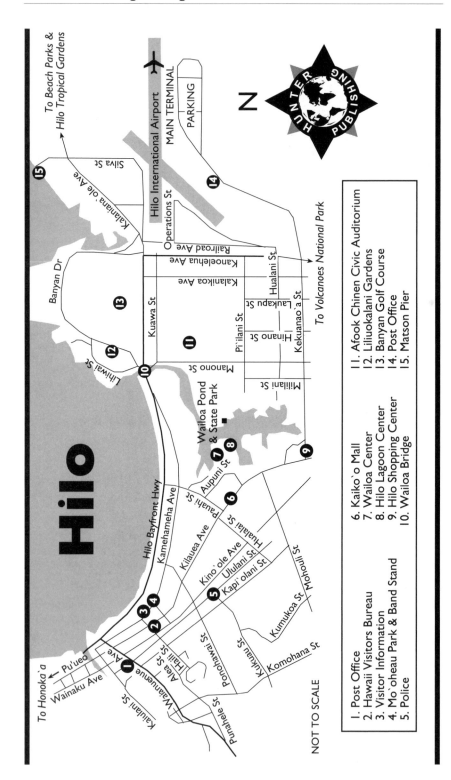

NOT TO SCALE

1. Post Office
2. Hawaii Visitors Bureau
3. Visitor Information
4. Mo'oheau Park & Band Stand
5. Police

6. Kaiko'o Mall
7. Wailoa Center
8. Hilo Lagoon Center
9. Hilo Shopping Center
10. Wailoa Bridge

11. Afook Chinen Civic Auditorium
12. Liliuokalani Gardens
13. Banyan Golf Course
14. Post Office
15. Matson Pier

from the early '90s covered several acres of land and destroyed roads, power lines, and many homes. The historic **Star of the Sea Painted Church** was rescued from the advancing lava flows and was moved to a location along the road just above the Kaimu area. Highway 132 leads east from Pahoa to **Cape Kumukahi Lighthouse** and terminates at the coast after intersecting with Highway 137. Then Highway 137 follows the southeast coast from Cape Kumukahi past **Issac Hale Beach Park**, **MacKenzie State Park**, **Opihikao** and **Kehena Beach** to its intersection with #130 at Kaimu. The road provides some spectacular rugged coastal views of this quiet, remote area of the Big Island.

■ Ka`u & South Point

The Ka`u District is probably the Big Island's most remote area. It covers a large portion of the south flank of **Mauna Loa**. The Hawai`i Belt Road 11 loops south from the Kona Coast and south from Volcanoes National Park to the southernmost tip of the United States at **Ka Lae, South Point**. The town of **Na`alehu**, in fact, lays claim to being the southernmost residential area of the US. Pahala town was a thriving sugar plantation community until the mill closed a couple of years ago. As in other parts of the island, the demise of sugar has wreaked havoc on the local economy.

The passage through Ka`u alternates with farming land, rugged coastal areas, hills, mountain slopes, dry upland forests and lava deserts. It's a sparsely populated area. The South Point Road leads 11 miles off from the main highway to **Ka Lae**, the South Point. At the end of the road are boat launching facilities used by local fishermen. There is also an old heiau (temple) and fishermen's shrine. From this area, a backcountry road along the coast leads to **Green Sand Beach**. Among the area's main attractions is Punalu`u **Black Sand Beach Park** and its resident population of Hawaiian green sea turtles, which are easily seen just offshore. **Manuka State Wayside Park** has a unique dry forest nature trail and small botanical garden. **Kauaha`ao Church** in Waiohinu dates from 1841 and is worth seeing.

■ Land Tours/Operators

There are several tour operators offering coach, van and 4WD vehicle half-day and full-day tours to all the major sights of the Big Island. These include Kona coffee farms and mills, beaches, Parker Ranch and Waimea, historic North Kohala, the Waipio Valley, Hamakua Coast waterfalls, Hilo area tropical flower botanical gardens, Hawai`i Volcanoes National Park, South Point. Check with any of the following operators for details. Tour rates vary with itinerary and origin. Standard half-day Kona Coast beach tour ranges from $25-35 per person. Full-day tour from Hilo to Hawai`i Volcanoes National Park is $45-75 per person; from Kona to the national park is $100 per person. Summit trip to Mauna Kea is $90 per person. A full-day Grand Circle Island tour from the Kona or Kohala Coast hotels is $55-65 per person.

Polynesian Adventure Tours, 74-5996V Pawai Place, Kailua-Kona, HI 96740, ☎ 808/329-8008. A full-day Grand Circle Island Tour from Kona and Kohala Coast hotels and a Hawai`i Volcano Adventure from Hilo hotels.

Roberts Hawai`i, PO Box 579, Kailua-Kona, HI 96740, ☎ 800/831-5541 or 808/329-KONA. A full-day Grand Circle Island Tour from Kona and Kohala Coast hotels, stopping at all the Big Island's major attractions.

Kipuka Tours, Hilo, Hawai`i, ☎ 800/663-9063 or 808/961-5082; e-mail kipuka@hilo.net. Full-day 4WD on/off-road tours from Hilo hotels to the Hilo-Volcano area, including Hilo town, waterfalls, caves, black sand beach, thermal hot springs, lava fields and Hawai`i Volcanoes National Park; picnic lunch included.

Hawaiian Eyes Land Tours, Hilo, Hawai`i, ☎ 808/937-2530 or 808/326-5661. Full-day 4WD custom land tours to the Big Island's unique environmental attractions. Tours take in the Mauna Kea summit, Volcanoes National Park, Mauna Loa volcanic landscapes, or the historic Kona and Kohala Coasts. Tours include full narration on history, culture, legends. Departures from Kona and Kohala Coast hotels; from Hilo hotels by arrangement.

Jack's Tours, 226 Kanoelehua Avenue, Hilo, HI 96720, ☎ 808/961-6666; 73-4770 Kanalani, Kailua-Kona, HI 96740, ☎ 808/329-2555. Half-day and full-day tours to the Big Island's major attractions, including Volcanoes National Park, historic Kona Coast, Hilo tropical botanical gardens, waterfalls.

Hawaiian Island Excursions, 75-195 Ala Onaona, Kailua-Kona, HI 96740, ☎ 808/329-0065. Half-day and full-day adventure tours to historic Kona Coast sites, Pu`uhonua O Honaunau National Historic Park, Kona coffee farms, Volcanoes National Park.

Adventures

The Big Island's Best Adventures

The Big Island has many unique adventures that will make your visit memorable and exciting. The following are a dozen of the best.

- Take a **helicopter flight over the volcano**.

- **Hike to the lava flow** at the end of Chain-of-Craters Road in Hawai`i Volcanoes National Park and see the flow into the ocean.

- Bike down the **Kohala Mountain Road** to the King Kamehameha Statue at Kapa`au.

- Take a tour on horseback, by wagon or 4WD vehicle through the majestic **Waipio Valley**.

- Kayak the **Kohala Mountain Irrigation Ditch**.

- Visit the **Pu`uhonua O Honaunau National Historical Park** to learn about ancient Hawaiian history and culture.

- Take the nature trail walk to **Akaka Falls** on the Hamakua Coast.

- Drive to **Mauna Kea Summit** and do the telescope observatory tour.

- Visit the **Hilo Tropical Botanical Gardens** and/or **Nani Mau Gardens**, two of Hilo's best tropical gardens.

- Take a self-guided tour/walk through **Lapakahi State Park**, site of an old Hawaiian fishing village.

- Take a **snorkel** cruise from Kona to the **Kealakekua Bay Marine Reserve**.

■ On Foot

The Big Island has a variety of hiking trails through the varied ecosystems – coastal beach, valley jungle, mountain rain forest, lava desert, and alpine mountain summit. Trails run through state forest reserves and parks, county parks, national park areas and remote coastal regions. Visitors can hike on their own or take a guided hiking adventure with one of the outfitters listed in the following section.

The Kohala Coast

Puako Petroglyph Fields Trails located at Holoholokai Beach Park next to the Orchid at Mauna Lani Hotel in the Mauna Lani Resort. Park in the parking lot. The trail is marked by a sign. The trail is about .5 mile one-way, 20 minutes, and goes through some dry forest and brush areas before coming to open lava fields and the petroglyph rock carvings. Stroll around the open areas and see the Hawaiian depictions of men, canoes, animals and other designs. This can be a very warm walk so take sunscreen, hat and water. The beach park is rocky, with small sandy patches, and is a good place to hunt for seashells among the coral rubble and rocks washed in by the surf.

King's Highway

King's Highway, the old Hawaiian trail that connected all the coastal settlements in ancient times, can still be accessed. One easy access point is on Waikoloa Resort Beach Drive just before the Kings' Shops Center. The rocky trail passes through the golf courses and petroglyph fields. The same trail can also be accessed at Mauna Lani Resort near the golf course clubhouse. The trail follows lava flows near the rugged coast. Any hike along this trail will be in hot, dry conditions on very rough lavarock surfaces, so prepare accordingly with good footwear, sunscreen, hat and water.

The Kona Coast

Kealakekua Bay and Captain Cook Monument is reached by a moderately difficult hiking trail from Highway 11 at Captain Cook town. This is a 2½-mile, three-hour round-trip. To locate the trail, turn off Highway 11 at Napo`opo`o Road to Kealakekua Bay. Just 100-yards from the turnoff is a dirt-gravel trail directly across from three big royal palm trees and running downslope between fence rows. Park along the road. This is the old wagon road leading to the former Kaawaloa settlement on the bay. The trail alternates from steep to level, from loose gravel to solid footing. It is also a warm sunny walk, so take hat, sunscreen and water.

The first part of the walk is under shade along the fence rows but the trail eventually comes to open lava fields. The hike back up is quite steep

Petroglyph field, Holoholokai Beach Park, Kohala Coast.

and tiring. As the road nears the bay, it passes through old stone foundations of the former village. The trail ends at the bay. There is a tall ce-
ment monument to Captain James Cook and a smaller plaque marking
the spot where he was killed by Hawaiians in a skirmish in 1779. On any
day there will be snorkel and dive boats filled with tourists anchored in
Kealakekua Bay offshore. They are frolicking in the waters of the Kealakekua Bay Underwater Marine Reserve with its varied marinelife.

Kaloko-Honokohau National Historic Park Trail is a coastal trail
still being developed. Distances vary from one to two miles, times from
one to two hours. You can access it three miles north of Kailua-Kona opposite Kaloko Industrial Area on a rough road just north of Honokohau
Boat Harbor. Hikers can also reach the park from the south side at
Honokohau Harbor. Turn right after entering the harbor and follow the
road to the end. The trail to the park starts opposite the large rock berm.
This park, 1,100 acres, spans two miles along the coast, encompassing
several old Hawaiian settlements. Resources include house foundations, fishing shrines, canoe landings, petroglyph rock carvings and
other archaeological sites. Nearby tidal pools and wetlands serve as a
preserve for migrant water birds and marine life. There are nice sandy
beach areas and much plant life native to this coastal ecosystem.
Restrooms are at Kaloko fishponds; no facilities otherwise. Take water
and snacks.

Hawai'i

Hawai`i Volcanoes National Park

DON'T MISS Hawai`i Volcanoes National Park has some of the Big Island's best hiking trails, from short and easy walks, to intermediate hikes, to overnight and multi-day backcountry treks. Hikers are advised to contact the **Superintendent, Hawai`i Volcanoes National Park**, Hawai`i 96718, ☎ 808/985-6000, or stop at the park's Kilauea Visitors Center for a map and details on hiking the park. Hikers are required to register and obtain permits for backcountry overnight hikes. Following are some of the park's most popular hikes.

Kilauea Iki Crater hiking trail.

Kilauea Iki is a moderate four-mile, two- to three-hour loop hike. Access is from Crater Rim Trail or Crater Rim Drive to the east of Kilauea Crater. The trail begins in young rain forest on the rim of the crater and leads down a 400-foot descent into Kilauea Iki Crater and across the crater floor. Watch your footing on the descent as some areas are loose rock and can be slippery. The trail across the crater floor is marked by stone cairns. There are steaming vents and cracks in the floor. Look for Pele's hair (the Hawaiian volcano fire goddess) – long slivers of olivine crystals from the lava that collect in the nooks and crannies of the jumbled rocks along the way. There are great views all around the immense cinder cone of Pu`u Pua`i, which erupted in 1959, creating this crater lava flow and the sheer vertical cliffs surrounding you. The trail leads up the opposite crater wall to the forest.

Devastation Trail is an easy, level one-mile, 30-minute walk on an asphalt paved trail across the edge of Pu`u Pua`i cinder cone formed by the 1959 eruption. The trail connects the parking lots of Kilauea Iki Overlook and Devastation Trailhead. The trail can be walked as a round-trip or one-way if a pickup is arranged at the other end. The trail follows along the edge of the ohia and tree fern forest, where it meets the barren cinder cone. The eruption destroyed much of the nearby forest, which was downwind of the eruption and was covered with cinders and pumice. The forest is now coming back. The area covered by the cinders and pumice is still stark, with numerous dead trees sticking up from the barren terrain.

Thurston Lava Tube is a .3-mile, 20-minute loop trail. Access it from the parking lot on Crater Rim Drive about two miles from Kilauea Visitors Center. This is one of the most popular attractions in the park, so expect it to be busy. The trail is asphalt paved and has a couple of steep sections but there are steps and handrails. It's often damp and rainy here and the trail can be slippery. The trail passes through dense ohia and tree fern forest as it descends into the lava tube. The tube is like a tunnel, 1,494 feet long, up to 22 feet wide and 20 feet high in places. Some areas are considerably lower and you must watch your head so you don't meet a rock. The tube is lighted but a flashlight would help as well. There are water puddles in the tube due to the natural percolation of rainwater from above and it can be quite cool and damp. The lava tube was created over 400 years ago when a flow formed an outer crust shell while the interior kept flowing. Once the lava drained away, the resulting lava tube remained intact. This is an enjoyable hike providing a closeup glimpse of the Hawaiian ohia and tree fern forest and a unique geological attraction.

Halema`uma`u Trail is a moderate three-mile one-way or seven-mile round-trip loop trail, three-six hours, to Halema`uma`u Crater in the Kilauea Caldera. Access the trail behind the Volcano House Hotel. The trail descends 500 feet through forest into Kilauea Caldera and crosses the floor to the Halema`uma`u Crater Overlook. The wind is usually brisk across the caldera and the sulfur gas smell is strong, making breathing difficult at times. Those with breathing difficulties should be cautious. There are panoramic vistas of the caldera, steaming vents and cracks, old lava flows and closeup views into still steaming Halema`uma`u Crater. Those hiking one-way can meet their pickup in the Halema`uma`u parking lot. Those doing the round-trip hike back to Volcano House Hotel can pick up the Byron Ledge Trail, which loops across the caldera and up to the Byron Ledge ridge, then back to the Volcano House Hotel.

Crater Rim Trail is a challenging 11-mile, day-long trek on varying terrain from forest trails to open, hot and windy lava rock trails; for experienced hikers only. The trail passes through a wide variety of geological and biological environments, circling the summit of Kilauea Caldera. The trail passes the Hawaiian Volcano Observatory and Jaggar Museum, Halema`uma`u Crater, near Devastation Trailhead and past Thurston Lava Tube, if you wanted to arrange a pickup and shorten the hike. On this full hike, you will see a cross-section of the entire sum-

Hawai`i

mit area, including its ohia and tree fern forests, dry open scrubland and desert, open lava fields, recent flow areas and craters. Bring water, food and be prepared for rain along the way. Sulfur gas fumes will be strong in the downwind southeast rift zone and Halema`uma`u areas.

Puu Loa Petroglyphs Trail is a 1½-mile round-trip, one- to two-hour, moderate walk over level to rolling lava fields. The trail varies from smooth to rough, sometimes over rocky or gravel sections. It is just off the Chain of Craters Road about 20 miles southeast of Kilauea Visitors Center on the coastal flatlands a few miles from the end of the highway, which is closed due to lava flows. The trail leads to fields of smooth pahoehoe lava mounds on which the petroglyphs were carved. There are many different types of petroglyphs in varying shapes, sizes and designs. Petroglyphs are fragile, so don't step on or damage these artworks in any way. Enjoy looking at them and even take some photos.

This is an open very breezy lava field with no shade trees. It can get very hot. Also this area is downwind of the eruption site just up the coast and volcanic sulfur fumes can be intense, so plan accordingly.

Mauna Iki/Footprints Trail is a moderate-to-difficult 8.8-mile, five- to six-hour hike through rocky, cinder trails of the Ka`u Desert. The trail is accessed off Highway 11 about nine miles southwest of Kilauea Visitors Center. It connects the Hilina Pali Road and Highway 11 and bisects the Ka`u Desert Trail. The trail allows hikers to cut hiking distances to certain points of interest in the Ka`u Desert and Hilina Pali areas. Extensions are possible for overnight camping treks via Ka`u Desert Trail, Hilina Pali Trail and Halape Trail. Camping permits from the park visitors center are required for these treks. The first .8 mile of the trail is an easy hike on sandy or cinder trails to the "Footprints" exhibit.

The Footprints

The footprints, preserved under glass, are supposedly those of Hawaiian warriors who gathered in the area in 1790 to battle with the forces of Kamehameha the Great for control of the island. The gathered warriors were overcome by fumes and volcanic dust from an eruption at Halema`uma`u Crater to the east. Their footprints were left hardened in the ash and the army dispersed.

Hikers who choose to continue on beyond the footprints exhibit follow the trail through the upper sections of the Ka`u Desert, taking in the unique and interesting desert ecosystem plants and geological formations such as cinder cones, craters and lava flow formations.

This is an area of extreme temperatures, sun and high winds. Caution is advised. Take hat, sunscreen, water and food.

Kipuka Puaulu (Bird Park) is 2½ miles west of the entrance to Hawai`i Volcanoes National Park and 1½ miles north of Highway 11 on the Mauna Loa Strip Road. This is an easy one-mile loop trail, an hour's walk, through a special ecological preserve and is one of the national park's most enjoyable walks. The "kipuka" is an "island" of native forest and rare plants surrounded by fairly recent lava flows that have isolated this forest glen from the rest of the nearby forest lands. The trail meanders through dense old growth forest and open meadowlands. There is some gentle slope and climb but overall it is an easy hike. The area is alive with native Hawaiian birdlife fluttering among the trees. Best to visit early mornings or late afternoons. This is a very tranquil, pleasantly cool and breezy place to enjoy the pleasures of one of Hawai`i's unique deep forest trails. Picnic tables and restrooms available.

Mauna Loa Summit Trail is at the end of Mauna Loa Strip Road (6,662-foot level), off Highway 11, 2½ miles west of the entrance to Hawai`i Volcanoes National Park. This is a strenuous 36.6-mile, four-day round-trip hike. It takes two days to climb the south rim of Mokuaweoweo Caldera at 13,250 feet. Hikers spend the first night in Red Hill Cabin (10,035 feet) and proceed to the summit shelter on the second day. It takes an additional half-day to hike around the caldera to the true summit at 13,677 feet.

This backcountry trek is for experienced hikers and backpackers only. Hikers are subjected to high winds, altitude sickness, snow and cold temperatures.

A shorter but equally difficult 13-mile, two-day round-trip hike begins at the Mauna Loa Weather Observatory at the 11,000-foot level on the north side, accessed via the Saddle Road. Before taking this trail, hikers are advised to spend the night in their cars at the end of the road near

Mauna Loa Mountain.

the observatory (no accommodations are available). This will acclimate your body to Mauna Loa's elevation. Good hikers can do the trail in one day, but it's better to spend the night at Mauna Loa. A backcountry camping permit is required for either trip; check with Kilauea Visitors Center. For information and cabin reservations, contact Hawai`i Volcanoes National Park visitor information at ☎ 808/985-6000.

Ka`u District

Ka Lae (South Point) and Green Sand Beach is a moderate six-mile round-trip, two-hour, coastal trail hike through open grassy areas following jeep trails. The area is reached via South Point Road which branches off Highway 11 about six miles west of Na`alehu town. South Point Road is a narrow mostly one-lane asphalt lane winding down 12 miles through open pasture country. It passes by the Kamao`a Wind Farm, an electricity generating facility using huge windmill-like turbines. The winds at Ka Lae (South Point) are usually brisk and continuous. Ka Lae is believed to be where the first Hawaiians landed around 400 AD in their early migrations across the Pacific. There are old canoe mooring holes in the rocks and the ruins of a fishermen's heiau (temple). Fishermen still use the area to moor their boats, but they hoist them up and down the high cliffs to the calm water below. The road turns east through the remnants of a World War II communications station, terminating at a small boat launching harbor about a mile or so east. This is the beginning of the coastal trailhead. It's three miles to Green Sand Beach through open rolling grasslands along the coast. Mahana Bay, where the beach is located, is marked by a high cliff promontory rising along the coast and is visible from a distance. A hazardous trail leads down to the beach. Rough waters and currents make it unsafe for water activities but it's a nice place to just picnic and relax. You can easily see why it's called Green Sand Beach due to the green olivine crystals in the sand. There are no trees or shade along this entire warm, breezy coastline so take hat, sunscreen, water and food.

Manuka Nature Trail is a moderate 2¼-mile, two-hour walk at the southwest tip of the Big Island's Ka`u District, very near the South Kona

District. You can reach it at Manuka State Wayside off Highway 11, just west of the 81-mile marker, or 81 miles from Hilo, roughly 40 miles from Kailua-Kona. This is a nice botanical garden park with ornamental trees and shrubs and wide grassy areas. There is a picnic pavilion and restrooms. The nature trail is a loop walk which climbs into a forest of native ohia lehua, tree ferns and pukiawe, plus kukui, guava and other introduced plants and trees. This is a hike through an upland dry forest ecosystem. You'll also see and hear a lot of birdlife here.

The Hamakua Coast, Hilo & Puna

DON'T **MISS** **Akaka Falls State Park** is a .5-mile loop trail, a half-hour walk, but allow time to enjoy this veritable Garden of Eden setting. Located 11 miles north of Hilo; turn off Highway 19 at Honomu to Highway 220, go through this small country town and about 3½ miles up the slope. The road terminates at the park. This is a moderately difficult walk only because there are some short steep sections to climb. The trail is hard surfaced all the way and steep sections have steps and/or handrails. The effort is well worth it to see a lush tropical rain forest with gushing streams and waterfalls. It's everyone's ideal of what the tropical beauty of Hawai`i is all about.

From the parking lot, head right down the loop trail as it meanders up, down and around the stream gorges of the park. There is lush tropical greenery all around, with several species of fragrant gingers, Hawaiian ti plants, wild banana, plumeria, hibiscus, bird of paradise, gardenias, azalea and many more. Crossing the first bridge, if you've taken the righthand route from the trailhead, you'll pass under a towering stand of giant bamboo. Further along, at the point where the trail makes a sharp left turn, is a small lookout for **Kahuna Falls**, a tumbling cascade that rolls down the north side of the canyon.

Follow the trail on up the ridge to the main attraction, the beautiful 420-foot **Akaka Falls**, which plummets down a sheer cliffside in veiled mists to Kolekole Stream below. There is a rain shelter at this lookout. It's a fine place to pause and soak in all the tropical beauty and lushness of Hawai`i. Continue on the trail back to the parking lot.

Banyan Drive and Liliuokalani Park is a one-mile walk, one hour or longer, depending on how long you pause to enjoy the stops along the way. This walk begins in Hilo near the Seaside Hotel and follows the loop around Waiakea Peninsula along "hotel row" to Liliuokalani Park. Banyan Drive is lined with giant banyan trees, hence its name. The trees were planted over a 40-year period beginning in 1933. Each was planted by a visiting celebrity of the day. Each tree carries a sign at its

Hawai`i

Reflecting pond, Liliuokalani Park, Hilo.

base with the name of the person who planted it and the date planted. VIPs who planted the famous trees include Babe Ruth, Amelia Earhart, President Franklin D. Roosevelt, Lincoln Ellsworth (famed Arctic explorer), author Fannie Hurst and several lesser notables. There is even a tree planted by some obscure US Senator named Richard Nixon.

The trees make a virtual tunnel along Banyan Drive as it loops past the hotels and restaurants to Liliuokalani Park. The park is on the shores of Hilo Bay. This Japanese garden park was named in honor of Hawai`i's last reigning monarch, Queen Liliuokalani. It was developed in the early 1900s as a memorial park to the immigrant Japanese who worked at the old Waiakea Sugar Plantation. The park features several magnificent Japanese stone lanterns, pavilions, an arching footbridge, a pavilion bridge, a ceremonial tea house and reflecting lagoons. It is one of Hawai`i's loveliest cultural parks, and it is free.

Kaumana Trail is a .5 mile, one-hour hike and connects with the Saddle Road #200 at two points, 17.4 and 19.8 miles from Hilo. The trail is a remnant of the old Puu Oo-Kaumana Trail, which was used as an access route between Hilo and the saddle area between Mauna Kea and Mauna Loa. It extends along the 1855 lava flow from about 5,200 feet elevation down to 4,800 feet. Vegetation on the lava flow is scrubby ohia and tree fern. Common native birds are readily sighted along the trail. It is suited for short nature hikes. Hikers can be dropped off at one end and picked up at the other.

Lava Tree State Park is an easy .8-mile loop trail, half an hour walk, about 25 miles from Hilo. Take Highway 11 south from Hilo, turn left at Keaau to Highway 130 south to Pahoa and then left onto Highway 132 about three miles to the park entrance. A 1790 lava flow from Kilauea Volcano covered the present site, which was a forest of ohia lehua trees. The lava destroyed the ohia trees and left a number of tree-shaped lava shells as the rapidly flowing lava drained away. The resulting "stumps" are almost like abstract sculptures in lava rock but are completely natural. They provide some truly bizarre formations. The ohia lehua tree with its puffy red or red/orange blossoms has made a comeback in the park. There are other ornamental trees, shrubs and flowering plants as well, including heliconia or lobster claw ginger, torch ginger, colorful crotons, bracken fern and tree ferns. This is an enjoyable level stroll through a tropical botanical garden. The park has restrooms and picnic shelters, but can have lots of mosquitoes as well; bug repellent is advised.

DON'T MISS **Waipio Valley** is on the Hamakua Coast just about 50 miles north of Hilo. Take Highway 19 to Honoka`a, about 40 miles, then Highway 240 north nine miles to Kukuihaele and the Waipio Valley State Park Lookout. Leave car in parking lot. There is a picture postcard view from the lookout of the valley's north wall, the beach and a great expanse of the valley floor. The **Waipio Valley Trail** is actually a .75-mile paved, narrow and extremely steep 4WD road leading to the valley floor. At the valley floor, the road turns right for another .75 mile on a narrow dirt, and if wet, muddy and rutted, lane to the mouth of the valley and Wailoa Stream. The beach here is good for picnics and relaxing but most of it lies on the other side of Wailoa Stream. There is a waterfall trailing off the south wall near the beach area.

Back at the junction, the road leads left into the valley. This road follows the stream and toward Hi`ilawe Falls. However, the topside streams are tapped for irrigation by the landowners above; thus there sometimes is little water for the waterfalls. Since much of Waipio Valley is privately owned, it's best to stick to the main road. This road has several stream crossings and passes by many taro patches. You may see resident taro farmers working in their fields. The valley is a wondrously lush green environment. There is wild guava and even papaya and bananas growing along the way. However far you wander, remember that you still have to return to the junc-

Off-road tours go through Waipio Valley streams.

Hawai`i

tion at the base of the valley cliff road and it's still .75 mile up and out of the valley.

The Waipio and Waimanu Valley Trail (Muliwai) leads north out of Waipio Valley. This is a difficult two- to three-day wilderness backpacking trip for experienced hikers, advisable only during the drier May to October period due to the flood-prone streams that must be crossed. The trail is an 18-mile round-trip from Waipio Valley to Waimanu Valley. It is accessed at the north end of Waipio Valley beach after fording Wailoa Stream. The trail is 100 yards from the beach in a forest at the base of the north wall cliff. This is a switchback "Z" trail up the 1,200-foot cliff and reaches the high coastal plateau between the two valleys. The trail crosses some 14 gulches and streams along this rugged coastline, passing through dense coastal rain forest. It can be heavily overgrown in places and can be muddy, rocky and slippery as well. There is a trail shelter suitable for picnicking and camping about two-thirds of the way to Waimanu. Be on the lookout for horses and pig-hunters who frequent the area. After an equally steep descent into Waimanu Valley, turn right toward the beach, ford the stream and locate a suitable camping spot on or near the beach. You need a camping permit from the Lands and Natural Resources Department, Forestry and Wildlife office (see address/contact under Information Sources on page 294). Any stream water used must be purified and/or boiled first.

Kalopa State Park in the Hamakua Forest Reserve is 42 miles north of Hilo on Highway 19, turning left at the Kalopa State Park sign just past the 39 mile marker. The park has rental cabins with water, cooking facilities. plus campgrounds and picnic shelters. This state park has a 100-acre block of native Hawaiian rain forest that is kept in its natural state as much as possible, limiting incursions of alien species, pigs, and other destructive animals. There are several enjoyable hiking trails throughout. The **Kalopa Native Forest Nature Trail** is an easy .7-mile loop trail, one-hour walk through a true Hawaiian rain forest. Trails are well marked, as are a number of tree and plant species. Pick up a trail guide at the trailhead near the parking lot. The nature trail is just opposite the cabins and leads into dark forest under towering ohia trees. The forest here also has large tree ferns, kolea, kopiko, olomea, pilo, ground ferns and much more. The **Kalopa Gulch Rim Loop** is a 2.8-mile, two-hour walk suitable for all hikers. Pick up a trail guide at the parking lot display. This walk is through a 1930s reforestation project planted to conserve land and soil that had been badly overgrazed and misused. Fast-growing non-native species were introduced, including blue gum, paper bark, silk oak, ironwood and swamp mahogany. This large standing forest is still thriving and a native Hawaiian forest is beginning to re-establish itself. The area has linking trails to the main loop trail and is a pleasant walk in the woods.

Hiking Resources

For guided hikes and excursions, contact any of the following for more information. Typical half-day wilderness or forest hikes range up to $135 per person; longer excursions are more. Shorter historic town walks of one-two hours are $15 per person. Check with operators for current rates and details.

Downtown Hilo Walking Tours are sponsored by the Lyman Museum and American Association of University Women. The free guided walking tours are conducted the third Saturday of each month and are one-two hours long. The tour includes sites like Kalakaua Park, in the center of downtown Hilo, originally conceived as a civic center by King Kalakaua. The park was the site of one of Hilo's first missionary stations dating from about 1825. Other places of historical interest included in the walking tour are Niolopa (the now closed Hilo Hotel), the old and new library buildings, the old federal building, Lyman Museum and others. Reservations can be made through **Lyman House Museum**, ☎ 808/935-5021; tours begin at the museum, 276 Haili Street, Hilo. As an alternative, call the museum or stop by and pick up a free map to do the walking tour on your own.

Hawai`i Forest & Trail Ltd., PO Box 2975, Kailua-Kona, HI 96745, ☎ 800/464-1993, 808/322-8881; e-mail hitrail@aloha.net. This outfitter offers naturalist-led hiking adventures to the Big Island's unique ecosystems, including rain forests, mountains, volcanoes and wildlife refuges. Hikers are led by a naturalist-guide through the primeval forest, with geologic wonders, incredible views and native Hawaiian flora and fauna. Hikes include snacks, lunch, beverages/water and equipment. They vary from two-four hours over moderate terrain. Groups are limited to 10 hikers to assure a personalized experience. Hotel pick-ups included. Reservations are essential.

Hawai`i

Hawaiian Walkways, PO Box 2193, Kamuela, HI 96743, ☎ 808/885-7759. This hiking outfitter offers a variety of half-day and full-day hikes over the Big Island's mountains and valleys and along its shorelines. Spectacular mountain and coastline vistas, secluded beaches, upland meadows, lush tropical rain forest, hidden pools and streams, fishponds and ancient Hawaiian petroglyphs or rock carvings are some of the features of these hiking tours. They also have special three-day/two-night camping hikes and other customized excursions by arrangement.

Arnott's Lodge Hiking Adventures, 98 Apapane Road, Hilo, HI 96720, ☎ 808/969-7097. This outfitter offers a number of small group hiking adventures to the Big Island's most significant natural attractions. There are adventure excursions to Mauna Kea summit, Hawai`i Volcanoes National Park, South Point's famed Black Sand Beach and Green Sand Beach, Puna on the Rift Zone, and Hilo Waterfalls, as well as custom hikes and expeditions. Contact them for details, schedule and availability.

Pacific Rim Tours, 75-5751 Kuakini Highway, #206, Kailua-Kona, HI 96740, ☎ 800/444-3756, 808/329-5556; e-mail tours@aloha.net. This outfitter operates interpretive hiking adventures in Big Island rain forest wilderness, volcanic deserts, secluded beaches and remote rugged coastal areas. Take in the scenic grandeur of Volcanoes National Park, unique flora and fauna in Hawai`i's forests, old Hawaiian heiau (temples) and archaeological sites, petroglyph rock carvings, while learning about the islands' history and culture.

Sierra Club, Hawai`i Chapter, Moku Loa Group, PO Box 1137, Hilo, HI 96721, ☎ 808/982-9023 or 961-6142. This group has regular outings, walks, hikes and excursions around the Big Island. Visitors may be able to join their activities. Call or write for information.

Golf Courses

The Big Island has widely acclaimed championship golf courses, some of which regularly host major pro tournaments, such as the PGA Senior Skins Tournament. There are also some exciting, unique public golf links as well. Greens fees at resort courses range from $60-160. Public course fees range from $10-30.

Kohala

Hapuna Golf Course, at Hapuna Beach Prince Hotel, Mauna Kea Resort, ☎ 808/880-3000. This is an 18-hole Arnold Palmer-designed championship course on naturally hilly coastal uplands with nice views of ocean and mountains.

Mauna Kea Beach Golf Course, at Mauna Kea Beach Hotel, Mauna Kea Resort, ☎ 808/882-7222. This championship course has won wide acclaim for excellence. Simply put, it's one of Hawai`i's finest.

Francis H. I`i Brown Golf Course, Mauna Lani Resort, ☎ 808/885-6655. This spectacular 36-hole layout has North and South courses. Several holes run alongside or over the ocean and rugged coastline. This is home to the annual PGA Senior Skins Tournament. It's a magnificent place to play.

Waikoloa Beach Golf Club, Waikoloa Beach Resort, ☎ 808/885-6060. This is an 18-hole course designed by master Robert Trent Jones Jr. and sits amid black lava flows and blue Pacific Ocean.

Waikoloa Resort Kings' Course, Waikoloa Beach Resort, ☎ 808/885-4647. This 18-hole layout was designed by Tom Weiskopf and Jay Morrish. It has a distinct open, windswept setting reminiscent of famed courses in Scotland. The brisk Waikoloa winds continuously massage the area. The course features some of the most challenging sand traps in Hawai`i.

Waikoloa Village Golf Club, in Waikoloa Village in the uplands above the Waikoloa Resort, ☎ 808/883-9621. This is a Robert Trent Jones Jr.-designed 18-hole layout, challenging for beginners as well as serious golfers.

Waimea Country Club, Mamalahoa Highway 19, two miles east of Waimea, ☎ 808/885-8777. This 18-hole layout is in the heart of Parker Ranch country and has rolling hilly terrain through former cattle pastures. Natural forest lines the fairways and is subject to breezy, foggy conditions when low cloud fronts blow through the area.

Kona

Kona Country Club, 78-7000 Alii Drive, Keauhou-Kona, ☎ 808/322-2595. There are two separate 18-hole courses. The Ocean Front runs oceanside and is surrounded by vacation condo units. The Ali`i Country Club runs upslope, providing spectacular ocean and coastal views.

Hawai`i

Makalei Hawai`i Country Club, 72-3890 Mamalahoa Highway 190, five miles upslope of Kailua-Kona town, ☎ 800/606-9606, 808/325-6625. This championship 18-hole course has a cool, breezy upland setting on the forested slopes of Mount Hualalai at a 2,000-foot elevation. Most holes play downhill through undulating fairways and challenging greens.

Hilo and Hamakua Coast

Hilo Municipal Golf Course, 340 Haihai Street, Hilo, ☎ 808/959-7711. This is an 18-hole public course operated by the County of Hawai`i. Heavy use from local golfers on weekends, with weekdays a bit slower. Fairways are subject to soggy conditions during periods of Hilo's famed heavy rains, which can be anytime. There is a lighted driving range for night use.

Naniloa Country Club, 120 Banyan Drive, on Hilo's hotel row, ☎ 808/935-3000. This is a short nine-hole, par-36 course. The short fairways wind between stands of ironwood trees and tend to have rocky patches or rocks hiding just under the turf surface, making for a lot of dings and nicks in balls and clubs. Play this only if there is no other alternative and you absolutely must play golf.

Hamakua Country Club, just below Highway 19 at Honoka`a, ☎ 808/775-7244. This is a nine-hole course over very sloping terrain. There are nice views of Honoka`a and the ocean. Turn off the highway next to the Union 76 gas station and proceed to the entrance.

Volcano/Ka`u District

Discovery Harbor Golf and Country Club, located in small village of Waiohinu, Ka`u District, ☎ 808/929-7353. This is a nice 18-hole course surrounded by a country residential subdivision in the remote southern area of the Big Island.

Sea Mountain Golf Course, at Punalu`u, Ka`u District, ☎ 808/928-6222. This is a very nice 18-hole championship course with carefully landscaped fairways, lots of greenery and flowering plants. Strong coastal breezes are a factor here. This is a very remote tranquil country setting, five miles from Pahala town.

Volcano Golf and Country Club, just west of the entrance to Hawai`i Volcanoes National Park, off Highway 11. This is a lush, green 18-hole course with a grand setting amid the rolling and colorful ohia lehua/fern forest and old lava flows. Narrow fairways make a challenge of each hole.

Tennis Courts

There are several public and private tennis courts and complexes on the Big Island. Many hotels and resorts have their own courts available for guest use and some are open to the public on a user fee basis. Some courts operated by the County of Hawai`i are lighted for night use. For a map detailing public tennis court locations around the island contact the **Department of Parks and Recreation**, County of Hawai`i, 25 Aupuni St., Hilo, HI 96720, ☎ 808/ 961-8311.

Public Tennis Courts
Hilo

Edith Kanakaole Tennis Stadium, Piilani and Kalanikoa Streets, ☎ 808/961-8720. Three indoor and five outdoor courts; hourly user fees apply; reservations suggested.

University of Hawai`i at Hilo Tennis Courts, 200 W. Kawili St., ☎ 808/974-7520. Six outdoor courts.

Public Park Courts
Hilo

Ainaola Park, Hakalau Park, Lincoln Park, Lokahi Park, Malama Park, Mohouli Park, Panaewa Park (most of these are right in the Hilo town area).

Hamakua District

Papa`aloa Park, Papa`aloa Village; Honoka`a Park, Honoka`a town.

Kohala District

Kamehameha Park, Kapa`au town; Waimea Park, Waimea town.

Kona District

Greenwell Park, Captain Cook town; Higashihara Park, Keauhou; Kailua Park, Old Kona Airport; Kailua Playground, Kuakini Highway near Kailua-Kona town.

Ka`u District

Na`alehu Park, Na`alehu town; Pahala School, Pahala Village.

Puna District

Kurtistown Park, Kurtistown; Shipman Park, junction of Volcano and Pahoa Highways, Keaau town.

Hawai`i

Private Courts Open to the Public

Private resort courts charge hourly fees ranging from $6-25. Check with resorts for details.

Kohala

Hilton Waikoloa Village, 69-425 Waikoloa Beach Drive, Kohala Coast, HI 96743, ☎ 800/HILTONS, 808/886-1234. Eight hard-surface courts, two clay courts and a tournament stadium; user fees apply.

Mauna Kea Beach Hotel, 62-100 Mauna Kea Beach Drive, Kohala Coast, HI 96743, ☎ 800/882-6060, 808/882-7222. The Tennis Complex features 13 hard-surface courts, none lighted; user fees apply.

Mauna Lani Bay Hotel & Bungalows, 68-1400 Mauna Lani Drive, Kohala Coast, HI 96743, ☎ 800/367-2323, 808/885-6622. Ten hard-surface courts; user fees apply.

Mauna Lani Racquet Club, Mauna Lani Drive, Kohala Coast, HI 96743, ☎ 808/885-7755. Six hard-surface courts, two grass courts and a stadium court with three courts lighted for night play; user fees apply; memberships available.

The Orchid at Mauna Lani, One North Kaniku Drive, Kohala Coast, HI 96743, ☎ 800/845-9905, 808/885-2000. Eleven hard-surface courts, seven lighted for night play, and a stadium court; user fees apply.

Outrigger Waikoloan Resort, 69-275 Waikoloa Beach Drive, Kohala Coast, HI 96743, ☎ 800/688-7444, 808/886-6789. Six hard-surface courts for day play only; user fees apply.

Kona

Keauhou Beach Hotel, 78-6740 Alii Drive, Keauhou-Kona, HI 96740, ☎ 800/446-8990, 808/322-3441. Six hard-surface courts, two lighted for night play; user fees apply.

King Kamehameha Kona Beach Resort, 75-5660 Palani Road, Kailua-Kona, HI 96740, ☎ 800/367-6060, 808/329-2911. Four hard-surface courts with two lighted for night play; user fees apply.

Royal Kona Resort Tennis Club, 75-5852 Alii Drive, Kailua-Kona, HI 96740, ☎ 800/774-KONA, 808/329-3111. Four hard-surface courts, three lighted for night play; user fees apply.

Shopping

The Big Island has everything from shopping malls with big name department stores and specialty boutiques to small town shops that carry a wide selection of locally produced fashions, arts and crafts, antiques and Big Island products.

Kona

The Stenciled Cottage, 74-5600 Pawai Place, Bldg. B, Kailua-Kona, HI 96740, ☎ 808/326-3224. This shop has a wide selection of local arts and crafts, specialty items, unique gifts.

**Hilo Hattie`s,** 75-5597A Palani Road, Kailua-Kona, HI 96740, ☎ 808/329-7200. This is Hawai`i's best known designer and manufacturer of stylish, bright and colorful island-style Alohawear and resortwear, including Aloha shirts for men and Hawaiian print muumuus for women, plus Aloha clothes for kids too.

Keauhou Shopping Center, 78-6831 Alii Drive, Keauhou-Kona, HI 96740, ☎ 808/322-3000. This center is anchored by KTA Superstore, Ace Hardware/Ben Franklin Crafts, Long's Drugs, restaurants, eateries, boutiques and specialty shops.

Kona Coast Shopping Center, 74-5588 Palani Road, Kailua-Kona, HI 96740, ☎ 808/326-2262. This center is anchored by KTA Superstore, Ross Store, local-style eateries and specialty shops.

Kona Inn Shopping Village, Alii Drive, Kailua-Kona, HI 96740, ☎ 808/329-6573. This resort center features restaurants, specialty boutiques, arts and crafts shops, activities desks, and resort wear shops, all in the heart of Kailua-Kona on Ali`i Drive.

Lanihau Center, 75-5595 Palani Road, Kailua-Kona, HI 96740, ☎ 808/329-3571. This center is anchored by Sack 'n Save Foods and Long's Drugs and has several restaurants and eateries, plus Waldenbooks and other specialty shops.

Kohala

As Hawi Turns, Akoni Pule Highway, Hawi town, North Kohala, ☎ 808/889-5023. This old country store is a fashion boutique with an interesting line of locally designed island-style women's fashions and accessories.

Waimea General Store, Parker Square Shopping Center, Highway 19, west edge of Waimea town, ☎ 808/885-4479. This shop has a nice selection of needlework and knitting supplies, cookery and kitchen products, books, toys, seasonal arts and crafts and lots more to browse.

Hawai`i

Kings' Shops, Waikoloa Beach Drive, Waikoloa Beach Resort, Kohala Coast, HI 96743, ☎ 808/886-8811. This resort center is anchored by Liberty House and Whalers General Store and has several other resort wear boutiques, specialty shops, gift shops, activities desks, and restaurants, including Roy's Waikoloa Bar & Grill, Big Island Steak House, Grand Palace Chinese Restaurant, Hama Yu Japanese Restaurant and a food court with several outlets.

Parker Square, 65-1279 Kawaihae Road #19, west edge of Waimea, ☎ 808/885-7178. This country-style ranch-themed complex features several specialty stores like Waimea General Store, Bentley's, Silk Road Gallery, Gallery of Great Things, Waimea Coffee & Co. and others.

Parker Ranch Shopping Center, Highway 19/#190 junction, Waimea, ☎ 808/885-7178. This country town mall is anchored by Sure Save Supermarket and has the Parker Ranch Store for ranch and western wear, several local boutiques, arts and crafts outlets and eateries like Big Island Coffee Co., Su's Thai Kitchenlli's Pizza.

Waimea Center, Highway 19, Waimea. This center is anchored by KTA Superstore and has several gift and specialty shops like Kamuela Kids, Kamuela Hat Co., Cook's Discoveries and several restaurants, including Maha's Café, Yong's Kai-Bi, Kamuela Deli and Great Wall Chop Suey.

Hilo

Hilo Hattie's, 111 E. Puainako St., Prince Kuhio Plaza, Hilo, HI 96720, ☎ 808/961-3077. Hawai`i's best known designer and manufacturer of colorful island-style fashions, including Aloha shirts for men and Hawaiian print muumuus for women, plus Aloha clothes for kids too.

Hilo Shopping Center, 345 Kekuanaoa St., Hilo, HI 96720, ☎ 808/935-6499. This refurbished mall has several specialty and gift shops plus travel agency, bank, bakery and restaurants.

Prince Kuhio Plaza, 111 E. Puainako, Hilo, HI 96720, ☎ 808/959-3555. This is Hilo's flagship mall, with several big name retailers like Liberty House, Sears and J.C. Penney's plus a number of other boutiques, shops and services, plus a food court with varied outlets.

Puainako Town Center, 2100 Kanoelehua, Hilo, HI 96720, ☎ 808/959-7309. This center is anchored by Payless Drugs and Sack 'N Save Supermarket and has several other specialty shops and restaurants like Ting Hao Mandarin Restaurant, Dotty's Coffee Shop and fast food outlets.

Hawaiiana Arts & Crafts

Abba Featherworks, 421 Makalika St., Hilo, ☎ 808/959-4987. Specializes in the intricate and colorful fine art of handmade Hawaiian feather leis and bands for hats, necklaces.

Alapaki's, Keauhou Shopping Center, Alii Drive and Kamehameha III Drive, Keauhou-Kona, ☎ 808/322-2007. A wide selection of Hawaiiana arts, crafts and woodcarvings.

Cook's Discoveries, Waimea Shopping Center, PO Box 6960, Kamuela, HI 96743, ☎ 808/885-3633. This small shop in the historic Spencer House carries a diverse selection of arts, crafts and jewelry, all by local artisans.

Dan De Luz Woods Inc., two locations: 64-1013 Mamalahoa Highway in Waimea, ☎ 808/885-5856; or PO Box 407, Kurtistown, HI 96760, shop is just past the 12-mile marker on Highway 11 near Mt. View village, ☎ 808/968-6607. This Big Island master wood carver has been creating beautiful one-of-a-kind wooden bowls, plaques and unique woodwork pieces for many years. His hand-turned and hard-carved work has to be seen to be appreciated. These beautiful art pieces made from native woods like koa, milo, monkeypod will be treasured for a lifetime.

Grass Shack, Highway 11, Kealakekua, Kona, ☎ 808/323-2877. This well known visitor stop carries a number of locally made Hawaiian arts and crafts like woven pandanus and coconut fiber hats, mats, slippers and placemats.

**Hulihe`e Palace Gift Shop,** 75-5718 Alii Drive, Kailua-Kona, HI 96740, ☎ 808/329-6558. On the grounds of Hulihe`e Palace, the former summer palace of Hawaiian royalty in the 1800s, this shop has a variety of locally made arts, authentic Hawaiiana and jewelry. Proceeds go to help maintain the palace museum and grounds.

Kimura Lauhala Shop, Old Mamalahoa Highway 180, Holualoa, Kona, just down the road from Holualoa's art colony, five miles above Kailua-Kona town, ☎ 808/324-0053. This small town family-run shop has a wide variety of handmade woven lauhala (pandanus) products like mats, baskets, hats, slippers, placemats and related crafts. You'll find authentic made-in-Hawai`i products here.

Big Island Woodworks Gallery, 308 Kamehameha Avenue, in the historic S. Hata Building, Hilo, ☎ 808/961-0400. This fine arts and crafts gallery has a beautiful display of handmade woodwork bowls, plaques, figures, carvings and crafts from Big Island woodworkers and artisans. Browse among a number of unique and beautiful pieces.

Kohala Koa Gallery, Highway 250 at 270, in Bamboo Restaurant Building, Hawi town, North Kohala, ☎ 808/889-0055. This small gallery shop has a nice selection of hand-turned wooden bowls and unique crafted woodcarvings.

Sig Zane Designs, 122 Kamehameha Avenue, Hilo, HI 96720, ☎ 808/935-7077. This local designer is noted for colorful Hawaiian-inspired natural print designs and colors for fabrics that are fashioned into women's dresses, muumuus, skirts and shirts.

Sugawara Lauhala & Gift Shop, 59 Kalakaua St., Hilo, ☎ 808/935-8071. This small family-operated Hawaiiana arts and crafts shop carries a good selection of lauhala (pandanus) woven baskets, hats, mats and slippers. The Sugawara sisters have been handcrafting these fine local gifts for years.

**Kama`aina Woods,** on Lehua Street downhill from the post office, Honoka`a, HI 96727, ☎ 808/775-7722. This small town shop and factory specializes in handmade koa bowls and other woodwork products.

Waimea Craft Mall, 67-1167 Mamalahoa Highway, across from the Waimea Shopping Center, Waimea, ☎ 808/887-0020. This artists' outlet has a wide assortment of arts and crafts, all done by local Big Island artisans. There are paintings, woodcarvings, candles, ceramics, picture frames, jewelry and much more.

Museums

Big Island museums capture the culture of Hawai`i from pre-western contact to the missionary days of the early 1800s, the development of the sugar industry in east Hawai`i, the coffee industry in Kona, ranching in Kamuela, and the influence of the immigrant ethnic groups.

Onizuka Space Center, Kona International Airport terminal, Kailua-Kona, HI 96740, ☎ 808/329-3441. This memorial museum of space flight and astronaut lore is dedicated to Hawai`i's own son, Astronaut Ellison S. Onizuka, who was lost aboard the 1986 space shuttle disaster at Cape Canaveral. Colonel Onizuka was born and raised in Kona and grew up on his family's coffee farm. The museum features memorabilia from his career in space exploration, including hands-on exhibits and a piece of "moon rock" donated by NASA.

Hulihee Palace Museum, 75-5718 Alii Drive, Kailua-Kona, HI 96740, ☎ 808/329-1877. This attractive and imposing beachside structure was built in 1838 and used as a summer residence by the ruling Hawaiian monarchs. The Palace is maintained by the Daughters of Hawai`i as a showcase of Hawaiian culture. The palace has some beautiful antique

Hawaiian furniture, original bedroom furnishings, antique handmade Hawaiian quilts and other memorabilia from the days of Hawaiian royalty.

Royal Aloha Coffee Mill & Museum, 160 Napo`opo`o Road, Captain Cook, HI 96704, ☎ 800/566-2269, 808/328-9851. This museum has educational displays and exhibits on the history of the Kona coffee industry. Enjoy a complimentary cup of coffee as you tour the museum and stop in the gift shop afterwards to browse a variety of fresh milled Kona coffee products.

Kamuela Museum, intersection of Highways 19 and 250 (Kohala Mountain Road), just west of Waimea town, ☎ 808/885-4724. This is a privately operated museum with a large collection of ancient Hawaiian weapons, World War II artifacts, furniture of Hawaiian royalty, and other art objects on display.

Kona Historical Society Museum, PO Box 398, Captain Cook, HI 96704, ☎ 808/323-2005. Housed in the historic Greenwell Store, a quarter-mile south of Kealakekua town on Highway 11, this old country store maintains an extensive collection of historic manuscripts, photographs, maps, artifacts and has regular exhibits on early Kona ranching, coffee farming, and life in the Kona District. KHS also conducts historical tours. These include: 1) A 1½-hour walking tour of historic Kailua-Kona village to experience Kailua's colorful past; 2) A 1½-hour walking tour of the historic Uchida Coffee Farm, circa 1925, listed on the National Register of Historic Places; 3) Specially arranged tours such as Captain Cook at Kealakekua Bay, and a Keauhou Archeological Tour.

Lyman House Memorial Museum, 276 Haili Street, Hilo, HI 96720, ☎ 808/935-5021. This is a New England-style missionary home built in 1839 for the Rev. David and Sarah Lyman, the first Christian missionaries to arrive in Hilo. Next door to the original Lyman House is the modern museum building, which holds a unique collection of memorabilia of early Hilo and Big Island lifestyles. Artifacts and memorabilia cover the pre-western contact era, the post-contact missionary and Hawaiian Monarchy period of the 1800s, then the 1900s. There are many cultural artifacts representing the ethnic groups that migrated to Hawai`i over the generations.

Parker Ranch Visitor Center and Historic Homes, in Parker Ranch Shopping Center, Highway 19, Waimea, ☎ 808/885-7655. The visitors center has a museum of ranch history and exhibits plus a film that details the history of cattle ranching in Hawai`i and the story of the Hawaiian "paniolo" (cowboy). The Historic Homes (☎ 885-5433) include

Parker Ranch country.

the 100-year-old main ranch house at Pu`uopelu and the 140-year-old New England-style Mana House built by John Palmer Parker I. The Mana House has an interior made of all Hawaiian koa wood. The Pu`uopelu home has a fine artwork and antique collection of the late Richard Smart, the ranch's last sole owner. The Historic Homes are located off Highway 190 just west of Waimea town.

Hunting

Hunters will enjoy an expedition to Big Island ranchlands, fields, forests and mountains in pursuit of big game or game birds. Hunters can go for wild boar, Mouflon sheep, or mountain goats, plus wild turkey, quail, pheasant, chukar or francolin partridge. The Big Island will provide thrills, action and a unique outdoor experience on a professionally guided hunting adventure. Check with either of the following hunting outfitters for details. Guided hunting excursions begin at about $500 per day for one hunter; extra hunters are $150 each to a maximum of four per party. Non-resident hunting license is $100.

Ginger Flower Charters, 73-4250A Kauhale, Kailua-Kona, HI 96740, ☎ 808/325-7600. Wild boar hunts, plus archery hunts for sheep and goat in season and game birds; deep sea fishing charters also arranged.

Hawai`i Hunting Tours, PO Box 58, Paauilo, HI 96776, ☎ 808/776-1666. Private custom hunts for sheep, wild boar, goat and game birds in the remote backcountry of Mauna Kea.

■ On Wheels

Big Island Biking Trails

Whatever your level of biking and whether you want an easy relaxing ride along a flat coastal trail or the challenge of a difficult mountain climb, you'll find a trail to call your own on the Big Island. In addition, you'll enjoy the scenic vistas and unspoiled panoramic views of the Big Island's less traveled off-road back-country trails and paths.

Walua Road is a few miles south of downtown Kailua-Kona on Kuakini Highway. Opposite the Kilohana/Komohana housing tract, turn inland on Lako Street. The trail begins above the Chevron gas station. This is a 6.4-mile round-trip, 45-minute ride, a paved trail running through housing subdivisions. The trail crosses residential streets, so be aware of local traffic. The ride climbs uphill gradually, from 400 feet to 1,200 feet elevation. There are panoramic ocean views and tropical landscaping the entire way. The ride back is downhill all the way.

Pine Trees trail is just south of Kona International Airport at the Natural Energy Lab of Hawai`i (NELHA) grounds. Turn into NELHA just before airport entrance and go about one mile to the coastline. This 6.4-mile round-trip trail, 1½ hours, follows along the sea coast with both north and south segments. The north trail begins 50 yards north of the parking lot. The lava trail soon turns to sandy beach road that winds along the coast for 1.2 miles. The trail ends at the Ho`ona Historical Preserve. Return to the parking lot and head south. Pick up the south trail where the road curves, then veer to the right and follow the beach trail for two miles. This is an easy ride for beginners.

Pohue Road trail is located in the North Kohala District between Hawi town and Mahukona. There are two access points. From the Kohala Mountain Road #250, turn onto Pohue Road just past the 17-mile marker. Follow the gravel road 50 yards, then turn right on a grassy road and go through the gate. From the Akoni Pule Highway 270, the coastal route north from Kawaihae, just past the 18-mile marker, turn inland on the access road. This country road maintained by the government features varied terrain and wonderful open views of ranchlands and Maui across the sea. Road surfaces vary from rocky cinder to dirt lanes across ranchlands. It's your choice to ride uphill or downhill. Either way is five miles, round-trip 10 miles. It takes a half-hour to ride down, one hour or more to ride up.

Old Puna Trail is located along the Puna coastline from Hawaiian Paradise Park subdivision north to Haena Beach. Head south from Hilo to the turnoff for Highway 130 at Keaau. Take #130 about 4½ miles, turn left on Kaloli Road and go another 4.2 miles to Beach Road. Head left on Beach Road and pick up the trail. It's still under development and is rough and rugged. With improvements it will be a smoother ride. The trail follows the old Puna trail, which linked the area with Hilo back in the 1800s. As the trail approaches Hilo, it skirts the airport. You'll ride through lush tropical forest, with fruit trees, flowers and bright foliage. 4WD trails branch off to fishing spots on the coast but these are rough trails to be avoided. You'll see Haena Beach nestled in evergreens and Norfolk Island pines. This is a 10-mile ride one-way, about three-four hours.

Mana Road is one of the Big Island's longer backcountry bike trails and goes around Mauna Kea, Hawai`i's tallest mountain at 13,769 feet. Follow the Saddle Road #200 up the mountain from either the Hilo or Kona side. Turn off at the Mauna Kea Access Road leading to the summit, just opposite a hunter check-in hut. Drive north on this road about two miles and turn right, east, on the dirt road and cross a cattle guard gate. From Waimea, the Mana Road access junction is on Mamalahoa Highway 19 just across from the Department of Hawaiian Home Lands complex. This is an upcountry trail linking Saddle Road and Waimea around the east and north sides of Mauna Kea. The distance is 45 miles either way and is an all-day six- eight-hour ride. Elevation changes from 3,000 to 6,500 feet.

The trek ranges from smooth level dirt or gravel road through cattle pastures to rough, rugged and rutted trail in dense upland forest. This is also a 4WD vehicle road used by hunters. There are unspoiled vistas of mountain slopes, forest and distant ranchlands, with stands of magnificent old koa trees throughout the upcountry pastures. Don't be surprised to come upon herds of cattle. They'll usually scatter upon seeing people. There are numerous cattle gates to pass through; be sure to close them all. There are a couple of cabins available to campers along the trail. Contact **State Forestry and Wildlife**, ☎ 808/974-4221. To bike it one-way, arrange to have someone meet you at the other end. You'll need lots of food and water, plus cool weather raingear.

Kulani Trails are located south of Hilo off Highway 11. At 4.2 miles south of Hilo, turn right onto Stainback Highway at sign for Panaewa Zoo. Continue 2.6 miles and turn right at Waiakea Arboretum. Take the first left off the highway and the first set of trails begins. This is a challenging dense forest ride on single track trails with lots of slippery conditions, roots, rocks, fallen logs and lots of mud, but it is a cool forest ride. There are majestic 100-foot eucalyptus trees all around. Distances and times vary; routes wind throughout the Waiakea Forest Reserve area.

Volcano Trails are located 30 miles south of Hilo and 97 miles south of Kona via Highway 11 at Hawai`i Volcanoes National Park. All paved roads in the park are open to bikers; some unpaved trails may be open at varied times. Check with park rangers at the entrance or visitors center and get a map. The 11-mile Crater Rim Drive circles Kilauea Volcano summit caldera and goes through tropical rain and fern forest, past steaming vents and smoking sulphur banks, craters and cinder cones. There are a number of short walks at places like Devastation Trail and Thurston Lava Tube, plus several craters and overlooks. The Chain of Craters Road winds downslope from Crater Rim Drive for over 20 miles to the recent eruption sites along the Kalapana Coast, the national park's southern boundary area. The road terminates where the latest lava flows have crossed it. If the eruption activity is still on, it's possible to see the steam plumes from where the lava enters the ocean. Visitors might also be able to see the lavaflows close up if rangers feel it is safe enough. Bikers can take

Lava flows into the ocean at Kamoamoa Beach, Volcanoes National Park.

this paved road, but be warned that it gets a lot of traffic and is a long climb back up.

Ainapo Trail is south of Hawai`i Volcanoes National Park on Highway 11. At 12.2 miles past the park entrance, turn right on the access road marked by a gravel turnout, gate, and Ainapo Trail Road sign. Bear right for about .1 mile. The ride is on dirt and grass double-track, gradually climbing through pasture, guava tree thickets and rocky outcroppings. One mile in is a gate and after another 3½ miles the road forks; keep right for another 4.4 miles to the Ainapo Trailhead. This section of the famed Ainapo Trail is for hikers only and leads to the summit of Mauna Loa. Bikers have to return at this point. There is a hiker's cabin about a 3½-hour hike up at the 7,750-foot level. To reserve the cabin, call **State Forestry & Wildlife, ☎** 808/974-4221. Bikers return by the same route. This ride is nine miles long, three hours up to the trailhead and one back down.

Kilohana Trail is accessed via the Saddle Road #200. Look for the Kilohana Hunter Check-in Station sign between mile markers 44 and 45 on the Saddle Road. Turn onto this gravel road and the trail begins on this northwest side of Mauna Kea. This is a 6.6-mile one-way ride for experienced riders only, about 1½ hours each way. The road climbs gradually

Hawai`i

on gravel, then dirt; eventually, it gets rough. At 2.2 miles, go right at the fork and this takes you to Ahumoa, a cinder cone at 7,042-feet elevation, with nice views of surrounding country. The road continues up, and you may have to walk part way, for another 3.1 miles to Pu`u La`au and a hunter's cabin surrounded by eucalyptus trees at 7,446 feet elevation. This is a good place to rest, picnic and enjoy the views before heading back down the same route.

Puna Coast Beach Road is accessed by heading south on Highway 11 out of Hilo and taking the Keaau turnoff, Highway 130, for 4.6 miles. Turn left on Kaloli Road in Hawaiian Paradise Park subdivision. Take Kaloli Road 4.2 miles downslope to Beach Road at the coast and turn right on Beach Road for another 1.2 miles. The old Puna trail begins here and runs 10½ miles one-way, about an hour or so ride. The ride is mostly level on a cinder and dirt road through fields of wild orchids and coastal rain forest. There are great views along this isolated and remote rugged coastal area. The dirt road ends at Kapoho, where one can continue on to the coastal settlements of Pohoiki, Opihikao and Kalapana areas via paved Highway 137, about another 12 miles. This would be advised only if you can arrange a pickup at the Kalapana end. Otherwise it's a long ride back the same route or via Pahoa town and Highway 130.

Some stretches of the island highway system lend themselves well to bike touring and you may want to give these a try.

Highway 240 from Honoka`a town to the Waipio Valley overlook is a 10-mile one-way ride through rolling hills and old sugar plantation lands along the Hamakua Coast. The road passes through the small plantation settlements of Kawela, Kapulena and Kukuihaele before reaching the top of Waipio Valley. It's a pleasant, easy ride with nice views of the north side of Waipio Valley.

DON'T MISS **Kohala Mountain Road #250** runs 20 miles up and over the Kohala Mountains between Waimea and Hawi. This is perhaps the Big Island's most scenic pastoral route, traveling through rolling ranch country, green mountains and pastures, herds of grazing cattle and sheep, and beautiful views of distant Kohala Coast areas. This is a narrow, winding road and is lined with ironwood trees that serve as a windbreak along the upper reaches where the Kohala winds can be brisk. Caution is advised; moderate in difficulty.

Highway 270 from Kapa`au to the Pololu Valley in North Kohala is a pleasant, easy eight-mile one-way ride through old sugar plantation country and lush open coastal hill country. It's a narrow, winding road so caution is advised. The area has several old plantation settlements with a distinct rural Hawaiian charm. Along the way, the road passes by the historic Wo On Store and Wo Tong Chinese Society Building dating from 1886, Keokea Beach Park, as well as several churches and other historic buildings.

Biking Resources

Several operators and outfitters offer beginner, intermediate and advanced biking adventures to different areas of the Big Island. Adventures range from two to four hours. Tour rates range from $50-105 depending on itinerary. Check with outfitters for details.

For more information on biking and trails on the Big Island or renting bikes and equipment, contact the following groups and organizations:

Peoples Advocacy for Trails Hawai`i (PATH), PO Box 62, Kailua-Kona, HI 96745, ☎ 808/326-9495; e-mail path@aloha.net; www.hialoha.com/path. This is a non-profit community group that advocates the development and improvement of more trails around the Big Island for non-motorized multi-use access.

Big Island Mountain Bike Trails, www.interpac.net:80/~mtbike/index.html.

Chris' Adventures, PO Box 869, Kula, HI 96790, ☎ 808/871-BIKE; www.lmg.com:80/maui/hykebyke.htm. This outfitter offers biking adventures on the Big Island. The *Kohala Mountain Adventure* lets you bike down a volcano with off-road options and snorkeling. The *Mauna Loa Challenge* is a challenging ride from the 11,000-foot level on 56 miles of rugged backcountry roads. The *Kona Coffee Trek* bikes from Kona's upslope coffee farm country down to magnificent Kealakekua Bay's historic sites, with snorkeling options. The *Big Islander Off Roader* goes from majestic Mauna Kea to scenic marvels of Waipio Valley or the Kohala Coast Trail. Rides range from half- to full-day.

Mauna Kea Mountain Bikes, PO Box 44672, Kamuela, HI 96743, ☎ 888/MTB-TOUR, 808/885-2091. This outfitter has biking adventures which provide some of the Big Island's best backcountry riding. Adventures range from two to four hours, covering six to 21 miles, depending on the route. The *Kohala Downhill* (Hawi) follows the scenic old Kohala Highway and along the Akonipule Highway. The *Mana Highway* (Kamuela) ride covers the spectacular upcountry ranch and rangelands of Mauna Kea. The *Mud Lane* (Waimea) ride is an advanced ride through rugged rain forest and backcountry trails. The *Mauna Kea Kamakaze* ride is on steep gravel and paved roadways starting from Mauna Kea's summit, 13,796 feet, and riding downhill, with incredible views all the way. All rides include full equipment and bike.

Hawaiian Pedals, 75-5744 Alii Drive, in Kona Inn Shopping Village, Kailua-Kona, HI 96740, ☎ 808/329-2294. This outfitter has a full range of road, touring and mountain bike rentals and equipment. They also offer several guided bike tours, including the Downhill Mountain Tour and Mauna Kea Tour, plus other rides to discover the hidden beauty, history and culture of the Big Island.

Dave's Bike and Triathlon Shop, 75-5669 Alii Drive, Kailua-Kona, HI 96740, ☎ 808/329-4522. This shop has a full line of road and mountain bike rentals and equipment and repairs.

Hilo Bike Hub, 318 E. Kawili Street, Hilo, HI 96720, ☎ 808/961-4452. This shop specializes in mountain bikes and related equipment and has a full line of rentals available; repairs.

B&L Bike & Sports, 75-5699 Kopiko Place, Kopiko Plaza, Kailua-Kona, HI 96740, ☎ 808/329-3309. This shop carries a full line of bikes and equipment and other sporting goods and gear. They have rental bikes and do repairs.

C & S Cycle and Surf, 64-1066 Mamalahoa Highway, Waimea, HI 96743, ☎ 808/885-5005. This bike and surf shop has a full line of bike rentals and related equipment, plus surfing equipment, snorkeling gear.

Red Sail Sports, Hilton Waikoloa Village, ☎ 808/886-2876; Hapuna Beach Prince Hotel, ☎ 808/880-1111. Both beach concession outlets can arrange bicycle rentals for hotel guests.

■ On Water

Beaches

 The Big Island of Hawai`i, as the youngest of the Hawaiian Islands geologically, has few fine sandy beaches in comparison to O`ahu, Kaua`i and Maui. Sandy beaches just haven't had enough time to develop completely around the island as yet. You can wait a few thousand years and give it another try or you can simply explore and discover the many fine beaches that do exist. Granted, several of the beaches may not be nice sand and tend to be coarse pebbles or are even rocky, but there are still several places around the island to enjoy beach activities and the ocean. Facilities and amenities vary at the parks, some have restrooms, showers, picnic pavilions, while some have no facilities. The following are some of the Big Island's better beaches.

The Kona Coast

Pu`uhonua O Honaunau National Historic Park at Honaunau Bay has a nice sandy pebble beach with rocky outcroppings. Beautiful stand of coconut palms as a background to the old Hawaiian heiau site and historic ruins of the park. Located at the end of Highway 160 off Highway 11, 20 miles south of Kailua-Kona town.

Napo`opo`o Beach Park is at the village of the same name which adjoins Kealakekua Bay. Located at the end of Kealakekua Bay access road off Highway 11 below Captain Cook town. Beach has limited parking and facilities. The bay is the site of Kealakekua Bay Marine Reserve and ruins of ancient Hikiau Heiau are near beach.

**Kahalu`u Beach Park** is on Ali`i Drive at Keauhou Bay just south of Kailua-Kona town next to the Keauhou Beach Hotel. This is a popular swimming and snorkeling site, with lots of reef fish in the water. Beach is black and white sand and pebbles. Concession stand, restrooms, picnic tables.

White Sands Beach Park is on Ali`i Drive four miles south of Kailua-Kona town. This is one of a few white sand beaches along this coastline. It's small and always busy. Winter storms wash the sand out and bring it back later, giving it the local name, "Magic Sands Beach."

Kamakahonu Beach is the small sandy pocket beach fronting the King Kamehameha Kona Beach Hotel and right next to Kailua Pier. Despite its small size, the beach gets lots of traffic, again due to the relative scarcity of nice sandy beaches on the Kona Coast.

Hawai`i

Kaloko-Honokohau National Historic Park is still under development, but visitors will find this new park worth a visit. Located three miles north of Kailua-Kona opposite Kaloko Industrial Area on an access road just north of Honokohau Boat Harbor. Nearby tidal wetlands serve as a waterbird preserve. Other historic and archaeological resources are found throughout the park. Nice sandy beach areas.

Kona Coast State Park is two miles north of Kona International Airport on Highway 19. A rough access road crosses open lava fields to reach the beach area. There is a high sand dune backing the beach and nice tidal pools for snorkeling and swimming. Restrooms, pavilion, showers.

The Kohala Coast

**Anaeho`omalu Beach** is one of the loveliest beaches on the Kohala Coast. Located at Waikoloa Beach Resort, off Waikoloa Beach Drive. It's a long crescent of golden sand and generally quiet water, small waves lapping the shore. Behind it is a stand of handsome coconut palms and the old fishponds, Ku`uali`i and Kahapapa, once reserved for Hawaiian royalty. The Outrigger Waikoloan Resort sits further back behind the fishponds. Adjacent park area has picnic tables, showers.

Hapuna Beach State Park is the Big Island's largest stretch of fine white sandy beach, over a half-mile long. Located off Puako Road adjacent to Mauna Kea Resort. Shallow waters slope gently to deeper offshore waters. Good swimming, snorkeling, bodysurfing and windsurfing. Full beach facilities include concession stand, picnic pavilions, restrooms, showers.

Kauna`oa Beach is perhaps better known at Mauna Kea Beach for the famous hotel that sits immediately behind it. Located at the end of Mauna Kea Drive. There is public access to this beautiful sandy crescent. Good swimming, boardsurfing and bodysurfing. Restrooms and showers on the beach. This beach was listed in the annual "Top 10 Best Beaches" national survey conducted by the University of Maryland. It was one of six beaches in the state so honored.

Spencer Beach Park is near the port village of Kawaihae and below Pu`ukohola Heiau National Historic Park just off Highway 270. This is a very nice sandy beach with gentle surf, perfect for small kids. There are restrooms, showers, picnic pavilions, tables.

The Hamakua Coast & Hilo

Waipio Valley Beach is at the mouth of the magnificent Waipio Valley at the end of Highway 240. A 4WD vehicle is needed to reach the valley

Mauna Kea Beach, Kohala Coast.

floor via the very steep, hazardous road down to the valley. The beach is a long black sand crescent bisected by the Waipio River.

Swimming is not advised at Waipio Valley Beach due to strong undertows and currents. Good for sunning, picnicking and beachcombing only. No facilities at this beach.

Laupahoehoe Point Park is off Highway 19 at Laupahoehoe via the access road to the point. The park is a lava rock peninsula jutting into the ocean. There is a small boat ramp here. The beach is mostly rocky pebbles and coral chunks. Park facilities include picnic pavilions, restrooms, showers. There is a monument to those lost in the 1946 tidal wave that swept away a school on the peninsula. It's a nice spot to enjoy ocean breezes and the tranquility of the Hamakua Coast.

Onekahakaha Beach Park is just off Kalanianaole Street in the Keaukaha area of east Hilo. The park has a protected sandy bottom swimming area for youngsters. It's a great spot for tide pool exploring. There are also picnic pavilions, restrooms and tables.

Leileiwi Beach Park is off Kalanianaole Street in the Keaukaha area of east Hilo. There is good swimming, snorkeling and surfing here. Lots of rocky outcroppings and quiet water pools for snorkeling. It's next to the Richardson Ocean Center, a marine education and aquatic display center open to the public.

Puna District

Kehena Beach is on Pohoiki Road, Highway 137, between Opihikao and the Kaimu/Kalapana junction with Highway 130. This is a broad expanse of fine black sand below the Kehena Lookout. Access is via a steep trail down the cliff face. This is a popular beach with swimmers and bodysurfers. This beach is undeveloped, with no facilities available.

Puala`a Park is 2½ miles south of junction of Highway 132 and 137 on the Kapoho coast southeast of Pahoa town. This recently developed park features a half-acre pond fed by thermal freshwater springs mixed with seawater.

Ka`u District

**Punalu`u Beach Park** is five miles south of Pahala town off Highway 11 at Punalu`u. This is a long fine black sand beach backed by low dunes and coconut palm trees. There is a small boat ramp facility at the east end.

Swimmers and snorkelers should be careful of going out too far due to strong currents sweeping the bay.

Hawaiian green sea turtles are very numerous in this bay and are easily seen as they surface and feed close into shore where they graze on sea weed. Showers, restrooms and picnic pavilion available.

Green Sand Beach is at Mahana Bay, reached via the end of South Point Road and a very rough four-mile round-trip coastal road. A 4WD vehicle is needed or one can hike in and out. Park your car where the good road ends and the coast trail begins. The beach is accessed by a steep and hazardous trail down the cliff side. The sand is tinted with volcanic olivine crystal grains which give it a distinctly green tinge and glassy luster.

The surf here is often rough, so swimming and snorkeling is advised only on calm days. There are no facilities of any kind.

Cruises, Sailing

Several operators offer cruise, sailing and submarine adventures, including whale watching cruises. Whale watching cruises begin at $45-55 per person. Submarine adventures begin at $60-80 per person. Sunset cocktail cruises begin at $25 per person.

Adventure Sailing, PO Box 44335, Kamuela, HI 96743, ☎ 800/726-7245, 808/326-5174. A variety of special cruises, including seasonal whale encounters, snorkeling explorations, coastal ecology cruises, sunset sails aboard the 50-foot Gulfstar *Maile.*

Atlantis Submarine, 75-5660 Palani Road, Hotel King Kamehameha, Kailua-Kona, HI 96740, ☎ 800/548-6262, 808/329-6626. These unique underwater cruises operate with a state-of-the-art submarine designed to take guests down to depths of 150 feet through Kona's fabulous underwater world. The cruises take you along Kona's colorful reefs where you get a fish-eye view of marine life. Morning and afternoon hourly departures Monday-Friday only are from Kailua Pier.

Hawai`i Sailing Company, 44-2050 Kaapahu Road, Paauilo, HI 96776, ☎ 808/776-1505. This cruise operator offers a number of half- and full-day sailings and special charters, including snorkeling cruises, seasonal whale watching cruises, picnic sails.

Lanakila Ventures, PO Box 2786, 75-5663 Palani Road, Kailua-Kona, HI 96745-2786, ☎ 808/326-6000. This large sailing trimaran has several daily sailings, including morning and afternoon snorkeling cruises, a dolphin/eco cruise, seasonal whale watching cruises, and sunset/dinner cruises. Snorkel gear, snacks, beverages included on all cruises.

Nautilus II, 75-5663 Palani Road, Kailua-Kona, HI 96740, ☎ 800/821-2210, 808/326-2003. Office directly across from the Kailua Pier. This undersea adventure uses a 58-foot, 49-passenger semi-submersible craft that cruises Kona's coral reefs for spectacular views of fish and reef-life. The spacious air-conditioned cabin has large windows for underwater viewing. There are several one-hour narrated cruises daily, departing from Kailua Pier. If you've never seen the underwater world of the coral reef first-hand and have always wanted to, then this is the adventure for you. This is an excellent educational tour for youngsters of all ages.

Whale Watch, PO Box 139, Holualoa, HI 96725, ☎ 808/322-0028; e-mail dmcswwa@interpac.net. These adventure cruises are operated by marine biologist and whale researcher, Captain Dan McSweeney, a long-time Kona resident. There are guaranteed whale sightings year-round, using vessels equipped with underwater windows for whale viewing. There are daily morning and afternoon three-hour cruises, departing Honokohau Harbor just north of Kailua-Kona town.

Westwind, PO Box 3541, Kailua-Kona, HI 96745, ☎ 808/936-3700. Daily sailing charters and sunset cruises along the beautiful Kona Coast aboard the 41-foot Islander-class *Westwind*. Cruises depart from Honokohau Harbor just north of Kailua-Kona town.

Snorkeling, Rafting

Several operators offer snorkeling and rafting cruises along the Kona Coast. Typical rates for a half-day snorkel cruise are $45-55 per person. Rates for a half-day raft adventure are $60-65 per person.

Body Glove, PO Box 4523, Kailua-Kona, HI 96745, ☎ 800/551-8911, 808/326-7122; e-mail bcruises@ate.net. This 55-foot trimaran offers daily departures from Kailua Pier for a 4½-hour sail, snorkel, and scuba dive cruise along the Kona Coast. Light breakfast and deli lunch included. Snorkel-diving adventure includes the Pawai Bay Marine Preserve just north of Kona, with its rich and varied marinelife and fish, underwater caves, arches and rock formations, dolphins, manta rays, sea turtles.

Fair Wind, 78-7130 Kaleiopapa Road, Kailua-Kona, HI 96740, ☎ 800/677-9461, 808/322-2788; e-mail fairwind@interpac.net; www.fair-wind.com. This sailing catamaran offers two daily snorkel and scuba diving cruises with instruction and snorkeling gear included. The luncheon cruise departs at 9AM and returns at 1:30PM. Cruise includes continental breakfast and burgers for lunch. The cruise visits Kealakekua Bay Marine Reserve for 2½ hours. The afternoon cruise departs at 1:45PM, returning at 4:45PM, snacks and beverages included. There is a charge for scuba diving tanks and gear. Cruises depart from Keauhou Bay pier.

Kamanu, 74-425 Kealakehe Parkway, #16, Kailua-Kona, HI 96740, ☎ 808/329-2021. This operator offers daily snorkeling cruises along the north Kona Coast to the Pawai Bay Marine Reserve aboard the 36-foot catamaran, *Kamanu*. Cruises are 3½ hours long and allow 1½ hours snorkeling time. Includes all snorkel gear, instruction, deli lunch and beverages. See an incredible range of marinelife, underwater seacaves, rock formations.

Captain Zodiac, PO Box 5612, Honokohau Harbor, Kealakehe Parkway, Kailua-Kona, HI 96740, ☎ 800/247-1484, 808/329-3199. Daily expeditions in motorized inflatable rubber white-water rafts along the

Kona Coast, taking in sea caves, old Hawaiian village sites, and snorkeling in Kealakekua Bay Marine Reserve on a four-hour cruise. Snorkel equipment and lunch included. There are morning and afternoon departures.

Fair Wind Raft Adventures, 78-7130 Kaleiopapa Road, Kailua-Kona, HI 96740, ☎ 800/677-9461, 808/322-2788; e-mail fairwind@interpac.net; www.fair-wind.com. This adventure cruise operator offers two daily raft adventures to snorkel and cruise the Kona Coast, Kealakekua Bay Marine Reserve and the calm waters of historic Honaunau Bay. See myriad marinelife, sea caves and lava tubes. Includes all snorkel gear, snacks-beverages, showers.

Sea Quest, PO Box 390292, Kailua-Kona, HI 96739, ☎ 808/322-3669 or 329-7238; e-mail Prime1@aloha.net. This operator offers snorkeling cruises with inflatable boats, taking in the remote areas between Keauhou Bay and Honaunau on the Kona Coast. The cruises visit sea caves, lava tubes, Captain Cook's Monument at Kealakekua Bay and the Pu`uhonua O Honaunau National Historic Park at Honaunau, with diving time allowed. Three- to four-hour adventures include snacks, beverages and snorkel gear.

Snorkel Bob's, 75-5831 Kahakai Road, Kailua-Kona, HI 96740, ☎ 808/329-0770. Snorkel equipment rentals by the day or week. Complete snorkeling equipment available, mask, fins, sterilized snorkel, underwater cameras, boogie boards.

Red Sail Sports, Hilton Waikoloa Village, ☎ 808/886-2876; Hapuna Beach Prince Hotel, ☎ 808/880-1111. This water sports beach shop has a full range of dive and snorkel equipment rentals and can also arrange cruises and dive/snorkel adventures.

Scuba Diving

Several outfitters offer scuba diving instructional programs and adventures on the Kona Coast. Typical one-tank dives begin at about $50 per person; two-tank dives begin at about $85 per person.

Aloha Dive Company, PO Box 4454, Kailua-Kona, HI 96745, ☎ 800/708-KONA, 808/325-5560. From beginning diving instruction to deep blue water dives. High adventure dives are custom arranged. Experience the thrill of tropical marinelife as you dive the outer edge of Hawai`i.

Big Island Divers, 75-5467 Kaiwi St., Kailua-Kona, HI 96740, ☎ 808/329-6068. A certified PADI dive center operating introductory dives, manta ray night dives, scuba charters, with a full line of equipment rentals.

Eco-Adventures, 75-5744 Alii Drive, Kona Inn Shopping Village, Kailua-Kona, HI 96740, ☎ 800/949-DIVE, 808/329-7116; e-mail ecodive@ilHawaii.net. A full range of snorkel, scuba dive and ecoadventure excursions, including daily blue water boat dives, night dives and special manta ray dives. Certified PADI instruction and equipment.

Nautilus Dive Center, 382 Kamehameha Avenue, Hilo, HI 96720, ☎ 808/935-6939. This PADI dive center offers scuba instruction and has scuba charter adventures to the unspoiled reefs of East Hawai`i. They also have a full line of equipment rentals.

Ecotropic Divers, PO Box 6276, Kamuela, HI 96743, ☎ 808/882-1544; e-mail eco@ecopacific.com. This PADI certified dive operator offers a variety of excursions, including standard day and night dives, snorkeling, snuba dives and whalewatching cruises. A full line of equipment rentals is also available.

East Hawai`i Divers, PO Box 2001, Pahoa, HI 96778, ☎ 808/965-7840. This outfitter offers NAUI certification instruction, plus guided shore dives island-wide to explore the Big Island's unspoiled reefs.

Kona Coast Divers, 75-5614 Palani Road, Kailua-Kona, HI 96740, ☎ 808/329-8802. A full range of dive charters and excursions, plus PADI instruction and equipment rentals.

Kohala Divers Ltd., Kawaihae Shopping Center, Kohala Coast, HI 96743, ☎ 808/882-7774; www.kohaladivers.com. This outfitter has a variety of dive charter excursions along the Kohala Coast and secluded bays and coves, plus PADI instruction and equipment rentals.

Ocean Spirit Diving Services, PO Box 5555, Kailua-Kona, HI 96745, ☎ 808/329-4710. This outfitter specializes in small group scuba dives with morning and afternoon adventures. They provide dive classes, introductory dives, snorkeling excursions.

Snuba Big Island, ☎ 808/326-7446. Snuba uses an underwater mask and breathing tube with the air source contained in a flotation raft that follows as you explore the underwater world. It allows you to explore the beautiful coral reefs without the heavy dive gear and training needed for scuba diving. Easier than snorkeling, it allows you to see and experience much more.

Kayaking, Parasailing

There are kayaking and parasailing adventures available on the Big Island. Three-hour ocean kayak rentals begin at about $20 per person; two-hour guided adventures begin at $40-50 per person. Mountain kayak cruises through old plantation irrigation ditches are $75 per person. Parasailing adventures are $42 for 400-foot elevation ride, $52 for 800-foot elevation.

Kohala Mountain Kayak, Kohala Ditch.

Kohala Mountain Kayak Cruise, PO Box 660, Kapa`au, HI 96755. ☎ 808/889-6922; www.kohala.net/kayak. This is one of the Big Island's most unusual kayaking adventures. It's a three-mile inflatable kayak cruise through the old Kohala Ditch built in 1905 to irrigate the sugar plantations of the North Kohala District. The three-hour float cruises the ditch, tunnels and flumes of the canal through open rain forest and mountain pastures, offering fantastic views. The original 22½-mile irrigation ditch was a major engineering feat of its time through the rugged gorges and valleys of North Kohala. Water from the ditch served the Kohala Sugar Plantation for 70 years until its demise in 1975. Snacks and cold/hot drinks included at the end of the cruise, plus a visit to a secluded waterfall and forest swimming hole. Cruises begin with a van ride from Kapa`au to the ditch site.

Kayak Historical Discovery Tours, 87-3187 Holomoku Road, Captain Cook, HI 96704, ☎ 808/328-8911. This outfitter provides kayak excursions along the Kona Coast and also has custom-arranged fully-outfitted two- to five-day kayak outings around the Big Island's scenic coastlines.

Ocean Safari's Kayak Tours & Rentals, Kailua-Kona, ☎ 808/326-4699.

Kona Boy Kayaks, 79-7491 Mamalahoa Highway, Kailua-Kona, HI 96740, ☎ 808/322-3600; e-mail kayaker@aloha.net. This outfitter offers a full range of kayak and snorkeling equipment rentals, half- and full day, plus overnight kayak excursions along the Kona Coast for snorkeling, exploring sea caves, reefs and marine life reserves.

Hawai`i

UFO Parasail, PO Box 5438, Kailua-Kona, HI 96745, ☎ 800/FLY-4UFO, ☎ 808/325-5UFO. Parasail adventures in Kona Bay and along the Kona Coast, with rides from 400-800 feet high for fantastic thrills and views. Hi-tech winch power boats provide dry takeoffs and landings. Parasailing is an adventure like no other.

Surfing & Windsurfing

The west side of the Big Island generally has better surfing and windsurfing than the rest of the island. The Kona and Kohala Coast beaches have the best overall wind and surf conditions favored by boarders, although there are a couple of beach areas in Hilo that produce good waves. Check with the following water sports concessions and surf shops for equipment rentals and information.

Ocean Sports, 69-275 Waikoloa Beach Drive, Outrigger Waikoloan Resort, Kohala Coast, HI 96743, ☎ 808/886-5555. This beach concession shop rents a wide selection of surfing, body surfing and windsurfing equipment.

Red Sail Sports, Hapuna Beach Prince Hotel, Kohala Coast, ☎ 808/880-1111; Hilton Waikoloa Village, Kohala Coast, ☎ 808/886-2876. These beach concession shops carry a full line of surfing and windsurfing equipment.

`A`ama Surf & Sport, 75-5741 Kuakini Highway, Kailua-Kona, HI 96740, ☎ 808/326-7890. A full assortment of surfing equipment.

Orchid Land Surfshop, 832 Kilauea Avenue, Hilo, HI 96720, ☎ 808/935-1533. Body boards, men's and women's sportswear and custom surfboards.

C & S Cycle and Surf, Mamalahoa Highway 19, Waimea, ☎ 808/885-5005. Surf and body boards, sportwear and water sports equipment.

Fishing - Deep Sea Charters

The Big Island is one of the best places for deep sea fishing. The Kona Coast is famous for its trophy-sized Pacific Blue Marlin and Yellowfin Ahi Tuna, plus dolphin (mahimahi), ono (wahoo) and other game fish. Kona is home to a number of annual deep sea fishing tournaments. The Kona International Billfish Tournament attracts teams from around the world who vie for top prizes in this "Superbowl" of fishing. A Big Island deep sea fishing expedition is sure to be memorable. For details, check with any of the following charter booking services or boats. Charter boat rates range from $175-295 for half-day, $275-450 for full-day. Share charters generally begin at about $65 per person for a half-day.

Kona Activities Center, PO Box 1035, Kailua-Kona, HI 96745, ☎ 800/367-5288, ☎ 808/329-3171.

Kona Charter Skippers Association, 75-5663 Palani Road, Kailua-Kona, HI 96740, ☎ 800/7MARLIN, 808/329-3600.

Kona Marina Sports Activities, 74-425 Kealakehe Parkway, Honokohau Harbor, PO Box 2398, Kailua-Kona, HI 96740, ☎ 808/329-1115; e-mail uki@ilHawaii.net.

The Charter Locker Activities, Kealakehe Parkway, Honokohau Harbor, Kailua-Kona, HI 96740, ☎ 808/326-2553.

The Charter Desk, Kealakehe Parkway, Honokohau Harbor, Kailua-Kona, HI 96740, ☎ 888/KONA4US, 808/329-5735.

Impulse **Charters,** 73-4343 Ama Ama St., Kailua-Kona, HI 96740, ☎ 808/325-7749. A 28-foot Topaz twin diesel boat.

Hapa Laka **Hawaiian Charters,** PO Box 2051, Kailua-Kona, HI 96745, ☎ 808/322-2229; a 21-foot custom-built boat.

Hanamana, PO Box 4239, Kailua-Kona, HI 96740, ☎ 808/322-1809 or 329-3493; a 37-foot custom aluminum boat.

Tara **Sportfishing,** PO Box 4363, Kailua-Kona, HI 96740, ☎ 808/325-5887; a 46-foot Hatteras fishing boat.

Anxious **Sportfishing,** 75-217 Nani Kailua Dr. #189, Kailua-Kona, HI 96740, ☎ 808/326-1229; a 33-foot Bertram fishing boat.

Illusions, PO Box 1816, Kamuela, HI 96743, ☎ 808/883-0180; a 39-foot Topaz Flybridge boat.

Pacific Blue, 74-5071 Kumakani, Kailua-Kona, HI 96740, ☎ 808/329-9468; a 40-foot Hatteras Sportfisher boat.

Hua Pala, 73-1089 Ahualani St., Kailua-Kona, HI 96740, ☎ 808/325-3277; 35-foot Uniflite fishing boat.

Intrepid, PO Box 5200, Kailua-Kona, HI 96745, ☎ 808/322-8012; a 38-foot Bertram fishing boat.

Layla, PO Box 5567, Kailua-Kona, HI 96745, ☎ 808/329-6899; a 31-foot Custom Innovator fishing boat.

Hawai'i

■ In the Air

Scenic Flightseeing & Helicopter Tours

 Big Island air tour and helicopter lines offer a variety of flightseeing adventure tours to Hawai`i Volcanoes National Park and volcanic eruption sites, the scenic Hamakua Coast rain forest, waterfalls and rugged coastline, beaches and secluded coves, the splendor of Waipio Valley, the Kohala Mountains, Mauna Kea's lunar landscape and astronomy observatories, and rolling upcountry ranchlands of the island. Depending on itinerary, standard airplane tours range from $69-119 per person; Circle Island tours begin at $169 per person. Bi-plane rides begin at $65 per person. Standard helicopter tours range from $99-130 per person; Circle Island tours range as high as $275 per person. Check with the following for details.

Big Island Air, ☎ 800/303-8868, 808/329-4868; e-mail bigisle@ilHawai`i.net. This charter airline offers Big Island air tours departing from Kona International Airport. There is a special *Circle Island / Volcano Tour, Sunset Volcano Tour*, and a *Super Saver Volcano Tour*. Additional air tours take in Maui.

Koa Air Service Hawai`i, Kona International Airport, ☎ 808/326-2288. A charter tour operator with air photo tours around the Big Island as well as rentals of Cessna aircraft.

Mokulele Flight Service, PO Box 342, Holualoa, HI 96725, Kona International Airport, ☎ 808/325-7070. Air photo tours by arrangement and rental of Cessna aircraft.

Classic Aviation Corporation, PO Box 1899, Kailua-Kona, HI 96745, Kona International Airport, ☎ 800/695-8100, 808/329-TOUR. Unique flying adventures in an open-cockpit 1935 WACO biplane reproduction. Enjoy incredible aerial views of the Big Island on a *Volcano Tour, Kona Coast Tour, Hamakua Coastline / Waterfall Tour with Volcano*, or special aerobatics such as loops, rolls, Cuban eights. You'll learn what flying by the seat of your pants is all about on this adventure! Tours available from either Kona or Hilo airports.

Island Hoppers, Hilo International Airport, Hilo, HI 96720, ☎ 808/969-2000; e-mail above@aloha.net. A small plane operator with deluxe air adventures. Each seat has a 360° view via large windows. Tour Mauna Kea, Kilauea Volcano, North Kohala, the scenic Hamakua Coast, Waipio Valley. Video of flight included.

Mauna Kea Helicopters, PO Box 1713, Kamuela, HI 96743, ☎ 800/400-HELI, ☎ 808/885-6400.

Kenai Helicopters Hawai`i, PO Box 4118, Kailua-Kona, HI 96745, ☎ 800/622-3144, 808/969-3131, 882-1851.

Safari Helicopters, Hilo International Airport, Hilo, HI 96720, ☎ 800/326-3356, 808/969-1259; e-mail safari@aloha.net; http://planet-Hawaii.com/~safari/.

Hawai`i Helicopters, Kona International Airport, Kailua-Kona, HI 96740, ☎ 800/367-7095, 808/329-4700.

Blue Hawaiian Helicopters, PO Box 384473, Waikoloa, HI 96732, Waikoloa Helipad and Hilo International Airport, ☎ 800/745-BLUE, 808/961-5600; www.blueHawaiian.com.

■ On Horseback

Trail Rides & Wagon Rides

Several outfitters offer horseback trail rides around the Big Island. Trail rides vary by countryside, terrain, landscape and scenery but all will provide a closeup view of the Big Island's unique environment. Rates vary by itinerary but for a basic two-hour trail ride they range from $50-75 per person.

King's Trail Rides O`Kona, 111 Mile Marker, Mamalahoa Highway, Kealakekua, HI 96750, ☎ 808/323-2388; e-mail bones@interpac.net; www.interpac.net/~hit/ktr.html. Ride, snorkel and have lunch at the Captain Cook's Monument on the shores of beautiful Kealakekua Bay in Kona; beautiful scenery and views of Kona Coast area.

Paniolo Riding Adventures, PO Box 363, Honoka`a, HI 96727, ☎ 808/889-5354. Open range riding adventures on an 11,000-acre working cattle ranch in the Kohala Mountains. Enjoy good horses and superb riding conditions through lush upcountry pasturelands with fantastic views and cool mountain breezes in a pristine outdoor Hawai`i setting. There are 2½-hour and four-hour rides.

**Waipio Na`alapa Trail Rides,** PO Box 992, Honoka`a, HI 96727, ☎ 808/775-0419. Take an adventure on horseback into old Hawai`i. Explore the magnificent Waipio Valley on the Big Island's Hamakua Coast, the historically significant Valley of Kings. This is a 2½-hour ride through lush tropical jungle trails on the valley floor, past working taro patches, giant waterfalls and many historic sites. Rides are subject to weather conditions. Call first for information.

Waipio on Horseback and Taro Farm, PO Box 183, Honoka`a, HI 96727, ☎ 808/775-7291. Take a personalized 2½-hour riding tour into the secluded Waipio Valley. Learn the history and culture of this once heavily populated valley of old Hawai`i. See working taro farms, lush jungle, meandering streams and gushing waterfalls. Rides are weather-dependent, so call for current conditions.

**Kohala Na`alapa Trail Rides,** PO Box 992, Honoka`a, HI 96727, ☎ 808/889-0022. This outfitter leads rides through 12,000 acres of working cattle and sheep ranch in the North Kohala Mountains at Kahua Ranch and Kohala Ranch. Open range riding across ranch pasturelands and the beautiful rolling hill country of North Kohala. Experience panoramic views of mountains and the distant Kohala Coast. Rides are 2½ hours long.

Waipio Valley Wagon Tours, PO Box 1340, Honoka`a, HI 96727, ☎ 808/775-9518. For those not inclined to horseback riding, this operator provides a great alternative. Enjoy a unique trip back in time on a comfortable mule-drawn wagon ride through the spectacular Waipio Valley, Hawai`i's famed Valley of the Kings. This adventure is fully narrated with the history and culture of the valley explained. See working taro farm patches, majestic waterfalls and cascading streams and the dense rain forest jungle of the valley floor. This is a 1½-hour tour.

Kohala Carriages, Old Halaula Mill Road, Kapa`au, HI 96755, ☎ 808/889-5955. This operator provides relaxing and comfortable country tours in an open-sided covered wagon drawn by a pair of giant Belgian draft horses. Take a ride back in North Kohala time. Explore the countryside where King Kamehameha was born and spent much of his younger years. Learn the history and culture of the area and enjoy lunch in a private park along the secluded coast.

■ Eco/Cultural Activities

The Kona Coast

**Pu`uhonua O Honaunau National Historical Park,** Highway 160, Honaunau Bay, Kona, ☎ 808/328-2288. This is the best preserved old Hawaiian heiau (temple) in the islands. Interpretive displays relate much of Hawai`i's ancient history and culture. The site has self-guided walking tours through a restored temple, wooden tiki images, rock heiau foundations, canoe sheds and an imposing rock wall enclosing the complex. In the old days, during war this site served as a place of refuge for the defeated and for those who broke traditional taboos. They sought the protection of the kahunas (priests) in this enclosure.

Amy B. H. Greenwell Ethnobotanical Garden, PO Box 1053, Captain Cook, HI 96704, ☎ 808/323-3318. Look for the sign just south of town. This 10-acre botanical garden is a project of Bishop Museum of Honolulu and is a living museum of traditional Hawaiian ethnobotany. There are many species of native Hawaiian food plants, medicinal plants. Docent or self-guided tours.

Ahuena Heiau is next to Kailua Pier and in front of the King Kamehameha Kona Beach Hotel in Kailua-Kona. This restored heiau (temple) and the surrounding grounds is where Kamehameha the Great ruled his realm after uniting the islands under one kingdom in 1795. It is believed that he spent many of his final days here before his death in 1819.

Kona Historical Tours, 81-6551 Mamalahoa Highway, Kealakekua, HI 96750, ☎ 808/323-2005. This is a tour company offering historical and cultural walking tours of Kailua-Kona village and a historical Kona coffee farm operation.

Bayview Kona Coffee Farm, PO Box 680, Honaunau-Kona, HI 96726, ☎ 800/662-5880, 808/328-9658; e-mail bayview@aloha.net. This farm is above Honaunau Bay just off Highway 160 near St. Benedict's Painted Church. See how coffee is farmed and milled on this family-operated coffee farm. Enjoy a cup of Kona brew as you browse through. A visitors center sells Kona coffee and coffee products.

Greenwell Farms, 81-6560 Mamalahoa Highway 11, Kealakekua, HI 96750, ☎ 808/323-2862. This mill and farm has daily visitor tours of the coffee groves and mill facilities.

Holualoa Kona Coffee Co., 77-6261 Mamalahoa Highway 11, Holualoa, HI 96725, ☎ 800/334-0348, 808/322-9937. This mill and farm welcomes visitors daily to tour the coffee farms and visit the mill.

Kona Coffee Emporium, 79-7098 Mamalahoa Highway 11, Captain Cook, HI 96704, ☎ 800/KONA4ME, 808/322-7717; e-mail kona@ilHawaii.net This coffee mill outlet has retail coffee sales and coffee espresso bar service.

Mauna Loa Royal Kona Coffee Visitors Center & Museum, 83-5427 Mamalahoa Highway, Captain Cook, HI 96704, ☎ 800/669-5633, 808/328-2511. This retail coffee shop and visitors center has a variety of Kona coffee and related products; free cup of coffee as you browse and enjoy the scenic view of Kealakekua Bay far below.

Hawai'i

The Kohala Coast

**Pu`ukohola Heiau National Historic Site,** Kawaihae, Kohala, ☎ 808/882-7218. This massive heiau (temple) was built by Kamehameha the Great in 1791 upon the advice of a priest who told him he would conquer all the islands of Hawai`i if he did so. By 1795, Kamehameha did conquer in war all the other islands except Kaua`i, which later acceded to his rule and recognized him as king. An interpretive display at the visitors center relates the entire story of the rise of Kamehameha the Great.

King Kamehameha Statue stands in front of the community center in Kapa`au, Highway 270 past Hawi town. It is decorated with long flower leis on June 11, King Kamehameha Day. The bronze cast statue was made in the 1880s in Paris and was intended for Honolulu. But the ship it was on sunk in the Falkland Islands in the South Atlantic en route to Hawai`i. A duplicate was made and later erected at Honolulu's Ali`iolani Hale, the Judiciary Building across from Iolani Palace. The original was eventually salvaged, restored and erected here in North Kohala, the birthplace of Kamehameha. A similar statue was also recently erected in Hilo's Wailoa State Park on the Hilo Bayfront.

King Kamehameha's Birthplace and Mo`okini Luakini Heiau are in far North Kohala. Just two miles west of Hawi town on Highway 270, turn off north and downslope on Upolu Airport Road. This road leads to tiny Upolu Point airstrip, a bumpy, narrow asphalt lane. At the airstrip, turn left down another bumpy dirt lane for 1½ miles. This road terminates at Kamehameha's Birthplace, now just rock foundation ruins that have been somewhat restored and marked with an interpretive sign. On a nearby knoll is the once-sacred Mo`okini Luakini Heiau. It was at this temple where the Hawaiian ali`i nui, the kings and ruling chiefs, prayed to their gods and offered human sacrifices in ceremonies. The temple, one of the largest on the Big Island, was built about 480 AD. Visitors are allowed to enter the heiau enclosure.

Lapakahi State Historical Park is on Highway 270 on the Kohala Coast 12 miles north of Kawaihae. This is the site of an old Hawaiian fishing village, now restored. There are stone wall foundations of houses, canoe sheds and other structures. Various sites are clearly marked and a trail guide brochure allows for an easy self-guided walk through the old village. The park has remnants of a family heiau, a fishing shrine, lamp stand, salt pans (depressions in rock) used to crystalize salt water, old fire pits, a water well and much more representing the old Hawaiian lifestyle.

Keck I and Keck II, telescopes on Mauna Kea.

The **Ellison Onizuka Center for International Astronomy** is at the 9,200-foot level on Mauna Kea. It's accessed via the Saddle Road #200 which links Hilo and Kona-Kohala over the plateau between Mauna Kea and Mauna Loa. Turn off Saddle Road onto the Mauna Kea Summit Road. The Onizuka Center is just over six miles up this road, which is paved but quite steep, with many sharp curves. The road from the Onizuka Center on up to the summit and the Mauna Kea Science Reserve is only partially paved and is mostly rough gravel and rutted. 4WD vehicles are required.

Weather can be dangerous anytime of year at this high elevation, with possible heavy snowfall and freezing temperatures in winter. Dress for cold weather. The 13,769-foot summit has extremely thin air and can be hazardous for those with breathing or heart conditions, as well as for pregnant women or young children. Call ahead and check on the current conditions and programs: **Onizuka Center,** ☎ 808/961-2180 or 935-7606.

Hawai`i

The Onizuka Center serves as base camp housing for the many scientists and astronomers working on research projects at the observatory telescopes on the summit. The Center has displays and programs on Mauna Kea and the various observatories. They conduct summit day tours on weekends and star gazing tours on weekend nights. Programs are free and open to the public, but are weather-dependent.

Ka`u District/Volcano

**Punalu`u Black Sand Beach Park** is five miles south of Pahala off Highway 11 at Ninole, Seamountain Resort/Golf Course. This wide black sand crescent is on the Punalu`u small boat harbor. The near off--shore waters have a large resident population of endangered Hawaiian green sea turtles that are easily seen as they forage the seaweed beds.

Swimming and snorkeling are possible, but extreme caution is necessary, as offshore currents can be strong in this bay.

Green Sand Beach Tours, Na`alehu, Hawai`i, ☎ 808/929-9664. This is a half-day guided tour from Na`alehu to the South Point's famed Green Sand Beach along the rugged coastal trail. The green sand comes from the volcanic olivine crystals eroded from the cinder cone, Pu`u O Mahana, surrounding the bay. It's one of Hawai`i's most unusual beaches.

Hawai`i Volcanoes National Park Visitors Center,** Volcano, Hawai`i, ☎ 808/985-6000. No visit to the volcano would be complete without a stop at the park headquarters museum and visitors center to see the natural history displays and to view the eruption film. Also take in **Thomas A. Jaggar Museum, next to the **Hawaiian Volcano Observatory** a couple of miles along the Crater Rim Drive. Here you can see videos of volcanic eruptions, geologic displays and working seismic equipment that monitors the volcanic activity for the adjacent observatory. There are fantastic overlook views into Kilauea Caldera and the distant Halema`uam`u Crater.

Volcano Winery is just south past the entrance to Hawai`i Volcanoes National Park. Turn right onto Volcano Golf Course Road and go about a half-mile past the golf course . ☎ 808/967-7772. This is not necessarily an eco/cultural activity, but for wine lovers it may prove interesting. This is the Big Island's only operating vineyard and winery. It offers blends of tropical fruit flavors and experimental grapes from its vineyards. Try samples of Lilikoi (passionfruit), Guava Chablis, Volcano Blush, Lehua Blossom Honey Wine and Symphony, its main product from the Symphony grape, a California hybrid.

Akatsuka Orchid Gardens, off Highway 11 just past the 22 mile marker, Volcano, HI 96785, ☎ 808/967-8234. This flower grower has a colorful display of orchid varieties, as well as cut flower sprays and potted plants in their retail shop; shipping available.

The Hamakua Coast/Hilo

Banyan trees line Hilo's hotel row and give it the name Banyan Drive. Most of these handsome spreading trees were planted 50 or more years ago by such VIPs as President Franklin D. Roosevelt, Amelia Earhart, Babe Ruth, Fannie Hurst and other notables of the era. There's even one planted by a then-aspiring politician named Richard Nixon. Each tree is marked accordingly.

Old Mamalahoa Highway Scenic Drive is just five miles north of Hilo at the intersection with Kalanianaole School. Old Highway 19 follows the rugged rain-forested Hamakua Coast for four miles, before linking back with the newer Highway 19. The scenic route takes in numerous gulches and coves as it winds through lovely lush coastal country with scenic views. Shower trees, royal poinciana, breadfruit, coconut, African tulip, and royal palms line the route much of the way. The old route passes through aged sugar plantation villages with melodious names such as Papaikou, Onomea, Pepeekeo, and Kawai Nui. It's definitely a scenic drive worth taking.

Liliuokalani Park is on Banyan Drive in the Waiakea Peninsula adjacent to the hotels and on the shore of Hilo Bay. This authentic Japanese garden park was named in honor of Hawai`i's last reigning monarch, Queen Liliuokalani. It was built in the early 1900s as a memorial to the immigrant Japanese who developed the old Waiakea Sugar Plantation. The park features several magnificent Japanese stone lanterns, pavilions, an arching footbridge, a tea house, and reflecting lagoons. It is one of Hawai`i's loveliest cultural parks and is a must-see in Hilo.

Suisan Fish Market Auction is on Hilo Bay at the mouth of the Wailoa River on Lihiwai Street on the other side of Liliuokalani Park from the Banyan Drive hotels. The auction is a colorful cultural experience and a must for Hilo visitors. Laid out for inspection is the tuna fishing fleet's catch of 50-100 lb. yellow fin tuna (ahi), mahimahi, and numerous colorful tropical fish, squid, and other seafood delicacies. The auction is conducted in a spirited multi-lingual pidgin English that gives an exotic

Hawai`i

Farmer's Market, Hilo.

atmosphere to the scene. The auction begins at 7 AM, Monday through Saturday. Closed Sunday. Free. Don't leave Hilo without experiencing this!

Hilo Farmers' Market has fruit and vegetable produce, tropical flowers and a flea-market under the tents on Wednesday, Saturday and Sunday mornings until noon. It takes place at the corner of Mamo Street and Kamehameha Avenue in downtown Hilo, across from Mo`oheau Park. It's a colorful, exciting event with bargains galore!

East Hawai`i Cultural Center, 141 Kalakaua Street, Hilo, ☎ 808/961-5711, opposite Kalakaua Park and the Post Office. The center is housed in the Old Police Station, a historic building constructed in 1932 and placed on the National Register of Historic Buildings and Places. It resembles a Hawaiian "hale" (house) of the 1800s with its hipped roof. The Center is dedicated to culture and the arts in East Hawai`i. Ongoing art gallery shows and exhibits are free and open to the public.

Panaewa Rain Forest Zoo, a couple of miles south of Hilo just off the Volcano Highway 11 on Mamaki Street, ☎ 808/959-7224, is open daily. This is one of Hilo's least known and most delightful free attractions. It is one of the few natural tropical rain forest zoos in the United States. The small facility is operated by the County of Hawai`i and features several rain forest species in natural environment enclosures. Among the animals on display are an African pygmy hippopotamus, water buffalo, rain forest monkeys, a tapir, jungle parrots, Hawaiian wild pigs, endangered Hawaiian birds like the Nene Goose, Hawaiian `Io (hawk), Pueo (owl) and Hawaiian Stilt. The zoo is a pleasant walk through natural rain forest with numerous flowering trees and shrubs. Colorful peacocks strut openly.

Mauna Loa Macadamia Nut Factory is three miles south of Hilo on the east side of Volcano Highway 11 and back through the orchards a couple of miles. ☎ 808/966-8618, open daily. Look for road signs marking the entrance. A visitors center provides free samples of Hawai`i's popular gourmet nuts and a wide variety of macadamia nut products are available for purchase. There is a free narrated factory tour.

Wailoa State Park-Wailoa Center is on the Wailoa River and behind Kamehameha Avenue and the Hilo Bayfront. Wailoa Park comprises the lands surrounding the Wailoa River and Waiakea Fish Pond. There are lots of picnic tables and several covered pavilions. Fishermen in rowboats are often seen floating around the pond angling for the abundant mullet fish. There are also a Vietnam Veterans War Memorial and a Tsunami (Tidal Wave) Memorial in the park. The park's most recent addition is a handsome statue of King Kamehameha the Great on the Hilo Bayfront side of the park off Kamehameha Avenue. The Wailoa Center in the park features free art exhibits, seasonal showings, and cultural displays by local artisans. Check the schedule at the Center for current show. Wailoa Park is a good place for a pleasant picnic lunch.

Waipio Valley Shuttle & Tours, PO Box 5128, Kukuihaele, HI 96727, ☎ 808/775-7121. This operator runs a shuttle service taking visitors from the top of Waipio down to the valley floor and to the beach at the mouth of the valley, returning at end of day or by arrangement. It's a practical way to get to/from the valley without the steep diffcult climb on the narrow roadway and perfect for day visitors wanting to see the valley on their own. They also provide narrated tours of the entire valley, relating the history and culture of Waipio and its taro farming.

Gardens

Hawai`i Tropical Botanical Garden, just north of Hilo on the four-mile scenic drive (old Highway 19), RR 143-A, Papaikou, HI 96781, ☎ 808/964-5233, is open daily. Nature trails meander through tropical rain forest, cross streams and waterfalls, and follow the rugged coast. Extensive collections of palms, bromeliads, gingers, exotic ornamentals and rare plants. Admission fee. A garden of joy for nature photographers.

Nani Mau Gardens, 421 Makalika Street, Hilo, just south of town, turn east off Volcano Highway, ☎ 808/959-3541, open daily. You can't miss the turn off the highway – just look for beautiful floral beds and displays on both sides of Makalika Street. From the highway, it's a half-mile to the gardens. There are some 20 acres of tropical foliage, flowers, trees and plants along with a waterfall, pond and Japanese Garden. Visitors can stroll on their own or opt for a tram tour through the grounds. The orchid greenhouse is spectacular, with many varieties of orchids in bloom. There is a large gift shop also; admission fee.

Big Island Tropical Gardens, 1477 Kalanianaole, Hilo, ☎ 808/961-6621, open daily. Stroll through gardens of exotic tropical flowers, including orchids, anthuriums, gingers. Free.

World Botanical Gardens is on Highway 19 north of Hilo and 2½ miles north of Honomu, just past the 16-mile marker, ☎ 808/963-5433; watch for sign. This is a newly developing botanical garden on 300 acres of former sugarcane fields. Improvements are in process, but the gardens are open on an admission fee basis. Many species of tropical ornamental plants, trees, fruit trees, and flowering plants are being established. The garden trails and nature walks include a lookout point at the spectacular triple cascades of Umauma Waterfalls.

Lodging

 The Big Island has a wide range of hotel, condominium and bed & breakfast accommodations to suit every budget. The rates below are for a standard double-occupancy room.

Accommodations Price Scale	
$	less than $100 per night
$$	$100-199 per night
$$$	$200-299 per night
$$$$	$300 and up per night

There is a real variety of hotels in Waikiki, ranging from budget-tourist class to world-class luxury. There are the big name international chains like Hilton, Hyatt and Sheraton, as well as properties from the local Outrigger, Aston, Castle and Marc groups, who operate hotels on all the Hawaiian Islands and offer lodgings to fit all budgets. Check the individual hotels below or for more details contact them directly: **Outrigger Hotels & Resorts,** ☎ 800-OUTRIGGER; **Aston Hotels & Resorts,** ☎ 800-922-7866; **Castle Resorts & Hotels,** ☎ 800-367-5004; **Marc Resorts Hawai`i,** ☎ 800-535-0085. A few independents are thrown in for good measure.

Bed & Breakfasts

The Big Island has a wide variety of B&Bs. Some are listed in the following lodging sections. You can also contact any of the following booking services for information on others.

■ **A`anene B&B Reservations,** PO Box 597, Volcano, HI 96785, ☎ 808/985-8673.

- **Go Native Hawai`i B&B,** PO Box 11418, Hilo, HI 96721, ☎ 800/662-8483, 808/935-4178.

- **Hawai`i's Best B&B,** PO Box 563, Kamuela, HI 96743, ☎ 800/262-9912, 808/885-4550; e-mail bestbnbs@interpac.net.

- **My Island B&B**, PO Box 100, Volcano, HI 96785, ☎ 808/967-7216 or 967-7110, fax 808/967-7719.

- **Volcano Reservations,** PO Box 998, Volcano, HI 96785, ☎ 800/736-7140, 808/967-7244.

The Kona Coast

Kanaloa at Kona, 78-261 Manukai Street, Kailua-Kona, ☎ 800/OUTRIGGER, 808/322-9625; e-mail reservations@outrigger.com; www.outrigger.com. This is a deluxe oceanfront condo complex on Keauhou Bay. 1/2BR suites are luxuriously appointed with all amenities. Complex has three pools, spas, tennis courts with golf, shopping and activities nearby. $$

King Kamehameha Kona Beach Hotel, 75-5660 Palani Road, Kailua-Kona, ☎ 800/367-6060, 808/329-2911. This Kailua-Kona landmark hotel fronts sandy, calm Kamakahonu Beach on Kailua Bay next to the pier at the head of the town's main street, Alii Drive. Rooms have a/c and TV. There are two restaurants, a cocktail lounge, tennis courts and lobby shopping mall. This is a standard tourist class hotel with a convenient location for all of Kona's attractions and activities. $$

Kona Village Resort, PO Box 1299, Kaupulehu-Kona, ☎ 800/367-5290, 808/325-5555; e-mail kvr@ilHawai`i.net. This is the Big Island's most unusual resort and is on the beach at Kahuwai Bay, Kaupulehu, 15 miles north of Kailua-Kona. The resort is comprised of 125 separate thatch-roofed "hale" bungalows. The hale reflect the traditional design of South Pacific Islands like Tahiti, Fiji, Samoa and the Marquesas. All have full modern conveniences except telephones and TV. The resort is set along the beach, with lush landscaping of trees and flowering plants. Birds abound everywhere. The most disturbing things about this resort will be the sound of birds singing in the morning and the rumble of surf at your front door. It is a magical place and well worth the premium rates charged. Rates include a Full American Plan with all meals. $$$$

Kona by the Sea, Kona by the Sea, 75-6106 Alii Drive, Kailua-Kona, ☎ 808/327-2300, 800/922-7866; www.aston-hotels.com. This is a well maintained, quiet, four-story condominium complex, great for families or groups. The spacious rooms are nicely appointed and have a/c, TV and fully-equipped kitchens. No sandy beach here, but there is a swimming pool, jacuzzi, adjoining grass yard for small children, sandy area with barbecue grills and lounge chairs. The ocean beach attracts local surfers and is a good place to watch the action. There is also a public salt water pool beyond the rock wall at the end of the property. $$

Royal Kona Resort, 75-5852 Alii Dr., Kailua-Kona, ☎ 808/329-3111, 800/774-KONA; e-mail rkr5433@isis.interpac.net; www.interpac.net/rkona. This is also a well-known Kona landmark and one of Kona's original modern tourist hotels. It sits on a rocky precipice jutting into Kailua Bay and affords a commanding view of the town and bay area. Rooms are neat, clean and include a/c, TV, refrigerator and coffee-tea maker. The hotel has a restaurant, cocktail lounge, swimming pool, tennis courts and shops. Good location, walking distance to town, shopping, dining. $$

Kona Reef, 75-5888 Alii Drive, Kailua-Kona, Castle Resorts ☎ 800/367-5004, 808/329-2959; www.castle-group.com. This condo complex has an oceanfront location on the sunny Kona Coast, with adjacent pocket sandy beach area. 1/2/3BR units are spacious and have full kitchens; pool, sun deck, spa, BBQ facilities available. Golf and tennis are nearby, with restaurants and shopping in walking distance. $$

Keauhou Beach Hotel, 78-6740 Alii Drive, Keauhou-Kona, ☎ 800/367-6025, 808/322-3441. This is a well-maintained 310-room hotel on the oceanfront. There's no sandy beach here but lots of tidal pools to explore marinelife; next door to Kahalu`u Beach Park. Rooms are spacious and clean, with a/c, TV, refrigerator. Good location a couple of miles down the coast from town. $$

White Sands Village, 74-6469 Alii Drive, Kailua-Kona, ☎ 800/367-5168 or 800/854-8843. This 108-unit condo complex has a few 1/2BR units in rental programs. Units have nice furnishings and a/c; tennis courts, pool, barbecue facilities on site. Complex is just across the road from White Sands Beach Park. $

Kona Hotel, PO Box 342, Holualoa Road, Holualoa, HI 96725, ☎ 808/324-1155. This country village hotel is family-operated and in Kona's famous coffee farm country on the slopes of Mt. Hualalai, seven miles from town. Nothing fancy here, but the Aloha spirit is warm and inviting. Simple budget rooms share bath facilities and a small lobby TV room. $

Hale Hoa, reservations through Hawai`i's Best B&Bs, ☎ 800/262-9912, 808/885-4550. This is a Polynesian-style pole house overlooking Kealakekua Bay. It has a nicely appointed interior, tropical-inspired furnishings, separate bedroom and full kitchen. There is also a wrap-around veranda complete with jacuzzi. Sleeps up to four people. $$

Hale Malia, reservations through Hawai`i's Best B&Bs, ☎ 800/262-9912, 808/885-4550. This modern well-furnished home has two oceanfront rooms which open to a wide veranda overlooking the sea. There is also a room with a small side view. Each room sleeps two. On an oceanfront location just two miles south of Kailua-Kona town. $$

Hale Maluhia, 76-770 Hualalai Road, Kailua-Kona, HI 96740, ☎ 800/559-6627, 808/329-5773; e-mail hawai-inns@aloha.net; www.Hawai`i-bnb.com/halemal.html. Located just three miles upslope from Kailua-Kona village, this is a large rambling home on one acre with outdoor spa, lanai, rec room, VCR, library. $

Hale Pueo, reservations through Hawai`i's Best B&Bs, ☎ 800/262-9912, 808/885-4550. This contemporary home is upslope at the 1,800-foot level on Mount Hualalai, 15 minutes from Kailua-Kona town. It features a downstairs guest studio with bright decor and ambiance. A pleasant lanai offers great views of the Kona Coast and sunsets. Sleeps four. $

Holualoa Inn B&B, PO Box 222, Holualoa, Kona, HI 96725, ☎ 808/324-1121, reservations through Hawai`i's Best B&Bs, ☎ 800/262-9912; e-mail holualoa@Hawai`i.net; www.konaweb.com. This attractive cedar home is on a 40-acre estate in the small, quiet village of Holualoa on the cool slopes of Mt. Hualalai in Kona. The estate is a former cattle ranch and coffee farm. There is a rooftop gazebo providing magnificent views of the surrounding countryside, the Kona Coast, and incredible sunsets. This is a very quiet, relaxing atmosphere. The four spacious and well-appointed guest rooms all have private bath. $$

Merryman's B&B, PO Box 474, 81-1031 Kepuka, Kealakekua, HI 96750, ☎ 800/545-4390, 808/323-2276; also through Hawai`i's Best B&Bs, ☎ 800/262-9912; e-mail merryman@ilHawai`i.net. This is a comfortable cedar home in rural Kealakekua, Kona. The four spacious guest rooms have ocean or garden views. Two rooms share a bath, one suite has private bath and a downstairs room has private bath, entrance and deck. Large open living room and front-back lanais; tropical gardens surround home. $

The Kohala Coast, North Kohala, Waimea

Jenny's Country Cottage, reservations through Hawai`i's Best B&Bs, ☎ 800/262-9912, 808/885-4550. This 100-year-old cottage features traditional koa furniture, a four-poster bed and quiet ambiance on four lush country acres about two miles from Kamuela town. Meandering lanes are great for walking in the cool, crisp air. $

Kamuela Inn, PO Box 1994, Kamuela, HI 96743, ☎ 808/885-4243. This country inn has 31 standard and kitchenette rooms, all with TV. A newer Mauna Kea Wing features several spacious, well-furnished rooms. The original wing's rooms are smaller and simpler, but very clean. Located in Waimea town near shopping, restaurants, area attractions, minutes from Kohala Coast resorts and beaches. $

Mountain Meadow Ranch B&B, PO Box 1361, Kamuela, HI 96743, ☎ 800/535-9376, 808/775-9376; e-mail wgeorge737@aol.com. Halfway between Kona and Hilo in upcountry Ahualoa above Honoka`a, the scenic pastures and majestic trees provide lots of country charm and atmosphere on this seven-acre estate. Easy access to Waipio Valley, Parker Ranch, Manua Kea, Honoka`a and Waimea towns. Two bedrooms sleep up to three people each; TV, sauna, solar-powered spa. $

**Pu`u Manu Cottage,** reservations through Hawai`i's Best B&Bs, ☎ 800/262-9912, 808/885-4550. This is a secluded country cottage in open pastureland three miles from town. A converted horse barn, it has a cozy fireplace and French doors that open to large deck and views of Mauna Kea. Sleeps four. $$

Elima Lani at Waikoloa Village, 68-3883 Lua Kula Street, Waikoloa, HI 96738; Castle Resorts ☎ 800/367-5004, 808/883-8288; www.castle-group.com. This condo complex is in the breezy cool upcountry of Waikoloa, five miles above the Kohala Coast resort area. There are beautiful surrounding views of Big Island mountains and coastline. Swimming pools, spa, sun deck, BBQ picnic facilities available, village golf course nearby. Comfortable well-furnished studio/1/2BR units have kitchens and all amenities. $

Makai Hale, reservations through Hawai`i's Best B&Bs, ☎ 800/262-9912, 808/885-4550. This is a lovely private home four miles from the island's best white sand beaches. The area has consistently fine weather and great ocean views. The guest B&B wing opens directly to the swimming pool and there are whale watching opportunities from December to May. $

Waimea Gardens Cottage, reservations through Hawai`i's Best B&Bs, ☎ 800/262-9912, 808/885-4550; e-mail bestbnb@aloha.net. This streamside cottage has two private units on 1½ acres. The cottage's Kohala and Waimea Wings have antique furnishings, patio French doors and decor, which lend a pleasant country atmosphere. Units sleep three each. $$

Kohala Village Inn , 55-514 Hawi Road, intersection of Highways 270 & 250, Hawi, North Kohala, HI 96719; reservations ☎ 808/ 889-0105 or 889-0419. This country-style inn is the only lodging available in the remote North Kohala district and offers basic, no-frills lodging. The 10 budget rooms are clean and simple; some can sleep up to six. The Kohala Village Restaurant next door has a meal discount for inn guests. Easy access to nearby Pololu Valley, Mo`okini Heiau, King Kamehameha Birthplace and statue, seasonal whale watching, and the quiet country charm of a small town rural area. $

Mauna Kea Beach Hotel, 62-100 Mauna Kea Beach Drive, Kamuela, HI 96743-9706, ☎ 800/882-6060, 808/882-7222. This 310-room hotel on Kauna`oa Bay is Hawai`i's foremost luxury hotel. Guests have access to all resort activities, including golf, tennis, pool, and beach sports. The MKB has a tradition of award-winning fine dining at its restaurants. This is a luxury-class full-service resort. $$$$

Mauna Lani Bay Hotel and Bungalows, 68-1400 Mauna Lani Drive, Kohala Coast, HI 96743-9796, ☎ 800/367-2323, 808/885-6622; e-mail maunalani@maunalani.com. This elegant 350-room oceanfront hotel sits amid a stark black lavaflow on beautiful Makaiwa Bay Beach. Most rooms have ocean views, some mountain views. Spacious rooms are luxuriously appointed with all amenities. House restaurants provide superb dining. Five private bungalows, each with its own swimming pool, spa and personal butler, provide the ultimate in service, for a price of course. All resort activities available. This is a luxury-class resort. $$$$

Mauna Lani Point Condominiums, 68-1310 Mauna Lani Drive, Mauna Lani Resort, Kohala Coast, HI 96743; Classic Resorts, ☎ 800/642-6284, 808/885-5022. This 116-unit complex sits next to the ocean on the fairways of Mauna Lani's renowned Francis I`i Brown South Golf Course. Units have either garden fairway or ocean fairway views. The units are well furnished and include large private Lana`is, living and dining areas, full kitchens and all amenities. $$$

Mauna Lani Terrace Condominium, Mauna Lani Resort, Kohala Coast, HI 96743; to South Kohala Management at ☎ 800/822-4252, 808/883-8500. These luxury units are adjacent to the Mauna Lani Bay Hotel. They are well maintained, with the tasteful decor and furnishings expected. Units have a/c and ceiling fan in living room, private Lana`is, wet bars, and complete laundry facilities. Easy access to the resort's world-class golf and tennis, health club and water sports. $$$

Hawai`i

Outrigger Waikoloan Resort, 69-275 Waikoloa Beach Drive, Kamuela, HI 96743-9763, ☎ 800/OUTRIGGER, 808/886-6789. This 547-room hotel is behind the beautiful Anaeho`omalu Bay Beach and lagoon amid a stark black lava flow. The rooms are small but pleasant and well furnished. The lobby is open and airy, with a lanai overlooking the pool and gardens. The hotel has restaurants, cocktail lounges, tennis courts, access to Waikoloa Resort golf courses and shops. With Anaeho`omalu Beach and its lovely fishponds fronting the hotel, this is one of the most beautiful settings along the Kohala Coast. $$

The Shores at Waikoloa, HC02 Box 5460, Waikoloa, HI 96743; South Kohala Management at ☎ 800/822-4252 or 808/883-8500, 808/885-5001. These spacious, well-furnished and comfortable 1/2/3BR units have a/c, with full kitchens, TV, laundry and other amenities. Perfect for families. Easy access to Waikoloa Beach Resort activities. $$$

The Vista Waikoloa, Waikoloa Beach Drive, Waikoloa Beach Resort, Waikoloa, HI 96743; South Kohala Management at ☎ 800/822-4252, 808/883-8500. This multi-building complex is right on Waikoloa Beach Drive between the Outrigger Waikoloan and Hilton Waikoloa Village and next to the golf course fairways. The spacious units have full kitchens and all amenities; easy access to all resort recreational facilities. $$$

Waimea Country Lodge, 65-1210 Lindsey Road, Kamuela, HI 96743; Castle Resorts, ☎ 800/367-5004, 808/885-4100. This small 21-unit country motel features spacious rooms with clean, pleasant furnishings, TV, and nice meadow and mountain views of Kamuela ranch country. Right in the heart of Kamuela town, adjacent to Paniolo Country Inn Restaurant and near shopping, other restaurants, area attractions. Just minutes to the Kohala Coast resorts and beaches. $

Hilo & the Hamakua Coast

Arnott's Lodge, 98 Apapane Road, Hilo, HI 96720, ☎ 800/368-8752, 808/969-7097. This backpackers' lodge is near Hilo's Keaukaha area beach parks and offers basic accommodations. Private and bunk rooms share bathrooms, a common kitchen and TV room. Some units have private kitchen and bath. Free airport shuttle service. Excursions and hiking tours arranged. $

Akaka Falls Inn B&B, PO Box 190, Honomu, HI 96728-0190, ☎ 808/963-5468. This pleasant, attractive B&B is in an old storefront building right on main street in Honomu on the way to Akaka Falls

State Park. The operation combines a gift and art gallery with an ice cream counter-deli-snack bar. $

Hale Lamalani, 27-703 Kaieie Homestead Road, Papaikou, HI 96781, ☎ 800/238-8BED, 808/964-5401; e-mail hihoney@ilHawaii.net; www.alohamall.com/hamakua/lamalani.htm. The "House of Heavenly Light" is 7½ miles north of Hilo and two miles upslope at the 1,000-foot elevation on Mauna Kea. Great views of mountain, ocean, volcano and bay views from a refurbished 1940s-era plantation-style home. Three comfortable guest rooms have views, shared bath, sundeck and lanai. $

Luana Ola B&B Cottages, PO Box 430, Honokaa, HI 96727, ☎ 800/357-7727, 808/775-7727; e-mail luana@aloha.net; www.stayHawaii.com/luana.html. These charming private cottages overlook sweeping ocean views on the high coastline of Honokaa town. Each has kitchenette, full bath, large porch, laundry facilities, phones and is wheelchair accessible. Guests can walk into historic old Honokaa town to shops, dining or to explore. $

Our Place-Papaikou's B&B, PO Box 469, 3 Mamalahoa Highway, Papaikou, HI 96781, ☎ 800/245-5250, 808/964-5250. Located four miles north of Hilo on Highway 19. This large cedar home has four guest rooms. Common open Lana`i to each bedroom overlooks a stream and tropical vegetation. Home has a library, fireplace, grand piano, cable TV/VCR; no smoking indoors. Easy access to area activities and attractions. $

Hale Kai, 111 Honolii Pali, Hilo, HI 96720, ☎ 808/935-6330. The home is on a bluff facing the ocean and Hilo Bay just two miles from downtown Hilo. There are three rooms with private baths and a separate apartment unit. Rooms face the ocean, except the loft room which has a side ocean view; pool, jacuzzi and patio. $$

Maureen's B&B, 1896 Kalanianaole, Hilo, HI 96720, ☎ 808/935-9018. This old family mansion (circa 1932) is in the Keaukaha area of Hilo, opposite James Kealoha Beach Park and four miles from town. The home is redwood and cedar, with a huge open-beam cathedral ceiling in the living room. Arched doorways and windows and dual staircases give this home a touch of New England; many antique furniture pieces, bookcases and artwork throughout. Five guest rooms available. Beach is right across the street. $

The Shipman House B&B, 131 Kai`ulani Street, Hilo, HI 96720, ☎ 800/MAP-THIS or 800/627-8447, 808/934-8002; e-mail bighouse@bigisland.com. This elegant Victorian-style home dates from

1900 and has been home to the Shipman family since 1901. It is on both the State and National Historic Registers. The main home features a wide wrap-around Lana`i and three-story rounded tower with conical roof. There are 5½ acres landscaped with tropical fruit trees and flowering plants. One guestroom in the main house; two guestrooms in the separate 1910 guesthouse. All rooms have ceiling fans, walk-in closets, private bath, TV and fridge. $$

Waipio Valley Hotel, 25 Malama Place, Hilo, HI 96720, ☎ 808/775-0368 in Waipio. This is one of the Big Island's most unusual hotels. Located in Waipio Valley, it is a very rustic inn providing only the bare essentials: a bed, toilet, and a cold shower. Guests bring their own food and share cooking facilities. The hotel is run by taro farmer, Tetsuo Araki, who lives in Hilo and drives back and forth. Contact him at the hotel or in Hilo at ☎ 808/935-7466. Four-wheel-drive transport is needed to get down the hazardous valley road or you can hike (two miles from top of the valley to the hotel) or get a ride with Waipio Valley Shuttle tours. A great place to hike and explore a tropical rain forest valley. Don't forget the mosquito lotion! Five guest rooms with twin beds are available. Advance reservations needed. $

Dolphin Bay Hotel, 333 Iliahi Street, Hilo, ☎ 808/935-1466. This small 18-unit hotel is in a quiet old residential area of Hilo four blocks from the downtown area and three blocks from Hilo Bay. Few amenities other than fans and TV; no room telephones. Kitchen facilities are included in all units. $

Hawai`i Naniloa Hotel , 93 Banyan Drive, Hilo, ☎ 800-367-5360, 808/969-3333. This 325-unit tower is a Hilo landmark, overlooking Hilo Bay. Spacious rooms have a/c and TV. Health spa, fitness center and resort pool are on grounds, golf course across the street. No beach, as the shoreline is rugged lavarock. Within walking distance of Coconut Island, Liliuokalani Park, Suisan Fish Auction. One of Hilo's nicest hotels. $$

Hilo Bay Hotel, 87 Banyan Drive, Hilo, ☎ 800/367-5102, 808/935-0861. This 145-unit budget hotel is right on Hilo Bay next to the Naniloa Hotel. Rooms have a/c and TV. Restaurant, lounge, gift shops are on grounds. No beach, as the shoreline is rugged lavarock; golf across the street and walking distance to Coconut Island, Liliuokalani Park, and Suisan Fish Auction. $

Hilo Hawaiian Hotel, 71 Banyan Drive, Hilo, Castle Resorts ☎ 800/367-5004, 808/935-9361; www.castle-group.com. This beautiful 286-room hotel fronts directly on Hilo Bay just behind Coconut Island. No sand beach, as the shoreline is rugged lavarock. The spacious rooms have a/c and TV. Queen's Court Restaurant has nightly themed buffets; cocktail lounge, meeting room, and shops are on grounds. Golf course across the street and walking distance to Coconut Island, Liliuokalani Park and Suisan Fish Auction. $$

Puna & Hawai`i Volcanoes National Park

Carson's Volcano Cottage B&B, PO Box 503, Volcano, HI 96785, ☎ 800/845-LAVA, 808/967-7683. There is one studio cottage and a three-room cottage; private bath, entrances and decks; kitchenettes. Room decor reflects Polynesian, Oriental, Country and Southwest themes. A hot tub on the main house deck is available for all guests; soak up the cool Volcano evenings. Close to national park activities, golf course, restaurants. $

Chalet Kilauea at Volcano B&B, PO Box 998, Volcano, HI 96785, ☎ 800/937-7786, 808/967-7786; e-mail bcHawaii@aol.com. Rooms have Pacific, African and European themes and there is a Treehouse suite and three separate nearby cottages – Ohia Holiday Cottage, Hapu`u Forest Cabin and Hoku Hawaiian House – which sleep up to six people. Relax in the hot tub, enjoy the fireplace, browse the library and wake up to a gourmet breakfast in the art deco dining room. Close to Hawai`i Volcanoes National Park, village, and restaurants. $

Country Goose, PO Box 597, Volcano, HI 96785, ☎ 800/238-7101, 808/967-7759; e-mail cgoose@interpac.net; www.Hawaii-bnb.com/congses.html. This home has 1BR with private bath and entry, king size bed and double futon quilt. Electric baseboard heat and electric blankets take the chill off the crisp Volcano air. Very peaceful and quiet setting. $

Hale Iki, reservations through Hawai`i's Best B&Bs, ☎ 800/262-9912, 808/885-4550. This cozy cabin is nestled in a fern forest in Volcano Village. It has a warm interior complete with wood-burning stove and full kitchen. There is also an oversized tub and a view through tall bay windows to the rain forest. Upstairs loft sleeps two. $$

Hale Ohia Cottages, PO Box 758, Volcano, HI 96785, ☎ 800/455-3803, 808/967-7986; or Hawai`i's Best B&Bs, ☎ 800/262-9912, 808/885-4550. This cottage offers 3 BRs and sleeps up to five people; kitchen, large living room and one tub-shower bath. A large covered deck has table, chairs and barbecue for cookouts. Near national park entrance, hiking trails, golf course. $

Hawai`i

Lokahi Lodge, PO Box 7, Volcano, HI 96785, ☎ 800/457-6924, 808/985-8647; or Hawai`i's Best B&Bs, ☎ 800/262-9912, 808/885-4550. This luxury four-room inn combines modern convenience with Volcano country charm. Located a mile from the national park, this plantation-style home has heated rooms, each with private bath. Wide veranda overlooks a lush native ohia forest. Each room sleeps four. $

Mountain View B&B, P.O Box 963, Kurtistown, HI 96760, ☎ 808/968-6868. This modern home is about 15 miles south of Hilo in the rolling farm and forestlands of the Mountain View village area. The home is on a large lot surrounded by forest and lush greenery. Noted Big Island artists, Linus and Jane Chao, have an art studio on the lower level, where they conduct art classes. Inquire about special art class/room packages. Special themed-decor rooms share bath. Easy access to shopping, dining and attractions of the Hilo area and Hawai`i Volcanoes National Park. $

My Island B&B, PO Box 100, Volcano, HI 96785, ☎ 808/967-7216/967-7110; e-mail myisland@ilHawaii.net; http://ilHawai`i.net/bnb/myisland. This historic century-old missionary-style home sits amidst a rambling botanical garden and fern forest jungle. Grounds are landscaped with collection of exotic plants from around the world. Comfortable rooms have various bed arrangements: singles, doubles, triples, and families. $

Kilauea Lodge, PO Box 116, Volcano Village, HI 96785, ☎ 808/967-7366; e-mail k-lodge@aloha.net. This is a rustic old YWCA camping lodge and dormitory built in 1938, which was renovated and reopened as a lodge and restaurant. Set amidst the quiet cool country air of Volcano Village near Hawai`i Volcanoes National Park headquarters and visitors center. There are 12 guest units, with private bathrooms and fireplaces and one private cottage. $$

Volcano House , PO Box 53, Hawai`i Volcanoes National Park, Hawai`i 96718, ☎ 808/967-7321. This 42-room hotel has a rustic country lodge atmosphere and generally spacious well-kept rooms. The quiet, cool volcano climate is invigorating and a pleasant change from Hawai`i's standard beach hotels. There is a cocktail lounge and the Ka Ohelo Dining Room overlooks Kilauea Caldera, providing great views as you have breakfast, lunch or dinner. The national park visitors center is directly opposite. $

Ka`u District & South Point

Bouganvillea B&B, PO Box 6045, Ocean View, HI 96704, ☎ 800/688-1763, 808/929-7089; e-mail peaceful@interpac.net; www.Hawaii-bnb.com/bougvl.html. This B&B features a pool, hiking, biking, views of the ocean and South Point, all in the quiet country of rural Ka`u. The operators are eager to share Hawai`i and the relaxing friendly atmosphere. Two guest rooms have private bath and entry. $

Hobbit House, Hawai`i's Best B&Bs, ☎ 800/262-9912, 808/885-4550. This home is near the remote southernmost town in the USA, Na`alehu, in the Ka`u District. It sits on a hilltop with sweeping vistas all the way to the coast. The guest suite has all the comforts and amenities, including a full kitchen. This is a tranquil country location. $$

South Point B&B, PO Box 6589, 92-1408 Donala Drive, Ocean View, HI 96737, ☎ 808/939-7466. This home offers guests quiet rooms, all with private entrance and bath. Guests can enjoy breakfast on the wraparound Lana`i while admiring the flowers and view of South Point and the ocean. Nearby attractions include Ka Lae (South Point), hiking to remote Green Sands Beach, golf at Discovery Harbor or Seamountain courses, and Volcanoes National Park, an easy 45-minute drive away. $

Shirakawa Motel, PO Box 467, Na`alehu, HI 96772, ☎ 808/929-7462. Promoted as "The Southernmost Motel in the USA.," this 13-unit country motel offers simple accommodations for relaxation, peace and quiet. It's nestled amidst the cool climate of a coffee tree grove and is surrounded by lush vegetation. The Shirakawa family combines the warmth of true old-fashioned Hawaiian hospitality with simple modern conveniences. No TV. This is a no frills, simple getaway for those wanting just the solitude of the countryside. $

Camping

■ County Camping Sites

 The County of Hawai`i maintains 11 parks around the island with designated camping sites. Facilities vary at the sites so it is best to check ahead. Tent camping only is available – no cabins. Minimal camping fees required to obtain camping permits; full information is available from **Department of Parks and Recreation**, County of Hawai`i, 25 Aupuni St., Hilo, HI 96720, ☎ 808/961-8311 or at the Kailua-Kona office, ☎ 808/327-3560.

Hawai`i

■ State Camping Sites

The State of Hawai`i maintains six designated camping sites around the Big Island. The parks and sites have either tent campgrounds, camping shelters, housekeeping cabins or group barracks-style accommodations. There are no fees to use state parks for picnicking or camping. However, permits are required for camping and there are standard minimal fees charged for use of shelters, cabins and group accommodations. Campgrounds and cabins are at **Hapuna Beach State Recreation Area, Kalopa State Recreation Area, Kilauea State Recreation Area, MacKenzie State Recreation Area, Manuka State Wayside** and **Mauna Kea State Recreation Area**. For reservations and information, contact: **Department of Land & Natural Resources**, Division of State Parks, Hawai`i District Office, PO Box 936, Hilo, HI 96720-0936, ☎ 808/974-6200.

■ National Park Camping Sites

Hawai`i Volcanoes National Park has three drive-in campgrounds available for campers with their own tents and gear. Each site has fireplaces, picnic tables and a pavilion shelter. No permit is needed and there is no fee for camping in the national park; camping is on a first-come, first-served basis. The park also maintains three simple backcountry cabins on Mauna Loa for hikers, but you must register at park headquarters for overnight stays. These cabins are in remote high-elevation areas where severe weather can occur, especially in winter. These are also on a first-come, first-served basis, but they are not heavily used and hikers can usually be accommodated. Check with park rangers for details. For camping information in the national park, contact: **Superintendent, Hawai`i Volcanoes National Park**, Volcano, HI 96718, ☎ 808/985-6000.

One national park campground, **Namakani Paio**, has some simple A-frame cabins that sleep four people and share a central restroom and shower facility. Cabins have an outdoor BBQ grill and picnic table. Standard minimal rates are charged for cabin rentals and include bed linens, blankets and towels. Reservations are made through the **Volcano House Hotel**, PO Box 53, Hawai`i Volcanoes National Park 96718, ☎ 808/967-7321.

Dining

 The Big Island of Hawai`i has a wide range of cuisines, restaurants, cafés and island eateries for the adventurous diner. Food ranges from five-star gourmet continental-international to delectable local-style plate lunches. Dining out will be a memorable part of your Big Island experience. The restaurant price ranges, as in the other island sections of this book are based on the average dinner meal, exclusive of tax, alcoholic beverages and desserts.

Dining Price Scale
$ . . . . under $10 per person
$$ . . . . $10-25 per person
$$$ . . . . $25 and up per person

■ Luaus

King Kamehameha Kona Beach Hotel, 75-5660 Palani Road, Kailua-Kona ☎ 808/329-2911; Island Breeze reservations, ☎ 808/326-4969 – call for times. The festivities begin with the arrival of torch bearers via canoe from Ahu`ea Heiau, King Kamehameha's temple fronting Kamakahonu Beach and the hotel grounds. The luau that follows is a feast of authentic Hawaiian foods and specialties from Oceania. A Polynesian performance of song and dance follows. It's all very colorful, touristy and good fun. Reservations required and Aloha attire preferred. $$$

Kona Village Resort, Kaupulehu-Kona ☎ 808/325-5555. The South Seas-style Kona Village Resort has one of the island's best luaus. The luau begins with the traditional removal of the roast pig from the imu (underground oven). Following this are cocktails and the luau feast, with an incredible buffet of Hawaiian and Polynesian foods, probably the grandest luau spread on the Big Island. A Polynesian performance of music and dance provides a stirring end to a memorable evening. Aloha attire preferred. $$$

Royal Kona Resort, 75-5852 Alii Drive, Kailua-Kona ☎ 808/329-3111 – call for times. The luau includes an Aloha shell lei greeting and continuous island entertainment. Prior to the luau, there is the traditional opening of the imu (underground oven) and removal of the roast pig. The lavish buffet with authentic Hawaiian foods includes an open bar. A

Polynesian review performance of song and dance follows. Reservations are suggested and Aloha attire preferred. $$$

■ Dinner Cruises

Capt. Beans' Dinner Cruise, PO Box 5199, Kailua-Kona, Hawai`i 96745-5199, ☎ 808/329-2955. This sunset dinner cruise onboard Capt. Beans' Polynesian-style sailing canoe departs Kailua Pier daily at 5:15PM. The cruise along the famous Kona Coast includes island entertainment, an open bar and all you can eat; adults 21 and over only, no children. Call for reservations and transportation pick-up at area hotels and condos. Aloha attire is preferred. $$$

Lanakila Ventures, Kailua Pier, Kailua-Kona, HI ☎ 808/326-6000. This twin-masted sailing yacht offers an Aloha Dinner Cruise with live entertainment as the boat cruises the coral reef waters along the Kona Coast at sunset. Reservations suggested. $$$

■ Restaurants

The Kona Coast

Bangkok Houses, 75-5626 Kuakini Highway, King Kamehameha Mall, Kailua-Kona, ☎ 808/329-7764. This is a bright clean and inviting dining room, complete with white tablecloths. The menu here is authentic Thai cuisine. They feature 100 selections from beef, chicken and seafood to veggie dishes. You can request the amount of spice from mild to extra hot. The curries are excellent. $$

Basil's Pizzeria & Ristorante, 75-5707 Alii Drive, Kailua-Kona, ☎ 808/326-7836. The menu here is all Italian with pizza, pasta, seafood, eggplant parmegiana, sausage and peppers, chicken cacciatore. $

Ocean View Inn is in the heart of Kailua-Kona at 75-5683 Alii Drive, just down from Kailua Pier, ☎ 808/329-9998. This is a popular family restaurant with the locals. The menu is extensive, with Chinese, American, and Hawaiian food. Decor and ambience are simple and nothing fancy, but the food is good and plentiful. Go early for dinner as it gets crowded rapidly. $

Sam Choy's Restaurant, 73-5576 Kauhola Bay 1, Kaloko Industrial Park near the airport, Kailua-Kona ☎ 808/326-1545. This is one of Kona's most popular "local style" eateries. Sam, chef-owner, is something of a local media celebrity and has two restaurants in Honolulu. The menu features excellent local-style cuisine with a distinct

Hawai`i/Pacific Regional accent. Such things as tomato beef, teriyaki steak, chicken stir fry, fried fish, lau lau and lomi salmon are staples and there are daily specials. It's a little hard to find, but turn into the Kaloko Industrial Area as if you're going to Costco. Look for the Kauhola Street sign to locate the building. Well worth the search. $

Teshima's Restaurant, Highway 11, Honalo, Kona, ☎ 808/322-9140, seven miles south of Kailua-Kona. This neat, clean family restaurant features friendly old-fashioned service by the Teshima family. Specialties are Japanese-American cuisine and local favorites and the menu has something for everyone. Nothing fancy here, just decent country café food. $

Thai Rin Restaurant is streetside in the Alii Sunset Plaza, 75-5799 Alii Drive, Kailua-Kona, ☎ 808/329-2929. This restaurant turns out great versions of trendy hot and spicy Thai cuisine. The menu features over two dozen items, including crispy fried noodles, chicken satay, three kinds of curry, spicy soups, Thai garlic shrimp, squid and much more. $

Kona Galley is on Alii Drive across from Kailua Pier, in the Seaside Shopping Mall upstairs, ☎ 808/329-5550. There are open-air views of Kailua Bay and nice sunsets. The continental-international menu features items like fresh catch, seafood, pasta, chicken, pizza, sandwiches. A nice location for casual dining. $$

Manna Korean BBQ, Crossroads Shopping Center, 75-1027 Henry, Kailua-Kona, ☎ 808/334-0880. This clean bright Korean lunch counter features generous servings of good Korean cuisine. Daily buffet hot table has kal bi, BBQ beef and chicken, chicken katsu, spicy pork, man doo, several soup and noodle dishes and other specials. Entrées get choice of four veggies and rice. This is a great bargain for good Korean food. $

Manago Hotel, Highway 11, Captain Cook, Kona, ☎ 808/323-2642. The dining room of this old family-operated hotel turns out good local-style food. There are Japanese-American specials like teriyaki, tempura, noodles, fried fish. No menu, just a chalkboard on the wall listing the day's fare. Good country-style cuisine. $

Hale Moana, Kaupulehu-Kona ☎ 808/325-5555 at the Kona Village Resort. This pleasant and airy dining room is the main restaurant for this South Seas-style resort. It overlooks the beach for lovely sunset dining and has an adjacent garden area for daily open-air lunch. The menu changes nightly and the cuisine includes American, European and Hawaiian accented specialties. Entrées include stir-fry shrimp, lobster and chicken with veggie noodles, mixed grill of steak, lamb chop and sausage, veal loin, roast duck, prime rib, pasta special and fresh island fish. The daily buffet lunch is a magnificent spread of salads, hot and cold entrées, grills and delectable desserts. Reservations required. $$$

Hale Samoa, Kaupulehu-Kona ☎ 808/325-5555 at the Kona Village Resort. This warm, intimate dining room features a Samoan motif complete with an outrigger canoe hanging from the ceiling and decorative crafts. The menu is surprisingly international and changes nightly. Entrées include fresh island fish, broiled prime striploin steak, lamb loin roast, buffalo filet, fresh opakapaka snapper and salmon, all done with an Asian-Pacific flair, plus a variety of creative appetizers, soups and salads. Attentive service in a romantic South Seas atmosphere is the tradition here. Gorgeous sunsets. Reservations are a must. $$

Oodles of Noodles, Crossroads Shopping Center, 75-1027 Henry, Kailua-Kona, ☎ 808/329-9222. This new eatery is the domain of Chef Amy Fergerson-Ota, noted local Kona resort chef. The menu features a number of exotic noodle dishes with creative preparations. Featured entrées include linguine puttanesca, seafood green curry cake noodle, Asian Peking duck, orzo risotto, curried coconut pork somen and much more. $$

Huggo's, 75-5828 Kahakai Road, Kailua-Kona ☎ 808/329-1493, next door to Royal Kona Resort. This open-air deck-style restaurant perched just above the shore and surf has the best location on Kailua Bay. Huggo's is one of those old-time restaurants that seems to have been there forever. They still serve up the freshest of island fish and seafood and excellent steaks. The mountain high dessert pies aren't bad either. Great sunsets go perfectly with great food. $$

The Kohala Coast, North Kohala, Waimea

Café Pesto, Kawaihae Center, Kawaihae ☎ 808/882-1071. This small Italian café offers a wide variety of pizza, pasta and risottos, hot sandwiches, calzones, and other specialties. $$

Great Wall Chop Suey, Waimea Center, Highway 19, Waimea, ☎ 808/885-7252. The Cantonese food offered is excellent in quality and quantity. There is a full selection of beef, pork, chicken, seafood, and noodle dishes. $

Maha's Café, Waimea Center, Highway 19, Waimea, in the historic Spencer House, ☎ 808/885-3633. This small café shares space with Cook's Discoveries, a unique Hawaiiana gift shop. The café specializes in light gourmet breakfasts, lunches and afternoon snacks. Lunch features Waipi`o Ways combo of broiled island fish and steamed taro, sweet potato, garden greens, plus fresh-made turkey, tuna, ahi, lamb or veggie sandwiches, Kohala Harvest chef's salad, and luscious desserts. $

Nori's Saimin Too, 64-1035 Mamalahoa Highway, Ululani Plaza, Waimea, ☎ 808/885-9133. This country diner, like their original Hilo outlet, features a wide variety of noodle dishes and take out items, including loco moco, BBQ chicken sticks, teriyaki beef, burgers, sandwiches and daily specials. $

Paniolo Country Inn, Kawaihae Road, Waimea, ☎ 808/885-4377. This country café has rustic ranch-style decor and ambiance. The menu features a variety of burgers and sandwiches, BBQ ribs, chicken, pasta, Mexican food, and pizza. There is a large collection of branding irons from Big Island ranches decorating the walls and a beautiful aquarium with Hawaiian reef fish that will interest youngsters. $$

Young's Kal-Bi, Waimea Center, Highway 19, Waimea, ☎ 808/885-8440. The main feature here is good Korean cuisine served in ample portions. The menu lists kal-bi ribs, BBQ beef, Korean chicken, chicken katsu, mandoo (Korean won ton), fish. Clean, attractive location, simple decor; eat here or take out. $

Edelweiss, Highway 19, Kawaihae Road, Waimea, ☎ 808/885-6800. This rustic chalet-style inn fits in with the cool upcountry ranch climate of Kamuela. It has a distinct Alpine air and features wonderful continental-international cuisine. Specialties include weinerschnitzel, Black Forest chicken, venison ragu, German sausage plates, veal, several varieties of fresh island seafood and other creative dishes. Master Chef Hans-Peter Hager ensures a pleasant dining experience. Great food and pleasant service. No reservations. Credit cards. $$

Kohala Village Restaurant, intersection of Hwys 250-270 in Hawi, ☎ 808/889-0105. This country coffee shop features sandwiches, salads, and entrées such as chicken stirfry, red pesto pasta, Honolulu fried noodles, fried rice, Oriental chicken salad. $

Kamuela Provision Company, Hilton Waikoloa Village, Kohala Coast, ☎ 808/885-1234. This lovely open-air restaurant situated on a bluff overlooks the Kohala Coast surf and shoreline. The decor is provincial Thailand-Malaysian, with greenery, artwork, and multi-leveled rooms much like a Thai-Malaysian house. The menu features Asian/Pacific-inspired seafood, steaks, fresh island fish, pasta and exotic desserts. Reservations suggested. $$

Batik, Mauna Kea Beach Hotel, Kohala Coast, ☎ 808/882-7222. This is the hotel's acclaimed fine dining room. The menu features European cuisine inspired by Provence, with many classic selections, plus creative appetizers, soups, and salads and an extensive wine list. First class service and a pleasant dining experience are standard. Reservations suggested. $$$

Bay Terrace, Bay Terrace, Mauna Lani Bay Hotel, Kohala Coast, ☎ 808/885-6622. This open-air garden terrace restaurant provides a delightful dining atmosphere. The menu is continental-international, featuring several choices of beef, fresh island fish, seafood, chicken, lamb, and other specialties. There is a daily lavish lunch buffet and the Sunday buffet is especially nice, with many Japanese and Oriental specialties. The Friday and Saturday night seafood buffet is excellent, with superb entrées, salads and dessert bar. Reservations recommended. $$$

Canoe House, Mauna Lani Bay Hotel, Kohala Coast, ☎ 808/885-6622. This pleasant open-air oceanside dining room specializes in Asian-Pacific cuisine. The food and service are superb. The menu features creative appetizers such as sashimi and poke, baby back ribs, Chinese won tons, eggplant curry; entrée selections include fresh seared mahi-mahi, hibachi salmon, pesto seared scallops, grilled marinated ono, New Zealand lamb chops, Thai seafood curry and many others. Reservations suggested; credit cards. $$$

Merriman's, Opelo Plaza, Highway 19, Waimea, ☎ 808/885-6822. This is Chef Peter Merriman's original Big Island restaurant. He is a leader in the Hawaiian Regional culinary trend of using local products in creative cookery. His Maui restaurant is also well known. The menu here features Parker Ranch prime rib (house special), fresh island fish, cioppino, steaks, veal, Kahua Ranch lamb, chicken and daily specials, plus appetizers, soups, salads and exotic desserts. Reservations suggested; credit cards. $$$

Roy's Waikoloa Bar & Grill, Waikoloa Beach Resort, Kings' Shops Center, ☎ 808/885-4321. This is Big Island outlet of celebrity chef Roy Yamaguchi's widely acclaimed restaurant chain. The cuisine is similar to the trendy local Regional Cuisine and culinary approach of his restaurants in Hawai`i and internationally. The emphasis is on combining fresh local products with creative cookery methods. The menu features such dishes as macadamia nut crusted mahimahi, sesame seared opakapaka, lemongrass shutome & blackened ahi, Mongolian lamb, garlic herb chicken. $$$

The Grill, The Orchid at Mauna Lani Hotel, Kohala Coast, ☎ 808/885-2000. This hotel fine dining room has the atmosphere of a plush country manor house and offers continental/Hawaiian Regional Cuisine. Menu selections include fresh pastas and appetizers, fresh island fish, steak, lamb, veal, Maine lobster, Hawaiian fisherman's stew. Fine service and quality cuisine are standards. Reservations suggested. $$$

The Pavilion, Mauna Kea Beach Hotel, Kohala Coast, ☎ 808/882-7222. This well-known dining room features creative continental-international gourmet cuisine. A complete wine selection complements the gourmet fare. Live contemporary dinner music lends a relaxed atmosphere to a pleasant evening. Reservations suggested. $$$

Tiare Room, Outrigger Waikoloan Resort, Kohala Coast, ☎ 808/885-6789. The contemporary elegant decor of this hotel fine dining room makes for a most pleasant ambiance. The menu features continental and international fare, including fresh island fish, Pacific salmon, lobster, beef tenderloin, New York steak, veal, lamb, venison, chicken and pasta, plus appetizers, soups and salads. Good food and attentive service. Reservations suggested; credit cards. $$$

Hilo & the Hamakua Coast

Jolene's Kau Kau Korner, in Honoka`a at the intersection of Lehua and Mamane Streets, ☎ 808/775-9498. This nicely renovated small town café is clean and bright with simple decor and lace window curtains. The menu features mahimahi, shrimp tempura, seafood platter, beef teriyaki, New York steak, captain's plate, chicken katsu, plus burgers, sandwiches, salads and desserts. $

Don's Grill, 485 Hinano Street, Hilo, ☎ 808/935-9099. This pleasant family restaurant is consistently one of Hilo's best inexpensive dining options. The menu features beef, chicken, pork chops, fish, sandwiches, burgers, soups and salads, daily specials and many local favorites. The house specialty is an excellent rotisseried chicken. Bright, clean, fast and courteous service, generally great food and very reasonable prices. $

Kay's Lunch Center, 684 Kilauea Avenue, Hilo, ☎ 808/968-1776. This local-style restaurant features Korean cuisine, including BBQ beef, short ribs, and a house-special crispy Korean chicken. Homemade cream cheese pies for dessert are wonderful. The decor and ambiance here are simple, nothing fancy, just generous servings of good, reasonably priced food. $

Ken's House of Pancakes, 1730 Kamehameha Avenue, Hilo, ☎ 808/935-8711, near Banyan Drive hotels. The menu features pancakes and breakfast items, plus a variety of American foods, sandwiches, and some local-style dishes. Popular with visitors as well as locals because it is open 24 hours a day, every day of the year. $

Hawai`i

Leung's Chop Suey House, 530 E. Lanikaula St., Hilo, ☎ 808/935-4066. This small Chinese kitchen is popular with local folks. Varied menu of Cantonese dishes and a buffet counter to select your own hot items. Cake noodles are a must! Not a fancy place but good food. $

New China Restaurant, 510 Kilauea Avenue, Hilo, ☎ 808/961-5677, next to Hawai`i Hardware Company. The menu features Cantonese and Hong Kong-style cuisine with a wide selection of beef, pork, chicken, duck, seafood, and noodle dishes. They feature some unusual items like abalone soup, lemon chicken, squid with green pepper and black beans. Try the pot stickers. Good food at reasonable prices in a clean, bright environment. $

Nihon Restaurant, 123 Lihiwai St., Hilo, ☎ 808/969-1133. This popular restaurant serves Japanese cuisine. Menu items include beef teriyaki, chicken katsu, fish misoyaki, donburi, noodles and fresh-made sushi. Open, airy rooms with Japanese decor and views of Hilo Bay. $$

Scruffles Restaurant, 1438 Kilauea Avenue, Hilo, ☎ 808/935-6664. This family coffee shop features local and international cuisines. Choices include burgers and sandwiches, curries, Mexican specials, pasta dishes, Korean, Japanese, and American specials like smoked chicken and BBQ ribs. Bright, attractive contemporary decor with booth or table seating. $

Ting Hao Mandarin Restaurant, Kanoelehua Avenue, ☎ 808/959-6288, in the Puainako Town Center. The menu here is authentic Mandarin Chinese. It features exotic spicy cuisine from Szechwan and Hunan, delicious non-spicy gourmet dishes from Taiwan, Beijing, and other areas of China, as well as healthy vegetarian delights. A real dining adventure. $

Café Pesto, 130 Kamehameha Avenue, Hilo, ☎ 808/969-6640. The Italian menu features a variety of pastas, appetizers, salads and sandwiches and the house special wood-fired pizzas, served with a variety of creative toppings. There is a bright contemporary decor in the old-fashioned high-ceiling room with open kitchen area. $$

Pescatore, corner of Keawe and Haili Streets, Hilo, ☎ 808/969-9090. The menu here features genuine Italian cuisine. Tasty soups, salads and appetizers complement a wonderful variety of creative seafood, chicken, veal, vegetarian and pasta dishes. The fresh-baked bread melts in your mouth. Warm woodwork decor, great food and pleasant service make this small eatery a real discovery. $$

Seaside, 1790 Kalanianaole St., Hilo, ☎ 808/935-8825. This small family-run restaurant is in the middle of Keaukaha's fish ponds area, where seafood for the table can't get any fresher. Local mullet, trout, and other fresh fish selections make up the menu. For fresh creative seafood, this is the place to go. $$

Topo Gigio's, 400 Hualani St., Waiakea Villas, Hilo, ☎ 808/961-5588. This small Italian restaurant has both inside and covered outside dining areas. The menu is heavy on creative pastas and Italian favorites. The inside room is a bit crowded. An antique toy collection lines the wall and hangs from the ceiling. Good food and good service. $$

Puna & Hawai`i Volcanoes National Park

Keaau Junction, Keaau Town Center, Keaau, ☎ 808/966-6885. This restaurant features a railroad-train theme with a menu of broiler selections, rotisseried chicken and south-of-the-border selections like tacos, burritos, tostadas, chimichangas and quesadillas, plus pizza and sandwiches. $

Luquin's Mexican Restaurant, Main Street, Pahoa, ☎ 808/965-9990. The emphasis here is Mexican food like tacos, burritos, enchiladas, botanas, soups, salads and other specialties. The decor is Mexican and contrasts with the rough exterior of the old wooden building in which it's located. This place will appeal to the adventurous diner who likes Mexican food. $

Naung Mai Thai Kitchen, Main Street, Pahoa, ☎ 808/965-8186. This small diner is in Pahoa's old town row of early buildings. The menu is authentic Thai cuisine, with red, green or yellow curry, seafood, chicken, evil jungle beef, pork specials and vegetarian dishes; also rice and noodles. Adventurous Thai food at reasonable prices. $

Kilauea Lodge Restaurant, Highway 11, Volcano Village, ☎ 808/967-7366. This cozy dining room is part of the Kilauea Lodge Bed & Breakfast operation. The menu is continental-international cuisine featuring fine seafood, beef, veal, and chicken selections, along with appetizers and salads. Good service, good food in a relaxed country lodge atmosphere. $$

The Godmother, Main Street, Pahoa, ☎ 808/965-0055. The menu here is Italian and features items like meatballs and pasta, ravioli, parmigiana, lasagna, fettuccine, piccata, marsala, scampi and special Godmother pork chops. Bright, clean, simple decor. $$

Ka`u District & South Point

Mark Twain Square, Highway 11 in Waiohinu, ☎ 808/929-7550. This is a family-run café and gift shop in an attractive early-Hawaiian-style building. It stands next to the Mark Twain monkey-pod tree planted by the famous author during his 1860s visit to Hawai`i. The café features good plate lunches, sandwiches, burgers, snacks, coffee, beverages. $

Volcano Country Club Restaurant, near Hawai`i Volcanoes National Park, just off Highway 11 at the 30-mile marker, ☎ 808/967-7721. This rustic dining room is in the golf course clubhouse and features a variety of sandwiches, beef, chicken, fish, and local-style favorites. Nice open, airy room, golf course views and good food. $

Ka Ohelo Room, in the Volcano House Hotel, Hawai`i Volcanoes National Park, ☎ 808/967-7321. The menu features continental and international cuisine from prime rib and steaks to fresh island fish and several types of pasta, plus soups, salads and appetizers. The dining room overlooks majestic Kilauea Caldera. The rustic country lodge atmosphere makes for a nice ambiance. Dining on the edge of the volcano adds a special charm to the generally good cuisine and pleasant service. $$

**Na`alehu Coffee Shop,** next to Na`alehu Shopping Center, Na`alehu, ☎ 808/929-7238. This old-fashioned country coffee shop serves up American-style food, including steaks, seafood, fresh island fish, chicken, sandwiches and salads. $$

Index

Adventure Guides
from Hunter Publishing

Extensively researched and with the very latest information, Adventure Guides are written by experienced authors. The focus is on outdoor activities – hiking, biking, rock climbing, horseback riding, downhill skiing, parasailing, scuba diving, backpacking, and waterskiing, among others – and these user-friendly books provide all the details you need, including prices. The best local outfitters are listed, along with contact numbers, addresses, e-mail and Web site information, and recommendations. The introductnion provides background on history, geography, climate, culture, when to go, transportation and planning. The guides then take a region-by-region approach, plunging into the heart of each area and the advenzzztures offered, with information on accommodations, shopping, restaurants for every budget, and festivals. All books have town and regional maps. Fully indexed.

ALASKA HIGHWAY

2nd Edition, Ed & Lynn Readicker-Henderson
"A comprehensive guide.... Plenty of background history and extensive bibliography."
Travel Reference Library on-line
The fascinating highway that passes settlements of the Tlingit and the Haida Indians, with stops at Anchorage, Tok, Skagway, Valdez, Denali National Park and more. Sidetrips and attractions en route, plus details on the Alaska Marine Hwy, Klondike Hwy, Top-of-the-World Hwy. Color photos. 400 pp, $16.95, 1-55650-824-7

BAHAMAS

2nd Edition, Blair Howard
Fully updated reports for Grand Bahama, Freeport, Eleuthera, Bimini, Andros, the Exumas, Nassau, New Providence Island, plus new sections on San Salvador, Long Island, Cat Island, the Acklins, the Inaguas and the Berry Islands. Mailboat schedules, package vacations and snorkeling trips by Jean-Michel Cousteau. 280 pp, $14.95, 1-55650-852-2

EXPLORE BELIZE

4th Edition, Harry S. Pariser

"Down-to-earth advice.... An excellent travel guide."
– *Library Journal*

Extensive coverage of the country's political, social and economic history, along with the plant and animal life. Encouraging you to mingle with the locals, Pariser entices you with descriptions of local dishes and festivals. Maps, color photos. 400 pp, $16.95, 1-55650-785-2

CANADA'S ATLANTIC PROVINCES

Barbara Radcliffe Rogers & Stillman Rogers

Pristine waters, rugged slopes, breathtaking seascapes, remote wilderness, sophisticated cities, and quaint, historic towns. Year-round adventures on the Fundy Coast, Acadian Peninsula, fjords of Gros Morne, Viking Trail & Vineland, Saint John River, Lord Baltimore's lost colony. Photos. 672 pp, $19.95, 1-55650-819-0

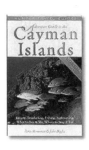

CAYMAN ISLANDS

Paris Permenter & John Bigley

The only comprehensive guidebook to Grand Cayman, Cayman Brac and Little Cayman. Encyclopedic listings of dive/snorkel operators, along with the best sites. Enjoy nighttime pony rides on a glorious beach, visit the turtle farms, prepare to get wet at staggering blowholes or just laze on a white sand beach. Color photos. 224 pp, $16.95, 1-55650-786-0

COASTAL ALASKA & THE INSIDE PASSAGE

3rd Edition, Lynn & Ed Readicker-Henderson

"A highly useful book." – *Travel Books Review*

Using the Alaska Marine Highway to visit Ketchikan, Bellingham, the Aleutians, Kodiak, Seldovia, Valdez, Seward, Homer, Cordova, Prince of Wales Island, Juneau, Gustavas, Sitka, Haines, Skagway. Glacier Bay, Tenakee. US and Canadian gateway cities profiled. 400 pp, $16.95, 1-55650-859-X

COLORADO
Steve Cohen

Adventures in the San Juan National Forest, Aspen, Vail, Mesa Verde National Park, The Sangre de Cristo Mountains, Denver, Boulder, Telluride, Colorado Springs and Durango, plus scores of smaller towns and attractions. Resident-author Cohen knows the state intimately.
296 pp, $15.95, 1-55680-724-0

COSTA RICA
3rd Edition, Harry S. Pariser

"... most comprehensive... Excellent sections on national parks, flora, fauna & history."
– *CompuServe Travel Forum*
Incredible detail on culture, plants, animals, where to stay & eat, as well as practicalities of travel. E-mail and Web site directory.
560 pp, $16.95, 1-55650-722-4

EXPLORE THE DOMINICAN REPUBLIC
3rd Edition, Harry S. Pariser

Virgin beaches, 16th-century Spanish ruins, the Caribbean's highest mountain, exotic wildlife, vast forests. Visit Santa Domingo, revel in Sosúa's European sophistication or explore the Samaná Peninsus jungle. Color.
340 pp, $15.95, 1-55650-814-X

FLORIDA KEYS & EVERGLADES
2nd Edition, Joyce & Jon Huber

"... vastly informative, absolutely user-friendly, chock full of information..." – Dr. Susan Cropper
"... practical & easy to use." – *Wilderness Southeast*
Canoe trails, airboat rides, nature hikes, Key West, diving, sailing, fishing. Color.
224 pp, $14.95, 1-55650-745-3

FLORIDA'S WEST COAST

Chelle Koster Walton

A guide to all the cities, towns, nature preserves, wilderness areas and sandy beaches that grace the Sunshine State's western shore. From Tampa Bay to Naples and Everglades National Park to Sanibel Island.

224 pp, $14.95, 1-55650-787-9

GEORGIA

Blair Howard

"Packed full of information on everything there is to see and do." – *Chattanooga Free Press*

From Atlanta to Savannah to Cumberland Island, this book walks you through antique-filled stores, around a five-story science museum and leads you on tours of old Southern plantations.

296 pp, $15.95, 1-55650-782-8

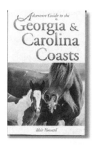

GEORGIA & CAROLINA COASTS

Blair Howard

"Provides details often omitted... geared to exploring the wild dunes, the historic districts, the joys..." – *Amazon.com Travel Expert*

Beaufort, Myrtle Beach, New Bern, Savannah, the Sea Islands, Hilton Head and Charleston.

288 pp, $15.95, 1-55650-747-X

GREAT SMOKY MOUNTAINS

Blair Howard

"The take-along guide." – *Bookwatch*

Includes overlapping Tennessee, Georgia, Virginia and N. Carolina, the Cherokee and Pisgah National Forests, Chattanooga and Knoxville. Scenic fall drives on the Blue Ridge Parkway.

288 pp, $15.95, 1-55650-720-8

HIGH SOUTHWEST
2nd Edition, Steve Cohen
"Exhaustive detail... [A] hefty, extremely thorough & very informative book." – *QuickTrips Newsletter*
"Plenty of maps/detail – an excellent guide."
– *Bookwatch*
Four Corners of NW New Mexico, SW Colorado, S Utah, N Arizona. Encyclopedic coverage.
376 pp, $15.95, 1-55650-723-2

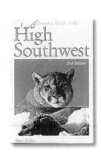

IDAHO
Genevieve Rowles
Snake River Plain, the Owyhee Mountains, Sawtooth National Recreation Area, the Lost River Range and the Salmon River Mountains. Comprehensive coverage of ski areas, as well as gold-panning excursions and activities for kids, all written by an author with a passion for Idaho.
352 pp, $16.95, 1-55650-789-5

THE LEEWARD ISLANDS
Antigua, St. Martin, St. Barts, St. Kitts, Nevis, Antigua, Barbuda
Paris Permenter & John Bigley
Far outdistances other guides. Recommended operators for day sails, island-hopping excursions, scuba dives, unique rainforest treks on verdant mountain slopes, and rugged four-wheel-drive trails.248 pp, $14.95, 1-55650-788-7

MICHIGAN
Kevin & Laurie Hillstrom
Year-round activities, all detailed here by resident authors. Port Huron-to-Mackinac Island Sailboat Race, Isle Royale National Park, Tour de Michigan cycling marathon. Also: canoeing, dogsledding and urban adventures.
360 pp, $16.95, 1-55650-820-4

NEVADA
Matt Purdue
Adventures throughout the state, from Winnemucca to Great Basin National Park, Ruby Mountain Wilderness to Angel Lake, from Cathedral Gorge State Park to the Las Vegas strip. Take your pick! 256 pp, $15.95, 1-55650-842-5

NEW HAMPSHIRE
Elizabeth L. Dugger
The Great North Woods, White Mountains, the Lakes Region, Dartmouth & Lake Sunapee, the Monadnock region, Merrimack Valley and the Seacoast Region. Beth Dugger finds the roads less traveled. 360 pp, $15.95, 1-55650-822-0

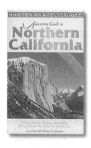

NORTHERN CALIFORNIA
Lee Foster & Mary Lou Janson
Waves lure surfers to Santa Cruz; heavy snowfall attracts skiers to Lake Tahoe; scuba divers relish Monterey Bay; horseback riders explore trails at Mammoth Lake. Travel the Big Sur and Monterey coasts, enjoy views of Yosemite and savor Wine Country. Resident authors. 360 pp, $$15.95, 1-55650-821-2

NORTHERN FLORIDA & THE PANHANDLE
Jim & Cynthia Tunstall
From the Georgia border south to Ocala National Forest and through the Panhandle. Swimming with dolphins and spelunking, plus Rails to Trails, a 47-mile hiking/biking path made of recycled rubber. 320 pp, $15.95, 1-55650-769-0

ORLANDO & CENTRAL FLORIDA
Disney World, the Space Coast, Tampa & Daytona
Jim & Cynthia Tunstall
Takes you to parts of Central Florida you never
knew existed. Tips about becoming an astronaut
(the real way and the smart way) and the hazards
of taking a nude vacation. Photos.
300 pp, $15.95, 1-55650-825-5

OKLAHOMA
Lynne Sullivan
The only full-sized comprehensive guidebook
covering Oklahoma from tip to toe. Explore the
rich history of the state's 250,000 Native
American residents, their lands and culture, with
details on powwows, historical reenactments, and
celebrations. The author also tells where, when
and how to bike, hike, float, fish, climb, ride and
explore, with full information on outfitters and
guides. Photos. 300 pages, $15.95, 1-55650-843-3

PACIFIC NORTHWEST
Don & Marjorie Young
Oregon, Washington, Victoria and Vancouver in
British Columbia, and California north of Eureka.
This region offers unlimited opportunities for the
adventure traveler. And this book tells you
where to find the best of them.
6 x 9 pbk, 360 pp, $16.95, 1-55650-844-1

PUERTO RICO
3rd Edition, Harry S. Pariser
"A quality book that covers all aspects... it's all
here & well done." – *The San Diego Tribune*
"... well researched. They include helpful facts...
filled with insightful tips." – *The Shoestring Traveler*. Crumbling watchtowers and fascinating folklore enchant visitors. Color photos.
344 pp, $15.95, 1-55650-749-6

SIERRA NEVADA
Wilbur H. Morrison & Matt Purdue
California's magnificent Sierra Nevada mountain range. The Pacific Crest Trail, Yosemite, Lake Tahoe, Mount Whitney, Mammoth Lakes, the John Muir Trail, King's Canyon and Sequoia – all are explored. Plus, excellent historical sections. An adventurer's playground awaits!
300 pp, $15.95, 1-55650-845-X

SOUTHEAST FLORIDA
Sharon Spence
Get soaked by crashing waves at twilight; canoe through mangroves; reel in a six-foot sailfish; or watch as a yellow-bellied turtle snuggles up to a gator. Interviews with the experts – scuba divers, sky divers, pilots, fishermen, bikers, balloonists, and park rangers. Color photos.
256 pp, $15.95, 1-55650-811-5

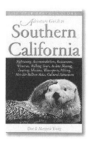

SOUTHERN CALIFORNIA
Don & Marge Young
Browse an art festival, peoplewatch at the beach, sportfish near offshore islands and see world-class performances by street entertainers. The Sierras offer a different adventure, with cable cars ready to whisk you to their peaks. A special section covers daytrips to Mexico.
400 pp, $16.95, 1-55650-791-7

TEXAS
Kimberly Young
Explore Austin, Houston, Dallas/Ft. Worth, San Antonio, Waco and all the places in-between, from Dripping Springs to Marble Falls. Angle for "the big one" at Highland Lakes, or try some offshore fishing. Tramp through the Big Thicket or paddle on Lake Texoma. Photos throughout.
380 pp, $15.95, 1-55650-812-3

VIRGIN ISLANDS
4th Edition, Harry S. Pariser

"Plenty of outdoor options.... All budgets are considered in a fine coverage that appeals to readers."
– Reviewer's Bookwatch
Every island in the Virgins. Valuable, candid opinions. St. Croix, St. John, St. Thomas, Tortola, Virgin Gorda, Anegada. Color. 368 pp, $16.95, 1-55650-746-1

VIRGINIA
Leonard M. Adkins

The Appalachian Trail winds over the state's eastern mountains. The Great Dismal Swamp offers biking, hiking and canoeing trails, and spectacular wildlife. Skyline Drive and the Blue Ridge Parkway – popular drives in spring and summer. Photos. 420 pp, $16.95, 1-55650-816-6

THE YUCATAN
Including Cancún & Cozumel
Bruce & June Conord

"... Honest evaluations. This book is the one not to leave home without." *– Time Off Magazine*
"... opens the doors to our enchanted Yucatán."
– Mexico Ministry of Tourism
Maya ruins, Spanish splendor. Deserted beaches, festivals, culinary delights. 376 pp, $15.95, 1-55650-792-5

All Hunter titles are available at bookstores nationwide or from the publisher. To order direct, send a check for the total of the book(s) ordered plus $3 shipping and handling to Hunter Publishing, 130 Campus Drive, Edison NJ 08818. Secure credit card orders may be made at the Hunter Web site, where you will also find in-depth descriptions of the hundreds of travel guides we offer.

ORDER FORM

Yes! Send the following *Adventure Guides*:

TITLE	ISBN #	PRICE	QUANTITY	TOTAL
	SUBTOTAL			
SHIPPING & HANDLING (United States only)				
(1-2 books, $3; 3-5 books, $5; 6-10 books, $8)				
ENCLOSED IS MY CHECK FOR				

NAME:

ADDRESS:

CITY:STATE:ZIP:

PHONE:

VISIT US ON THE WORLD WIDE WEB

http://www.hunterpublishing.com

You'll find our full range of travel guides to all corners of the globe, with descriptions, reviews, author profiles and pictures. Our Alive Guide series includes guides to Aruba, Bonaire & Curaçao, St. Martin & St. Barts, Cancún & Cozumel and other Caribbean destinations. Romantic Weekends guides explore destinations from New England to Virginia, New York to Texas. Charming Small Hotel Guides cover Italy, Venice, Tuscany, Spain, France, Britain, Paris, Germany, Switzerland, Southern France, New England, Austria and Florida – all in full color. Hundreds of other books are described, ranging from Best Dives of the Caribbean to Battlefields of the Civil War and The African-American Travel Guide. Books may be purchased on-line through our secure credit card transaction system or by check.